THE AIR OF REALITY
NEW ESSAYS ON
HENRY JAMES

THE AIR OF REALITY

NEW ESSAYS ON

HENRY JAMES

Edited by
JOHN GOODE

'One can speak best from one's own taste, and I may therefore venture to say that the air of reality (solidity of specification) seems to me to be the supreme virtue of a novel – the merit on which all its other merits . . . helplessly and submissively depend.'

Henry James, 'The Art of Fiction' (1884)

METHUEN & CO LTD
LONDON

First published in 1972 by
Methuen & Co Ltd
11 New Fetter Lane London EC4
© *1972 Methuen & Co Ltd*
Printed in Great Britain
by W & J Mackay Limited, Chatham

SBN 416 12480 1

Distributed in the USA by
HARPER & ROW PUBLISHERS, INC.
BARNES & NOBLE IMPORT DIVISION

CONTENTS

INTRODUCTION

JOHN GOODE

I don't think I need to be apologetic about offering another book on James. The individual essays justify themselves. But, in addition, the project itself had its origin in a feeling that the quantity of writing about James isn't by any means matched by the quality. I felt that the great period of James criticism came to an end by the mid fifties, and that the books one is grateful for since then – Poirier, Anderson, Holland, for example – are both rare and, for one reason or another, severely limited – the first by the chosen field, the other two by intense and narrow commitments. Most of what remains, when it isn't pure rubbish (and James has attracted more than his fair share of that) has either been abstractly formalistic or coolly appropriative, so that the characteristic stance of Jamesian criticism tends to be either that of the displaced philologist or of the unassailable moral comforter. Remarkably detached from the general discourse of literary criticism, it has been and remains highly vulnerable to the kind of attack Geismar attempted to mount. His book was disappointing, partly because it wasn't consistent or controlled or discriminating enough, but also because the word 'cult' offered too much credit to the latest phase of James criticism. James has been less worshipped than processed; the endless exegeses are little manufactures.

The earlier generation I have indicated was not like this. For it, James was a critical *case*, not to be appropriated or carved up into rhetorical devices, but to be confronted often problematically in terms of larger values. When we think of Fergusson, Arvin, Wilson, Troy, Winters, Leavis, Kettle, Bewley and Dupee, we recall an urgent debate on a number of issues pertinent to James and beyond him too – a debate with aesthetic, social and moral implications which, if it led to some blindness and much unleashing of prejudice, led also to most of the insights that readers of James can profit by, because, it is obvious, for such critics the question of Henry James was still a real one.

It is a real one still because his work will always pose basic problems of value and significance. But it is particularly urgent now because these problems have an important bearing on the development of literary criticism. The most striking feature of our discipline is that it has remained so inflexibly and, especially in England in the last decade, increasingly committed to an embattled position – one which, if it appears in various guises, as the liberal imagination as well as minority culture, consistently appropriates literature to prop up the crumbling dualisms of post-Romantic culture. Individual and society, culture and history, experience and ideology, 'fiction' and 'reality', love and knowledge – so much of the work of the last decades has been devoted to holding these terms apart. It's a commitment analysed most fully by Raymond Williams[1] who also makes the connexion between it and criticism's most characteristic technique – the close reading which gives emphasis to a special definition of maturity resembling what Lawrence termed a 'knowing in apartness'. Awareness becomes all, and if the formula is reversed in a campaign against dryness, this is only to play the same game, to leave unchallenged the structure of estrangement. It's a structure which can't really account for James, although he is usually seen as its consummate product (one still gets people claiming that James's fiction affirms 'the autonomy of self'). You either have to make severe reservations about the later James, like Leavis and Harvey, or read him with an effort of heroic ingenuity – like Bayley. For one thing, as a number of essays in this book demonstrate and discuss, the mode of critical awareness is so fully represented in the novels that the reader is overreached by the character (and often the character is morally distant in other ways). James, in other words, exposes and places and therefore historicizes the kind of 'maturity' criticism endorses. But more than this, he puts all modes of knowing, including love, in social relationship. One of the affirmations Williams makes about James is that his novels are concerned with some of the 'deepest' and some of the 'coarsest' human problems: the essays which follow make clear, I think, not only how true that is, but also how close the deep and the coarse lie together.

Of course, I do not wish to commit my own act of appropriation of James or of the contributions which follow. Not everybody who has written here would subscribe to these generalizations, and I do not believe that James *demonstrates*, even implicitly, such a position. I only claim that a critical confrontation with James must call in question the prevailing stance of literary studies. I did not, of course, prescribe any method or line, and the techniques employed range from highly developed analysis to detailed historical placing. What I did suggest was that the book as a whole should have what M. H. Abrams calls a 'mimetic orientation' – that we might profit most by asking questions about the relationship of the work to the world it takes account of.

I won't insult either the reader or the contributors by introducing each item with a vapid generalization. However, I need to say something about the selection of topics – or rather about the exclusion of others. As a general principle, I wished to give essays the space they needed even though it meant omitting some important areas of James. The exclusions are based on various criteria: one is simply evaluative (I don't think that *The Princess Casamassima*, for example, deserves the close attention it has frequently had, and I think that *The Spoils of Poynton* is overestimated). Secondly, there are texts which have had so much attention (I am thinking above all, of course, of *The Portrait of a Lady*, but also – proportionately – *The Europeans* and *The Turn of the Screw*) that it seemed better to make way for other more neglected or more problematic works. Finally, other texts were reluctantly left out only because they couldn't neatly be fitted in: I would have liked, for example, to have had something on some of the tales and on the last unfinished works. More positively, it seemed important to give certain novels an attention they had not been accorded (*The American*, *The Bostonians*, *The Tragic Muse*), to extricate others from a simplifying moralistic criticism (*Washington Square*, *What Maisie Knew*, *The Awkward Age*), and to submit those which are habitually disputed to fresh scrutiny. I realize, of course, that it wouldn't take much ingenuity to use the same criteria to produce a different list, but I think that the one presented here makes for as full an airing of the crucial problems as is possible within the limits of one volume.

Unless otherwise stated in the notes at the end of each chapter, quotations are taken from *The Novels and Stories of Henry James*, edited by Percy Lubbock, London, 1921–3, 35 volumes. The following abbreviations are used in the notes:

Letters = *The Letters of Henry James*, edited by Percy Lubbock, London, 1920, 2 volumes.

Notebooks = *The Notebooks of Henry James*, edited by F. O. Matthiessen and K. B. Murdock, New York, 1947.

Selected Letters = *Selected Letters of Henry James*, edited by Leon Edel, London, 1956.

The two unpublished letters to Mrs Humphry Ward quoted on pp. 120 and 139 are quoted by permission of the Clifton Waller Barrett Library, University of Virginia (the Henry James Collection). The unpublished letters to Aldrich (p. 111) and William James (p. 167) are quoted by permission of the Harvard College Library (© 1972 Alexander R. James). We are grateful to Professor Leon Edel for his co-operation in respect of this material.

I should like to thank Mrs J. Chennells, Mrs D. Medhurst and Miss D. Pullen for their help in the preparation of this book.

Notes

1. Most relevantly in *The English Novel from Dickens to Lawrence*, London, 1970.

I

The American

R. W. BUTTERFIELD

'I have written my story from Newman's side of the wall', James told William Dean Howells in a letter, shortly after completing *The American*.[1] Thirty years later, in the Preface to the New York edition of the novel, he was to write:

> If Newman was attaching enough, I must have argued, his tangle would be sensible enough; for the interest of everything is all that it is *his* vision, *his* conception, *his* interpretation: at the window of his wide, quite sufficiently wide, consciousness we are seated, from that admirable position we 'assist'. He therefore supremely matters; all the rest matters only as he feels it, treats it, meets it.[2]

He perhaps exaggerates the 'sufficient width' of Newman's consciousness, preferring at this point neither to draw attention to the frequent gaps between that consciousness and the author's, nor to remark upon the extent to which so much of the comedy is to be found in Newman's misreadings and incomprehensions. Nonetheless, this is, indisputably, Newman's book, Newman's story, Newman's education through experience; and the first questions concern his identity and his role. Who is he? Who and what does he represent?

Named by his parents after Christopher Columbus, he is of course, most clearly and simply, new American man, setting out on his reverse voyage of discovery from the New World, which is old and familiar to him, to the Old World, which is entirely strange. Unlike his creator, he is not a metropolitan Easterner who has continually felt an affinity with Europe; he is still, in many characteristic respects, a Westward-stepping pioneer merely turned about, a distant relative of Natty Bumppo and Davy Crockett, a 'great Western Barbarian, stepping forth in his innocence and might, gazing a while at this poor effete Old World, and then swooping down on it'. His gestures and psychological 'shape' are in the most literal sense spacious and expansive, in contrast with a Europe that is confined and enclosed. We meet him within the typically European limited space of the Museum, 'his head thrown back and his legs outstretched . . . in profound enjoyment of his posture', the body at full stretch of that 'wide range' which Valentin envies in him. Claire attracts him immediately, because her 'face had . . . a range of expression as delightfully vast as the wind-streaked, cloud-flecked distance on a Western prairie'. On occasions 'he performed the movement which was so frequent with him, and which was always a sort of symbol of his taking mental possession of a scene – he extended his legs'; the mythic Westerner, it might be, a gigantic Crockett or Boone, striding to take possession, whether 'mental' or proprietary, of his territory. In similar spirit he makes as little concession as possible to the necessity of being fenced in and roofed over. He prefers 'very large rooms' that are 'light and brilliant and lofty . . . in which you wanted to keep your hat on', habitations perhaps rather pathetically reminiscent of the wide and empty plains. Valentin's rooms, on the other hand, are 'low, dusky, contracted, and crowded'; the Bellegardes' houses are barricaded against the open world by high walls and iron gates, that in the Rue de L'Université reminding Newman of a convent, and their country home seeming to him to be 'like a Chinese penitentiary'; whilst in losing Claire, her American fiancé suffers not only the pain of loss, but also feels the shock of horror at the thought of her being shut in, imprisoned, deprived in her retreat of physical expanse and movement.

A prototypical Westerner, drawn by an author who had scarcely penetrated the cultural wilderness west of Manhattan Island, Newman has perched 'on rail fences in young Western towns, in the twilight . . . with humorous loafers and obscure fortune-seekers', and 'sat with Western humorists in knots round cast-iron stoves, and seen "tall" stories grow taller without toppling over'. He is also portrayed within a symbolic tradition still more generalized, being recognized by Mr Babcock, the intellectual and introspective New Englander, as 'one of nature's noblemen'.[3] And when Valentin has pointed out to him the perhaps insuperable inconvenience of his lack of a title, Newman himself insists: 'But I say I am noble'. To the opposition between the new Western American and the old Europeans can be added, then, an element of the romantic contrast between an unofficial *natural* nobility and an official *social* nobility which masks a profound spiritual ignobility. (However, the nobility which the young Madame de Bellegarde discerns in him and which persuades her briefly to honour him with the title of Duke of California, in compensation for the misfortune of having been born an American, is doubtless a quality more financial than natural, she herself being avowedly on her 'knees to money'.)

Newman is also 'a child of nature',[4] with respect to his incomprehension, at least initially, of elaborate social convention, and with respect to his unease and confusion upon entering the aesthetic universe. The novel opens in the Louvre, a microcosmic expression of all Europe's differences from uncharted, unformalized, extra-historical, and aesthetically virgin America. In this unfamiliar territory, Newman is suffering from an 'aesthetic headache', for 'Raphael and Titian and Rubens were a new kind of arithmetic, and they inspired our friend, for the first time in his life, with a vague self-mistrust'. Like his partial model, Mark Twain, who had toured Europe in 1867, the year before Newman's adventure, and who had given an extensive account of his responses in *Innocents Abroad*, Newman is far more interested in the narrative content of a picture than in its formal totality, and is continually disposed to translate the subject of a painting back from the canvas to its original source of inspiration in the natural and human world.[5] Veronese's *Marriage-Feast of Cana*, for instance, 'satisfied his conception, which was ambitious, of what a splended banquet should be'. Though he studiously consults his Baedeker, he approaches European high culture not as something to be aesthetically and historically apprehended, but as a landscape spread out before him, an unexplored territory, to be covered, devoured, staked out. He wishes to see 'the finest pictures and handsomest churches'; and, in the case of churches, on his summer tour he manages to consume 'some four hundred and seventy'. If the aesthetic dimension is at first alien and troublesome to this 'child of nature', how much more drastically so is the intricate construct of European *social* forms and conventions, whose sacrosanct 'differences' he can hardly perceive. With 'his stock of ready-made formulas and phrases . . . the scantiest', he is alternately bewildered by and contemptuous of all this 'mere gallantry and compliments and nonsense'. However, it is worth noting here that whereas 'the first green leaves of Long Island'[6] (the natural world) had provided the background scenery for his earlier spiritual transformation, it is the Cathedral of Notre-Dame (the aesthetic and historical world) which he felt 'was the best place he could be in' for the meditation at the close of the novel, which led to his self-release from the limitations of an avenger's psychology. This difference may serve as a measure of the extent to which Newman has changed from being some kind of untutored child of nature, whose profoundest emotions find their appropriate accompaniment in the natural world, into a man whose sensibility at a moment of intense pressure can powerfully respond to Europe's non-natural world, artificial, aesthetic, historical.

Twain's travel book can provide a further descriptive term for the essential Newman. He too is an 'innocent abroad'. Not altogether, of course, for he comes to Europe with 'an eye in which innocence and experience were singularly blended'; but that experience must be very largely financial, and social and psychological only in so far as he might well be able to gauge accurately how many of the 'business virtues' a new acquaintance possessed. At first, 'the complex Parisian world about him seemed a very simple affair'; he is to learn how disastrously mistaken he is in this ascription of simplicity. It is especially the Nioches, those representative Parisians inhabiting the amorphous terrain where the petty bourgeoisie and the *demi-mondaines* briefly intermingle, who act as disabusers of his simplifying innocence. Gullible and 'trustful', his immediate impression of the artfully deceptive Noémie is that she is 'so honest. Beauty, talent, virtue; she combined everything!' Talent she certainly has, but not quite of the kind that Newman first believed he discerned. So radical is his misinterpretation of her, and so sharp is the lesson she teaches him, that by the time he meets her in London in the following year, truly 'a sadder and a wiser man' now, she has come to seem to him 'an odious blot upon the face of nature'. As for her moth-eaten, dog-eared father, it is a still longer time before Valentin and the evidence of Newman's own eyes can together convince him that M. Nioche's moral disapproval of his daughter runs a poor second to his liking for the material advantages her coquetry brings him. Above all, though, it is the Bellegarde family who lead him along the briary path from innocence to experience, from a 'general hospitality to the chances of life' to the imagination of evil and disaster. 'You will never understand', exclaims Valentin early on in their friendship, momentarily irritated by the possibility of Newman's never recognizing the complexity of things fully enough to appreciate the younger Bellegarde's generosity. Perhaps he never does completely 'understand', but by the end it is as much a matter of choice as of inability. And of course the irony of the novel, both comic and tragic, is chiefly located in Newman's 'innocent' impercipience and incomprehension (admittedly an increasingly wilful incomprehension) of aristocratic etiquette and values. One example may suffice by way of illustration: Madame de Bellegarde's insistence on giving the engagement party in her house rather than in Newman's apartment seemed to the American

> a handsome proposal, and such proposals always touched the sources of his good-nature. He said to Madame de Bellegarde that he should be glad to come on the 25th or any other day, and that it mattered very little whether he met his friends at her house or at his own. I have said that Newman was observant, but it must be admitted that on this occasion he failed to notice a certain delicate glance which passed between Madame de Bellegarde and the marquis, and which we may presume to have been a commentary upon the innocence displayed in the latter clause of his speech. (Ch. 14)

Gradually, as events force Newman to look more closely and to delve more deeply into human behaviour and motives, such blithe innocence is lost to him, such sweet unconsciousness is lifted. In this context, it should be noted that *The American* changes character, as Newman's vulnerable naïvety develops into a self-protective awareness. It begins as a novel that is 'realistic' in its social observation and narrative material, yet one that is seen chiefly through the eyes of a man who has a 'romantic' (and thus, in some sense, false) vision of Europe, a vision altogether too benign and 'innocent'. It concludes as a novel in which melodramatic and 'romantic' events (duels, dark

secrets, devilish glances, murders, flights into convents) expose the
'reality' of Europe, which Newman now sees, in all its thickness and
complexity of history and evil, beneath the deceptive surface of
appearances. Romanticized social realism becomes psychologically
realistic romance, and in so changing and becoming it seems to me
that *The American* actually escapes and transcends the rather simpler
opposition between realism and romance which so concerned James
in his Preface to the New York edition.

New American man, 'Western Barbarian', 'nature's nobleman',
'child of nature', 'innocent abroad': to this configuration of nineteenth-century mythic roles, one further variant may be added – that
is, the American as optimist. Newman has known hard times; once

> failure seemed inexorably his portion; ill-luck became his bed-fellow,
> and whatever he touched he turned, not to gold, but to ashes . . . there
> seemed to him something stronger in life than his own will. (Ch. 2)

But the indignation he had felt at this 'impertinent force', which
threatened any optimism, challenged his control over events, and
tempted him into the sin of failure, had inflamed his zeal and
hardened his determination. Irritated by 'fatality in misery', he
'buffeted his way into smooth waters'; his optimism carried him to
success; and his success proved the virtue of his optimism, bore
witness that optimism was the right and natural emotional condition.
One of Newman's earliest exchanges with M. Nioche nicely polarizes
New World buoyancy and Old World defeatism (both speakers, it
should be remembered, having been on the same side of the economic
fence, as businessmen, as capitalists):

> 'Do I understand you to say that you have had reverses?' asked
> Newman.
> 'Reverses? Oh, sir, misfortunes – terrible.'
> 'Unsuccessful in business, eh?'
> 'Very unsuccessful, sir.'
> 'Oh, never fear, you'll get on your legs again,' said Newman cheerily.
> The old man drooped his head on one side and looked at him with an
> expression of pain, as if this were an unfeeling jest. (Ch. 1)

Newman's optimism in economic matters is but one aspect,

albeit the most important as far as the prehistory of the narrative is concerned, of an emotional hue that colours his every attitude. Possessed of a 'vast sunny immunity' from depression, he lives in a steady mood of 'good-humoured prosperity', demands of his prospective language tutor, M. Nioche, that their conversation be 'cheerful', 'bright', and 'lively', and responds only to paintings that are 'bright and gay'. (He would assuredly have approved of Howells's dictum of the moment that 'truthfulness to American life requires a note of cheerfulness'.) Through experiences which include the death of his closest European friend, and the death-to-worldly-life of the woman he loves, Newman comes to know not only despair, but perhaps more significantly a dull melancholy, and to realize, in the face of malevolent power and evil, the superficiality, the falsity, the sheer bland irrelevance of his earlier optimism.

Newman is no literary man. 'The newspapers form his principal reading'; he has 'never read a novel'; and he conducts his 'correspondence altogether by telegram'. None the less, his ignorance of literary culture need not deter one from locating him on the periphery at least of an intellectual territory inhabited, for all their great differences, by Whitman, Twain and Howells – at any rate in their younger days before each underwent his separate, cautionary disillusionment. He is placed there by those qualities of his outlined above – variously, by his initial optimism, his sentimental cheeriness, his denial or unawareness of evil, his 'naturalness' and spontaneity, his discomfort in the presence of artifice, and his dislike of elaborate convention. He is of his time and of his place, a product and an expression of the American mid nineteenth century, of a social and intellectual history characterized, for instance, by the Westward Movement, by the gospel of Manifest Destiny, and by the Transcendentalist departure from orthodox Christianity and the concomitant evasion of the problem of evil. However, like his more literary counterparts he did not spring suddenly and fully formed in all his informality upon the historical landscape. He, like them, has evidently behind him the massive Protestant heritage. He is representatively Protestant in Catholic Europe. And, unlike the writers, he is an extraordinarily clear illustration of the intertwining of the spiritual and the economic orders. Newman stands at the nexus of Protestantism and capitalism.

He is not of course, in any important sense, a symptom of that relatively specific phenomenon, the decline in the nineteenth century (indeed through the eighteenth century also) of New England Puritan culture, its dogmatic zeal sliding into a diffident earnestness, its fiery intellectual passion dwindling into little more than Mr Babcock's heartburn. He is no Bostonian. His good manners are genial rather than genteel. And he considers the possibility of being 'compelled to live in Boston' as but an appropriately severe punishment for Tom Tristram's cultural treason. Boston, or at least Dorchester, Massachusetts, has its spokesman in *The American* in the shape of Babcock, the depressingly worthy Unitarian minister, who briefly accompanies Newman on his summer tour of Holland, Germany and Italy. But Babcock functions only in extreme contrast to Newman, as a means of defining, by his cautious asceticism, his thin-spiritedness, and his relentless seriousness, all that Newman is not. They are so different, in fact, that eventually Babcock cannot 'take' Newman any more than the Bellegardes can, and leaves him in Venice with the intense plea that his easy-going acquaintance 'remember that Life and Art *are* extremely serious'.

Babcock is a faded heir of the Puritan divines, similarly intellectual and cultivated, and similarly gripped in 'his secret soul' by a detestation of corrupt and splendid Europe. Newman is no such direct descendant; but he is sufficiently imbued with a Protestant psychology to find Catholicism completely, incomprehensibly foreign. His religious ardour is not warm enough for him to feel towards Rome any burning hatred; indeed, his religious emotion is apparently so cool that he is essentially a kind of proto-secular man, whose references to life 'here below' are merely typical of Protestantism at a certain stage of sentimental disintegration. But the loose system of values, which he has inherited from Protestantism and its diffusion, and which characterizes him as individualistic, moralistic, practical and activist, does render him quite incapable of understanding a religion which appears to him to be one solely of forms, rituals, and mystical withdrawal. 'He will die in the best sentiments. . . . The curé was quite satisfied', observes M. de Grosjoyaux, as Valentin sinks towards death in the next room. ' "Heaven forgive us!" groaned Newman. "I would rather the doctor were satisfied." ' M. de

Grosjoyauz's fellow second at the duel, M. Ledoux, was also 'a great Catholic, and Newman thought him a queer mixture'. One of the most witty implications of the gulf between the mind of the American Protestant and that of the European Catholic is contained in the following exchange between Newman and Valentin:

> 'Are you very religious?' asked Newman, in a tone which gave the enquiry a grotesque effect.
>
> M. de Bellegarde evidently appreciated the comical element in the question, but he looked at Newman a moment with extreme soberness. 'I am a very good Catholic. I respect the Church. I adore the blessed Virgin. I fear the Devil.' (Ch. 7)

A more painful expression of the same mental gap is Newman's agonizing incomprehension of Claire's retreat into the convent.

> He had never let the fact of her Catholicism trouble him; Catholicism to him was nothing but a name, and to express a mistrust of the form in which her religious feelings had moulded themselves would have seemed to him on his own part a rather pretentious affectation of Protestant zeal. If such superb white flowers as that could bloom in Catholic soil, the soil was not insalubrious. But it was one thing to be Catholic, and another to turn nun – on your hands! There was something lugubriously comical in the way Newman's thoroughly contemporaneous optimism was confronted with this dusky old-world expedient. To see a woman made for him and for motherhood to his children juggled away in this tragic travesty – it was a thing to rub one's eyes over, a nightmare, an illusion, a hoax. (Ch. 21)

However, by far the most important effect of Newman's cultural background is manifested in his attitude towards work, in his proud subscription to the Protestant work ethic. Continually, Newman is drawn to emphasize the opposition between an America that works and a Europe that plays, between an America in which work is a supreme virtue and a Europe for which work is an activity faintly indecent and scarcely mentionable. The terms of the opposition are of course contained exclusively within the circle of privilege, the world of wealth, accrued or inherited, which is simultaneously removed from and directly productive of the proliferating areas of real oppression and exploitation. Even the Nioches are no exception; M.

Nioche is merely 'a reduced capitalist', a potential exploiter turned parasite upon the dallying aristocracy. The real working-classes are invisible – albeit to a slightly lesser extent than in many of James's later novels – from the windows of the apartments along wide boulevards and the drawing-rooms overlooking private courtyards that Newman frequents. The closest we come to a glimpse of them is of those who are the immediate appendages of aristocratic and bourgeois life, the servants arranged in the shadows, the waiters hovering for a tip, the cab-drivers racing back and forth with their whimsical fares. Only to the hypersensitive listener are there hints of the communards or of the human material that had played its essential part in Newman's coming out 'successful in copper' and 'pretty square in leather'. This is an argument conducted solely between those whose interests are ultimately, beyond the barricades, the same: between aspirant, aggressive bourgeois and entrenched, defensive aristocracy; between 'progressive' entrepreneur and 'conservative' landowner; between new money and old blood. And reference to the barricades is neither sensational nor irrelevant. Had Newman stayed a few months longer in Paris, he might have discovered some common ground with the Marquis de Bellegarde at the time of the Commune.

The confines of the dialogue duly recognized, it is certainly the case that Newman's sense of his difference from the Parisians with whom he comes in contact is acute and persistent. The contrast is impressed upon us within a few moments of meeting him, when, sampling the unfamiliar, spectatorial leisure of the pavement café, he is asked by Tom Tristram how he has made his money:

> Newman had pushed his hat back from his forehead, folded his arms, and stretched his legs. He listened to the music, he looked about him at the bustling crowd, at the plashing fountains, at the nurses and the babies. 'I have worked!' he answered at last. (Ch. 2)

The implicit reprimand is addressed not only to playful Paris, but also to the languid and indolent Tristram, who has in effect, in Newman's view, betrayed America's industrious ideals. Later, he proposes his 'proud consciousness of honest toil' as cause and explanation of the easy contentment that Valentin envies in him. The ease

comes from a clear conscience, a grateful awareness of personal virtue
– the double virtue of work and success. His inner tranquillity,
though, would not long survive on the boulevards. He has come to
Paris to 'have a good time', to 'loaf', to *relax* – no, to be precise, he
has come less to do these things than to learn how to do them, or even
to find out whether he can learn how to do them. He will surely fail
to learn these other rhythms; his restless Puritanical urges are too
strong. 'I am a good worker . . . but I rather think I am a poor
loafer,' he almost boasts. To the Marquis de Bellegarde, representatively the aristocrat disdainful of any form of remunerative employment, he stresses but does not exaggerate his conflicting attitudes
and emotional temper:

> Paris is a very good place for idle people. . . . But I am not an idler. I
> try to be, but I can't manage it; it goes against the grain. My business
> habits are too deep-seated. . . . I miss my business activity. You see, I
> began to earn my living when I was almost a baby, and until a few
> months ago I have never had my hand off the plough. Elegant leisure
> comes hard. (Ch. 10)

He is feeling the first itches of the need to return to office, factory,
and stock exchange.

It will be noticed that Newman in talking of his work habits uses
phrases like 'hands on the plough' and 'honest toil' derived from
manual labour. Now it is obviously the case that many successful
American capitalists, of fact and of fiction, have started on their
journeys from rags to riches (their 'inevitable' journeys, Valentin
remarks) with their hands on the plough or the axe or the pick.
Presumably Newman, whom at the age of fourteen 'necessity had
taken . . . by his slim young shoulders', was no exception; although,
significantly, there is no specific reference to such activity. But the
point to be made here is that to Newman, for all such fine plain
phrases, work is indistinguishable from the making of money. Apart
from its profitability, the nature of the work, its substantive quality,
interests him scarcely more than it does the Bellegardes.

> It must be admitted, rather nakedly, that Christopher Newman's sole
> aim in life had been to make money; what he had been placed in the
> world for was, to his own perception, simply to wrest a fortune, the

bigger the better, from defiant opportunity. This idea completely filled his horizon and satisfied his imagination. Upon the uses of money, upon what one might do with a life into which one had succeeded in injecting the golden stream, he had up to his thirty-fifth year very scantily reflected. Life had been for him an open game, and he had played for high stakes. He had won at last and carried off his winnings; and now what was he to do with them? (Ch. 2)

There it is exactly, in those last two sentences: he had gambled, he had speculated, and he had won. Such has been his 'honest toil', his 'plough'. Newman provides a marvellously lucid illustration (of which James may not have been entirely and continuously conscious) of the interrelationship and mutual encouragement of the capitalist economy and Protestant values. The capitalist justifies and celebrates his activity by insistent reference to the work ethic; the protestant conscience, listening to the gospel of work, urges on the individual capitalist initiative; the goad is the fear of failure and the consequent guilt; the success is the reward and the proof of virtue; and, all the while, the fact that 'work', however tiring or ulcerating it may be, is essentially the process of the capitalist economy is disguised by a heart-stirring rhetoric of 'honest toil' and the sweat and grime of scantly rewarded physical labour. The financier becomes a 'toiler', and the genuine ploughman a figure for the necessary inspiriting rhetoric.

So, proudly and placidly says Newman: 'I have worked'; or again, 'I can't say I have had any specialty. My specialty has been to make the largest possible fortune in the shortest possible time.' He has pursued this almost patriotic aim so unrelentingly that on his own admission, 'I have never had time to feel things. I have had to *do* them, to make myself felt.' This imbalance within him, by implication one that is typically American, is to be harshly corrected in Paris. For a time it might be said that he continues in his familiar mould, since the story seems to concern less his feelings for Claire, notwithstanding his sentimental idealization of her, than the necessity to make himself felt, with the full weight of his money, by the Bellegardes. But it ends with Newman, his deepest emotions aroused and then thwarted, learning amongst other hard lessons that the dominion of his will and of its chief instrument, his money, is not infinite. Or to put it simply and bluntly, he learns that money cannot buy everything.

That his approach to the world has been entirely pecuniary is clear from the first word we hear him utter: 'Combien?' It is 'the single word which constituted the strength of his French vocabulary'. More than that, it is a word from the only language he knows at all fluently, the language of money. It is a brilliant opening, this enquiry into price in the museum of the Louvre; it is a compression of the whole conflict between Europe and America. America will attempt to buy Europe, or, in this initial instance of Noémie's copy of a Madonna, at least an imitation of Europe. 'Dynamic' America will make a bid for 'stagnant' Europe. Europe though tempted, will resist. To Newman everything, everybody, must have a price, must be up for sale. The acquisition does not demand any especial ruthlessness; it is just, for him, the unquestioned way of moving through the world. 'The world, to his sense, was a great bazaar, where one might stroll about and purchase handsome things.' Thus, although he can talk of the wife for whom he is seeking in terms of a familiar bourgeois romantic idolatry, as an object to be revered and almost worshipped, he can also woo her with the 'great directness and firmness' of a financier engaged in a takeover operation, and can speak of her in purely proprietary terms as something to be paid for and possessed, as the 'best article in the market', and as 'the *thing* best worth having' (my italics).[7] As a result, whilst the larger part of our sympathies is extended towards Newman in his loss of Claire, as towards one whose generous and genuine emotions have been crushed by evil and destructive forces, we feel at the same time that a necessary penalty has been exacted – one that could not have been exacted if the marriage had finally taken place – for that earlier omnivorous acquisitiveness.[8]

This acquisitiveness should not at all be mistaken for miserliness or any slow, persistent, accumulative avarice. Newman is a big money-maker, but he is also a big spender. And the difference between the American economy and psychology, on the one hand, and the less flexible and spectacular French counterparts, on the other, is reflected in the contrast between Newman's largesse and fondness for 'treating' people, and the 'thriftiness' and 'delicate frugalities' of bourgeois Paris. His generosity in financial matters relates closely to the one further aspect of his character which needs to be mentioned in the context of his Americanness – this being his egalitarianism, the 'genuinely democratic assumptions' of this 'great strapping demo-crat'. In these qualities we are again to read him as typically Ameri-can, and to see his holding of such attitudes as in no way incompatible with his situation as a successful self-made capitalist. First of all, his is obviously the egalitarianism of opportunity rather than of con-dition. Secondly, it is an egalitarianism mainly for the already privi-leged, in that it would open with money doors that breeding and heritage would keep closed. Thirdly, it is little more (although in Legitimist Parisian circles it is precious enough as this) than an easy affability of manner towards servants and waiters, an 'unprecedented approachableness'. (In other words, it is a cast of mind that sets in motion no radical politics. His kindness towards Mrs Bread in em-ploying her and thus freeing her from the Bellegardes in no way alters her own conception of a servant as 'a mysteriously projected machine'.) In effect, his egalitarianism is a further reflection, mani-fested here in social terms, of that openness and expansiveness which are also conveyed, geographically, in Newman the free-roaming Westerner, and, economically, in Newman the capitalist in a *laissez-faire* economy. It is the social manner of one unused to restriction of movement, whether physical or financial – the manner of a citizen of the 'free country'.

However individualized, however distinctive and idiosyncratic, Newman is first and foremost a figure allegorical in conception, a personification of American values, 'habits of mind and feeling', and economic and social formation. He is the New Man in the Old World; creature of the virgin Western spaces in a cramped and crowded Paris, dense with history; the *naïf* and innocent amongst the sophisti-cated and experienced; spontaneous 'natural man' amongst the formal and conventional. He is a democrat with open arms con-fronted by an exclusive aristocracy; an heir of the Protestant con-science in a world of Catholics who have fought for the Pope; a parvenu, who had 'to earn [his] living when [he] was almost a baby', loose amongst families paralysed by the sense of their own past, beginning 'somewhere in the ninth century, under Charlemagne'; a self-made financial man of an expanding commercial Republic face to face with reactionary Royalist landowners, frozen behind history. He is the American Protestant individualist displayed in his economic guise as the Capitalist. The hero of *The American* is all these things before he is Christopher Newman, with his 'clear, cold gray' eyes and 'rather abundant mustache', who falls in love with Claire de Cintré.

That he is so has not been fully enough appreciated by those several readers who have judged Newman to be 'incredible', 'unreal', 'ridiculous', 'false', 'artificial', or 'romanticized'.[9] No Westerner, it has been claimed, who had known San Francisco in the first boom years, and presumably 'bleeding Kansas', silver-strike Nevada, gold-rush California, and the cut-throat world of the competing railroads, could have been so well-mannered and so pleasantly at ease, for all the 'missed jokes', in the drawing-rooms of Ultramontane Paris; no pre-eminently successful rival of such immediate contemporaries as Daniel Drew, Jim Fisk, Jay Gould, Collis P. Huntington, John Pierpont Morgan, Leland Stanford, Cornelius Vanderbilt, and the Rockefellers, could have been, even given the change of heart on Long Island, so trusting, thoughtful, sweet-tempered, generous-spirited, and unprepared for devious machinations.[10] Says Newman to Claire: 'I honestly believe I have no hidden vices or nasty tricks. I am kind! kind! kind!' And we believe him – that is, we believe that he believes it of himself.

Now, certainly, in the original version of *The American* there are some glaring and obtrusive improbabilities, which James 'corrected' for the New York edition; for instance, the information that Newman's vast fortune had been carved out in less than three years, since he had come out of the Civil War 'penniless' – three years, during which he had involved himself in copper, railroads, oil, leather, wash-tubs, and various other unmentioned and unmentionable commodities, in some of which he had been 'a hopeless fizzle'. But such inaccuracies of detail apart, the objections to which I have referred seem to me to be trivial. The book's interest and the irony, comic and tragic, lie less in Newman, as specific man with all his eccentricities and peculiarities, than in Newman, the American. Christopher Newman is the typical, the archetypal, American, the complex of characteristically American attitudes, values, modes of perception, experiences. That the role he plays as American associates him with, variously, Davy Crockett as striding Westerner and Jim Fisk or Jay Gould as speculator and financier, whilst he is at the same time in his particular individuality scarcely compatible with our images of those legendary-historical figures, is a measure of the extent to which his conception is as much generic and allegorical as it is specific and realistic.

Newman's is not the only name with allegorical overtones. Those of most of the Parisians he meets suggest that the bearers play a role that is allegorical, at least in part. For Newman, Claire, who most memorably appears 'dressed in white', is the bright, clear light entering his life, which previously, he has come to think, had 'a rather graceless and sordid mien' (cf. *Roderick Hudson's* Christina Light). In the novel her emotional journey, from imprisonment within widowhood and her family household, outwards to the freedom offered by Newman, and back to the confinement of the convent, is indeed *curved*, as the surname, de Cintré, which she bears from her earlier marriage, signifies. The guardians, the custodians, the watch-dogs over this beauty, an epitome of the beauty and richness of Europe, are the Bellegardes. The Marquis's forename, Urbain, testifies to his being the highly polished city aristocrat in opposition to the rough and rugged 'child of nature'. His younger brother, Valentin, presides, a light-hearted patron saint, over Newman's love affair and, like his Roman namesake before him, dies a martyr in some sense to a code and a set of principles, however ridiculously debased; whilst Newman's other chief advocate, Mrs Tristram, is obviously associated by her name with doomed romantic love, especially at this time of frequent re-creations of the medieval story – by Arnold, Tennyson, Wagner, and shortly by Swinburne. Finally, in this context, the faithful servant, the stuff of plain decency in this world of elaborate corruption, is named, with heavy aptness, Mrs Bread.[11]

Tom Tristram exists as a warning to Newman, and to James himself as he formally begins his expatriation, of the dangers of a complete and permanent uprooting. He remains here, though, little more than a sketch of the rootless man, a practice drawing for the more substantial portraits which were to follow.[12] Through him James confronts the less admirable aspects of the radical rejection of America and of the casual denial of the American heritage. Uprooted from the nourishing native soil, Tristram has lost all the characteristic American virtues, which Newman still possesses, and has become 'shamefully idle, spiritless, sensual, snobbish', and in physical appearance 'corpulent and rosy'. But, in losing his American qualities, he has absorbed little in compensation from Europe. He is still aesthetically blind – to the Louvre ('I don't call this Paris!'), to Italy, an 'awful country', and to the subtle beauty of Claire de Cintré.[13] He spends much of his time at the club playing poker with fellow-Americans, while at the same time his sense of America is of something 'little better than a vulgar smell'. The only wisdom he possesses is a kind of common-sensical cynicism which accounts for his lack of surprise at the failure of Newman's quest. He is the embodiment of misspent leisure, of utterly wasted and dissipated energy, whose wife punishes him with contempt and banishment to the sidelines of any important conversation. And although with his amiability and his lack of malice he is essentially 'a good fellow', whose dislike of the mean-spirited Bellegardes is intense, he is also, Newman feels, 'a rather degenerate mortal', a cautionary example for Americans, like Newman and James, who have just taken up residence in Europe. There is in the rootless Tristram no chance of growth, and by the end of his time in Paris Newman has come to feel that he has 'outgrown . . . completely the phase of equal friendship with Tom Tristram'. Hedonist and philistine, he is the creation of a James who was both a Protestant moralist and a cosmopolitan aesthete.

Mrs Tristram, like her husband, provides a hint of later and more complete characters. She is an early version of the confidante, of the *ficelle*. With regard to the main action, Newman's courtship of Claire, she is its initial instigator, its intermediary assistant, and its retrospective commentator and interpreter. While her liking and concern for Newman and Claire are genuine, and while the part she plays in the affairs of their hearts is benevolent and constructive, she is also driven by self-interested motives, the interest being that of a social experiment undertaken by a connoisseur of manners and social nuance. Reviewing with her the failure of his endeavour, Newman asks:

'Was it from curiosity that you urged me to try and marry her?'

'A little,' said Mrs Tristram, growing still more audacious. Newman gave her the one angry look he had been destined ever to give her, turned away and took up his hat. She watched him a moment, and then she said, 'That sounds very cruel, but it is less so than it sounds. Curiosity has a share in almost everything I do. I wanted very much to see, first, whether such a marriage could actually take place; second, what would happen if it should take place.'

'So you didn't believe,' said Newman, resentfully.

'Yes, I believed – I believed that it would take place, and that you would be happy. Otherwise I should have been, among my speculations, a very heartless creature. *But*', she continued, laying her hand upon Newman's arm and hazarding a grave smile, 'it was the highest flight ever taken by a tolerably bold imagination!' (Ch. 25)

This element of 'heartless', objective experimentalism she shares with Newman's other well-wishers – with the young Marquise, and with Valentin. All three are trapped, at various stages of discontent, within their leisured situations; all are either saved or prevented, by either money or status, from 'doing' anything. Mrs Tristram's lively intelligence, elsewhere unfulfilled and scarcely challenged, exercises itself playing social chequers, with her friends as the pieces. The feather-brained, 'silly, thirstily-smiling' Marquise – that 'ferocious democrat' for whom democracy means a readiness to flirt with Newman – that 'revolutionary' whose principal revolutionary ambition is to attend the students' Bal Bullier – looks upon Newman's courtship as a possible respite from her chronic ennui, a promising momentary relief from the oppressive tedium of her own marriage. Even Newman's beloved Valentin, early accorded by his aristocratic station no option of activity but to fight for the Pope, having dutifully 'received an apostolic flesh-wound', returns to Paris and to a boulevardier's voyeurism. Noémie Nioche, Mme Dandelard, Newman, Claire: for all Valentin's sweetness and generosity of temper, each of these is in some respect but grist to the mill of his unemployed intellect. His association with Mme Dandelard he explains with disarming honesty:

I am watching the process. I am curious to see just how things will go. Yes I know what you are going to say: this horrible Paris hardens one's

heart. But it quickens one's wits, and it ends by teaching one a refinement of observation! To see this little woman's little drama play itself
out, now, is, for me, an intellectual pleasure. (Ch. 7)

(James himself was at this time talking of 'beastly Paris' and of 'the
superiority of English culture and the English mind to the French'.)[14]
And quite revelling in his permanent condition of torpor, he admits
to Newman that the American's affair

> will be more than amusing . . . it will be inspiring. I look at it from my
> point of view, and you from yours. After all, anything for a change!
> And only yesterday I was yawning so as to dislocate my jaw, and
> declaring that there was nothing new under the sun![15] If it isn't new to
> see you come into the family as a suitor, I am very much mistaken. Let
> me say that, my dear fellow; I won't call it anything else, bad or good;
> I will simply call it *new*. (Ch. 8)

Even though Mrs Tristram, the Marquise, and Valentin are to a
greater or lesser extent on Newman's 'side' (and hence on ours), this
aspect of their involvement on his behalf makes for a damning
critique of aristocratic and high bourgeois leisure, and of a society
on whose polished upper surface such dangerous, 'heartless' games
are played. James himself knew from childhood a life of equivalent
leisure, inherited wealth, and material ease, but the world of the
deeply serious and responsible New York and Boston intelligentsia
was a far, disapproving cry from that of Haussmann's boulevards and
the Rue de L'Université. (Perhaps it is also possible to see in the
figure of Valentin, who from the first holds such a romantic attraction
for Newman and yet simultaneously alarms him with his dispassionate objectivity, a dim reflection of the person of Flaubert, for whom at
this time James had similarly ambiguous feelings, a mixture of
fascination and repulsion at his 'coldness'.)[16]

A willingness, like that of Mrs Tristram and of Valentin, to
manipulate others for their own entertainment must always be
potentially destructive of emotion. As such it is but an aspect, a mild
version of that deathliness which, as James would have us see it,
permeates the whole of Parisian society. In *The American* Europe is
undeniably a kind of death. Its essential character is lethal. And

against it the American Newman, for all his defects, offers an equally undeniable life, a manifest sunny 'vitality'. Death squats in a corner of the European soul, ready to make of every European either a victim or a killer. A recent expatriate, James in Europe is literally dicing with death.

Take M. Nioche, that 'exquisite image of shabby gentility'. His façade of programmatic respectability and moral alertness is, variously, impenetrable to Newman and transparent to Valentin. Behind that façade there is a hideously clashing interior of spiritual defeat ('I have no spirit, and when you have no spirit you must keep quiet'), self-disgust, self-pity, half-hearted self-righteousness, a shrieking – though barely audible – hatred of his daughter, and yet at the same time an irresistible greed for the material ease and comfort which her successful coquetry will bring him. French bourgeois society and the French economy are neither flexible nor resilient enough to sow in this 'reduced capitalist' the continuously self-renewing optimism on which Newman flourishes; hence his fatalism, in spite and indeed because of his inability to think in any terms other than those of the slow social climb, of clambering unsteadily upwards in the wake of his daughter's petticoats, in the hope that she will lead him to a measure of 'respectability' in the shadows of *le grand monde's* amours. A good petit bourgeois, he has learned no ambition other than economic accumulation and modest social aspiration; baulked, 'reversed' financially, he still has no vision beyond or outside the social elevator. Economic acquisitiveness, membership in a demarcated and rigid society and token bourgeois morality make for insoluble, internal contradiction, which in terms of personality must entail a total hypocrisy. Suffering from a kind of quiescent hysteria, M. Nioche lives a lie – a lie that has killed his spirit.

His daughter is alive enough. Indeed her liveliness, on which her father leeches as his only remaining capital, is part cause of his spiritual vacancy or death. Like Mrs Tristram, but in an entirely 'heartless' manner, Noémie is a skilful manipulator, a player with human pawns, from the moment she sets out, with her copy-paintings and, later, her strategic 'sudden frankness' about their mediocrity, to hook a piece of Newman or of his money, to the time when the basic destructiveness of her role is exposed in her responsibility for the death of Valentin, her frustrated lover, or, in turn, her 'user'. 'I don't care who does which, so long as you make a scene,' she cries; and Valentin, obedient to a deadly honour, provokes a duel and goes off to die. She had first seemed to Newman, the personification of 'beauty, talent [and] virtue', dazzled as he was by all things European, and worshipful of all apparently 'respectable' women. Soon even the American innocent can recognize that this worldly-wise child of European experience has 'simply never had any' innocence. Later he will not dispute with a titillated Valentin that her soul is hard enough, has sufficient of the stuff of death in it, to make her 'capable of looking at a man strangled without changing colour'. And finally for Newman, simultaneously Protestant moralist, natural man, and grief-stricken friend of the martyred Valentin, she becomes 'an odious blot upon the face of nature', a spot where murder has been done. But however unsympathetic, however irredeemably callous Noémie may be, we still feel that it is less her who is to blame than the Europe which has made her what she is. In other words, her viciousness is product rather than essence.

Europe, then, is death for the young Henry James, who, having chosen expatriation, becomes therefore a kind of social and cultural necrophiliac, a less physiological Poe. And of course this European death is most fully incorporated within the whole Bellegarde family, the type of Europe, as Newman of America – a Europe which, as the necessary inverse of America according to the dictates of this romantic mythology, is authoritarian, hierarchic, inflexible, exclusive, aristocratic, and Catholic. The only distinction within that world is between the 'good' Bellegardes who are murdered (either literally or metaphorically) and the 'bad' Bellegardes who murder.

To the extent that he has repudiated the values (or perhaps, more precisely, the characteristics) of the Bellegardes, Valentin has embraced life. He is outward-looking, 'completely void of introspection'; he is 'expansive', 'irresistibly entertaining and enlivening'; indeed he is 'intensely alive – frankly, ardently, gallantly alive'. And yet there is no outlet for all this personal vitality. His social status allows him no means of expressing or developing his liveliness, with the result that he drifts upon his open-ended curiosity to the languor of the perpetual consumer, the ennui of the habitual spectator. He is directed inexorably towards death, albeit initially but a living death. Newman offers him the escape route: America. And Valentin, 'half ironical and half curious', is momentarily 'fascinated by Newman's plain prose version of the legend of Eldorado'. But *The American* is conceived within a design too complex and pessimistic to allow for such a simple escape: if Valentin could have made a new life in America, Newman could have married Claire. Valentin is trapped within Europe; and the irony is to be found in the fact that the trap is partly of his own making. Immediately after toying with the glittering temptation of Eldorado, Valentin returns to Noémie's box at the opera purposefully to instigate the duel of honour, which is retrospectively to be tantamount both to his suicide and to his murder by something like 'the spirit of Europe'. He dies at dawn and in spring. But no hint of rebirth accompanies his funeral. There is merely the greater ironic poignancy that such a fine young life, which had kicked so gaily against the pricks of aristocratic Europe, has been snuffed out.

Just as Newman points the American way out to Valentin, so does he propose that possibility to Claire – and of course far more completely and insistently. Of the major characters in the book Claire has seemed to many readers to be the least satisfactorily imagined. James's problem with Claire was to create a woman impressive enough to infatuate Newman, less by physical beauty than by conspicuous distinction of personality; and at the same time to make her passive, timorous, and helpless enough to be a victim of her destructive society. In the end, it cannot be denied that he fails his own challenge. It *is* difficult to 'square' the woman who has in the earlier chapters 'in combination, all the brilliant things that he dreamed of finding', and whose mere presence dominated every gathering, so that 'she entirely occupied and filled one's vision', with the woman who so suddenly relinquishes Newman, fearfully obedient to her mother's 'authority'. And yet, in retrospect, the very colourlessness and partial inconsistency in her portrayal may seem entirely appropriate (perhaps almost accidentally). For again we see vitality suppressed, and the free flow of personality interrupted – 'rendered inconsistent', it could even be said; so that as Claire fades from the centre of the stage to invisibility behind the walls of the convent, she illustrates all too evidently the inescapable, slow negation of life by aristocratic and haut bourgeois Europe.

In conversation with Newman about the future, Valentin playfully predicts that 'I shall turn monk. Seriously, I think I shall tie a rope round my waist and go into a monastery.' He dies before the prediction can be fulfilled; and yet its essence is fulfilled, for Valentin conceives of monasticism as unambiguously a means of dying, as a convenient method of disposing of the body, when, as he puts it, the appetite for living has been lost and the pot of life has cracked. Similarly, Claire's flight beyond the clutches of her murderous relatives to the Carmelite nunnery in the Rue d'Enfer is the most effective form of death this side of the grave. And it is not only Newman who thinks of her course of action in terms of death. Claire herself recognizes the suicidal implications of her retreat. Breaking off her engagement to Newman, she begs him to let her 'go in peace. I can't call it peace – it's death. But let me bury myself.' In addition, the address of the monastery is sufficient clue to the absence of any hope. To all intents and purposes her life is closed for her as finally as is Valentin's. There is no sense of a different order of life, a continuing spiritual life, in James's descriptions of the convent. It is a place 'dumb, deaf, inanimate . . . barren . . . dead', where 'the days and years of the future would pile themselves above her like the huge immovable slab of a tomb'.[17] To the murders of the old Marquis and Valentin has been added, effectively, the murder of Claire – or, if one wishes to see in Claire's final decision a vestige of resoluteness, one may say that she chooses to reveal to her family the real death, the denial of the possibility of living, at the heart of their 'way of life'.

'They' are of course specifically old Madame de Bellegarde and her son Urbain, the present Marquis. In their every characteristic they are inverse reflections, within this still relatively simplistic mythology of international differences, of the American Newman: aristocrats whose lineage goes 'back, back, back'; royalists attempting to deny eighty years of history since the French Revolution; Catholics who would surely wish to deny Protestantism too; despisers of work and of the necessity to work, whether that work be sheer labour or the profiteering of 'a commercial person'; people of 'forms and phrases and postures', whose tight, controlled mouths are 'conservative orifices'; rigidly exclusive people, enclosed behind iron gates and stone walls in houses which immediately remind Newman of convents, as convents will later call to mind the tomb.

By choice petrified in the past, they are simultaneously embodiments and dealers of death, their evil consisting chiefly in their simply not allowing life to take place, either in themselves or in others. The Marquis is characterized by a 'stony' or a 'wooden' absence of life. He is writing a book on the significant subject of 'The Princesses of France Who Never Married', and who therefore, it may be generally assumed, never gave birth to new life. In the Marquis that deadly stiffness of manner and iciness of heart are drawn for the most part with the tools of comedy; the devil, though fearsome enough to be detested, is ultimately contemptible and ludicrous. Against him from beginning to end all James's formidable comic armoury is relentlessly directed, and it is a delightful experience to be on hand to watch the process of ridicule:[18]

> The next time [Newman] saw M. de Bellegarde he attempted to call his attention to some of the brilliant features of the time. The marquis presently replied that he had but a single political conviction, which was enough for him: he believed in the divine right of Henry of Bourbon, Fifth of his name, to the throne of France. Newman stared, and after this he ceased to talk politics with M. de Bellegarde. He was not horrified nor scandalized, he was not even amused; he felt as he should have felt if he had discovered in M. de Bellegarde a taste for certain oddities of diet; an appetite, for instance, for fishbones or nutshells. Under these circumstances, of course, he would never have broached dietary questions with him.   (Ch. 13)

Madame de Bellegarde's evil, on the other hand, is derived from a rather different imaginative tradition, one that is more purely melodramatic and at times tentatively heroic. She is a distant kinswoman of Lucifer, or a much closer relative of Hawthorne's intimates of the devil – Mistress Hibbins, Chillingworth, Westervelt.[19] Her authority, unlike the Marquis's, is assured and effective; and though it is perhaps Newman's greatest combative triumph to feel certain that 'she *is* scared! she *is* scared!', he finally has to admit to her 'grit' and her 'steel-cold pluck'. ' "Damn it, she *is* plucky," said Newman, and he walked home with a slight sense of being balked. She was so inexpressibly defiant.' He can soon decide that this pluck may be 'only a very superior style of brazen assurance'. But such a recognition of course lights exactly upon a crucial element of her evil. For the opposition between the Bellegardes and Newman (between Europe and America) is in part the opposition between style and content, between surface and interior, between manners and morals. For James, the post-Protestant moralist, style alone, exquisite formality, was long to remain a clear shape of evil (e.g. Gilbert Osmond) – just as for James, the aesthete and sophisticate, content alone, indiscriminate emotional expenditure was to remain sure ground for tragic folly (e.g. Daisy Miller).

Madame de Bellegarde's evil is most flamboyantly manifested in the murder of her husband. The murder is undeniably melodramatic, as critics of this particular incident have always charged. The drawing-room in which the comedy of manners is being played is suddenly draped with the trappings of gothic horror. Yet the incident, though narratively 'shaking', represents more a heightening of effect, an accentuation, a crescendo of emphasis, than an inexcusably abrupt change in the character of the book. For what is the murder of the old Marquis but an extension into the literal and the physical of the metaphorical and spiritual murder that has been done to Claire, to Valentin, and differently to Newman? The murder is a melodramatic but entirely apt metaphor for the total deathliness of aristocratic Europe, its own murderer, its own victim.

The Bellegardes, mother and son, and the Europe of which they are the quintessence, are the creations of a patriotic and loyalist James, whose American heritage was, variously, Protestant, moralist, democratic, industrious, and indeed, with respect specifically to his father, politically radical and metaphysically visionary. Parasitic and tyrannical, they are creations who in their odiousness bear witness to the intense guilt felt by the expatriate novice. For it is surely the very intensity of this guilt that necessitates the stereotyped character of the conflict and the allegorical polarization. Europe must be as vicious as possible, the American as decent as possible, for James to punish himself sufficiently for his cultural treason. And yet at the same time Europe must have wisdom and beauty enough, and the American be in certain important respects limited and imperceptive enough, to account for, if not quite justify, the refusal to return home. If Newman were to be Henry James, in other words if we were to identify with him whole-heartedly, adopt his *point of view*, James would have to follow Newman back to America. So, for all James's claims in his Preface, our vision cannot always be Newman's. It may be the case that we always stand beside Newman to look at the Marquis in exactly the same spirit of amused detestation, and generally at Madame de Bellegarde, and sometimes at Valentin. But we also spend much of the time sharing jokes that he misses with Valentin, with Mrs Tristram, and even occasionally with Madame de Bellegarde. If we have any single perch from which we watch, it is above the whole tragi-comic shambles in the august company of the omniscient author.

Where is this perch? Where do we place ourselves? Certainly not in France amongst the Bellegardes, depraved and doomed, and the Nioches, corrupted and contemptible. Nor in America: we have laughed at Newman's expense and scorned his proprietary attitudes too often to measure Europe from those shores. In effect, we sway in mid Atlantic, now leaning West, now tilting back East. Or perhaps we can make the literal suffice as metaphorical and decide by way of compromise to settle on an island off the European continent – to go, like James, to England and finish the book there.

But of course, within the narrative context of *The American*, England is not offered as any kind of solution; Newman, as far as we know, merely passes through England, one melancholy, disenchanted summer. The conclusions of *The American* are unmistakably pessi-mistic, even if for the most part lightly and humourously so. Europe is Death; but American 'life' is not so fine that it can be allowed to reinvigorate Europe. There can be no solution, no resolution; in the simplest terms there can be no happy ending. What begins as a comedy of mutual incomprehension must end as a tragedy of dual unfulfilment. Europe, whose waning power can be only repressive, is rightly doomed. America, whose rising power can be only aggressive, is deservedly defeated.[20] Europe is beyond salvation. But America has not (yet?) the saving grace. It may be the New World. It is not the New Word.

A note on the editions

On 1 November 1875, Henry James, who had recently arrived in London, began a letter to his family in Cambridge, Massachusetts, with the following large proclamation: 'I take possession of the old world – I inhale it – I appropriate it!'[21] Within the month, having established himself in Paris, James had begun the writing of *The American*, whose hero in the earlier pages of the novel speaks often in similarly grandiose terms. For several months afterwards he continued to own to these enthusiastic appetites, announcing to Howells in a letter of 28 May 1876 that he was

> turning into an old, and very contented, Parisian: I feel as if I had struck roots into the Parisian soil, and were likely to let them grow tangled and tenacious there.[22]

Later in the same letter, however, he did admit that 'of pure Parisianism I see absolutely nothing', and elsewhere he confessed to feeling excluded from 'the half-dozen charming houses to which it would be pleasant to go of an evening'.[23] Christopher Newman may have been in a position on occasions to turn down dinner invitations from the Princess Borealska, but his story, like James's, is more completely one of exclusion by the scarcely breachable walls of aristocratic houses, convents, and 'polite conversation'. By 29 July James was telling his brother, William, that

> my last layer of resistance to a long-encroaching weariness and satiety with the French mind and its utterance has fallen from me like a garment. I have done with 'em, forever, and am turning English all over. . . . I have got nothing important out of Paris nor am likely to.[24]

Thus, during the months in which he was engaged upon the writing of *The American*, the course of James's own responses to 'the old world' to a considerable extent dictated his hero's progress from initial indiscriminate ardour to final disaffection and the resolve 'to stay away forever'. As Leon Edel has said: 'there was an almost excessive flow of daily incident from life into his book without prior assimilation of it.'[25]

Newman is of course importantly distinct from James – as Westerner, as financier, as stranger to Europe, as self-vaunted 'doer' rather than 'feeler' or 'thinker' or 'writer'. But his situation, his plight, the swing of his emotional pendulum, are sufficiently close to the author's to account for the fine 'free play of so much unchallenged instinct' that made James thoroughly nostalgic when he came to write, over thirty years later, the Preface for the New York edition. The portrayal of Newman, especially in the earlier chapters before the specific events of his story departed from James's own immediate experience, has a freshness and an unhampered fluency which surely are directly owing to the intensity of the author's identification with his character. 'I have written my story from Newman's side of the wall', he confirmed to Howells; and in the Preface he retrospectively imagined a still closer relationship, that of 'a tall, protective, good-natured elder brother'.[26]

When James was preparing the New York edition of his works in the years 1907–9, the novel that he revised most extensively was *The American*. The revisions, the rewriting of whole sections, the invention of an ending considerably different in inflection from that of the original, have left us, if not quite with two books, at least with more than one. The versions are of course similar enough in broad outlines of narrative and thematic conception to create few problems with respect to general discussion and evaluation. The problems arise very largely over quotation. Regularly, units from the phrase to the paragraph vary either slightly or radically, with the changes having an effect in the context either slight or radical.

In my essay in nearly all cases it would have been possible to cite the variant quotation in the footnotes; and this of course would have been obligatory, if differences between the two texts had especially concerned me. But I have felt that the process would be both tiresome and tiring for the reader – and admittedly for myself! I have therefore chosen, with only the rarest of exceptions, to refer solely to the original edition, which is the important book of *one* writer, a young man working out of his immediate experience, rather than of *two*, an old man looking over the shoulder of a younger and attempting persistently to 'correct' and improve upon him.

Notes

1. Letter of 30 March 1877, *Selected Letters*, p. 99.
2. *The Art of the Novel*, edited by R. P. Blackmur, New York, 1934, p. 37.
3. *The American*, London, 1921 ed., p. 80. The first edition is more vague. The equivalent passage reads: 'Newman was an excellent, generous fellow; Mr Babcock sometimes said to himself that he was a *noble* fellow.'
4. Thus, in the New York edition, Mrs Tristram conceives of him. The first edition reads: 'She told him that he was "horribly Western", but in this compliment the adverb was tinged with insincerity.' It is noticeable that James was obviously concerned in his revision to bring out the romantic primitivist elements in the conception of Newman, which were only implicit in the original edition.
5. For instance, Twain writes that 'I discovered that if I were to stay there a month, I should still find myself looking at the people instead of the in-animate objects on exhibition.' And just as Newman 'had often admired the copy much more than the original', so Twain 'could not help noticing how superior the copies were to the original'.
6. The contemporary Whitman's Long Island, it is not entirely irrelevant to observe.
7. In the revised edition the proprietary aspect is brought out even more strongly, and a wife becomes 'the best kind of property to hold'.
8. We feel this in spite of the fact that Newman has to a considerable extent repudiated his own past and has come to recognize that it had 'a rather graceless and sordid mien'. For as the author, drawing back from Newman for a moment, goes on to comment with uncharacteristic brutality of language: 'It is very well to sneer at money-getting after you have filled your pockets, and Newman, it may be said, should have begun somewhat earlier to moralize thus delicately' (Ch. 5).
9. The first three adjectives quoted are applied to the portraiture of Newman by F. R. Leavis, *The Great Tradition*, London, 1962, pp. 141-2; the latter three by Maxwell Geismar; *Henry James and his Cult*, London, 1964, p. 25. Constance Rourke, *American Humour*, New York, 1931, p. 189, is much more sensitive towards James's intentions, recognizing that his purpose was 'that of drawing the large, the generic, American character . . . the composite type'.
10. See in particular John Robert Moore, 'An Imperfection in the Art of Henry James', *Nineteenth Century Fiction*, xiii, no. 4, March 1959. Moore finds ridiculous the contrast between the dupe, deceived by Noémie, and the ruthless businessman; and he is unconvinced by Newman's secularism, on the grounds that the West was dogmatically Protestant.
11. John A. Clair, '*The American*: A reinterpretation', *PMLA*, lxxiv, 1959, with the aid of some ingenious detective work, concludes: 'Mrs Bread, the true

mother of Claire de Cintré, was a blackmailer claiming both Newman and the Marquise de Bellegarde as victims. . . . Newman, by dint of his characteristic American *naïveté* and his opacity as a judge of character, was completely "taken in" by her ruse. . . . Claire's refusal to accept Newman in marriage came as a direct result of her having been informed by the Bellegardes of her true parents. . . . Claire de Cintré, the tragic heroine, refuses to marry Newman because of her illegitimate birth.' His suggestions are entertaining, but will not stand up to scrutiny.

12. Nevertheless, one of this century's most famous American literary expatriates, T. S. Eliot, has written of his admiration for the portrait and has surmised that only an American can truly appreciate him: T. S. Eliot, 'A Prediction in Regard to Three English Authors', *Vanity Fair*, February 1924, reprinted in Leon Edel (ed.), *Henry James: A Collection of Critical Essays*, Englewood Cliffs, New Jersey, 1963, pp. 55–6.

13. Elements of the Mark Twain of *Innocents Abroad* appear in Tom Tristram as well as in Newman. For instance, in the Tristram who exclaims: 'Hang it, I don't care for pictures; I prefer the reality!'

14. See Leon Edel, *Henry James: The Conquest of London, 1870–83*, London, 1962, p. 221.

15. One is inevitably and appropriately reminded of a later celebrated American novel about American expatriate life in a world-weary Paris. Its author, of course, was Ernest Hemingway, an ardent admirer of Henry James, and the novel was *The Sun Also Rises*, whose title was taken from the same chapter of *Ecclesiastes* as Valentin's languid declaration 'that there was nothing new under the sun'.

16. Edel, *Conquest of London*, p. 227.

17. I cannot therefore agree with those who, like R. P. Blackmur in his introduction to the Laurel paperback edition of *The American* (New York, 1960), wish to emphasize, in some kind of optimistic manner, the element of victory in Claire's renunciation of secular life.

18. Richard Poirier, *The Comic Sense of Henry James*, London, 1960, p. 56, expresses it well: James's irony is 'often affectionately and even begrudgingly . . . directed at such characters as . . . Newman. . . . But the full force of James's comedy, his broadest humour and most emphatic satire, is saved for those people, like the Bellegardes, who hamper the impulse towards "freedom" of James's heroes and heroines.'

19. In the New York edition she is even described at the time of her final meeting with Newman as emitting a 'satanic hiss'.

20. Or, as Constance Rourke, op. cit.., pp. 201–3, well expresses it, of this book written in the middle of the corrupt and violently disillusioning 'gilded age': 'Defeat had become at last an essential part of the national portraiture. . . . Defeat for the American adventurer was new, at least in wide transcription. . . . [But] the outcome . . . was in a sense the traditional outcome, for triumph

was comprised in it; but the sphere had altered from outer circumstances to the realm of the mind and the spirit.'

21. Quoted in Edel, *Conquest of London*, p. 200.
22. *Letters*, vol. 1, p. 48.
23. Edel, *Conquest of London*, p. 228.
24. *Selected Letters*, p. 78.
25. Edel, *Conquest of London*, p. 248.
26. Aged 32 at the time of beginning the original, James gave to his 'elder brother' the accessible age of 36. In his middle sixties at the time of revision, he could raise Newman's age quite drastically to 42.

2

Washington Square

JOHN LUCAS

I

Perhaps the first impression one takes from *Washington Square* is of its unmistakable brilliance. For the novel has about it an entirely justified self-confidence and sureness both in style and the handling of events. James, you feel, is nowhere more certain of his powers than in *Washington Square*, and much of his poise must come from his sure sense of an audience (the point I am making is not affected by the fact that such a sense was largely misguided). Take any sentence and you note its easy certainty of tone: you are made to feel that James is absolutely confident of his effects. For example: 'Marion Almond was a pretty little person of seventeen, with a very small figure and a very big sash, to the elegance of whose manners matrimony had nothing to add.' The tone of that sentence seems to me typical, even though, as I shall suggest, the unruffled search for the comic that it implies can come to seem strikingly at variance with the situations being treated.

The comic brilliance is, however, everywhere. It is there, for example, in the dialogue between Catherine and Arthur Townsend, on the occasion of his bringing his cousin, Morris, to Washington Square:

'My cousin asked me to bring him, or I shouldn't have taken the liberty. He seemed to want very much to come; you know he's awfully sociable. I told him I wanted to ask you first, but he said Mrs Penniman had invited him. He isn't particular what he says when he wants to come somewhere. But Mrs Penniman seems to think it's all right.'

'We are very glad to see him,' said Catherine. And she wished to talk more about him, but she hardly knew what to say. 'I never saw him before,' she went on presently.

Arthur Townsend stared.

'Why, he told me he talked with you for over half an hour the other night.'

'I mean before the other night. That was the first time.'

'Oh, he has been away from New York – he has been all round the world. He doesn't know many people here, but he's very sociable, and he wants to know everyone.'

'Everyone?' said Catherine.

'Well, I mean all the good ones. All the pretty young ladies – like Mrs Penniman!' And Arthur Townsend gave a private laugh.

'My aunt likes him very much,' said Catherine.

'Most people like him – he's so brilliant.'

'He's more like a foreigner,' Catherine suggested.

'Well, I never knew a foreigner,' said young Townsend, in a tone which seemed to indicate that his ignorance had been optional.

'Neither have I,' Catherine confessed, with more humility. 'They say they are generally brilliant,' she added, vaguely.

'Well, the people of this city are clever enough for me. I know some of them that think they are too clever for me; but they ain't.'

'I suppose you can't be too clever,' said Catherine, still with humility.

'I don't know. I know some people that call my cousin too clever.' (Ch. 5)

Much of *Washington Square* is conducted through dialogue and James was justly proud of his achievement in this respect. For the comedy implicit in the exchange I have quoted is both satisfying in itself and fully relevant to the novel's concerns. It tells us so much: of Mrs Penniman's prompt readiness to create a romance for Catherine; of Catherine's involvement with Morris Townsend; of his past. And we learn a good deal more. For everything that is said is controlled by the social tone, so that *what* is said is inseparable from *how* it's said. The conversation that occurs between Arthur and Catherine is only possible within a definite social context, and it is in the way James makes the context palpable that so much of the brilliance of *Washington Square* lies. That is why, of course, there is not a great deal of point in comparing James's novel with *Eugénie Grandet*. For as the title of Balzac's novel implies, his focus is on the girl herself, whereas

James is directing attention towards the social context that shapes his novel's events. To come to the crux of the matter by a slightly different route, one might say that *Washington Square* is best seen as a novel in the tradition that Jane Austen's fiction inaugurates. Its drama depends on the range and subtlety of James's presentation of social relationships, with all that that implies of tone, habits of deference, poise, conscious civility, calculated decorum: all those elements, in short, in which certain lives are given definitive shape and to which they can become forfeit.

James's social world is, of course, America. More precisely, it is a certain area of New York city. And for Ezra Pound at least the unerring rightness of James's rendering of his milieu is not something that aliens can fully recognize. 'No one but an American', Pound says, 'can ever know, really know, how good he is at bottom, how good his "America" is.' And he goes on:

> No Englishman can, and in less degree can any continental, or in fact anyone whose family was not living on, say, West 23rd Street in the old set-back two-story-porched red brick vine-covered houses, etc. when Henry James was being a small boy on East 23rd Street; no one whose ancestors had not been presidents or professors or founders of Ha'vawd College or something of that sort, or had not heard of a time when people lived on 14th Street, or had know of some one living in Lexington or Newton 'Old Place' or somewhere of that sort in New England, or had heard of the New York that produced 'Fanny', New York the jocular and uncritical, or of people who danced with General Grant or something of that sort, would quite know *Washington Square* or *The Europeans* to be so autochthonous, so authentic to the conditions. They might believe the things to be 'real', but they would not know how closely they correspond to an external reality.[1]

Pound may be overstating the case, but he is surely right in wanting to insist on James's concern to render his milieu with the kind of accuracy and intensity that one associates with the presentation of Highbury and Mansfield Park.

The point needs some stressing, I think, because of the apparently widespread critical agreement that New York isn't of any great importance to the novel. When James was working on the book he wrote to William Dean Howells:

I sympathize even less with your protest against the idea that it takes an old civilization to set a novelist in motion – a proposition that seems to me so true as to be a truism. It is on manners, customs, usages, habits, forms, upon all things matured and established, that a novelist lives – they are the very stuff his work is made of; and in saying that in the absence of those 'dreary and worn-out paraphernalia' which I enumerate as being wanting in American society, 'we have simply the whole of human life left', you beg (to my sense) the question. I should say we had just so much less of it as these same 'paraphernalia' represent, and I think they represent an enormous quantity of it.

Richard Poirier quotes this letter in his excellent book on James, but he does so only to argue that it supports his case that 'the public status of characters in *Washington Square* depends not at all on their social place or nationality, and is wholly a matter of their similarity to stock characters in stage melodrama and the fairy tale.'[2] My own feeling is that the novel itself everywhere contradicts Poirier's thesis, and that if characters *do* become like stock types in stage melodrama and fairy tale – and I agree that they do – it is because they see themselves called on to play parts created by their self-conscious awareness of what their society requires of them. And this applies just as much to Dr Sloper as it does to Morris Townsend, as I shall try to establish. It is for this reason that I find F. W. Dupee's remarks on the novel so odd.

> It is not essential to *Washington Square* that its scene is America. The Old New York setting is lovely but insubstantial, an atmosphere and no more; and so familiar seems the fable of the girl jilted by her fortune-hunting suitor that we are surprised to learn from James's notebooks that he was following quite closely an actual incident related to him by Fanny Kemble.[3]

Dupee is without doubt quite right to note the familiarity of James's theme. It is indeed an old one. But *Washington Square* differs very importantly from the numerous sentimental novels where the theme had been thoroughly at home. For James's novel is a perfect blending of his 'gaping habit' before life – his rendering of events without interference – and what can be regarded as his crucial desire to make the ordinary interesting. And here it is worth noting the reasons he gives, in an essay of 1876, for disliking the Goncourts:

They inevitably went into 'realism', but realism for them has been altogether a matter of taste – a studio question, as it were. They also find the disagreeable particularly characteristic, and there is something odd in seeing these elegant erudites bring their highly complex and artificial method – the fruit of culture, and leisure, and luxury – to bear upon the crudities and maladies of life, and pick out choice morsels of available misery upon their gold pen-points.[4]

It is not impossible to imagine those words being applied to James's own later fiction. It would, of course, be unfair: but not outrageous. But it *would* be outrageous to apply them to *Washington Square*. For what *Washington Square* reveals, among other things, is James's relentless and detailed study of very ordinary goings-on in a particular society. The life he draws on is unspectacular, mundane; as mundane, shall we say, as the life that Crabbe treats in *Procrastination*, or which Jane Austen studies in *Persuasion*. In all three cases it is the fineness of analysis, the subtlety of enquiry that creates great art. Speaking of Stendhal, James noted that he felt 'as soon as he began to observe, that character, manners and civilization are explained by circumstances, and that in the way of observing and collecting circumstances there was a great work to be done'.[5] *Washington Square* is best seen, I think, as a study of circumstances that will sufficiently explain why its people are what they are, behave as they do. There is nothing artificial in James's method. On the contrary, it has about it the feel of inevitable rightness that springs from the certainty with which he can place everyone in the environment that so takes his attention and which, if it doesn't amount to the manners, customs, usages, habits and forms that he found in the European novel, is certainly the next best thing. His care over the rendering of context explains, I think, why he could so surely speak of Hawthorne as pure, simple, unsophisticated, and why he could rightly characterize *The Marble Faun* as incurring the penalty 'of seeming factitious and unauthoritative, which is always the result of an artist's attempt to project himself into an atmosphere in which he has not a transmitted and inherited property'.[6]

To go back to the dialogue from which I have already quoted, it is worth noting how carefully Morris is socially placed by what James has his characters say. When Arthur explains that Morris had asked

him to bring him, and when he explains that Mrs Penniman has
given the idea her blessing, we are bound to notice the social offence
that Morris is giving and the way in which he is playing the part of
interloper, pretending to a social position that he doesn't in fact have.
Arthur's words reveal that Morris has got to Washington Square
either by lying or by accepting the socially irresponsible methods of
Mrs Penniman, and we never lose sight of Morris's social wrongness.
That he plays a part only makes more apparent the fact that he is
acting out the requirements that society places upon him. His name
makes very clear how we are to take him. He does not belong to the
Square, the then-fashionable centre of New York, but to the town's
end, where indeed Dr Sloper has to go when he wants to see Townsend's sister, Mrs Montgomery. And Morris is the inevitable product
of the society which tries to exclude him and in which he tries to be
included. He is not a male equivalent of Becky Sharpe, but certainly
all that he is and does depends on the society with which he has to
deal. So that D. W. Jefferson's remark that Morris Townsend is
'obviously shallow and rootless from the outset; neither he nor our
knowledge of him undergoes any development' manages to be at once
wrong (since Morris, as we shall see, *does* develop), irrelevant (since
we aren't meant to see him as a mysterious figure) and absurd (since
it reveals that Jefferson hasn't at all understood the novel's concern
with circumstance).[7] It is, however, true that Morris is out of place
in Washington Square. His brilliance may not be that of the foreigner,
but it is certainly not native, natural, to New York society. And the
unnaturalness is made apparent in James's beautifully deft rendering
of Morris's indifference to the codes of behaviour that mark the
society into which he has intruded. Take, for example, his proposal
to Catherine that she shall meet him in the Square, since he can't
come to the house where he has been insulted:

> She hesitated awhile; then at last – 'You must come to the house,'
> she said; 'I am not afraid of that.'
> 'I would rather it were in the Square,' the young man urged. 'You
> know how empty it is, often. No one will see us.'
> 'I don't care who sees us. But leave me now.'
> He left her resignedly; he had got what he wanted. . . . Her father
> said nothing. . . . Mrs Penniman also was silent; Morris Townsend had

told her that her niece preferred, unromantically, an interview in a
chintz-covered parlour to a sentimental tryst beside a fountain sheeted
with dead leaves, and she was lost in wonderment at the oddity – almost
the perversity – of the choice.   (Ch. 9)

The irony that attends Mrs Penniman's pondering the perversity of
Catherine's choice is, admittedly, a simple one, but it does help to
pinpoint the impropriety of Morris's suggestion – 'You know how
empty it is, often. No one will see us.' To understand from where
James took his sense of how to render the socially indecorous one
would have to go back to something like Jane Austen's study of the
relationship between Jane Fairfax and Frank Churchill. And to say
this is to suggest that *Washington Square* is very much a novel in an
established mode, not so much because of its subject but because of
its treatment of that subject. Indeed, it might even seem to come
close to pastiche of Jane Austen. But what saves it from that is
James's aloof distaste for the society he presents. There is a cool,
detached and scalpel-sharp dissection of society at work in this novel,
a kind of ironic ruthlessness that compares favourably with James's
rendering of English society in, say, *The Portrait of a Lady*, which is
unintentionally much nearer to pastiche in its treatment of English
society. Finely though James writes about Lord Warburton, for
example, one is aware that he is there dealing in an atmosphere 'in
which he has not a transmitted and inherited property'. But there can
be no temptation to apply his criticism of Hawthorne to *Washington
Square*.

   To pick almost at random. How brilliantly he shows Morris's
abandoning of 'manner' when he is in Mrs Penniman's company,
since with her the young man does not need to keep up his act. And
how Morris's coarseness comes out in conversation with her (and by
coarseness I don't mean merely social ineptitude). There is the
occasion when he meets Mrs Penniman just before Catherine's trip
to Europe. Mrs Penniman tells him they must walk where they will
not be observed:

   Morris was not in high good-humour, and his response to this speech
   was not particularly gallant. 'I don't flatter myself we shall be much
   observed anywhere.' Then he turned recklessly towards the centre of

town. 'I hope you have come to tell me that he has knocked under,' he went on.

'I am afraid I am not altogether a harbinger of good; and yet, too, I am to a certain extent a messenger of peace. I have been thinking a great deal, Mr Townsend,' said Mrs Penniman.

'You think too much.'

'I suppose I do; but I can't help it, my mind is so terribly active. When I give myself, I give myself. I pay the penalty in my headaches, my famous headaches – a perfect circlet of pain! But I carry it as a queen carries her crown. Would you believe that I have one now? I wouldn't, however, have missed our rendezvous for anything. I have something very important to tell you.'

'Well, let's have it,' said Morris. (Ch. 21)

It is part of the more obvious comedy of the novel that while Mrs Penniman acts at her finest with Morris he doesn't act with her at all. Really, he hardly needs to: Mrs Penniman's notion of romance so fully takes in anything that is opposed to social decorum that she has no room to observe or understand the implications of Morris's behaviour:

> Mrs Penniman's real hope was that the girl would make a secret marriage, at which she should officiate as bride's woman or duenna. She had a vision of this ceremony being performed in some subterranean chapel; subterranean chapels in New York were not frequent, but Mrs Penniman's imagination was not chilled by trifles; and of the guilty couple – she liked to think of poor Catherine and her suitor as the guilty couple – being shuffled away in a fast-whirling vehicle to some obscure lodging in the suburbs, where she would pay them (in a thick veil) clandestine visits; where they would endure a period of romantic privation; and when ultimately, after she should have been their earthly providence, their intercessor, their advocate, and their medium of communication with the world, they would be reconciled to her brother in an artistic tableau, in which she herself should be somehow the central figure. (Ch. 15)

The absurdities hinted at in Mrs Penniman's name (the pennilessness that causes her to batten on to the Sloper household, and the simpering interest in men which makes her a prime cause of Catherine's miserable love-affair) are fully present in this passage. And always her behaviour springs directly from her desire to act out a chosen role which – further irony – Dr Sloper, in his kindness at taking her in, has made more possible. Mrs Penniman is a very stupid woman, comically stupid, but also dangerously stupid. The comedy surrounding her depends to a large extent on the neatness with which James catches her nuances of speech – the phrases and habits of expression that she borrows from cheap novel and play. She takes an interest in the 'sentimental shadows' of what she sees as Catherine's 'drama'; she wishes the 'plot to thicken'; she advises Catherine to act – 'in your situation the great thing is to act'; she tells her niece that 'if you succumb to the dread of your father's wrath . . . I don't know what will become of us'; and when Catherine tells her not to make any more appointments with Morris, 'Mrs Penniman rose with considerable majesty. "My poor child, are you jealous of me?" she asked.' Her danger lies precisely in her stupidity, the romantic notions which close her mind to the nature of Morris's act.

It is, of course, Dr Sloper who sees through Morris:

> 'He is not what I call a gentleman; he has not the soul of one. He is extremely insinuating; but it is a vulgar nature. I saw through it in a minute. He is altogether too familiar – I hate familiarity. He is a plausible coxcomb.'
>
> 'Ah, well,' said Mrs Almond, 'if you make up your mind so easily, it's a great advantage.'
>
> 'I don't make up my mind easily. What I tell you is the result of thirty years of observation; and in order to be able to form that judgement in a single evening, I have had to spend a lifetime in study.'
>
> 'Very possibly you are right. But the thing is for Catherine to see it.'
>
> 'I will present her with a pair of spectacles!' said the Doctor. (Ch. 7)

Sloper speaks with authority here, but this kind of authority is a judgement on him as much as on Morris. For Sloper has spent thirty years taking care to become a gentleman. He has moved up town to Washington Square and he has used his intelligence to get himself a rich wife. Sloper is something of a fortune-hunter himself. Which is why, as Richard Poirier points out, he is perfectly positioned to understand Morris's type.

James draws attention to the Doctor's fear of vulgarity: 'He had a dread of vulgarity, and even a theory that it was increasing in the society around him.' But he also lets us realize that there is a considerable streak of vulgarity in the Doctor. And in the ways in which James fillets out this vulgarity we can see something of that aloof and disenchanted gaze which he turns onto the 'best' society of *Washington Square*. Sloper's vulgarity lies essentially in the rigid mask of irony which he identifies with urbanity and which he clamps onto himself, assuming it to be proper for his position. Like Morris, Sloper plays a part in society, and it is one that causes him to become his own victim, as in the crucial conversation with Morris at Mrs Almond's. The conversation takes place partly because of Sloper's uneasy suspicion that he might 'appear ridiculous to this young man, whose private perception of incongruities he suspected of being keen'. Morris tells the Doctor that he has only his good right arm by which to earn work. The Doctor's irony – his social front – comes into play.

> 'You are too modest,' said the Doctor. 'In addition to your good right arm you have your subtle brain. I know nothing of you but what I see; but I see by your physiognomy that you are extremely intelligent.'
>
> 'Ah,' Townsend murmured, 'I don't know what to answer you when you say that. You advise me, then, not to despair?'
>
> And he looked at his interlocutor as if the question might have a double meaning. The Doctor caught the look and weighed it a moment before he replied. 'I should be very sorry to admit that a robust and well-disposed of young man need ever despair. If he doesn't succeed in one thing, he can try another. Only, I should add, he should choose his line with discretion.'
>
> 'Ah, yes, with discretion,' Morris Townsend repeated, sympathetically. 'Well, I have been indiscreet, formerly; but I think I have got over it. I am very steady now.' And he stood for a moment, looking down at his remarkably neat shoes. Then at last, 'Were you kindly intending to propose something for my advantage?' he inquired, looking up and smiling.   (Ch. 9)

Sloper is caught out and his irony made to look very vulnerable at this moment. And it is his own fault. He has shown his vulgarity in wanting to outwit Morris. In playing the other man's game he has lost. (One might note in passing that it is very like Osmond's conversation with Rosier in *Portrait*, where Osmond's very marked distaste for being vulgar in fact commits him to vulgarity.)

For Sloper, as for Osmond, fear of vulgarity is fear of losing social poise, which in turn means fear of losing the ironic possibilities of any moment. This is very finely caught in a scene between the Doctor and Catherine, just before they go to Europe. Catherine tells him that

> '. . . if I don't obey you, I ought not to live with you – to enjoy your kindness and protection.'
>
> This striking argument gave the Doctor a sudden sense of having underestimated his daughter; it seemed even more than worthy of a young woman who had revealed the quality of unaggressive obstinacy. But it displeased him – displeased him deeply, and he signified as much. 'That idea is in very bad taste,' he said. 'Did you get it from Mr Townsend?'
>
> 'Oh no; it's my own,' said Catherine, eagerly.
>
> 'Keep it to yourself, then,' her father answered, more than ever determined she should go to Europe.   (Ch. 22)

It is very subtly done, the way James modulates the Doctor's awareness of the possibility of loss into a matter of taste. And of course taste is involved, for if Catherine leaves him his social reputation is bound to suffer. Taking her to Europe is therefore his way of educating her into good taste – making her see how socially impossible marriage with Townsend would be. More than that, the trip is to make her see how much her father needs her. For what we are allowed to recognize behind his words about taste is his very real feeling for Catherine, although it is a feeling constantly at the mercy of his irony. His better self, that is, is inhibited by the social mask. That is why James can bring off the master-stroke of the Doctor's effort to break through to un-ironic communication with his daughter in the lonely Alpine village. As Poirier has pointed out, this is a melodramatic scene in which there is no hint of parody, but I think it not enough merely to remark that Sloper's 'intensities at this moment seem to arise from a compelling emotional necessity'.[8] They do, of course, but it is possible to be more precise than Poirier wants to be and to say why the scene is so right, why it rings so true. The reason for the Doctor's confession – for that is what it amounts to – is surely that at last he feels sufficiently remote from that social context which seemed to require of him a permanence of ironic posture to dare to tell Catherine more of the truth than he has ever before been able to show her:

The Doctor looked up and down the valley, swinging his stick; then he said to her, in the same low tone,

'I am very angry.'

She wondered what he meant – whether he wished to frighten her. If he did, the place was well chosen: this hard, melancholy dell, abandoned by the summer light, made her feel her loneliness. She looked around her, and her heart grew cold; for a moment her fear was great. But she could think of nothing to say, save to murmur, gently, 'I am sorry.'

'You try my patience,' her father went on, 'and you ought to know what I am. I am not a very good man. Though I am very smooth externally, at bottom I am very passionate; and I assure you I can be very hard.'

She could not think why he told her these things. Had he brought her there on purpose, and was it part of a plan? What was the plan? Catherine asked herself. Was it to startle her suddenly into a retraction – to take an advantage of her by dread? Dread of what? The place was ugly and lonely, but the place could do her no harm. There was a kind of still intensity about her father which made him dangerous, but Catherine hardly went so far as to say that it might be part of his plan to fasten his hand – the neat, fine, supple hand of a distinguished physician – in her throat. Nevertheless, she receded a step. 'I am sure you can be anything you please,' she said; and it was her simple belief.

'I am very angry,' he replied, more sharply.

'Why has it taken you so suddenly?'

'It has not taken me suddenly. I have been raging inwardly for the last six months. But just now this seemed a good place to flare out. It's so quiet, and we are alone.' (Ch. 24)

It is without doubt a very remarkable scene, remarkable above all for the fact that because Catherine and the Doctor are removed from any social context – 'we are alone' – he can drag out truths about himself and his feelings for his daughter which she cannot possibly understand. There is really terrible irony in his remark 'you ought to know what I am'. For Catherine has no chance of knowing what he is, as her reply makes him realize: ' "I am sure you can be anything you please." "I am very angry," he replied, more sharply.' Angry because he has to face the bleak certainty that she can never understand him. He has been only too successful in meeting the requirements of his social position, has become finally trapped by Catherine's unshake-able belief in him as the supreme ironist. She cannot know that the mask is not the actuality. The acts which society demands of people are beyond her comprehension. Being the only truthful person in the novel she cannot see that Morris is playing a part, and she cannot see that her father is playing a part also. Whereas because the two men are very conscious of the roles they act out they understand each other perfectly well.

2

But at this point we need to take deeper soundings of James's art and of the subtleties that allow him to perceive and exploit such gaps as appear in the differences between how Sloper customarily presents himself and how, at the one moment I have analysed, he is revealed. In his first essay on Balzac, James remarked that

> If, instead of committing to paper impossible imaginary tales, he could have stood for a while in some other relation to the society about him than that of a scribbler, it would have been a very great gain. The general defect of his manner . . . is the absence of fresh air, of the trace of disinterested observation. . . .[9]

Disinterested observation is one of the most obvious and satisfying features of *Washington Square*, and it connects with a habit of mind that is familiar enough, the Jamesian insistence that the novelist should be an invisible narrator of his own tales. Nor is this simply a personal preference. The fact is that James believes that the deepest kind of realism can be attained only by the novelist's refusal to inter-cede, to let plot dictate to probabilities, or to let moral approval or disapproval cloud his sense of telling it like it is. He makes the point succinctly in his review of Froude's *Short Studies on Great Subjects*:

> In history it is impossible to view individuals singly, and this point constitutes the chief greatness of the study. We are compelled to look at them in connexion with their antecedents, their ancestors, their con-temporaries, their circumstances. To judge them morally we are obliged to push our enquiry through a concatenation of causes and effects in which, from their delicate nature, enquiry very soon becomes impracti-cable, and thus we are reduced to talking sentiment. Nothing is more

surprising than the alertness with which writers like Mr Froude are ready to pronounce upon the moral character of historical persons, and their readiness to make vague moral epithets stand in lieu of real psychological facts.[10]

These sentences can be linked to the remark about Stendhal which I have already quoted. Taken together they provide a sure indication of James's unwillingness to use vague moral epithets of any of the characters of *Washington Square*. Nor is this to suggest that his art may be seen in terms that he used to criticize Gautier's poetry, of an atmosphere 'unweighted with a moral presence . . . unstirred by the breath of reflection'.[11] The point is rather that James's way of presenting character in terms of circumstance forbids us the easily satisfying kinds of judgement which a lesser artist would offer. In *Washington Square* the concatenation of causes and effects by which individuality becomes asserted is far too complex to allow us fairly to make such statements as that the novel is about 'a bad case of parental despotism', even though at least one critic has seen the novel in those terms. To judge Sloper as a despot is merely to become trapped in Mrs Penniman's view of him, and to have to feel that there may be justice in her concealing Morris's letters to Catherine inside her own. And though it is with Sloper that a simplistic view is most damaging, it inhibits an understanding of all the characters. I want to touch on some of the ways in which James's 'disinterested observation' allows him to focus on the damage which is done to Catherine while forbidding us the satisfaction of swift judgement on those who do the damage.

Mrs Penniman is a good example. She is silly, vapid, romantic, quite incapable of understanding the damage she is doing to Catherine. Yet how much conspires to give her the kind of influence by which she creates harm! The Doctor's kindness in giving her a home, Catherine's susceptibility, Morris Townsend's willingness to take advantage of her, Sloper's own deliberate over-acting of the role to which he knows she has assigned him and which strengthens her sense of doing right – all contribute to this end. The comedy of observation sets before us these complications and their results. Without them, Mrs Penniman would be helpless:

> She was romantic; she was sentimental; she had a passion for little
> secrets and mysteries – a very innocent passion, for her secrets had
> hitherto always been as unpractical as addled eggs. She was not
> absolutely veracious; but this defect was of no great consequence, for
> she had never had anything to conceal.   (Ch. 2)

Marvellous, the way the balanced phrases and sentences show at once
Mrs Penniman's potential for harm and her actual ineffectiveness.
And, as the paragraph continues, the sinuous process of the syntax
begins to entwine her with her brother and alert us to Mrs Penniman's future role:

> Mrs Penniman had never had a lover, but her brother, who was very
> shrewd, understood her turn of mind. 'When Catherine is about seven-
> teen,' he said to himself, 'Lavinia will try to persuade her that some
> young man with a moustache is in love with her. It will be quite untrue;
> no young man, with a moustache or without, will ever be in love with
> Catherine. But Lavinia will take it up and talk about it . . . Catherine
> won't see it, and won't believe it, fortunately for her peace of mind;
> poor Catherine isn't romantic.'

But the problem is, after all, one that eludes the Doctor's shrewdness.
He doesn't bargain for a young man who actually presents himself as
a lover. He may understand his sister's character but he is quite
unable to prevent the consequences of her operations when those are
helped by a turn of events he can't control.

It would be boring – and unnecessary – to work through the novel
in this way; and my purpose in drawing attention to the paragraph
quoted above is only to provide an indication of the subtleties of
James's mind, as it works to unravel something as inevitable as the
happenings in *Washington Square* which don't allow for a simple
moral response on our part.

But I do want to continue to point out the way in which the
inevitabilities come about, dictated as they are by the opportunities
which individuals create out of their need to take their place in a
social context – for I don't at all want to get away from that. What
Morris and Dr Sloper do is inextricably bound up with what they are;
the social outsider trying to get in, and the social celebrity anxious
not to lose his poise, his tone. Only because of the selfishness that

these acts involve can Mrs Penniman be so powerful – and she is very powerful. When Morris continues to see Catherine after the Doctor has made clear his disapproval of the young man, we are told:

> Mrs Penniman delighted of all things in a drama, and she flattered herself that a drama would now be enacted. Combining as she did the zeal of the prompter with the impatience of the spectator, she had long since done her utmost to pull up the curtain. She, too, expected to figure in the performance – to be the confidante, the Chorus, to speak the epilogue. It may even be said that there were times when she lost sight altogether of the modest heroine of the play in the contemplation of certain great scenes which would naturally occur between the hero and herself. (Ch. 10)

I have already mentioned that in *Washington Square* people are forced to play their parts in assuming social roles, and this passage makes it obvious that the imagery of the theatre, of the drama, is functional to the novel's purpose; people are always being caught out in gestures, and their being so enables that subtle investigation of the gap between the act and the actuality which James manages so finely. Mrs Penniman indeed is caught out time and again: in the oyster saloon, for example; but also, of course, in the drama that takes place in her mind, for that is the most obvious example in the novel of the gap between the act and the actuality.

But if the gap is great for us, for Mrs Penniman it doesn't really exist, and the confusions of her mind show themselves in the comic manner of James's disinterested observer – the narrator – through which her behaviour is recorded:

After Dr Sloper has turned Townsend down, we are told:

> Mrs Penniman took too much satisfaction in the sentimental shadows of this little drama to have, for the moment, any great interest in dissipating them. She wished the plot to thicken, and the advice she gave her niece tended, in her own imagination, to produce this result. It was rather incoherent counsel, and from one day to another it contradicted itself; but it was pervaded by an earnest desire that Catherine should do something striking. 'You must act, my dear; in your situation the great thing is to act,' said Mrs Penniman, who found her niece altogether beneath her opportunities. (Ch. 15)

The act she requires is, of course, one that Catherine isn't capable of – divided as she is between Morris and her father – but it is very important in the novel that acting and choice do not go together. For if we take the play on the word 'act' as we are meant to, we can see that for the other involved characters 'acting' is a way of avoiding choice; they aim to escape from their dilemmas by the assumption of a role which will free them from painful decisions, or from facing the truth.

And it is here, therefore, that the triumph of disinterested observations shows itself most forcefully. The comic manner shows us how unmistakably at odds with actuality the acts are. There is, for example, the moment when, after Morris's desertion of Catherine, the girl attempts to keep the disaster to herself:

> . . . her innocent arts were of little avail before a person of the rare perspicacity of Mrs Penniman. This lady easily saw that she was agitated, and if there was any agitation going forward, Mrs Penniman was not a person to forfeit her natural share in it.   (Ch. 30)

There the manner becomes consciously inadequate to deal with the shattering nature of Catherine's loss, and it is so because of the inadequacy of Mrs Penniman herself. Chapter 30 is, in fact, a good example of the triumph of James's method. It features what might be called a showdown between Mrs Penniman and Catherine, except that given the individuals a showdown is not really possible. Instead, Mrs Penniman is caught out in a series of ridiculously inadequate gestures:

> 'My plans have not changed!' said Catherine, with a little laugh.
> 'Ah, but Mr Townsend's have,' her aunt answered, very gently.
> 'What do you mean?'
> There was an impervious brevity in the tone of this enquiry, against which Mrs Penniman felt bound to protest. . . . 'Ah well,' she said 'if he hasn't told you!. . . .' and she turned away.
> Catherine watched her a moment in silence; then she hurried after her, stopping her before she reached the door. 'Told me what? What do you mean? What are you hinting at and threatening me with?'
> 'Isn't it broken off?' asked Mrs Penniman.
> 'My engagement? Not in the least!'
> 'I beg your pardon in that case. I have spoken too soon!'

'Too soon? Soon or late,' Catherine broke out, 'you speak foolishly and cruelly.'

And when the girl finally tells her aunt 'Why can't you leave me alone? I was afraid you would spoil everything; for you *do* spoil everything you touch!' we are told that Mrs Penniman 'was scared and bewildered'; and she tells Catherine 'Do you scold me for talking to him? I'm sure we never talked of anything but you.'

At the end of the chapter, Mrs Penniman's stupidity again comes out as she gives away – without realizing that she is involving herself – that she and Townsend had been in the plot together.

> Catherine . . . spoke at last as if she had not heard or understood her.
> 'It has been a regular plan, then. He has broken it off deliberately; he has given me up.'
> 'For the present, dear Catherine; he has put it off, only.'
> 'He has left me alone,' Catherine went on.
> 'Haven't you *me*' asked Mrs Penniman with some solemnity.

As I have said, the comic manner won't let us see Mrs Penniman as morally evil. She is shown as too 'bewildered' for that, too caught out between act and actuality; and we know indeed that although she prods Townsend on towards the series of actions which combine with others to create the disaster, she doesn't really understand the full force of what she is doing. So, for example, when Morris takes seriously her plan of a quick marriage – the drama of which appeals to her – we are told 'She was a little frightened, but she went on with considerable boldness'. And that is the most that can be urged against Mrs Penniman. She is sometimes a little frightened.

But the comic manner in Chapter 30 allows of something more considerable than just an understanding of Mrs Penniman's inadequacy. For there is also the awfulness of Catherine's isolation, the terrible feeling of desolate loneliness that results from her giving up her father for Morris, who for that reason gives her up, without the hope of Mrs Penniman to turn to as reasonable friend. When Mrs Penniman asks 'Haven't you *me*' the comedy moves away from the absurdity of her remark to the pathos of Catherine's final loneliness. But to see how that is brought about, we need to look at Morris for a moment and *his* inadequacy, *his* act.

I have said that this act is forced on him by the social context in which he finds himself, and that the Doctor sees through it to a correct judgement of him. But Morris is in the happy situation of being a reasonably good actor, before a very appreciative audience: for neither Mrs Penniman nor Catherine sees through the act, since for different reasons neither has any cause to suspect it. Still, we can see Morris time and again being caught out. James's gaping habit allows him to reveal to us what is hidden from many of the characters. This is neatly shown when Catherine tells Morris that her father had said the young man was interested in her money.

> 'He told me to tell you . . . that if I marry without his consent, I shall not inherit a penny of his fortune. He made a great point of this. He seemed to think – he seemed to think – '
> Morris flushed, as any young man of spirit might have flushed at an imputation of baseness. 'What did he seem to think?'
> 'That it would make a difference.'
> 'It *will* make a difference – in many things. . . . But it will make none in my affection.'
> 'We shall not want the money,' said Catherine; 'for you know I have a good deal myself.'
> 'Yes, my dear girl, I know you have something. And he can't touch that.'
> 'He would never,' said Catherine. 'My mother left it to me.'
> Morris was silent awhile. 'He was very positive about this was he?' he asked at last. 'He thought such a message would annoy me terribly and make me throw off the mask, eh?'
> 'I don't know what he thought,' said Catherine sadly.
> 'Please tell him that I care for his message as much as for that!' And Morris snapped his fingers sonorously.   (Ch. 20)

Though Catherine doesn't notice Morris's slip in saying that the message was intended to 'make me throw off the mask, eh?' we do. Morris is not really a *very* good actor: the finger-snapping is so obvious a gesture. Equally obvious is his notion of the scene that Catherine and her father might play out in Europe, a scene in which the Doctor would be won over to his future son-in-law:

> . . . over there, among beautiful scenes and noble monuments, perhaps the old gentleman would be softened. . . . He might be touched by her

gentleness, her patience, her willingness to make any sacrifice but *that* one; and if she should appeal to him some day, in some celebrated spot – in Italy, say, in the evening; in Venice, in a gondola, by moonlight – if she should be a little clever about it, and touch the right chord, perhaps he would fold her in his arms, and tell her that he forgave her. (Ch. 23)

When Catherine realizes that Morris has left her, we are told that 'it seemed to her that a mask had suddenly fallen from his face'. I do not need to underline the implications of that phrase; but I do want to examine for a moment the presentation of Morris's dramatic inadequacy, by means of which the mask is seen to fall. Their last scene together takes place in Chapter 29 (it is worth drawing attention, by the way, to the manner in which James hurries the crisis up; the feeling of relentless exposure to the events as they pile up is quite extraordinary, I think, and helps to show how he creates the awareness for the reader of Catherine's very sudden fall into misery). In that chapter, Morris tries to retain a grip on events that are rapidly passing beyond his control. Indeed he'd already guessed that they would. Like Mrs Penniman he has become a little frightened at the prospect of what he has done to Catherine; and he tries to get her aunt to prepare the girl for their separation. He is, in fact, the coward that his allowing her to be the one to break the news of their proposed engagement to her father had shown; and in what he says we can sense the fright he feels at having discovered the unpredictability of his captive audience – Catherine – and his inability to deal with her response to his act (something of the same trick is worked in the scene between Owen Gereth and Fleda Vetch in Chapter 16 of *The Spoils of Poynton*, where Owen discovers to his amazement that Fleda is in love with him).

> 'Prepare her – try and ease me off.'
> Mrs Penniman stopped, looking at him very solemnly.
> 'My poor Morris, do you know how much she loves you?'
> 'No, I don't. I don't want to know. I have always tried to keep from knowing. It would be too painful.'
> 'She will suffer much,' said Mrs Penniman.
> 'You must console her. If you are as good a friend to me as you pretend to be, you will manage it.' (Ch. 28)

The cowardice is particularly present in his last meeting with Catherine. Here his act breaks down completely, and he is revealed as pathetically inadequate. Catherine tries to get him to promise to come and see her the following day:

> 'If I am prevented from coming tomorrow, you will say I have deceived you,' he said.
> 'How can you be prevented? You can come if you will.'
> 'I am a busy man – I am not a dangler!' cried Morris, sternly. His voice was so hard and unnatural that, with a helpless look at him, she turned away; and then he quickly laid his hand on the door knob. He felt as if he were absolutely running away from her. But in an instant she was close to him again, and murmuring in a tone none the less penetrating for being low, 'Morris, you are going to leave me.'
> 'Yes, for a little while.'
> 'For how long?'
> 'Till you are reasonable again.'
> 'I shall never be reasonable, in that way.' And she tried to keep him longer; it was almost a struggle. 'Think of what I have done!' she broke out. 'Morris, I have given up everything.'
> 'You shall have everything back.'
> 'You wouldn't say that if you didn't mean something. What is it? – what has happened? – what have I done? – what has changed you?'
> 'I will write to you – that is better,' Morris stammered.
> 'Ah, you won't come back!' she cried, bursting into tears.
> 'Dear Catherine,' he said, 'don't believe that. I promise you that you shall see me again.' And he managed to get away, and to close the door behind him.   (Ch. 29)

This very moving scene is the more remarkable in that we become aware that for the first time Morris has something like genuine feeling for Catherine; his inadequacy stems in fact from that feeling. The reason is that he has suddenly found that entanglement with her doesn't mean that he can comfortably 'know' who she is, and that even Catherine is a far more complex person than he had bothered to think her. What makes his act so inadequate is that he can't cope with this knowledge. He has depended on his own idea of Catherine, but more on his act, and when he sees its effect he is incapable of improvising successfully. His gestures are caught, and his act becomes – even to himself – disgraceful. Both he and

Mrs Penniman have brought Catherine to life, and they don't realize the complications of this until it is too late.

And for all his cleverness Dr Sloper is also inadequate. He too is caught out in his gestures; for he also acts out his role, and it creates complications over which he has no control. Sloper, as we have seen, comes to realize that he needs his daughter, and he dares to approach telling her of his love for her. That one should have to put the matter in such a way suggests, of course, his inadequacy; but it's an inadequacy of which Sloper himself becomes aware as he acts out his role of deserted father. I have in mind the scene between Catherine and himself in which she tells him that she hasn't given Morris up. Just how he acts his part comes out in what he says to her in reply to her remark 'But we can wait a long time':

> 'Of course, you can wait till I die, if you like.'
> Catherine gave a cry of natural horror.
> 'Your engagement will have one delightful effect upon you; it will make you extremely impatient for that event.'   (Ch. 18)

What one is meant to notice here is, I think, the vulgarity of the Doctor's act, of which at one moment, indeed, he himself becomes aware. Catherine says to him ' "If I don't marry before your death, I will not after." . . . "Do you mean that for an impertinence?" he enquired; an inquiry of which, as he made it, he quite perceived the grossness.'

As with Mrs Penniman and Morris, so with Sloper. All three are caught out because of Catherine's ability to surprise them with an unexpected (but to us, entirely natural) response. Faced with this, the Doctor cannot improvise, and he has therefore to fall back on the vulgarity of pathos. This is pointed up by the deliberate over-writing at the end of the chapter, which emphasizes the self-consciously melodramatic note in the Doctor's performance, and catches him out in his cliché posturing.

> He went to the door and opened it for her to go out. The movement gave her a terrible sense of his turning her off. 'It will be only once, for the present,' she added, lingering a moment.
> 'Exactly as you choose,' he repeated, standing there with his hand on the door. 'I have told you what I think. If you see him, you will be

an ungrateful, cruel child; you will have given your old father the
greatest pain of his life.'

This was more than the poor girl could bear; her tears overflowed,
and she moved towards her grimly consistent parent with a pitiful cry.
Her hands were raised in supplication, but he sternly evaded this appeal.

But when, just before they go to Europe, he repeats his act of calculated pathos, we realize that it has a kind of necessity for him. It is the
only way he can bring himself to hint at his true feelings for her. And
because he cannot entirely free himself from the grip of irony, he is
forced to turn pathos into bathos. Only outside all social context, as
I have pointed out, dare he drop irony, drop the act. As it is, in that
pre-Europe scene, Catherine says that she must tell Townsend she is
going.

> Her father fixed his cold eyes upon her. 'If you mean that you had
> better ask his leave, all that remains to me is to hope he will give it.'
> The girl was sharply touched by the pathetic ring of the words; it
> was the most calculated, the most dramatic little speech the Doctor had
> ever uttered.   (Ch. 22)

Of course, the fact that the Doctor doesn't grow nearer his
daughter during their European tour leads to their ultimate estrangement and to the resumption of that ironic pose which entails, for
example, the supremely vicious moment when he raises his hat to her
after she has finally lost Morris. A moment such as that is both
dramatically right and extremely shocking. Right, because it is
exactly how he *would* behave; shocking, because it crystallizes the
damage he has done to himself and to her, and indicates the vast gulf
that now separates them. And no talk about tyranny or despotism will
do justice to the complexities that James has unravelled in his study
of the father-daughter relationship.

I come back to an earlier point. *Washington Square* resists simple
moral attitudes and judgements. Not even the terrible stagnation of
Catherine at the end of the book – one notices how often the word
'rigid' is used of her in the last pages, as though she has become
arrested at a certain point forever – not even this allows us to bandy
about terms like 'evil' in describing Morris or Mrs Penniman or the
Doctor. Not, anyway, unless we are prepared to see their inade-

quacies as evil. And this is really the nub of the matter. For the brilliance of James's novel depends on the way in which its comic surface is played off against the tragic events, so that nothing strident is allowed to substitute for its unruffled and sure study of circumstance, of context, of concatenation of cause and effect. It is the ordinariness which is so extraordinary about *Washington Square*.

Notes

1. *Literary Essays of Ezra Pound*, edited by T. S. Eliot, London, 1954, p. 302.
2. R. Poirier, *The Comic Sense of Henry James*, London, 1967, pp. 165–7.
3. F. W. Dupee, *Henry James*, London, 1951, p. 63.
4. *Literary Reviews and Essays*, edited by A. Mordell, New York, 1957, pp. 158–9.
5. Ibid., p. 153.
6. *Hawthorne*, New York, 1966 ed., pp. 142, 155.
7. D. W. Jefferson, *Henry James and the Modern Reader*, London, 1964, p. 106. Jefferson's pages on *Washington Square* are quite the worst I have come across on the novel, though not noticeably inferior to the rest of his book.
8. Poirier, op. cit., p. 172.
9. *French Poets and Novelists*, New York, 1964 ed., p. 70.
10. *Literary Reviews*, p. 273.
11. Ibid., p. 96.

3

The Bostonians

DAVID HOWARD

'In any case,' he said, 'it was just personal.' F. Scott Fitzgerald, *The Great Gatsby*.

'Try to be one of the people on whom nothing is lost!' Henry James, 'The Art of Fiction'.

'I prefer free unions.' Verena Tarrant.

The Bostonians is a novel about union, even 'The Union'. What becomes unified is not altogether clear, partly because the word in the novel, as in American history, points consistently to battle. The employment of Miss Birdseye's serene, unifying, dying vision is characteristic:

> Three minutes later Miss Birdseye, looking up from her letter, saw them move together through the bristling garden and traverse a gap in the old fence which enclosed the further side of it. They passed into the ancient shipyard which lay beyond, and which was now a mere vague, grass-grown approach to the waterside, bestrewn with a few remnants of the supererogatory timber. She saw them stroll forward to the edge of the bay and stand there, taking the soft breeze in their faces. She watched them a little, and it warmed her heart to see the stiff-necked young Southerner led captive by a daughter of New England trained in the right school, who would impose her opinions in their integrity. Considering how prejudiced he must have been he was certainly behaving very well; even at that distance Miss Birdseye dimly made out that there was something positively humble in the way he invited Verena Tarrant to seat herself on a low pile of weather-blacked planks, which constituted the principle furniture of the place, and something, perhaps, just a trifle too expressive of righteous triumph in the manner in which the girl put the suggestion by and stood where she liked, a

little proudly, turning a good deal away from him. Miss Birdseye could see as much as this, but she couldn't hear, so that she didn't know what it was that made Verena turn suddenly back to him, at something he said. If she had known, perhaps his observation would have struck her as less singular – under the circumstances in which these two young persons met – than it may appear to the reader.

'They have accepted one of my articles; I think it's the best.' (Ch. 36)[1]

This is explicitly as well as gently an image of the union of North and South, or more correctly, through these eyes, an image of triumphant reconstruction, the daughter of New England 'imposing' her opinions. As we know, the opposite is true. Ransom, in achieving the publication of his most reactionary opinions, those already tried out on Verena, now feels qualified to pursue their marriage, to take Verena on fully, and through her the other Bostonian, Olive Chancellor. He is the carpetbagger in reverse. The South wins the war.

Both versions are combative and public. If Miss Birdseye had heard Ransom's remark she would have been less surprised than the reader at such an opening for lovers' talk. These are two performers in a performing world. (There is, of course, an assumption that what is going on in this part of the novel is some kind of triumph of love, of personal feelings, which I shall look at later.)

The detail of this scene is important. The superannuated ship-building town fits the superannuated reformer. And both combine to give a sense of the heroic New England that is gone. But the hints of desolation, of waste and debris and aftermath (even possibly of Ransom's ruined plantation, the South wasted by war) go further than this. The 'poverty' of the scene is an American one. The un-formed, blurred vision – Miss Birdseye's spectacles are notoriously ineffective – a vision involving nonetheless a serene complacent unifying, goes naturally with the casual unformed or decreated 'American scene'. But there is more than one attitude to this scene in the novel, just as there is more than one attitude to unions both private and public.

I want first to glance at some of the obvious 'American scenes' in the book, to connect the descriptive detail of this Marmion section with the detailed rendering of New York and Boston. There are other elements this scene takes up: the earlier Miss Birdseye of course, although she turns out to be a personification of debris and disarray; at least two other episodes of false serenity – Ransom almost lulled into the acceptance of Mrs Luna as a wife (Ch. 24), and Olive giving herself momentarily to Burrage's world of wealth, taste, and collecting, where human life ceased to be a battle (Ch. 18). And we must connect this approaching death, of the 'heroic' and 'sublime' Miss Birdseye, with the central meditation on death and battle in the Harvard Memorial Hall. But the convenient way into the novel is through other explicitly American scenes.

There is a particular view of Boston from Olive Chancellor's windows which comes very early in the novel, and recurs several times. The view of the Back Bay comes first via Ransom, who has little 'artistic sense' but finds its combination of spires, factory chimneys, masts, brackish water 'too big for a river and too small for a bay', and modern houses, 'picturesque' and 'almost romantic' (Ch. 3). The Bostonians are proud of this view too, always, according to Mrs Luna, 'giving you the Back Bay to look at, and then taking credit for it', so that it is not merely a question of Ransom exposing a provincial sensibility in the city of culture. He assists at a typical, in some ways rather mean, American scene, and that response and scene are rather coldly presented.

The sense of a distance between this American view and James's tone is more evident when this same scene reappears through Verena's eyes. There has been a change of season, and there is much more detail, but it is recognizably the same:

> . . . the long, low bridge that crawled, on its staggering posts, across the Charles; the casual patches of ice and snow; the desolate suburban horizons, peeled and made bald by the rigour of the season; the general hard, cold void of the prospect; the extrusion, at Charlestown, at Cambridge, of a few chimneys and steeples, straight, sordid tubes of factories and engine-shops, or spare, heavenward finger of the New England meeting-house. There was something inexorable in the poverty of the scene, shameful in the meanness of its details, which gave a collective impression of boards and tin and frozen earth, sheds and rotting piles, railway-lines striding flat across a thoroughfare of puddles,

and tracks of the humbler, the universal horse-car, traversing obliquely this path of danger; loose fences, vacant lots, mounds of refuse, yards bestrewn with iron pipes, telegraph poles, and bare wooden backs of places. Verena thought such a view lovely. . . .   (Ch. 20)

It is wrong to stop the quotation there of course, but doing so does bring out this distance I mentioned; leaving it like this makes of it an almost appalling separation. The passage goes on:

. . . and she was by no means without excuse when, as the afternoon closed, the ugly picture was tinted with a clear, cold rosiness. The air, in its windless chill, seemed to tinkle like a crystal, the faintest gradations of tone were perceptible in the sky, the west became deep and delicate, everything grew doubly distinct before taking on the dimness of evening. There were pink flushes on snow, 'tender' reflections in patches of stiffened marsh, sounds of car-bells, no longer vulgar, but almost silvery, on the long bridge, lonely outlines of distant dusky undulations against the fading glow.

The view at sunset does qualify, and this in fact had already been hinted at in the earlier view of it through Ransom's eyes. But there is a severe discrimination at work here which appears to condemn both Ransom and Verena. Unlike the 'real' Bostonian, Olive, they don't know when to look. They are really 'without excuse', especially because the transformation of ugliness – 'poverty', 'meanness', 'refuse', etc. – is so great: 'car-bells, no longer vulgar, but almost silvery'. The American scene is vulgar, rarely rescued by silver sound or rosy light. Like Miss Peabody, though, with her 'delicate, dirty, democratic little hand', it fades or dies rather well. Yet a few pages later there is the most intensely vulgar scene in the novel, the scene of Ransom's New York life. Here there is no fading light to work magical transformations. Instead there is the positive assertion of vigorous ugliness, of triumphant jumble and debris, of participation in a 'rank civilization' (I quote only a fragment):

The house had a red, rusty face, and faded green shutters, of which the slats were limp and at variance with each other. In one of the lower windows was suspended a fly-blown card, with the words 'Table Board' affixed in letters cut (not very neatly) out of coloured paper, of graduated tints, and surrounded with a small band of stamped gilt. The two sides of the shop were protected by an immense pent-house shed, which projected over a greasy pavement and was supported by wooden posts fixed in the curbstone. Beneath it, on the dislocated flags, barrels and baskets were freely and picturesquely grouped; an open cellarway yawned beneath the feet of those who might pause to gaze too fondly on the savoury wares displayed in the window; a strong odour of smoked fish, combined with a fragrance of molasses, hung about the spot; the pavement, toward the gutter, was fringed with dirty panniers, heaped with potatoes, carrots, and onions; and a smart, bright waggon, with the horse detached from the shafts, drawn up on the edge of the abominable road (it contained holes and ruts a foot deep, and im-memorial accumulations of stagnant mud), imparted an idle, rural, pastoral air to a scene otherwise perhaps expressive of rank civilization. (Ch. 21)

In spite of that final cautious note there is real excitement and relish here, an almost visceral closeness. The word 'picturesque' is inadequate: the scene invites not distance but exploration and dis-covery, a peering – even a falling – into one fascinating hole or box or cage after another. The excitement of the response is most clearly indicated later in the passage with the glimpse of the Elevated Rail-way 'overhanging the transverse longitudinal street, which it darkened and smothered with the immeasurable spinal column and myriad clutching paws of an antediluvian monster'.

One of the striking things about the whole passage is that James is being frankly personal and also apparently frankly irrelevant. The Dutch grocery is mentioned 'not on account of any particular in-fluence it may have had on the life or thoughts of Basil Ransom, but for old acquaintance sake and that of local colour'. Then he adds (with an echo of 'The Art of Fiction') 'besides which, a figure is nothing without a setting', and this is immediately set aside by 'our young man came and went every day, with rather an indifferent, unperceiv-ing step, it is true, among the objects I have briefly designated' – how different from Hyacinth Robinson. This setting seems to exist not for Ransom but for no purpose at all, or for a novel or part of a novel which is not going to be written:

If the opportunity were not denied me here, I should like to give some account of Basil Ransom's interior, of certain curious persons of both sexes, for the most part not favourites of fortune, who had found an obscure asylum there . . . . (Ch. 21)

However sceptically one takes that 'I should like', and one has to bear in mind the American magazine public,[2] this passage as far as it goes has great force. One thinks here of course of James's dalliance with naturalism and the Dickensian, and of the ambitions of *The Princess Casamassima*. Within this novel one is made very aware of what James won't touch: both Ransom's bohemian life in New York and that southern setting which includes 'something almost African' (Ch. 1); and also, the crucial case, Verena's setting. It is not my intention in this essay to go into the relation of Verena to the feminist movement in America in the 1870s. Andrew Sinclair's suggestion that she is a pale reflection of Victoria Woodhull, however questionable it may be, sufficiently points to how much of the extraordinary world of reform in this period is not there.[3] But I think we have to put the issue of figure and setting in a different way.

The question is whether James wanted to give her any setting at all. 'A figure is nothing without a setting', but we have just seen James refuse to find Ransom 'among the objects I have briefly designated'. This may be a reluctance or inability to explore certain areas of life, comparable with the failure to find in *The Princess Casamassima* 'the real thing'. But it begins to look more than that if we remember that this setting is not a setting at all in one sense. It is the most powerful of the 'American scenes' I have been quoting. And its power comes from letting the promiscuous detail and sensation have its head 'without excuse', as was implied of Verena. Its debris is so assertive it doesn't need justification either by a certain slant of light or a certain kind of hero, or indeed any furtherance of the novel. James without design is without excuse. It is not simply that this American scene triumphs over an art of fiction, of 'setting': it is almost wilfully irrelevant and indifferent. Setting and figure and author are liberated. The book, having turned from Boston, is on holiday.

But if the novel escapes at this point, however briefly, from a certain kind of discrimination of the ugliness and the 'poverty' of the American scene, it looks relevant, however destructively, to a larger design. For the visual vulgarity of America is only one part of a general and increasing American vulgarity. I do not want to dwell on this too long. It is very explicit in the novel and is brilliantly done. The assurance in the handling of the New York fashionable world, for example, is remarkable. My enquiry is into possible complexities of attitude towards this vulgarity. In the same way I shall neglect the particular reform questions, especially the woman question (as James does himself), for a more general sense of their American character. This should lead us to the elusive Verena, the crucial case as I have suggested for relation of figure to 'setting', now in the wider sense of 'the age'.

The obvious focus for a sense of the age are Ransom's remarks in Chapter 34. But although they give one version of contemporary mediocrity, and Ransom sees it as his task to rescue Verena from that mediocrity, he is in no clear way James's spokesman. To call him, as James does immediately afterwards, 'poor fellow', and to write of the 'ugliness' of his profession of faith, may well be irony at the expense of Verena and the age – 'Mr Ransom, I assure you this is an age of conscience.' But it is more likely that, given the consistent handling of Ransom, the irony is cutting both ways. Like Miss Birdseye he finds it difficult to recover from earlier severe treatment: for instance, 'five thousand, ten thousand, fifteen thousand a year? There was a richness to our panting young man in the smallest of these figures'; and 'he was conscious at bottom of a bigger stomach than all the culture of Charles Street could fill.' The sardonic handling persists into the New York section of the book: 'where should he find the twenty-dollar greenbacks which it was his ambition to transmit from time to time to his female relations, confined so constantly to a farinaceous diet?' His pronounced values are male, martial, anti-democratic, and stoical:

> it's a feminine, a nervous, hysterical, chattering, canting age, an age of hollow phrases and false delicacy and exaggerated solicitudes and coddled sensibilities, which, if we don't look out, will usher in the reign of mediocrity, of the feeblest and flattest and the most pretentious that has ever been. The masculine character, the ability to dare and endure, to know and yet not fear reality, to look the world in the face and take it for what it is – a very queer and partly very base mixture – that is what I want to preserve, as I may say, to recover. (Ch. 34)

Now this is not so much argument as oratory. Verena finds herself listening to the eloquence, the man, rather than the ideas. We know that voice, kept back for most of the book, comes from a 'large stomach' and a great ambition for success. It has that sincerity. And it is of course typical of the novel that relationships are conducted in this way. Ransom's resentment against women is natural, given his experience since leaving the South. He has found women in control wherever he has gone. The Olive Chancellors, Mrs Farrinders, Mrs Burrages, and Mrs Lunas, have the wealth or power or both. And their men are non-existent or weak – Olive's brothers, for example, were killed in the war. Like any other 'failure' or minority group he needs a conspiracy theory, but this hardly makes that theory the summation of the book's view of 'the age'.

Rather, given James's generally sardonic handling of him, he himself is part of the age. It's illuminating to compare him to Olive Chancellor in this respect. In terms of his statement *she* is the age, the enemy. But they are in the book the two chief discriminators of the age. They share a sense of how much 'trash' there is in it. They regret a lost heroic American past and posit the recovery of nobler human values of daring and suffering. The exactly comparable statement of Olive's views comes earlier in the book:

> Olive had a standing quarrel with the levity, the good-nature, of the judgements of the day; many of them seemed to her weak to imbecility, losing sight of all measures and standards, lavishing superlatives, delighted to be fooled. The age seemed to her to be relaxed and demoralized, and I believe she looked to the influx of the great feminine element to make it feel and speak more sharply. (Ch. 16)

Putting these two passages together most clearly reveals the irony of James's design. There is a very similar diagnosis and sense of the mediocrity of the age, with exactly opposite treatment: 'the masculine character', 'the great feminine element'.

Olive, on this occasion, has been talking to Matthias Pardon, the journalist with hair 'precociously white'. His 'gossip's view of great tendencies' personifies the age for her. And I would have thought that it is to the world of Matthias Pardon, and Selah Tarrant, we have to look for the most consistent portrait of the age. There are two passages on Tarrant and Pardon in Chapters 13 and 16 written in the brilliant manner of the first half of the novel which especially have a firm satirical confidence. In the first passage James comments that to Selah Tarrant 'human existence . . . was a huge publicity' which combined happily with the need for 'receipts' (Ch. 13). But it's the description of Pardon which catches 'the age' most ambitiously:

He had small, fair features, remarkably neat, and pretty eyes, and a moustache that he caressed, and an air of juvenility much at variance with his grizzled locks, and the free familiar reference in which he was apt to indulge in his career as a journalist. His friends knew that in spite of his delicacy and his prattle he was what they called a live man; his appearance was perfectly reconcilable with a large degree of literary enterprise. It should be explained that for the most part they attached to this idea the same meaning as Selah Tarrant – a state of intimacy with the newspapers, the cultivation of the great arts of publicity. For this ingenuous son of his age all distinction between the person and the artist had ceased to exist; the writer was personal, the person food for newsboys, and everything and everyone were every one's business. All things, with him, referred themselves to print, and print meant simply infinite reporting, a promptitude of announcement, abusive when necessary, or even when not, about his fellow-citizens. He poured contumely on their private life, on their personal appearance, with the best conscience in the world. His faith, again, was the faith of Selah Tarrant – that being in the newspapers is a condition of bliss, and that it would be fastidious to question the terms of the privilege. He was an *enfant de la balle*, as the French say; he had begun his career, at the age of fourteen, by going the rounds of the hotels, to cull flowers from the big, greasy registers which lie on the marble counters; and he might flatter himself that he had contributed in his measure, and on behalf of a vigilant public opinion, the pride of a democratic State, to the great end of preventing the American citizen from attempting clandestine journeys. Since then he had ascended other steps of the same ladder; he was the most brilliant young interviewer on the Boston press. He was particularly successful in drawing out the ladies; he had condensed into shorthand many of the most celebrated women of his time – some of these daughters of fame were very voluminous – and he was supposed to have a remarkably insinuating way of waiting upon *prime donne* and actresses the morning after their arrival, or sometimes the very evening, while their luggage was being brought up. He was only twenty-eight years old, and, with his hoary head, was a thoroughly modern young man; he had no idea of not taking advantage of all the modern conveniences. He regarded the mission of mankind upon earth as a perpetual evolution of telegrams; everything to him was very much the same, he had no sense of proportion or quality; but the newest thing was what came nearest exciting in his mind the sentiment of respect. (Ch. 16)

The particularization and the representativeness are superbly managed here, especially in the use of the wise child motif. (The passage does have a slightly different kind of power if we remember the trouble James ran into for being personal about Elizabeth Peabody, the model for Mrs Birdseye, and the way in which the injunction to the novelist to be 'one of the people on whom nothing is lost' in 'The Art of Fiction' is just as much a reporter's watchword as a novelist's.)

We have to remember then – perhaps James doesn't sufficiently remind us – that Pardon is as important a contender for Verena's hand as anyone else. Ransom and Olive are rivals but they both seek to rescue Verena from Pardon's world, which in many ways is her natural world. But then we come to James's major irony. Both Ransom and Olive have a partial discriminatory intelligence which enables them to see through the world of publicity. But like most other characters in the novel, with the notable exception of Dr Prance who is doing real and quiet work, they both seek a place in it, and in the end both have compromised with it. Olive plans to 'launch' Verena finally with Pardon's co-operation. Ransom has had his best article accepted. They both of course distinguish *their* public role from the world of publicity. They will offer the best article. But I don't think the book allows this kind of distinction final weight. Certainly the climax, with its vulgar public squabbling, can't. The point in Ransom's case is most economically made in the brilliant comic scene with Mrs Luna and Pardon before the Music Hall finale. Mrs Luna finds herself unwillingly providing material for the world of publicity – 'What Miss Chancellor's Family Think About It':

> 'If you have the impertinence to publish a word about me, or to mention my name in print, I will come to your office and make such a scene!'

'Dearest lady, that would be a godsend!' Mr Pardon cried, enthusiastically; but he put his note-book back into his pocket.

'Have you made an exhaustive search for Miss Tarrant?' Basil Ransom asked of him. Mr Pardon, at this inquiry, eyed him with a sudden, familiar archness, expressive of the idea of competition; so that Ransom added: 'You needn't be afraid, I'm not a reporter.'

'I didn't know but what you had come on from New York.'

'So I have – but not as the representative of a newspaper.'

'Fancy his taking you – ' Mrs Luna murmured, with indignation. (Ch. 40)

We are surely here meant to relish this mistaken identity because it makes a point about Ransom, which is not Mrs Luna's: that he is not so distinguishable. Ransom of course is taken for 'one of us' in various ways in the book. Not the least embarassing is that lady's way, claiming him as part of her own coarse, wealthy, Europeanized conservatism. He is not the reporter from New York, although in a sense he has from the beginning been gathering material; rather, fluid American character that he is, despite his 'stiffness', that is one of his possibilities. Certainly at this stage of the novel he feels himself to be on his way in his own part of the world of publicity.

All this will seem to avoid the main question of Ransom and Verena's mutual love, his desire to remove Verena from this 'detestable' world, and his influence in giving her – the first one to do so – a private identity, a sense of a self other than the continuously public self of her upbringing and life, a self, predictably, of a genuine domestic and familial vocation. But it seemed best to come at this in the way I have done in order not to confuse Ransom's public role with Verena's. Ransom doesn't stand for contempt of public life, except in so far as he stands for contempt of life in general, the queer and base mixture; but he is against women's involvement in it. 'He had always had a desire for public life; to cause one's ideas to be embodied in national conduct appeared to him the highest form of human enjoyment' (Ch. 21). Verena is offered the private life of a public man.

Nevertheless it may be argued that Ransom stands for personal values against the world of publicity. The difficulty with a word like 'personal', certainly much used by James, is that it can get a blanket endorsement – what could be of value which was not personal? – which can obscure the complexity of what it is pointing to. The use of the word in 'The Art of Fiction' for example, or in the essay on Daudet, is ambiguous, probably contradictory. In *The Bostonians* the word usually operates against the vocabulary of public life. The key moment in the development of the love of Ransom and Verena comes when she says his interest in her is not 'controversial' but 'personal'. Again, Olive's disqualification for public life is that – in Ransom's view, like all women – she takes things too personally, too hard.

One of the simplest readings the book offers is as a backstage drama – will the show go on? The anticipation here of *The Tragic Muse* is relevant but can be misleading. In that complex novel the performing art transcends and transforms the meanness of life, especially women's life, and the meanness of lesser arts, including the art of politics. In *The Bostonians* there is no secure world of discrimination and art, the actresses are more likely to be 'variety'. But there is this powerful element in the novel of a felt need to escape from the confinement of the personal, from private sensation, into contact with 'life', especially the life in 'the social dusk of that mysterious democracy'. 'I'm sick of the Back Bay', cries Olive.

It may be objected that, in noting this markedly Hawthorne-like aspect of the novel, I am really generalizing from Olive's particular 'problem' as wealthy guilty spinster, and in doing so possibly confusing the private, in terms of isolation, with the personal, with its necessary additional 'relationships'. Certainly what the novel does and was intended to do is to show 'one of those friendships between women which are so common in New England'.[4] This relationship is in different ways 'life' for both women, and it may be supposed to be a perverse version of the personal, disguised in the language of self-sacrifice and dedication. But this is rather stale ground, that of public activity and reform always being definable in terms of indirect or thwarted 'personal' desires.

But are we then to assume that the love of Verena and Ransom is 'really' personal in some sense? – heterosexual being better than lesbian, in spite of its grotesque variants in the book such as the Farrinders ('and his name was Amaria'), or Selah Tarrant's 'association' with Ada T. P. Foat?

Eventually it comes to the question of the nature of the relationship, the union. And uncertainties and forebodings about that do not spring from the novel's grim last sentence alone: 'It is to be feared that with the union, so far from brilliant, into which she was about to enter, these [tears] were not the last she was destined to shed.' If this is the most substantial relationship in the book (although one would have to say that the Olive–Verena affair is the more subtle, also involving as it does a rationale of free union), it is because it takes up and confirms what all other 'unions' point to: dominance for one partner, defeat for the other. That is the force of sexuality in the novel. Olive's sense, which James delicately guesses at, of Verena exhibiting women's 'hideous weakness – their predestined subjection to man's larger and grosser insistence' (Ch. 39) agrees with Ransom's attitude toward Verena (beneath his politeness): 'she was tremendously open to attack, she was meant for love, she was meant for him' (Ch. 36).

But the sexual sense of 'personal' in this relationship combines with the public as well as being opposed to it. Over another 'queer' American private life, another 'fiasco', looms the encompassing fiasco of the Civil War, the war of union, with the lurking irony of Ransom's championship of 'minority rights'. And it is Ransom's dedication to a cause, his forlorn but powerful hope of public success, that is part of his persuasion of her.

It is typical of the novel's procedure that this persuasion takes place in public (all their courting is done this way, except for those limited hours in Marmion), in the characteristic American scene of Central Park, under the gaze of the unemployed, 'the children of disappointment from across the sea'. It's the first time that Ransom lets go his bantering tone and speaks sincerely, from the stomach as it were – he is virtually unemployed himself at this time. She is partly won, as I have already suggested, by oratory, greater public conviction. For her to submit in that way is not surprising – it is not after all so odd a match for a daughter of the lecturing-circuit to make.

James thought of naming the novel after her, but who is Verena? Verena is a great creation, she makes *The Bostonians* plural in its greatness, gives the novel a compensating and complementary generosity along with its sardonic and satirical verve. Sometimes it is the idea of her that is great, rather than the embodiment. James does not always know how far to go with her or how much sceptical qualification to introduce. But even these reservations pick on something almost necessary to her presence.

Who she is is really part of the question of whom she is taken to be, whom she is made to be. She enters the book as the passive instrument of her father, and leaves 'enslaved' by Ransom. 'She had always done everything that people asked', 'it was in her nature to be easily submissive, to like being overborne'. Like Priscilla in Hawthorne's *The Blithedale Romance* she waits to be possessed, to be created. But that parallel is immediately disturbing. Hawthorne's 'gentle parasite' draws on the energies of other people. Verena's submission, sexual or otherwise, involves her as a source of energy, a capturable vitality.

For Olive she is 'life', particularly the life, 'the romance of the people'. She is that 'poor girl' Olive has been looking for, whom she will raise, and who will answer that need 'to know everything that lies beneath and out of sight'. In her first appearance in the novel she is eager and restless, 'not a quiet girl'. With her extraordinary red hair and bizarre dress (James shows her interest in dressing up at several points in the novel) she appears 'theatrical', but 'naturally theatrical'. Her performance at Miss Birdseye's is 'fresh' and 'pure', 'an intensely personal exhibition'. For Ransom

> the necessity of her nature was not to make converts to a ridiculous cause, but to emit those charming notes of her voice, to stand in those free young attitudes, to shake her braided locks like a naiad rising from the waves, to please everyone who came near her and to be happy that she pleased. (Ch. 8)

'All her desire was to learn' and 'she was ever-curious about the world'. She had 'no particular feeling about herself; she only cared, as yet, for outside things.' As you came to know her 'you would have wondered immensely how she came to issue from such a pair' as the Tarrants.

To Olive (in an unusually socialist moment):

> she was so strange, so different from the girls one usually met, seemed to belong to some queer gipsy-land or transcendental Bohemia. With her bright, vulgar clothes, her salient appearance, she might have been a

rope-dancer or a fortune-teller; and this had the immense merit, for Olive, that it appeared to make her belong to the 'people', threw her into the social dusk of that mysterious democracy which Miss Chancellor held that the fortunate classes know so little about, and with which (in a future possibly very near) they will have to count.   (Ch. 11)

Verena 'had moved her as she never had been moved'.

She was also 'a creature of unlimited generosity' who 'never held back'. Her 'gift' was a mystery, 'dropped straight from heaven' – nothing to do with her awful parents, her 'queer' life and background. She has survived that 'perfectly uncontaminated, and she would never be touched by evil' in spite of announcements like 'I prefer free unions'. She smiled at everyone, she 'likes the individual'.

There is a 'characteristic raciness of speech' in her.[5] She is 'the most extraordinary mixture of eagerness and docility', her success is 'simply to have been made as she was made'. Olive welcomes her as an innocent 'flower of the great Democracy', without vulgarity, coming from 'the poorest, humblest people', 'the very obscure', the only persons 'safe' from vulgarity. Yet she is 'miraculous', a 'whim of the creative force'. 'There were people like that, fresh from the hand of Omnipotence' (Ch. 15).

She flirts, or rather this is 'the subtle feminine desire to please'. 'There were so many things she hadn't yet learned to dislike.' She represented 'the consummate innocence of the American girl'. 'The very stones of the street – all the dumb things of nature – might find a voice to talk to you' (Ch. 17). She enables both Olive and Ransom to speak. She wants to 'intellectually command all life' but she is not 'naturally concentrated' like Olive. She jokes – turns the sacred formulae of feminist success into pleasantries. She is of 'many pieces', 'irresponsible', but she can 'kindle, flame up . . . resolve herself into a magical voice, become again the pure young sybil'. In entering the partnership with Olive she was attracted by 'the vision of new social horizons, the sense of novelty, and the love of change'. She 'put forth a beautiful energy'. She lacks pride, she is 'free from private self-reference',

> her bright mildness glided over the many traps that life sets for our consistency . . . everything fresh and fair renewed itself in her with

extraordinary facility, everything ugly and tiresome evaporated as soon as it touched her. (Ch. 20)

Under Olive's care she 'assimilated all delicacies and absorbed all traditions'. She could 'do anything she tried'.

Mrs Luna thinks her a third-rate adventuress, 'trash'. At his second meeting with her Ransom finds she has a 'fantastic fairness', she is an actress making a 'scene' of anything. She has a natural oratory and the 'air of being a public figure', but in this she is 'genial' not 'dogmatic'. She was 'honest and natural' but with 'queer, bad lecture-blood in her veins . . . a touching, ingenuous victim, unconscious of the pernicious forces which were hurrying her to her ruin' (Ch. 26). She is like an actress or singer, an 'improvisatrice . . . a chastened, modern, American version . . . a New England Corinna'.

She is 'meant for love'. She has a great power of enjoyment, she responds in New York to 'the infinite possibilities of a great city'. She was made to enjoy rather than suffer, there is the 'epicurean' in her, the impulse to 'live only for the hour'. She proves 'by the answering, familiar brightness with which she looked out on the lamp-lighted streets that, whatever theory might be entertained as to the genesis of her talent and her personal nature, the blood of the lecture-going, night-walking Tarrants did distinctly flow in her veins' (Ch. 31).

She resists protection: 'I must take everything that comes. I mustn't be afraid.' She is 'a good thing' to get hold of, 'the latest thing', someone who 'might easily have a big career', 'an article for which there was more and more demand' (an intellectually third-rate article in Ransom's opinion). Ransom tells her, 'I don't know where you come from nor how you came to be what you are, but you are outside and above all vulgarizing influences' (Ch. 34).

As the book nears its close James himself takes up her analysis much more, writing of 'her peculiar frankness' and 'the extraordinary generosity with which she would expose herself, give herself away, turn herself inside out, for the satisfaction of a person who made demands of her' (Ch. 37). She was 'always passion' (whether in love or for the feminist cause), but without a great capacity for suffering:

With her light, bright texture, her complacent responsiveness, her genial, graceful, ornamental cast, her desire to keep on pleasing others at the time when a force she had never felt before was pushing her to please herself, poor Verena lived in those days in a state of moral tension – with a sense of being strained and aching – which she didn't betray more only because it was absolutely not in her power to look desperate. (Ch. 38)

She had only a 'hothouse loyalty' to Olive and her cause, and eventually, like those other poor girls, there was a 'Charlie' to take her off.

James's sceptical note in that last extended quotation has its own complexities. The '*light*, bright texture . . . *complacent* responsiveness' are being measured against Olive's suffering, her capacity to take things too hard. *Her* morbidity makes desperation always at her disposal. The irony of a force 'pushing her to please herself' is clearer, especially as that 'force' has told Verena that 'what is most agreeable to women is to be agreeable to men'.

Given that general sense of Verena, however much 'of many pieces' it is, it becomes clearer still that Verena in love with Ransom is a defeated Verena. Like Fitzgerald's Gatsby, also a 'son of God', her discovery of personal love is limiting and destructive (far more so than the relationship with Olive). And what it limits or destroys is what James's lyrical tone in presenting her so often manifests, something personal in a different sense, her 'gift', what is responsive and vivifying in her nature.

And that love, that separable self, is closely related to the repeated attempts, very evident in the combined impressions of her I have quoted, to find her 'essence', to separate her from her background, her 'setting' – her parents, her class, the world of publicity, the whole vulgar American scene. She is both representative of the age and uniquely separable from it, and we are continually watching her in the novel being taken both ways. The comedy of these attempts is that they keep reopening the satirically settled question of the American scene. It gives that scene, the 'age', a perpetual second chance. And that chance can't be defined merely in terms of vulgar car-bells sounding almost silvery. It's the chance of Verena's indiscriminate vision itself, that power to make all things, including Ransom and Olive, speak, to make all things live.

This Orphic role, together with other religious and legendary associations – Minerva, 'fresh from the hand of Omnipotence' – how-

ever playful, give her a mythic potentiality. But her human variousness remains dominant. Her force is not that of a transcendent
presence; not so much a second coming, more an American second
chance, a superhumanized possibility, a Whitmanesque 'song of
myself' and 'democratic vista', a creative innocence like that of Huck
Finn's, both close to and separate from the world of the confidence
trickster and the adventurer.[6]

Her defeat then is naturally associated with the Civil War. It is in
the visit with Ransom to the Harvard Memorial Hall that her self-
consciousness begins. At the start of this episode her talk – about her
attendance at the Women's Convention – is typically gay and earnest:
'We had some tremendously earnest discussions, which it would have
been a benefit to you to hear, or any man who doesn't think we can
rise to the highest point. Then we had some refreshment – we con-
sumed quantities of ice-cream!' And it is also typically impersonal
about her success – 'it had no more manner about it than if it concerned the goddess Minerva'. In Ransom's imagination of the scene
she is 'ruined', the victim of a hall 'filled with carpet-baggers'. And
it is the intensity of this concern which shows and provokes her
discovery: 'See here, Mr Ransom, do you know what strikes me? . . .
The interest you take in me isn't really controversial – a bit. It's quite
personal!' (Ch. 25)

This new sense of the personal is interrupted by Ransom's contemplation of the Hall, which draws from James one of his most
apparently unequivocal passages in the book:

> The effect of the place is singularly noble and solemn, and it is im-
> possible to feel it without a lifting of the heart. It stands there for duty
> and honour, it speaks of sacrifice and example, seems a kind of temple
> to youth, manhood, generosity. Most of them were young, all were in
> their prime, and all of them had fallen; this simple idea hovers before
> the visitor and makes him read with tenderness each name and place –
> names often without other history, and forgotten Southern battles. For
> Ransom these things were not a challenge nor a taunt; they touched him
> with respect, with the sentiment of beauty. He was capable of being a
> generous foeman, and he forgot, now, the whole question of sides and
> parties; the simple emotion of the old fighting-time came back to him,
> and the monument around him seemed an embodiment of that memory;

it arched over friends as well as enemies, the victims of defeat as well as
the sons of triumph.   (Ch. 25)

Then as their own discussion intensifies, over the question of whether
Verena will tell Olive of their meeting, their relationship fits with this
heroic American past:

> 'I tell her everything,' said the girl; and now as soon as she had spoken,
> she blushed. He stood before her, tracing a figure on the mosaic pave-
> ment with his cane, conscious that in a moment they had become more
> intimate. They were discussing their affairs, which had nothing to do
> with the heroic symbols that surrounded them; but their affairs had
> suddenly grown so serious that there was no want of decency in their
> lingering there for the purpose.   (Ch. 25)

We surely connect Verena with this 'temple' to youth and generosity, this dedication and sacrifice, exclusively male as it is; and make
the connexion not only in terms of her own cause, and the struggle
of men and women, but also in what is becoming more serious to her
at this moment, the 'intimate' personal battle with Ransom and Olive.
The Civil War, the war for the Union, elsewhere described as 'one of
the biggest failures that history commemorates, an immense national
fiasco', is solemnized (as it is from this period on in America) with a
transcendental generosity, a slightly hollow effort of reconciliation –
'the victims of defeat as well as the sons of triumph'.

This solemn reconciliation is the setting for Verena's own kind of
reconciliation, her 'feminine logic': 'It is very beautiful – but I think
it is very dreadful, if it wasn't so majestic, I would have it pulled
down.' She objects to the glorification of bloodshed, the male martial
sacrament of sacrifice. But she responds, she partially submits, as she
will later to Ransom's intensity. As their own intimate battle starts,
her own sacrificial role is prepared. And as the chapter proceeds
Ransom begins to assert his newly-felt power, his 'man's brutality'
over her.

The Hall, then, operates both as a solemn memorial of an heroic
American past, a past contrasting with a mediocre modern age, and
as an ironic image of union. Here as everywhere in the novel the idea
of union, whether private or public, leads to conflict, and either
victory or defeat. The escape, 'after the battle had ceased', is

momentary, rhetorical and delusory, except as death's 'sacrifice'.

Yet Verena stands for an alternative, not an escape, within the unmemorialized world. She is not after all a heroine. Her thinking is not like Ransom's or Olive's. She *is* superficial, she *is* absurd. 'The truth had changed sides.' She changes her mind. She 'liked herself better'. There is something reassuring in that, and in James's refusal to make her 'tragic', to go for the full resonance of the innocent child-victim, as in *What Maisie Knew* or even *Daisy Miller*. There is nothing sacred in her defeat. There is something reassuringly mean in it, and in her (and their) prospects. If this is loss of innocence it is not *the* loss of innocence. A girl without a setting, or too many settings, too many changes of mind, cannot be that symbolic. Nothing American can be that symbolic.

The solemn temple appears in a different form at the end of the novel. The Boston Music Hall is the final meeting place for the trains of imagery of battle and religious apotheosis, and where they reach their most dramatic, and in some ways most vulgar, expression. Ransom fights his last daring battle of a campaign which has become increasingly desperate. This includes one carefully placed reference to him imagining himself in the role of Lincoln's assassin (Ch. 41). Like Olive he is prepared for martyrdom.

The temple of course is dedicated to the world of publicity, to the launching of 'the latest thing' into the mediocre age. But that is more Olive's and Ransom's view of it; both conceive of themselves as defying the mob. But it's Verena again who won't allow the re-actionary image of the democracy to cohere:

> 'And what will the people do? Listen, listen!'
> 'Your father is ceasing to interest them. They'll howl and thump, according to their nature.'
> 'Ah, their nature's fine!' (Ch. 42)

In the brilliantly rendered final fiasco, the refought battle of North and South, Verena's idea persists in the midst of contending parties. There is nothing final about the ending of the novel – we are not sure what will become of the Ransoms. More immediately, we may not be sure what will happen to Olive. 'I am going to be hissed, hooted, and insulted.' But the people may give her a voice.

In *The Bostonians* James wanted to write 'a very American tale', and in looking back at it towards the end of his life he found he had written a very 'curious' one. To search for the representative and come up with the curious is characteristically Jamesian. It could be a shorthand for what goes wrong with *The Princess Casamassima*. But it is the achievement of *The Bostonians* to convince of the curiosity of the very American, and, if Verena is given her full value, to celebrate that curiosity, sardonically but also generously.

Notes

1. All quotations are taken from the Chiltern Library edition, London, 1952, which follows the text of the first book edition of *The Bostonians* (1886).
2. For magazines like *Century* this public would be mainly feminine, or 'family' and therefore feminized. In so far as they perhaps deny James the opportunity for a certain kind of fiction, a 'masculine' fiction, this passage would be evidence for James's endorsement of Ransom's attack, later in the book, of the age as 'feminized'.
3. Andrew Sinclair, *The Better Half, The Emancipation of the American Woman*, London, 1966, pp. 263–8. For a life of Victoria Woodhull see Johanna Johnston, *Mrs Satan, the incredible saga of Victoria Woodhull*, London, 1967.
4. *Notebooks*, p. 47.
5. See Chapter 13 for an extended example of Verena's raciness.
6. *The Bostonians* first appeared in *Century*, beginning in February 1885. Extracts from Mark Twain's *The Adventures of Huckleberry Finn* appeared in *Century* during the same period.

4

The reference of
The Tragic Muse

D. J. GORDON and JOHN STOKES

1 *A holiday in Paris: premises and method*

The first movement of the book ends when the Dormers, Lady Agnes, Grace, Biddy and Nick, return to London from their short visit to Paris in spring or early summer. They, their friends, and those whom they unexpectedly meet, encounter too Paris itself. And Paris, where they are all together, implies, always, a London, in background or foreground. Here is the frame or constantly present point of reference: relationship to Paris/London being an agent in precipitating and defining the situations of the persons: the physical presence of the city, light and air, exteriors and interiors, private and public, institutions of private or public life, holding both history and the extant moment of the English, or more or less English group: who have in common, whether the Dormers or Peter Sherringham, Julia Dallow or Gabriel Nash, or the Rooths, mother and daughter, that in and towards Paris all are, in their ways, transients; and towards London, all, except Julia Dallow, uncertain of their places. Disclosures are partial and delayed.

We begin with the Dormers, seen from a distance, by a remote observer, as objects in an exhibition of objects. They are characterized generally by 'Englishness'. Information about who and what they are is given gradually, in brief instalments related to some moment of crisis, more or less important: it is not until Chapter 5 that we are given twin biographies of Nick and Peter Sherringham, which also connect and contrast the young men, as their walk through

Paris (to which these histories come as coda) has done already. Biddy
is left to make what she can of Gabriel Nash, until her brother
chooses to give him a name, and a reluctant partial report that raises
as many questions as it answers. She, and we, have to wait till the
lunch party to hear anything about those two women who had been
with Nash when brother and sister met him among the sculptures.
What Nick's pressing, present trouble is, we learn bit by bit through
his encounters with his family, with the sculptures, Paris, Sherringham, Gabriel Nash: the immediate climax being reached in Chapter
9 in that walk with Nash to Notre-Dame. Peter Sherringham is late
for lunch: for Lady Agnes, fearful of martyrdom, this is consonant
with the uncertainty of her son's movements and intentions, and even
of Julia Dallow's – who is a name and a topic of conversation or
allusion which partly reveals her, and partly the Dormers: a partial
disclosure that is carried on after she does eventually appear at dinner,
and later. Delayed and partial knowledge or disclosure are essential
for this novel, which begins with uncertainties and issues in them.

Encounters are between persons who do not understand each
other, though they may think they do (and may be of the same family),
or between one who understands and one or others who do not, or
between those who partially understand. Encounters may be with a
member of a specially defined extraneous group – represented by
Madame Carré – or with someone whose group cannot easily be
identified. Lady Agnes does not understand Nick, although he understands her. Biddy does not understand Nick, although she wants to.
Peter thinks he understands Nick, and, in part, does. Gabriel Nash is
certain he understands Nick and the Rooths and Madame Carré and
Julia Dallow. He does and he does not. Biddy is not the only person
who does not understand who or what Gabriel Nash is: finding a
label for Nash is an instructive and integral game which will tell us
more about the players than about Nash. Such uncertainties or misunderstandings – who and what are the Rooths? – are they even
English? – is even Peter Sherringham sufficiently English? – have to
do with social identities or roles and with names or signs that define
and therefore identify, so limiting or eliminating the uncomfortable
realm of the unfamiliar. Or they have to do with generalizations, or
propositions, or formulas that act like *names* for both persons and

activities. Such definitions may be correct or incorrect; and the validity of the social process by which we name and therefore impose an identity, and also the consequent connexions between 'being' and 'doing' are subject to examination.

The dialogue works towards the establishing or offering of such generalizations or definitions. Working through incomplete encounters, its characteristic method is the transposition or translation of a term or phrase, used by one person as proposition or formula, into a sense or application that the other can understand or misunderstand: which is, among other things, one of the classical methods of wit or paradox or aphorism, modes long taken – and rightly – to mark this novel.

Generated through such encounters, generalization or formula or name operates structurally: here, displayed and maintained with strict logic, is the prime articulation of the novel. It is the insistent appearance of such generalizations that makes *The Tragic Muse* seem more 'didactic' or 'programmatic' or 'theoretical' than the two other major novels that occupied James in this decade, *The Princess Casamassima* and *The Bostonians*. Yet these generalizations, with their extensions and developments, are proffered within situations of discussion; and it is the situations we must attend to and the picking out and testing of the generalizations. It may be that the situation, or the game, is more important than any result that can be called victory or defeat; and that generalizations that apparently come out as 'true' will have the region or confines of their 'truth' sharply drawn for us; and, will, after all, be held suspended in uncertainty. The generalizations, the way they emerge, their fate, are structural and give then, as they must, the tone of the novel, which is playful – games are being played – ironic, or comic: in a way that anticipates the sequence of stories about writers, and their public, that is to follow immediately – and indeed, overlaps *The Tragic Muse*. This has seemed to be – happily – the only way James could deal with his own situation (and not only his own in the eighties and nineties); but it precedes *Guy Domville*, and all that that disclosure meant.

And it is precisely through the reference of generalizations and their contexts in situations of discussion that James manages to make *The Tragic Muse* 'topical' – granted perhaps the rather large sense that Dickens, say, or George Eliot would allow to 'topicality' – in a way that *The Princess Casamassima* and *The Bostonians* are not. Generalization and situation can, that is, be referred to arguments and attitudes or points of view that have been familiar, or fairly familiar, to a certain audience, or audiences, over a decade or more. And encounters, generation of generalizations, situations of discussion, suspended or inconclusive conclusions, minister also to James's obvious wish to produce a syncretic work, an anthology if you like, one that could take in what could be, and what was being said in the large and serious field that, for good reasons, he wished at this moment to concern himself with.

One of James's problems was how to connect the story of the public or political life, and therefore the story of Julia, with the story of art and the life of art. Those objects at the Salon, sculptures in the sunny air where the English visitors are sitting, or pictures hung indoors, can be made to point to both. The absent Julia can, obtrusively, be connected with objects, beautiful objects, by Lady Agnes and Grace; but Nick rejects this offered link between himself and Julia: the taste, the intelligence that brought those objects together was not Julia's but her dead husband's. The Salon shows not a 'collection' but objects made by living artists. Through these we are to be led into generalizations, not so much about the worth of those new things as about the conditions that produced them, the conditions which must be available for the life and work of the artist. Biddy, biddable, innocent, offers a first proposition:

> 'The subject doesn't matter; it's the treatment, the treatment!' Biddy announced, in a voice like the tinkle of a silver bell.[1]

Falling from Biddy's lips this tinkles like a dropped formula, a stock response to the subject/treatment dilemma, coming as though she had learnt it by heart even in the presumably discreet studios where she was allowed to study 'modelling'. Nick brushes it aside, affectionately. His answer to his mother indicates here, among these tangible signs, responses, presuppositions, phrases that are to conduct us through James's principal enquiry:

This place is an immense stimulus to me; it refreshes me, excites me, it's such an exhibition of artistic life. It's full of ideas, full of refinements; it gives one such an impression of artistic experience. They try everything, they feel everything. While you were looking at the murders, apparently, I observed an immense deal of curious and interesting work. ... All art is one – remember that, Biddy dear. ... It's the same great, many-headed effort, and any ground that's gained by an individual, any spark that's struck in any province, is of use and of suggestion to all the others. We are all in the same boat.

Effort and work are what preoccupy Nick. Biddy, though she would like to, does not understand him; and, strolling among those objects, he transposes her jargon, or their mother's vocabulary, into the context of this effort and of the general conditions that must support it. 'Ideas' – what Biddy hopes to find for her modelling, the 'capacity for ideas' which she hopes she has – are put alongside *application*; her own *trying* becomes *trying seriously*; and definition of the crucial adverb is put into a paradox that translates Lady Agnes's position into its opposite: art is good, or acceptable to Lady Agnes when it is bad, which means when it is the affair of odd hours, a distraction like a game:

> The only thing that can justify it, the effort to carry it as far as one can (which you can't do without time and singleness of purpose), she regards as just the dangerous, the criminal element. ...

Biddy translates Nick's meaning into *professional* – that is what her mother doesn't want one to become; and Nick accepts the word. Professional is a social definition of what he meant, and could become (with still other social nuances) *work*, something one spends one's life on and tries to earn one's living by: Biddy immediately introduces 'Your own work – your painting'. But this is a light sense of *work* which Nick rejects, for himself. Painting has never been his *work*: 'if it had ... I should stick to it.' A set of terms has been erected, generated by occasion, by this sort of dialogue based on incomprehension (though in this case, sympathetic); and these are to persist. That a moment has been reached is marked by closing the dialogue and introducing a summary account of Nick Dormer's long transactions with Paris. His awareness of what the exhibits at the Salon stand for involves now the whole city. What he responds to is a manifold, comprising garden, shadows of summer clouds, the white images, provocative, 'hard in their crudity', even the rattle of plates in the restaurant. For this too is part of the contagion of Paris, that has always offered so many suggestions in the way of art; and now especially offers – the earlier phrase is repeated – 'a sense of artistic life': studios, companionships, youth, 'and a multitudinous newness, forever reviving and the diffusion of a hundred talents, ingenuities, experiments'. What the artistic life means as an activity is still his preoccupation. He felt that the exhibition 'would help him to settle something'; and he associates 'the idea of help' with a man whom he sees approaching. This is Gabriel Nash.

There is a major transposition from Nick's terms, *artistic life* or *life of art* and its glimpsed conditions, to *life as art*, with its proposed terms and conditions. Gabriel Nash offers this. Biddy cannot understand Nash, any more than she can identify or place him, except as a 'gentleman', or any more than she can identify even the nationality of the two silent women who were with him as they met. She can only try to understand, by finding some named role or formula that will bring Nash somewhere within a known world. Nick's part is to question, to welcome, neither to accept nor deny. Nash appears, as it were, from nowhere, to Nick who has not seen or heard of him for a long time: that he should move in what seems to others – not to himself – a cloud of uncertainty is essential to his full presentation. Nick's questions permit Nash to talk about himself – not in riddles or evasions, as Biddy may think, but in generalizations; for Nash is his own case, his own text, illustrating a new set of rules to live by.

Nash redefines and revalues accepted kinds of human activity, both art and politics, together with the conditions of their practice: he offers another sort of activity – in his definition as final. His premise is a version of what *experience* is; and this involves both the individual and his social relationships.

Nash's refusal to allow that he lives in the nineteenth century, or in London rather than in Samarkand, is the same as his refusal to allow that he either likes or dislikes English art. He is refusing any *formula* or social definition or *generalization*. And this he does in the name of *feeling*. 'They try everything, they feel everything,' Nick had said of the French artists; and Nash says 'We must feel everything, everything we can. We are here for that.' Nick's *feeling* had immediate reference to the artistic experience and the work that comes out of it. Nash's *feeling* is absolute, referring to nothing beyond itself: for there is nothing else that we have. In the one life we know, we have only our *impressions*. *Impressions* becomes the word for what our consciousness is made up of, and these impressions had better be agreeable ones:

> the happy moments of our consciousness – the multiplication of those moments. We must save as many as possible from the dark gulf.

Generalization loses its normal sense and is only admissible as autobiography (what I do) – 'My only generalizations are my actions' – and 'my behaviour' (what I do) is my feelings. This is not passive acceptance of anything that may come. If *feeling* modulates into *impressions*, and *impressions* modulate into the restrictive *agreeable impressions* ('happy moments'), these in turn are translatable into *the beautiful*. Our *feelings* are *behaviour* because we are capable of 'shades of impression, of appreciation', *appreciation* being a faculty we have, 'a special sense' that can be trained and extended so that we can get hold of the *beautiful*. With these words, *consciousness*, *impressions*, and *appreciation* we have a new vocabulary that connects with Nick's as he reflected on the life of art. Nick's question has to be (we are still among the sculptures): What does all this produce? And Nash's answer is, in his terms an inescapable one: he makes himself: 'I am a fine consequence.' 'Are you an aesthete?' Biddy asks. But that is only another name, a definition operating within the social reference which the 'I' denies:

> Ah, there's one of the formulas! That's walking in one's hat! I've *no* profession, my dear young lady. I've no *état civil*. These things are part of the complicated ingenious machinery.... Merely to be is such a *métier*; to live is such an art; to feel is such a career!

So the major transposition is effected. Such terms refer back to and reverse Nick's relating of the *serious* and the *professional* in the life of art; and refer also to the conditions of the political life. Biddy had introduced that life as an alternative choice to Nash's: Nick's choice to put right wrongs, abuses and sufferings. This has been dismissed as belonging to the *formulas* or the complicated social machines that are opposed to the free movements of the individual consciousness. Politics – returning to the vocabulary of *function*, and to an application that would horrify Lady Agnes – is

> a trade like any other, and a method of making one's way which society certainly condones.

But the *observer* – and thus Nick assigns a known role to Nash – engaged in distinguishing his *shades* must himself be involved in the world of *naming*. Nash agrees: he has his *terminology* (a set of names), and this is his *style* (a word that goes with *appreciation*); but *style* is wholly individual, which means wholly private. To function for the convenience of others means that the names, or signs or style must become grosser; and the shades, which are what truly distinguish, must go. And here the conditions of the practice of art and politics meet. And so too Nash has given up his own art, writing.

Nash has used, for himself, the vocabulary of the critic of art or literature: the notion that *style* is the man reaches its conclusion that style cannot be a vehicle of social relation. He is both in a role – critic, observer – and is denying it. And he does not observe that he is still as fond of generalizations as Nick says he had been while at Oxford. In the name of the final freedom of the isolate consciousness we are offered generally applicable rules for conduct.

Nash, then, reduces the political life to an affair of words, of Nick's speeches coming, like literature, within the orbit of his word 'style', and subject to the same condemnation: 'style' being essentially private and individual, both politics and literature must suffer corruption because they have to do with communication, with an audience, and so with the convenience of others, and so with the realm of machinery, both operating through names or formulas which, by identifying, thereby falsify. Politics, like literature, is excluded from the realm of doing, of *action*, of the true *métier*, behaviour being feeling; or from the realm of art, for the true *métier* is to *be*: the true work of art (the fine consequence) being myself. When Nash concludes that politics (meaning, this time, being a 'great statesman') is 'a trade like any other', and a method of making one's way which society certainly condones, 'he is taking up *work*' (which itself went with *professional*), which Nick had used as both a description of an essential condition of the life of art and a social definition of the artist's occupation ('my work' – 'my occupation'), refusing, as we saw, to accept the word, in either application for himself, as painter.

There are other ways of defining the conditions of the *public life* (or the political life). What Lady Agnes offers as Nash, Nick and Biddy stroll and talk is a version of these conditions that must (as Nash's do) guide our expectations about how this story is to be presented. What Lady Agnes knows is that the inescapable condition of the political or public life is *money*:

> 'It's all very well to say that in public life money isn't necessary, as it used to be. . . . Those who say so don't know anything about it. It's always necessary. . . .'
> 'I dare say; but there's the fact – isn't there? – that poor papa had so little.'
> 'Yes, and there's the fact that it killed him!'
> These words came out with a strange, quick little flare of passion.

If Nick is to have money he has to get it from someone. There are two sources, Julia and Mr Carteret. It is left for the graceless Grace to say outright what Nick's marriage to Julia would be for all of them – 'she would be so nice to us' – and to assume that 'Mr Carteret will always help him'. Lady Agnes knows only uncertainties: that she does not really know what Nick is, that his relationship with Julia is not to be taken for granted; that Mr Carteret's bounty depends on Nick being *serious*, of which his marriage to Julia would be a sign: money goes to money.

> If Nick becomes rich, Charles Carteret will make him more so. If he doesn't, he won't give him a shilling.

Lady Agnes does know that Julia and Mr Carteret have existences of their own, but this is only to know that there are limits to the ways in which they can be used. She accepts without hesitation Julia's function in the impending by-election at Harsh, as does Julia's brother,

Peter Sherringham, who takes it for granted when he brings the news to Lady Agnes. Their language dangerously assumes and portends a relation of ownership. Julia 'undertakes' to bring Nick in. And to pay the bill: 'I think that's her idea.' 'Delightful Julia!' Lady Agnes ejaculated. Julia will leave Paris 'for her man'. 'Her man?' – Lady Agnes's question means more to us than Peter's answer covers: 'the fellow that stands, whoever he is; especially if he's Nick.' Neither the naked cash basis, nor the sort of relationship this involves, affects for a moment Lady Agnes's version of the value of the political or public life. For her this value is wholly comprehended in Nick's relationship to his father, which is the relationship to a *name*: 'One of the greatest, simply.' And Lady Agnes's version will be expanded to become one of the kinds of *tradition* with which the novel is concerned.

'Poor Julia, how you do work her!: this is Nick's recognition that his mother and sister have cast Julia for a specific instrumental role, which would imply that he, in his turn, is to serve Julia's purpose, and demonstrate the conditions of his political life. ' "Julia wants me? I'm much obliged to her!" . . . "Where's the money to come from?" "The money? Why, from Jul—" Grace began, but immediately caught her mother's eye.' *Harsh* as a name is a joke to Gabriel Nash, but its realities are harsh enough for Nick, and for the English system. 'It belongs very largely to my cousin, Mrs Dallow.' 'But I thought we had no more pocket boroughs' is Nash's immediate translation. Nash, at this luncheon party, playing his part as visitor from Samarkand, can now go on with his devaluation of the political life. Surely a pocket borough fills your pockets? Surely only a bribe would induce a man to go into Parliament? Accused of thinking politics dreadful his answer is 'only inferior. . . . Everything is relative.'

It is characteristic of Nash's technique that the particular statement should be offered as an application of the wider generalization, and that this supporting generalization should be put forward as aphorism or epigram, and in a manner that assumes general acceptance, as of a commonplace. By now 'everything is relative' as a general measure of value was sufficiently commonplace, as Nash knows perfectly well, but he is playing a familiar role at this moment. And also to introduce this cliché is to bring into action his doctrine of experience, of which that phrase is an essential postulate. It helps him to continue his devaluation of politics, for only that application of the phrase is picked up, by Lady Agnes ('Inferior to what?'); but it will pass into and support the ways in which Nash evaluates art.

One of the purposes of the complex game played around this luncheon table is to establish a major theme: the theatre – actor, scene, play – as art, and in connexions with the political life, with other sorts of art, with questions about experience; and from the beginning, to establish the whole question of the theatre in a situation of dispute and controversy.

That the theatre would eventually come was adumbrated when Biddy, attempting to identify Gabriel Nash, saw him as a musician or an actor, and saw the younger of the two women with him as a dancer. The luncheon-table conversation opens formally with a life/theatre comparison from Nash. Tactically, this leads straight to money – 'The world isn't got up regardless of expense'; it also introduces a theme in his doctrine of experience: an economical stage procession shows the same figures appearing again and again, and this is an analogue for the 'repetition' and 'recurrence' that we haven't yet abolished 'in the study of how to live'. This is another way of talking about 'moment' or 'moments'. The actual theatre comes in through Nash's first account of those unexplained women, and passes immediately from the individual case – the girl wants to go on the stage – into generalizations so extreme that they enclose all the positions that Nash and Peter Sherringham will in due course state and enact. Nash is not helping the girl because he considers the theatre 'the lowest of the arts' – although the *Théâtre français* is a greater institution than the House of Commons:

> 'I agree with you there!' laughed Sherringham; 'all the more that I don't consider the dramatic art a low one. On the contrary, it seems to me to include all the others.'

Those great polemical assertions made – Nash acknowledges them as a 'view' – Peter's are kept till later for formal restatement. Lady Agnes seizes on what she understands: is it really better for a gentleman to be an actor?

Better than being a politician? Ah, comedian for comedian, isn't the actor more honest?

What a gentleman is to do is a question that Julia Dallow is soon to ask Nick. In answer here, Lady Agnes can only invoke Nick's 'great father' – for that image is the only value she knows in the realm of political action, the assumptions of class and family being her furthest generalizations. Nick's response is partial and only a *perhaps*, but he accepts Nash's predicated value: his own father was 'an honest man', and perhaps that is why he could not endure (or died of) the political life. Actor and politician have this in common, that they can only function in relation to an audience; that to catch this audience both speak and feign 'parts' that have been written and devised for them by others – they must be what they are not. *Honesty* is in relationship to 'part' and words and audience; the actor sets out to deceive no one (to interpret Nash); the politician's art, if he would succeed, is to deceive, radically. The comedian is the more honest man, yet *comedian for comedian* devalues both activities. Nash allows the actor more grace, certainly, but just a little more, and in this comparison.

Acting and its conditions (the theatre) are to become the central paradigmatic instance of the artist's life, with all those questions about how the actress becomes an actress, what she brings, and what she must acquire; and this must involve enquiry not only into the formation of the actress, but into what James, fascinated by the problem, called elsewhere the *nature d'actrice*; and brings too an enquiry, which James would not have admitted to be either separate or grander, into what the actress *does*, and what her art achieves: into, that is, the nature or meaning of her art, and into those necessary limitations which are imposed by those very conditions – the theatre depending as it does on several fixed relationships under which, as things are, it is practised. Those skirmishes, tentative beginnings, at the luncheon table are to prepare us for the general and special developments of Nick's concern with the life of art and with Nash's rejection of art. Nash has already moved into position about the theatre and so has Peter Sherringham: these topics are to be in their hands.

They turn, these topics, on two women: on the aspirant actress, Miriam Rooth, the younger of those two women who walked with

Nash among the sculptures and whom he so rapidly got rid of; and, counterposed to Miriam, the great achieved artist, the aged Carré, of the *Théâtre français*, whose past is legend, whose present is still potent, and who is to be brought together with Miriam when she hears the young woman 'say' something, so that she can pronounce judgement on her.

The tale of the Rooths is Gabriel Nash's; and it will serve more than one purpose. There is his report of Mrs Rooth's account of her splendid origins. This is fiction: Mrs Rooth has as much to do with truth as her daughter (who will have a good deal to do with it) will have to do with ruth. If Mrs Rooth's tale were true – it interests Lady Agnes – it would perhaps be less important for the aspiring actress than what Nash has learned or inferred about the facts. These have to do with Miriam's formal education – mostly bits and pieces of languages picked up during mother and daughter's cheap peregrinations through Europe; and we are to take this with Nash's confident claim that Miriam is stupid. And, more importantly, these facts have to do with Miriam's inheritance. Biddy, at first sight, had imagined Miriam as a particularly violent dancer; and Miriam has this of the Old Testament about her (and perhaps, proleptically, more, for Miriam, the sacred dancer, offended the Lord by conspiring to betray his servant, and was smitten by leprosy), that her Christian name indicates her father's faith: his surname had been Roth; and Miriam is half a Jewess. Of her name Peter Sherringham says immediately: 'It is as good as Rachel Félix' – and so Rachel, the Tragic Muse of painters and writers, first appears: that child of a Jewish pedlar, trailed across Europe, uneducated, whose legend is to be so powerful a presence, a reference for achievement and a touchstone for theory. With Rooth's Jewishness went a taste for collecting (Julia Dallow's husband had it, on a grander scale), and some skill in music ('like most of his species'); in fact he had the *artistic temperament*; but this phrase is given to Mrs Rooth, which puts its seriousness in doubt, and James uses it very gingerly as an explanation or description of the artist's nature. But there is no doubt that this paternal and racial inheritance was to count for Miriam.

The exchange turning on Carré is explicitly put forward as a rehearsal of currently familiar positions. Thus Nash accuses

Sherringham of using the language of the *feuilletons*, and Sherringham accuses Nash of using an attitude and arguments in vogue among the *raffinés*. Sherringham particularly refers to Nash's insistence on the poverty of the modern dramatic form, as compared with the novel.

The older dramatists, Nash argues, had an easier task: to represent a simpler civilization in which man expressed himself directly and violently in action and passion. But today 'What can you do with a character, with an idea, with a feeling, between dinner and the suburban trains?' Nash is, in part, defining 'modernity' in the sense of what the modern dramatist has to deal with. He is also giving a reason why the achievement even of a Carré must be limited. When Sherringham says that to watch her was

> an education of the taste, an enlargement of one's knowledge

we are certainly to believe him, but we are also to believe Nash's rejoinder:

> She did what she could, poor woman, but in what belittling, coarsening conditions! . . . The dramatist shows us so little, is so hampered by his audience, is restricted to so poor an analysis.

Even a Carré is limited, like the dramatist, by what he calls 'the essentially brutal nature of the modern audience'. 'Theatre' is tending to split into two: here Sherringham's concern is for *acting*, Nash's for what the actor has to work with.

Nash's attack on the actual conditions of theatrical performance (even his reference to the time-tables of the last suburban trains), which mark the infrangible limits of the dramatist's (and therefore of the actor's) art, is anything but new or esoteric. Yet it can serve as a consistent extension of his earlier declarations. The criterion of theatrical representation is *success*: there are not many bad actors because most of them succeed in 'that business', 'more easily and completely than in anything else'. Such success – money or satisfied vanity for the actor, or just money for managers and stage carpenters – depends wholly on giving the gross audience what it wants. The theatre is indeed 'a commercial and social convenience'. But the repetition of that word *convenience* and this insistence on the theatre's corrupting dependence takes us back to Nash on the art of writing, or the life of politics – which were condemned for precisely this same reason: the inevitable corruption of those other dealers in words, through the audience which they who properly exist as individuals are tied to – and tied therefore to the realm of convenience, formulas, generalizations.

Nash has another, equally consistent, version of why he has to come to reject the theatre, but this position is more radical, for it carries forward Nash's basic doctrine of experience. This step comes in the shape of still another generalization, turned by repetition into a formula. Nash first met the Rooths when Mrs Rooth was selling off her husband's objects. Those included pots, and at that time Nash was collecting pots. 'It was a little phase – we have our little phases, haven't we? . . . and I have come out on the other side.' And of his earlier enthusiasm for the theatre he says:

> Oh, I used to be of your way of feeling. . . . It's a phase like another. I've been through it. . . .

This connects with 'everything is relative'; and *phase* is an extension of *moment* or *moments*. Repetition or recurrence is fatal: happy *moments*, or a *phase*, had their value, but cannot retain it. We must move on: the moments must be multiplied.

Nick's admonition to Biddy that 'all the arts are one' had specific reference to the artist's necessary effort to carry his art further, and had involved no direct comparison between what artists *make*, with paint or stone or words. Peter's assertion that the 'dramatic art' includes all the others had been left unelaborated except for his justification of Carré; and that rests on a certain assumption about the unity of the arts based, like Nick's, in terms of effort, and on one, but not the only view of what the actor actually does.

> It's not easy . . . to produce, completely, any artistic effect . . . and those that the actor produces are among the most moving we know.

Part of the argument that Sherringham needs he offers to Nick after lunch as they stroll by themselves, aimlessly, through the streets. Nash had first used *represent* about what the dramatist does, and in its general sense of 'shewing forth' (drama as 'mirror' of its age). This is the word Sherringham uses as the basis of his argument, applying it, however, principally to the actor's art (the dramatist provides material for him to work on):

> I am fond of representation – the representation of life: I like it better, I think, than the real thing. You like it, too, so you have no right to cast the stone. You like it best done one way and I another; and our preference, on either side, has a deep root in us. There is a fascination to me in the way the actor does it, when his talent (ah! he must have that!) has been highly trained (ah! it must *be* that!). The things he can do, in this effort at representation (with the dramatist to give him his lift) seem to me innumerable – he can carry it to a delicacy! – and I take great pleasure in observing them, in recognizing them, and comparing them. It's an amusement like another: I don't pretend to call it by any exalted name; but in this vale of friction it will serve. One can lose one's self in it, and it has this recommendation (in common, I suppose, with the study of the other arts), that the further you go in it, the more you find. So I go rather far, if you will. But is it the principal sign one knows me by?

This is formally set out: the generalizations offer that restricted part of the argument about the unity of the arts that the novel will most require. They insist, again, on the process of *doing*, and introduce terms relative to this (*talent*, *training*) – which are almost immediately to be picked up in the case of Miriam – and relative to the critic's activity (*observe*, *recognize*, *compare*), which Peter claims for himself; and they offer no *justification* for the taste – it is more than this – for one or other kind. The vital suggestion that the 'representation' may be preferred to the 'real', is informally, almost casually, brought in.

This formal explicit argument is constructed to introduce the first formal explicit statement of Nick's situation:

> The idea of representation fascinates you, but in your case it's representation in oils – or do you practice water-colours too? You even go much further than I, for I study my art of predilection only in the works of others. . . . You're a painter, possibly a great one; but I'm not an actor.

Peter's argument is a piece of self-defence; the accusation he thinks he has to meet, which forces him to the formal statement and to its application to Nick, is an extension of the concern with *naming* or *identification*.

This begins with questions about Gabriel Nash ('He sounds like an Elizabethan dramatist,' Peter says) and what he is: an ass, in Peter's version, or a real case for enquiry into what might prevent 'the whole man from being as good as his parts', in Nick's. So to the luncheon dispute about the theatre, and Nick's

> ... the old sign one knew you best by: your permanent stall at the *Français* ....

and to Peter's argument, and to his final question, repeating Nick's phrase as a question. In language – used however lightly – that associates him with Nash and the critics ('I ought to discriminate ... I always want the further distinction, the last analysis'), Nick answers yes. And the dialogue is brought to a conclusion through a return to Nash, which is a return to the problem of defining him (or distinguishing him).

> Most people have a lot of attributes and appendages that dress them up and superscribe them, and what I like him for is that he hasn't any at all.

Sign, superscription: holy writ has been called in to extend the vocabulary available for proofs or tokens of identity. Peter's self-justifying declaration, which is also a way of asking by what sign Nick is best known, leads into brief companion biographies of the two young men, held up till now so that they should go with this revealing formal declaration: from indications we move to statement.

The biography of Nick is not simple. It is a comment on the conditions and values of the political, or public, life, in a specified English setting.

Political life is a function of family and class situation, and in turn guarantees that situation; it can only be exercised through money and can bring safety through money or alliance with money. Lady Agnes has already shown, vividly, that she knows this. Nick's great father – that great name – was a younger son; he had inherited baronetcy and property from his elder brother; Nick himself is the younger son. Bricket, 'that moderate property', is in the hands of his elder brother; that 'pleasant white house' (no great house of stone, let alone marble) is let, while the heir neglects his family and devotes himself to big-game shooting: an occupation approved of by a society which the narrator – the tone is plain – does not approve of. Lady Agnes's jointure is not 'an incitement to grandeur'. There is no dower house for her and her daughters, and no proper town house; she has to live in Calcutta Gardens, in a 'gabled, latticed house in a creditable quarter, though it was still a little raw, of the temperate zone of London'. This, in London, and dated by the speculative builder's name, is the precarious edge of the world; largely dependent on Mr Carteret's 'convenient cheques', it is to be 'in a general way' his mother's and his sisters's 'providence', as Mr Carteret is his. Lady Agnes's anxieties are real. The Dormers are in danger.

That the political life is proper to a gentleman is, we know, the limit of Lady Agnes' generalization; the content and value of the activity lie in its connexion with – and this would include the family – Nick's duty to maintain his father's name: which is also a kind of property he would bring to a contest in Harsh, balancing – in his mother's eyes – Julia's gifts. What Nick's father actually *did* to achieve 'greatness' we are not quite clear about: to leave us uncertain, and to define the achievement through Mr Carteret, or newspaper allusion or other report, are ways both of reducing the political life and of relating it socially – indirectly to class and directly to the media of publicity.

Mr Carteret's generosity to Nick (but Lady Agnes has already foretold its terms) springs from devotion to the great name: he has nothing more real (except his money).

> He had never married, espousing nothing more reproductive than Sir Nicholas's views (he used to write letters to *The Times* in favour of them). . . .

That parenthesis suggests, again, that politics is an ephemeral verbal activity, and the summary of Nick's first success also gives this:

> . . . the fresh cleverness of his speeches, tinted with young idealism and yet sticking sufficiently to the question (the burning question, it has since burnt out). . . . There had been leaders in the newspapers about it. . . .

The death-bed scene, when father dedicates son to the carrying on of his work, is treated in just the same way. We learn of it indirectly. Lady Agnes knew that Sir Nicholas's charge had been

> a solemn communication of ideas on the highest national questions (she had reason to believe he had touched on those of external as well as of domestic and of colonial policy). . . . It was work cut out for a lifetime, and that 'co-ordinating power in relation to detail', which was one of the great characteristics of Sir Nicholas's high distinction (the most analytic of the weekly papers was always talking about it), had enabled him to rescue the prospect from any shade of vagueness or ambiguity.

The streets of Paris meant Nick's last hours of freedom, he felt. Later, with Julia Dallow, he comes out to the boulevard and to Paris at night: crowds, lights, sounds, 'tokens of a great traffic of pleasure, that night-aspect of Paris which represents it as a huge market of sensations'. Light and murmur, through the windows of Julia Dallow's sitting-room, accompany Nick's dialogue with her. But she cannot interest herself except for a moment in all this. She is 'awfully tired' of the city; to visit France for her is to transfer a social life from one place to another, and her France is never cut off from London, the true centre of activity, or from Harsh; and these both mean political activity.

When Nick is eventually alone with Julia he has to tell her that he will gratefully accept the chance of standing for Harsh; and their dialogue is part of his enquiry into the gracefulness of her mind, and into the relationship between her imperiousness and her generosity. He will try to find out whether Julia has any more notion of what the political life means than, for example, his mother has; and this will involve the other question.

Julia aligns herself with Mr Carteret in the world that Lady Agnes recognizes. And though Julia does not like Nick to compare her with Lady Agnes, whom from the security of her riches she can patronize and organize, it is there that she belongs; for Lady Agnes, anxious now, dependent in her meagre substance, had shown high competence – 'ideas' – in the organization of the public life of a public man. Julia's price for making Lady Agnes's stay in Paris comfortable (carriages and presents) is the silent expectation that the Dormer ladies will do precisely what they are told. In politics *winning* is Julia's concern; and she will expect to be paid for her help, just as much as Mr Carteret will for those cheques that will meet the election expenses. Julia's payment will come as *success*: the success that will make her mistress of a successful political salon. For that, Nick tells her, is what she really wants, because she, no more than Lady Agnes, has 'an idea . . . to call an idea'. And *serious* and *work*, words that for Julia belong to the business of winning the election, are according to the usage of Lady Agnes, and not according to Nick's reference of them, in that first dialogue with Biddy.

Elections are won by making speeches (and by newspaper reports that degrade even the speeches). Nick is good at this activity:

> 'I've got the cursed humbugging trick of it. I speak beautifully. I can turn it on, a fine flood of it, at the shortest notice. The better it is the worse it is, the kind is so inferior. It has nothing to do with the truth or the search for it; nothing to do with intelligence, or candour, or honour. It's an appeal to everything that for one's self one despises,' the young man went on – 'to stupidity, to ignorance, to density, to the love of names and phrases, the love of hollow, idiotic words, of shutting the eyes tight and making a noise. Do men who respect each other or themselves talk to each other that way?'

Nick himself has been evasive enough, or playful, or oblique, or tangential, about both politics and art; but this speech here is a passionate declaration, not patient of any ambiguous reading. And the verbal art is still further reduced; words are not even *names* and *phrases*, they compose an idiot's tale of what is *hollow*, merely *noise*.

Julia, reaching after 'ideas', can only answer with unexamined words that might well come from a speech or an editorial, only to find Nick translating them into the reality or meaning of a situation. Her 'the good of the country' turns out to mean keeping the Tories out, and helping to prevent them doing whatever it is they want to do; and this is really what our organized political game is all about, whichever party is playing it. Her 'the simple idea that one ought to do something or other for one's country' Nick brings down to the irreducible reality of the individual act: 'there is one thing one can always do for his country, which is not to be afraid.' Her 'when it's for the country . . . for *them*' as justifying the use of other people's money to meet expenses receives the disenchanted answer 'when they get it back' – as Mr Carteret and Julia will, in their ways. Realizing that they have been speaking different languages Julia finally asks

Pray, isn't a gentleman to do anything, to be anything?

Doing and *being* are bound together, and the doing defines the being. But the *doing* means for Julia aspiring 'to serve the State' – which Nick renders (and we need not avoid the ambiguity of his word) as 'to make his political fortune'. Lady Agnes would have recognized Julia's words. Nick's parting suggestion that there are other ways of *doing*, that he, for example, is very fond of painting, gets only a gesture refusing to take him seriously. But Gabriel Nash had already raised the question of *being* and *doing*.

Carré has been renowned for half a century: she is Art itself, defined in a certain way, conscious of this, wholly confident that there is no other. Against the questions or innocuities of Mrs Rooth, Carré stands four-square, stable, 'classical' or historical as the Maison de Molière (or the Maison Carré). We approach her through history: the walls of her drawing-room are hung, as though it were a theatrical museum, with a lifetime's trophies, letters, or gifts, or wreaths, or diadems. Gabriel Nash wanders round looking at them. Nick sees her early portraits and wonders curiously how she manages to have been alive then, and alive now. Peter knows what this and Carré mean. She is art as tradition, taught and transmitted by master to pupil: Carré's art and her most celebrated parts go back to a great comédienne of the early years of the century. She also, by her survival, testifies to his theory that the actor's art is now in decadence, going down into vulgarity. The narrator, himself, establishes for us the final limits of this art and life and history – the little room is a museum, but there is something missing from it: 'clappings which . . . could now only be present as a silence'. This version of the life of art at its greatest is 'the history of a mask, of a squeak, a record of movements in the air'. A skull placed here in the formal composition is to remind us, in the presence of greatness, both of Carré's insistencies on what this art's instruments are, and of its transitoriness. She *is* insistent: she understands perfectly; in her way she is as rigid as Lady Agnes or Julia, as dependent on definition; but this may be – the question will expand – a necessary condition of the life of art.

Nick is almost embarrassed to hear the kind of life that Miriam might lead discussed in the girl's presence, but he reflects that the echoes of such discussions seem to linger 'in the egotistical little room'. The general questions, that is, are considered by Carré either not at all, or as having been settled once and for all, or as having to do only with the single question of what the girl's potentialities as an artist are. There is a turning of discussions we have heard before, but with a new specificity of application. The large questions come from Mrs Rooth, who cannot separate the notion of her daughter's becoming an actress (she knows the pressing need) from questions about 'life' and conduct; and these will find a form in that Paris/London contrast which the very presentation of Carré is also designed to indicate. On one side is the old artist whose Paris may be going, on the other the mother, whose age is as indeterminate as her origins, whose London is certainly unreal: lies, fantasy, ambition. Between the two women, the three men offer attitudes whose differences are also set out through reference to the cities.

> You mix things up, *chère madame*, and I have it on my heart to tell you so.

When Madame Carré says this to Mrs Rooth she is bringing out that she knows perfectly well what the essential point in their relation is. She goes on:

> I believe it's rather the case with you other English, and I have never been able to learn that either your morality or your talent is the gainer by it. To be too respectable to go where things are done best is, in my opinion, to be very vicious indeed; and to do them badly in order to preserve your virtue is to fall into a grossness more shocking than any other. To do them well is virtue enough, and not to make a mess of it the only respectability. That's hard enough to merit Paradise. Everything else is base humbug! *Voilà*, *chère madame*, the answer I have for your scruples!

What Carré knows is her *métier*. 'Morality' works only within the *métier*. Mrs Rooth's worries about respectability – 'we are very very respectable' – or about the possibility of her daughter having to represent a bad woman, or the thankfulness with which she can fall back on Shakespeare's purity: all this is not only silly, it is plain irrelevance. If the English stage can offer all that Mrs Rooth wants, so much the better for England. But *'je ne connais qu'une scène – la nôtre.'* Nash agrees. Peter agrees, but thinks something might be done for London. Gabriel Nash, who agrees with Carré anyhow, is quick to indicate the relevance of what she has been saying to Nick's situation. Nick, agreeing in his turn that Carré has shown 'an intelligence of the question', is annoyed that Nash should think that the position is new to him, and proceeds to make his own translation for Mrs Rooth:

> In other words, your daughter must find her safeguard in the artistic conscience.

Mrs Rooth understands neither version. This does not prevent her from uttering her own:

> Oh, a fine artistic life – what indeed is more beautiful?

This is rather worse than Biddy's chatter about subject and treatment. Nor does Mrs Rooth mean by 'earnest' or 'serious' what Carré does.

Carré's generalization is sufficiently central. Here it covers her objections to Mrs Rooth's account of the gifts or accomplishments that Miriam has to offer to the stage, which is the immediate question. Miriam is 'educated': she knows English, French, Italian, German. Carré's rejoinder is that in that case the girl had better be a governess: only the right education matters, and one language is enough provided Miriam can speak it. She has, her mother claims, a 'voice' of rare beauty; Carré replies

> Ah, then, if she has intelligence she has every gift.

Mrs Rooth's answer is that Miriam has 'a most poetic mind'. To that piece of English mixing-things-up Carré does not even reply.

The history of a squeak, the narrator has warned us. At Carré's first words – she is a red-faced woman in a wig with beady eyes –

Gabriel Nash exclaims, '*Ah, la voix de Célimène!*' What Carré is listening for, what she will judge on, what Nick is listening to, is Miriam's voice. The scene enforces this from start to finish. Miriam does very badly. Her training – to the French woman – has been grotesque: a few lessons from a retired English actress and from an Italian tragedian. At the moment her voice is impossible. The problem is whether there is something there, a note, an inflection that could be disengaged. Peter is more willing to find this quality than Carré, but, by the end of the scene, she too is willing to find something – from whatever motives, for it may well be that the old woman believes that Miriam's youth and her beauty and the interest of these young men will assure her a future, anyhow.

This beauty is not obvious. At first sight Peter finds that her face expresses no 'sentiment', even her obvious terror shows itself only as a kind of stupidity. But at the same moment he sees that the head is good. 'The head is very good', Carré repeats a moment later. The eyes are 'fine', 'deep', 'sombre'. When Miriam prepares for the first time to speak a part there is an immediate sense of a great physical presence. Her face now appears 'pale and regular, with a strange, strong, tragic beauty'. Forcing herself to speak:

> . . . she frowned portentously; her low forehead overhung her eyes; the eyes themselves, in shadow, stared, splendid and cold, and her hands clinched themselves at her sides. She looked austere and terrible, and during this moment she was an incarnation the vividness of which drew from Sherringham a stifled cry. '*Elle est bien belle – ah, ça!*' murmured the old actress; and in the pause which still preceded the issue of sound from the girl's lips Peter turned to his kinsman and said in a low tone:
> 'You must paint her just like that.'
> 'Like that?'
> 'As the Tragic Muse.'

Nick has looked at Carré with the painter's observation, he has been alive to Miriam's possibilities as a model, and he will repeat his hope that she may one day sit for him. At this moment he says nothing. Nor does Gabriel Nash (who is going to spend most of the time looking out of the window). This incarnation has its effect only on the old professional, and on the critic who works within the realm of that profession. Yet for Carré that surprised recognition was not necessarily the recognition of a talent for the stage. Here professional and critic – the latter, in spite of his understanding, is an amateur – are almost on different sides. The 'plastic quality' is the only sign of a vocation that Peter can find in Miriam; and this is something he has learnt to distrust. It is a 'gift' that may lead to nothing. And he knows that it is something that Carré discounts almost completely as an element of the 'histrionic nature', unless it is accompanied by more important attributes. At the extreme, Peter and Carré's dispute has been about the respective contributions of 'gifts', which he has championed, and 'unwearying study', which she has championed. The test case they had both used was Rachel. Peter had cited Rachel as a pre-eminent example of the great artist made by her 'natural endowment'. Carré had insisted that Rachel, although she had a voice and an eye, was 'essentially formed by work, unremitting and ferocious work'. But of course Carré had added, 'Rachel wasn't a *bête*: that's a gift, if you like!' This means, in the appropriate vocabulary, that Rachel had 'intelligence'. About Miriam's 'intelligence' Carré is doubtful. It is Mrs Rooth who thinks that Miriam has 'ideas': 'She gets them from you' is Carré's reply. 'Ideas' are certainly what is needed, and go with 'intelligence' and not being a *bête*: so far it has been Biddy who hoped to find them. Work, work, practise, practise, is the injunction she leaves her with, whatever future she may see for the girl. It is not she but Gabriel Nash who supposes that the voice, when it's worth anything, 'comes from the heart'.

At Peter's tea-party Miriam is presented to an English audience, whose standards and knowledge are very different from those of Carré, as Peter well knows; and, given that audience – people whom a rising young diplomat might well, though a shade dangerously, invite – Miriam is a success. This is a general misunderstanding, but for some of those present the occasion also serves to bring out other misunderstandings of which they are hardly aware, or it worsens those already established.

Biddy, who is 'immensely struck' by the recital, sees Miriam as a phenomenon that she must try (and Biddy always tries) to understand; but their conversation is about Nick:

'If your brother's an artist, I don't understand how he's in Parliament.'

'Oh, he isn't in Parliament now; we only hope he will be.'

'Oh, I see.'

'And he isn't an artist, either,' Biddy felt herself conscientiously bound to subjoin.

'Then he isn't anything,' said Miss Rooth.

'Well – he's immensely clever.'

When Nash is alone with Julia the misunderstanding, on her part, is total. Nash has already involved himself in Nick's problems, although they have yet to be fully expounded to him. Julia's involvement with Nick is of a different order. It is not enquiring, nor does it 'extend tolerances to others'. Her affection is of the kind that 'isolates and simplifies its object'. She is 'rigidly direct'; her desires for Nick are an expression of what she desires for herself; that rigidity controls her responses to anyone or anything outside of those particular desires, including Nash. His attack on the recent social pretensions of actors, an extended version of earlier remarks, meets no response. Elaborate discussions of the artistic life, as held at Carré's or, as here, of the lives that artists lead, have for Julia no meaning whatsoever, even when Nash obliquely refers them to Nick. And when her belated enquiry (yet another attempt to place the speaker) 'Are you an artist?' receives the apparently unhelpful answer 'I work in life', Julia turns away.

This is absolute failure. Other failures are recorded by the application of certain words to certain people, when those words have quite different meanings for the speaker and listener. By the company in general, Miriam is thought to be 'clever and successful'. She is not. Miriam's comment on Nick, 'he isn't anything', is met by Biddy's 'he's immensely clever', which hangs in the air. Nash is introduced to Julia by Nick as 'one of the cleverest men he knew'; she doesn't find him so. When they discuss Julia, Grace misunderstands Nash by apparently agreeing with him:

'Ah, she's very charming,' said Grace.

'She's very beautiful,' Nash rejoined.

'And very clever,' Miss Dormer continued.

'Very, very intelligent.'

To accord 'intelligence' does not advance agreement unless it is known what that person is intelligent about, which requires an agreement about what he is or what he does. Ambiguity in epithet or description is part of ambiguity of identity, and can be resolved only by a definition of identity, or of intention and practice.

Nick has arranged to meet Nash late in the evening and the two young men abandon modern Paris, Haussman's Paris of the *grands boulevards*, the *ville lumière*, for the *quartiers sérieux*, that older, dustier city: here they 'look, emphasize, compare'. Julia Dallow, to Nash, is a 'beautiful specimen' of the English garden flower, a 'product' of 'high cultivation' and 'much tending'; she has the 'completeness' that is always satisfying; she will never 'understand' him. Nor, Nick says, does he. This is precisely the mark or sign of Nash's relationships: the puzzles are made by those others – it is he who is 'simple'. He has a 'little system' which requires he should be 'just the same to everyone'; but *they* depend on the newcomer defining himself by knowing the right password, joining their side, their 'camp or religion'. He claims – in so far as his mode of qualification, of puzzled self-depreciation allows – that he has

> . . . no interest of my own to push, no nostrum to advertise, no power to conciliate, no axe to grind. I'm not a savage – ah, far from it – but I really think I'm perfectly independent.

'Little system' is *manner*, this treating everyone in the same way (which may, muddled as we are, seem to be impertinence); that it *is* a *system* in fact relates him – he accepts Nick's challenge – to the rest who also work by system; and Nash will also turn this round (to the politician) by claiming that by his consistent application of it he may become 'a perceptible force of good'. His system involves the making of no concessions whatever to those who expect him to name and align himself (and he had given up literature because that involved concessions and compromises): he will never never concede that 'we are only here for dreariness': 'modern slang', says Nick, which might be applied to virtue, decency, charity, perseverance, courage, honour. Such qualities Nash does not exclude as part of life. On the contrary, they are *subjects* or materials, like any others: *dreariness* is a matter of *treatment* (or lack of it):

> Life consists of the personal experiments of each of us, and the point of an experiment is that it shall succeed.

What we contribute is our treatment of the material, our rendering of the text, our style. Biddy's parroted formula – which Nick had rejected – is picked up, and sophisticated by extension to include the possibilities of that word 'style' (which goes with 'manner') which had puzzled Biddy. The first application, here, is to literature, and we ourselves become texts: difficult to read, because a sense of 'style' is so rare, but that's no reason why we should not try to write our best (be Macaulays, Ruskins, Renans). *That* is contribution, the 'great thing' we can offer. 'One has one's form' – that word, too, can pass from one reference to another; and Nash 'is not afraid of putting all life' into his, including honour, courage, charity – 'I'll only do them good' (Nick has told Biddy that this is what Nash would do for them – like the sculptures in the Salon). 'Style', which is 'a personal manner', belongs to a way of talking about art. So Nick follows Nash. This is his attempt: art is difficult, there is always more to learn, polishing, refining; but his direction is right, 'towards the beautiful'. Beauty is really present, concrete, certain, against Nash's games of translation; and Nick gestures to Notre-Dame, rising now in front of the young men: instance and focus of their exchanges, forcing explorations of definitions to what is admission of a dilemma. Notre-Dame is a visual fact, like the streets of old Paris. It is, however, a great deliberated artefact, with the qualities of 'simplification' (under the night sky) and 'large, full composition'. Nick's reference is immediately to the artistic life:

> How it straightens things out and blows away one's vapours – anything that's *done*! . . . The great point is to do something. . . .

'Done' is carried out to its necessary appropriate end: he had left Julia asking whether a gentleman wasn't to *do* or *be* (in her synonyms) anything; and Nash turns the word against him, to the very reference of that scene. Nick can't build cathedrals out of words. The poets do, yes – they make cathedrals out of words, Nick has said. But the vocabulary can be seen shifting again within that fluid bound:

> *Their* words are ideas – their words are images, enchanting collocations and unforgettable signs. But the verbiage of parliamentary speeches!

Great 'structures' – Nick adds this word – can be made in materials other than stone, timber, painted glass. The great artefact, immobile yet with, it seems, all the movement of some ship, is there for criticism, admiration, discussion; and there is comfort in Nash's 'response', his appreciation, exhibited by his own signs, of the 'great effect', the freedom of his 'feeling' and the utterance of his 'impression', his 'natural intelligence of everything of that kind'. In the great presence Nick can rest, soothed and joyful, 'as if it had been the temple of a faith so dear to him that there was peace and security in its precinct'. In a small café, away from the work of art, the dialogue continues: the terms are of those relations and signs that society, or the world, recognizes. Nash 'goes about his business, like any good citizen'. Nick's concerns are with 'do', 'accomplish', 'do anything', 'produce', 'go for', with 'the old false measure of success', as Nash tells him; with 'life', yes, but as so signed and marked. It is again a question of transpositions. Nash's 'business' is 'the spectacle of the world'; and this is not inconsistent with his search for what in this spectacle is 'charming'.

> Last year I heard of such a delightful little spot: a place where a wild fig tree grows in the south wall, the outer side, of an old Spanish city . . . I lay on the first green grass – I liked it.

This is 'doing' and 'accomplishment': it is the accomplishment of happiness through 'feelings' and 'sensations' – 'It's rare to have them . . . I go after them – when I judge they won't hurt anyone.' He takes his stand on his 'nature' or 'disposition'; and on 'liberty' which, with 'spontaneity' and 'enjoyment', goes with 'being natural'. Nick's open disclosure of his crisis or dilemma is being prepared for – Notre-Dame had been a determining sign for him – but he can only come to it through those other signs or definitions of 'life' which Nash transposes, or refuses, outright; and Notre-Dame was a thing 'done', in more senses than one. He is – he declares – committed to stand again for Parliament. What he wants is to be a painter – 'Isn't that the aesthetic life?' But he would want the 'aesthetic life', the 'little system' to be identified by those signs that mark the other.

> 'There will be precious little beauty if I produce nothing but daubs.'
> 'Ah, you cling to the old false measure of success. I must cure you of that. . . .'

The act is its own justification:

> There will be the beauty of having been disinterested and independent; of having taken the world the free, brave, personal way.

A life effort, certainly; but Nick would not now be satisfied without the visible result: he would want to paint 'decently'. If he were to produce only daubs, Nash would find him a still more interesting 'case'. As it is, with all that weighs him down and makes him seem, even to himself, so improbable, so freakish – his Philistine family, his traditions, his training, his circumstances, his career, the effect of his giving it up, even his own prejudices – these are enough to make him 'a magnificent case'. The last words are:

> 'It's her place, she'll put me in. . . .'
> 'Baleful woman! But I'll pull you out!'

Peter has already confessed his devotion to the particular art of representation practised by the actor, and, in conversation with Nash and Nick, has countered their generalizations with those of his own. His involvement with Miriam is also to provide him with a case, in two ways. Miriam, first of all, may have talent, and Peter will not resist the opportunity to observe and contribute to her development and training. She is also, he becomes convinced, a fine example of the artistic temperament, the *nature d'actrice*. He will now explore the relationship between talent and temperament, and become increasingly trapped between his admiration for the one and his fascination with the other.

Two full chapters describe this involvement, and indicate the kinds of relationship possible between them; these in turn invoke wider implications about the personalities and habits of actors, and their art of representation. The prime revelation comes early on, but is to be repeated again and again:

It came over him suddenly that so far from there being any question of her having the histrionic nature, she simply had it in such perfection that she was always acting; that her existence was a series of parts assumed for the moment, each changed for the next, before the perpetual mirror of some curiosity or admiration or wonder – some spectatorship that she perceived or imagined in the people about her. Interested as he had ever been in the profession of which she was potentially an ornament, this idea startled him by its novelty and even lent, on the spot, a formidable, a really appalling character to Miriam Rooth.

This perception is a generalized extension to include the whole personality of his even earlier prophetic distaste for what the actress does, a distaste that he had notably failed to communicate to Miriam. That outburst had related to Nash's equation of politician with actor, in terms of what they are both obliged to become for their respective audiences:

> 'You're a strange girl.'
> '*Je crois bien!* Doesn't one have to be, to want to go and exhibit one's self to a loathsome crowd, on a platform, with trumpets and a big drum, for money – to parade one's body and one's soul?'
> Sherringham looked at her a moment: her face changed constantly; now there was a little flush and a noble delicacy in it.
> 'Give it up; you're too good for it,' he said, abruptly.
> 'Never, never – never till I'm pelted!'

His revulsion coexists with a real, if incomplete, understanding of what the actress aspires to, and how she must learn her trade. 'If you see the things to do, the art of doing them will come, if you hammer away. The great point is to see them.' The contradictions in his own mind are fed by a susceptibility to Miriam's charm, 'communicative, persuasive, familiar, egotistical', which he responds to even when disturbed by its apparent inconsistency. Proof of her devotion to, and understanding of, her art, and her desire to 'do what's difficult' he can find; what he looks for is 'intelligence', and at times recognizes that essential as part of what disturbs him. 'All reflection is affectation, and all acting is reflection.' There remains the difficulty of finding in her charm, the excellence of her presentation of herself, signs that she has gained from her varied experience anything other than material for representation.

> He made indeed without difficulty the reflection that her life might have taught her the reality of things, at the same time that he could scarcely help thinking it clever of her to have so persistently declined the lesson. She appeared to have put it by with a deprecating, ladylike smile – a plea of being too soft and bland for experience.

These questions are clearly irrelevant to the immediate concerns of Carré or Miriam herself. They lead Peter finally to postulate 'something vulgar in the histrionic conscience', that must be reconciled with his first conviction that

> The actor's talent was essentially a gift, a thing by itself, implanted, instinctive, accidental, equally unconnected with intellect and with virtue – Sherringham was completely of that opinion; but it seemed to him no contradiction to consider at the same time that intellect (leaving virtue, for the moment, out of the question) might be brought into fruitful relation with it.

By flinching from Carré's uncompromising comments on Miriam's talent, Peter has revealed himself as an amateur among professionals:

> . . . she has relieved herself, with the rare cynicism of the artist, all the crudity, the irony and intensity of a discussion of esoteric things, of personal mysteries, of methods and secrets.

This world 'of mysteries, of methods and secrets', where hard logical passion is applied to the personal, is where Miriam belongs: she is already professional. But at first Peter can safely observe her, 'the spectacle of the young lady's genius', without risk either to his career or his emotions. Those dangers will arise when observation becomes involvement, and even then there are kinds of involvement:

> Certainly, however, she seemed to belong to him very much indeed, as she sat facing him in the Paris café, in her youth, her beauty and her talkative confidence. This degree of possession was highly agreeable to him. . . .

The object of dispassionate criticism might easily become a protégé, might even become what he possessed, and the possessed might become the used – 'she was the instrument, and incontestably a fine one, that had come to his hand' – or, if the revulsion prove too great, the protected – 'give it up'.

When Peter ponders Miriam's nature, 'affected, contradictious', he does so in terms which we already know.

> Was this succession of phases a sign that she really possessed the cele-brated artistic temperament, the nature that made people provoking and interesting?

This recalls the language of Nash, and, as before, it is applied to the life of the mind, and invokes a doctrine of experience. Significantly the language returns when Peter and Miriam discuss an actor's diction and manner, what is called his style. Peter is very precise about this: 'I mean any style that *is* a style, that is a system, an art, that contributes a positive beauty to utterance.' Comparisons are made with Nash, whom Peter describes, despite that person's refusal to admit of any audience, as very like an actor, with his 'affectations and histrionics'.

We come back to the question of the conscious exhibition of the self that it seems the actor must indulge, which Peter both fears and disapproves of, although he does extol a 'personal' style that can be so rarely achieved under the conditions of the modern theatre. The 'personal style' is that of an actor alone, unencumbered by the stage carpenter and costumier, and is now to be found only in the poor countries, most of all in Italy – 'it's a human exhibition, not a mechanical one'. But at the same time we are being led inexorably to a paradox. It may be that even the unencumbered human exhibition requires the multiple personality of the actor. If that is so, then the personal, the essential component of style, must also require the 'nature', the feigning honesty. The 'nature' might be the natural.

Peter's dislike of the modern theatre recalls that of Nash, because both, for reasons of different and varying complexity, resent the public demands that make up conditions for the practice, and are suspicious even of the practice itself.

> . . . you could afford to be vague only if you hadn't a responsibility. He had fine ideas, but she was to do the acting, that is the application of

them, and not he; and application was always of necessity a sort of vulgarization, a smaller thing than theory.

Such alignments of opinion reverberate against each other, and are still part of the strategy of the novel. Apparently similar formulas from opposed or dissimilar characters tell us something about both characters and formulas. Miriam's vulgar 'I go in for the book of life' echoes disturbingly, but does not repeat, Nash's remark to Julia, 'I work in life'.

Miriam, too, is both like and not like her mother, as Peter realizes, for both are concerned with fictions. The mother 'took everything for the sense, or behaved as if she did, caring above all for the subject and the romance'; the daughter 'hungry for the manner and the art of it, the presentation and the vividness'. The one makes 'the true seem fictive'; the other's 'effort was to make the fictive true'.

These speculations of Peter's *are* dangerous, but as long as he is able to preserve his role of critic and contribute only his judgement and knowledge he is, in part, protected. Then Miriam 'belongs' to him only as a talent and a potential.

> He reflected ingeniously that he owed his escape to a peculiar cause – the fact that they had together a positive outside object. Objective, as it were, was all their communion; not personal and selfish, but a matter of art and business and discussion.

This is 'the pure exorcism of art'; but it is not to last long. Once away from Miriam and the distancing discussions of technique and business, Peter discovers that he has not escaped: 'He *was* in love with her: he had been in love with her from the first hour.'

Exploring the labyrinth of Miriam's personality and situation, Peter becomes trapped himself.

The return from Paris, the 'huge market for sensations', to England means for Nick fresh confrontations with an inheritance whose images and traditions are to be compared with those of Paris, and the next part of the novel is much concerned with those traditions as maintained by persons and place. But there is repetition and extension of previous matter: the subdued but repeated pun on 'represent', and the reappearance of words such as 'work' and 'success' in other contexts. The practical ramifications of money and its relationship to 'freedom' which have so far only been asserted by Lady Agnes, now become her desperate and immediate concern: 'What freedom *is* there in being poor?'

The political life is to be devalued in terms of its actualities rather than its inherent possibilities; although the actualities are related to traditions of their own, fallen or mechanical as these may have become. Nick's distrust of his own rhetorical skill may or may not express an absolute valuation of the political life. His 'double nature' certainly contributes to a further delay of the great decision, but his versatility and imagination obscure and complicate the value of the opposing claim. It is left open whether or not, despite all this, politics might once have, and might still, present a serious alternative. That conclusion is to be delayed, like many others, until, or perhaps beyond, the end of the novel. For the moment the instances that are offered of the political life, personalities and practices, continue a devaluation already suggested by Nash to an attentive Nick in Paris.

Julia, we have been told, is 'rigid and singular'. There is now a full concentration on Nick's very different ambiguity, his 'double personality', his 'sympathy' and his ability to participate in the lives of others. But it is these abilities that direct him towards activity and postponement rather than action. Nick's double nature rises to challenges and the chances for activity, and works well with Julia's compulsive organizing. His tactful suppression of dangerous thoughts that might frighten his mother and Julia is, apart from the occasional hint, consistent. Activity and action predicate different kinds of achievement. The work of the politician is singular, continuous and, given its particular terms, automatic; the work of the artist that Nick is drawn to demands an individual appreciation.

Although these sections of the novel lack the density of reference to be found in those dealing with art, the images and characteristics of the political life are offered as a formal counterpoint, whose inadequacies the seemingly neutral narrator alludes to by a re-application of terms already introduced and an unapologetic exploration of Nick's nature. As before, the transposition of terms and images is a way of bringing two worlds together, as well as revealing their differences.

2 *Representation: cases and topics*

'I profess', James was to write, so much later, in his *Preface*:

a certain vagueness of remembrance in respect to the origin and growth of *The Tragic Muse*, which appeared in the *Atlantic Monthly* again, beginning January 1889 and running on, inordinately, several months beyond its proper twelve. If it be ever of interest and profit to put one's finger on the productive germ of a work of art, and if in fact a lucid account of any such work involves that prime identification, I can but look on the present fiction as a poor fatherless and motherless, a sort of unregistered and unacknowledged birth. I fail to recover my previous first moment of consciousness of the idea to which it was to give form; to recognize in it – as I like to do in general – the effect of some particular sharp impression or concussion. I call such remembered glimmers always precious, because without them comes no clear vision of what one may have intended, and without that vision no straight measure of what one may have succeeded in doing. What I make out from furthest back is that I must have had from still further back, must in fact practically have always had, the happy thought of some dramatic picture of the 'artist-life' and of the difficult terms on which it is at the best secured and enjoyed, the general question of its having to be not altogether easily paid for. To 'do something about art' – art, that is, as a human complication and a social stumbling block – must have been for me early a good deal of a nursed intention, the conflict between art and 'the world' striking me thus betimes as one of the half-dozen great primary motives. I remember even having taken for granted with this fond inveteracy that no one of these pregnant themes was likely to prove under the test more full of matter. This being the case, meanwhile, what would all experience have done but enrich one's conviction? – since if, on the one hand, I had gained a more and more intimate view of the nature of art and the conditions therewith imposed, so the world was a conception that clearly required, and that would for ever continue to take, any amount of filling-in. The happy and fruitful truth, at all events, was that there was opposition – why there *should* be was another matter – and that the opposition would beget an infinity of situations. What had doubtless occurred in fact, moreover, was that just this question of the essence and the reasons of the opposition had shown itself to demand the light of experience; so that to the growth of experience, truly, the treatment of the subject had yielded. It had waited for that advantage.[2]

James could only pick on Thomas Bailey Aldrich's invitation to write a serial as giving him the necessary 'jog'. What he does vividly remember, and what comes first to his mind is the 'sinister effect' the novel, coming after *The Bostonians* and *The Princess Casamassima*, had on his public success. And he either remembers or reconstructs (his verbs are a little difficult) certain problems he met with or must have met with in the course of composition, notably the business of fitting together Nick Dormer's and Miriam Rooth's stories. And also the physical presence of the two cities that saw the beginning and ending of the writing, from the 'good fog-filtered Kensington mornings' and the 'wide west window' that offered 'a half-grey, half-flushed expanse of London life' to the hotel bedroom in Paris 'during the autumn of 1889, with the Exposition du Centenaire about to end'. That is a true memory, for the novel does live between the two cities. Yet this was not the first time that James had attempted some dramatic picture of the 'artist-life'. And since the publication of the *Notebooks* in 1947, we have known of more than one 'concussion'. It has been observed that the passage on Herbert Pratt in the long notebook entry of November/December 1881 has to do with Gabriel Nash. In June 1884 there is the entry recording James's talk with Mrs Humphry Ward about an idea of hers for a story about an actress; and Mr Edel and Mr Cargill[3] have observed the relevance of Mrs Ward's short novel, *Miss Bretherton*, published in the December of that same year; and of James's exchange of letters with Mrs Ward. In 1884, too, James paid a very important visit to Paris; this Mr Edel has described, and he has, justly, connected it with that celebrated essay on 'The Art of Fiction' which James published in September 1884, and republished in *Partial Portraits* in 1888; and this essay must, in turn, be connected with *The Tragic Muse*. Also from the *Notebooks* we must take that impression of Bartet in her *loge* at the *Théâtre français* recalled on 2 February 1889, while he was actually at work on the novel.

Mr Edel reports that James had begun to plan the novel as early as the winter of 1886, while he was preparing to move – as he did in March 1887 – to that flat in Kensington with its wide west window. On 23 July 1887, James told Grace Norton that he was just beginning a novel.[4] By 3 March 1888 he was promising Aldrich a serial for the

Atlantic that would run for the whole of 1889; and his letter shows that he had already, however tentatively, discussed with Aldrich a project that was to become *The Tragic Muse*, although he was not yet quite certain of its scope, except that there was to be an actress, and that

> ... probably the thing will bear the name I gave you, 'The Tragic Muse'.[5]

Having forgotten, perhaps, his letter of more than a year earlier, he told Grace Norton on 30 September that he had been busy 'getting launched' on the novel, which had now become 'long', and whose real reach was perhaps not even yet fully defined. So much for a minimal and partial narrative.

James had almost entirely forgotten, too, what should have been obvious about this novel: its topicality. His text about the life of art was indeed personal, and demonstrated views that he had come to hold deeply; but they were worked out through James's own long involvement with other current views and controversies about the life of art, and the theory as well as the practice of art. *The Tragic Muse* was not the only text on offer on this subject, and comes as a contribution to debate. Its topicality, then, was both 'personal' for James, and 'public'. *The Tragic Muse* is 'topical', as *The Bostonians* and *The Princess Casamassima* are 'topical', but is more precisely and obviously so than either (for good, or evil) in the way it relates to moment and debate. It can also be read as an attempt by James to 'broaden his scope' and extend his audience. To do the latter it notoriously failed. 'Topicality' had not helped in the earlier cases. The closer topical relations of *The Tragic Muse* involved in fact a closer restriction of audience. The public world that *The Tragic Muse* comes from and points to is the world of the 'serious' papers, reviews and quarterlies. It was, indeed, a serious and important world, and definable because it was small and unified through class, culture, function.

To that small world, in the early summer of 1884 when James called on her, Mrs Humphry Ward, just at the start of her career, conspicuously belonged by inheritance, avocation and gift. Her husband had given up his Oxford Fellowship to join the staff of *The Times*, and in November 1882 they had settled in Russell Square. Mrs Ward's position was soon and easily consolidated. She had already done a good deal of miscellaneous writing and reviewing; through John Morley's friendship she had been contributing to the *Pall Mall Gazette*; she reviewed regularly for *The Times*; and in March 1883 Morley had invited her to contribute a literary article, or *causerie*, once a month to *Macmillan's Magazine*. The last of these, published in June 1885, was a full-scale article on *Marius The Epicurean*, a delicate and obviously important assignment. But fiction had been her aim, and when James – who had known the family almost since their arrival in London – went to see her, what she talked to him about, as she talked to others, was the scheme for her first and very short novel, *Miss Bretherton*, although we cannot be sure that James knew that her intention was so definite. *Miss Bretherton* was written in six weeks later that summer, and was published in the first days of December 1884.

This is how James recorded that conversation:

June 19th. Mrs H. Ward mentioned the other day to me an idea of hers for a story which might be made interesting – as a study of the histrionic character. A young actress is an object of much attention and a great deal of criticism from a man who loves the stage (he oughtn't to be a *professional* critic) and finally, though she doesn't satisfy him at all, artistically, loves the girl herself. He thinks something more may be made of her, though he doesn't quite see what: he works over her, gives her ideas, etc. Finally (she is slow in developing, though full of ambition), she takes one, and begins to mount, to become a celebrity. She goes beyond him, she leaves him looking after her and wondering. She begins where he ends – soars away and is lost to him. The interest, I say, would be as a study of a certain particular *nature d'actrice*: a very curious sort of nature to reproduce. The girl I see to be very crude, etc. The thing a confirmation of Mrs Kemble's theory that the dramatic gift is a thing by itself – implying of necessity no *general* superiority of mind. The strong nature, the personal quality, vanity, etc., of the girl: her artistic being, so vivid, yet so purely instinctive. Ignorant, illiterate. Rachel.[6]

Down to 'soars away and is lost to him' James is recounting what Mrs

Ward said about her idea. Although she was to change her mind about the ending we can still see in the novel the persistence of this original plan. To James's notion of what the *donnée* should reveal, we must return.

When *Miss Bretherton* came out he was sufficiently interested to go and talk to Mrs Ward about it, and to send a fairly long letter as well; his polite but firm qualifications confirm an already strong involvement in her idea:

> I think your idea, your situation interesting in a high degree, and I further think you have drawn many of the notes of its meaning, its beauty. The private history of the public woman (so to speak), the drama of her feelings, heart, soul, personal relations, and the shock, conflict, complication between those things and her publicity, her career, ambition, artist's life – this has always seemed to me a tempting, challenging subject. It seems to me, however, that as I said, you have rather limited yourself – you have seen that concussion too simply, refused perhaps even to face it. . . . I am capable of wishing that the actress had been carried away from Kendal altogether: carried away by the current of her artistic life, the sudden growth of her power, and the excitement, the ferocity and egotism (those of the artist realizing success I mean; I allude merely to the natural normal dose of those elements) which the effort to create, to 'arrive' (once she had a glimpse of her possible successes) would have brought with it. (Excuse that abominable sentence.) Isabel, the Isabel you describe, has too much to spare for Kendal – Kendal being what he is; and one doesn't feel her, see her, enough, as the pushing actress, the *cabotine*. She lapses toward him as if she were a failure, whereas you make her out a great success. No, she wouldn't have thought so much of him, at such a time as that, – though very possibly she would have come back to him later. You have endeavoured to make us feel her 'respectability' at the same time as her talent, her artistic nature, but in taking care to preserve the former, you have rather sacrificed the latter.[7]

Whatever James had in 1908 forgotten or did not wish to admit, *Miss Bretherton* must formally figure as a source for *The Tragic Muse*.

Miss Bretherton opens with the opening of the London season, the private view of the Royal Academy, and the few recorded events happen within the timetable of the social calendar: what it assumes is here and now, absolute contemporaneity. Miss Bretherton is as modest, as virtuous, as she is beautiful. London Society loves actresses. But Isabel Bretherton comes to know an inner circle which finds in her beauty and all the human virtues. The trouble, they hold, is that she can't act, and that her success is a wholly personal one. She is, they find, quite uneducated, and more concerned to show that an actress can be a good woman than with the triumphs of art; and even Forbes, the painter, who represents, in this circle, the public that looks only for beauty and charm, is alarmed when Miss Bretherton discloses her vulgar and uninstructed taste in painting. When Wallace, a writer friend, discovers with horror Miss Bretherton's determination to play the main role in a Romantic tragedy he has written, which he knows is beyond her, he asks Kendal, the main spokesman of the group and a scholar of French Literature, to persuade her to abandon the idea. Kendal tries to do so, and is compelled by Miss Bretherton's own candour to tell her what they truly think of her art. He then retires to Surrey to meditate on his realization that he is in love with her. She goes to Venice, where she meets Kendal's sister and her French husband, Paul de Chateauvieux. Immensely impressed by Miss Bretherton they take her education in hand; Paul de Chateauvieux begins to instruct her, intensively, in the literature and art of the theatre – and with great success. Wallace, also in Venice, has witnessed this education and its results – a reading of Juliet was one – and returns to London, having given Miss Bretherton his play, *Elvira*. Pausing only in Paris for some private lessons from an eminent French actor, Miss Bretherton returns to London. *Elvira* succeeds immensely with both publics, outer and inner. Kendal is left reflecting that Miss Bretherton has now passed beyond his reach. But suddenly he is called to his sister's bedside; and her last words of appeal determine him at least to make his offer. He does so; and at the moment of her real success, Miss Bretherton abandons art for marriage with the man who first made her recognize how inadequate her art had been. (And so she escapes, Mrs Ward makes clear, a public life she was physically and nervously unable to sustain.)

Even such a deliberately limited summary of *Miss Bretherton* must show that we are in close proximity to *The Tragic Muse*. To come closer we must first follow the working of Mrs Ward's procedure. Six months after publication the *Contemporary*'s reviewer was to be

surprised at *Miss Bretherton*'s popularity. There was no great need
for surprise: the 'case' of Mrs Ward is immensely instructive, for her
role was to mediate between that group who furnished the materials
for the 'serious' papers, the great reviews, and that group who read
them, and, in a wider ring, those capable of being influenced by those
instructed readers. These, essentially, are the 'outer' and the 'inner'
audiences of *Miss Bretherton*. Her huge success was to depend on
seizing the effective 'topic' and on finding a fictionally acceptable
vehicle for it, her gift for *vulgarization*. Just as in *Robert Elsmere* the
great 'topic', faith, is fictionalized by dramatizing the 'case' of T. H.
Green.

Miss Bretherton is nothing if not topical: as topical as any article
in that week's papers. Mrs Ward had under her eyes both a 'case' and
a context, and the reviewers very soon pointed it out. The *Pall Mall
Gazette* for 6 December – the day after James had called - has a
notice headed 'The Mary Anderson Myth' which begins

> Who was it set a-going an absurd rumour that the heroine of Mrs
> Ward's novel was no other than her friend Miss Mary Anderson, drawn
> to the life . . . ?

and goes on to list the 'vital and essential differences' that 'raise the
portrait of Isabel Bretherton from the rank of literary photography to
that of creative fiction'. All this is intended as irony; during the next
few weeks the 'myth' was a talking point in the national press.

> It is a leaf out of the actual living present; a study of today; a piece of
> London life clipped out no later than yesterday . . . her talk is such as
> may be heard in the drawing-rooms of cultivated women, where
> educated men resort. . . .

said the *Daily News* on Christmas Day.

Mary Anderson had opened her first London season in September
1883 at Irving's temporarily vacant Lyceum, accompanied by her
mother, for duenna, and her brother, and announced by immense
publicity – that word was just beginning on its modern career, as
James, among many others, testifies – involving the distribution of
thousands of photographs. She had visited England once before, in
1878, but privately as a tourist during a holiday that took her, pri-

marily, to Paris, where both Ristori and Bernhardt received her and praised, it seems, the private recitations she gave them, for their 'originality'. In 1883 she was only twenty-four, very beautiful (in the 'classical' manner), very respectable, and *dévote* – nothing was allowed to interfere with her attendance at mass. Social acceptance and success seem to have been immediate; and not only with lion-hunting hostesses, but in those circles where the World, Intellectuals and Artists might meet. Thus, towards the end of her first season, intending to put on a new *Romeo and Juliet* in the winter of 1884, and planning an appropriate preliminary visit to Italy:

> It was at Mrs Humphry Ward's house that, meeting James Russell Lowell for the first time, I mentioned to him our proposed trip to Verona. . . . The conversation which followed between Henry James and Mr Lowell made me all the more eager to start for the land of sunshine and song. . . .[8]

If Mary Anderson's rise had been remarkably rapid, her whole stage career was dramatically short. Her last season in England was in 1888, her last tour of America – dangerously marked by signs of physical and nervous collapse – followed immediately; her marriage in 1890 really did mean retirement.

Mary Anderson in London, as we shall see, fitted very precisely into certain schemes of expectation and desire: a set of intellectual *positions prises* could attach themselves to her. As Shaw said:

> No: Our Mary was not a beauty merely: she was an ideal. We made a type of her, just as we made a type of Mr Gladstone. . . .[9]

In other words Miss Anderson, in her personality, her acting, her reception was indeed a 'case', and Mrs Ward was so far wholly justified.

The discussion about Miss Anderson's 'case' may be sampled in a convenient anthology of reviews, favourable and unfavourable, which its well-informed author included in the little brochure intended for the actress's second season.[10]

In London the pattern obviously depends, in part at least, on which papers and which audiences, and on which critics, and on their audiences. She is a 'case' because she is a success; she is a success in part because of the publicity, as *The Times* sourly noted. Or as the *Morning Post* put it, more magniloquent: 'Borne on the wings of an enthusiastic press, the fame of Miss Anderson's loveliness had reached our shores long before her own arrival.' From the celebrated opening tableau in *Ingomar* (1 September 1883) onwards, the *Standard*, the *Daily News*, even the *Morning Post*, even *The Times* found occasion for superlatives about Parthenia's 'classic grace', the 'classic beauty of her features and the perfect moulding of her figure', her 'plastic grace' and 'ideal beauty'.

But the argument against Miss Anderson was powerfully and consistently made from the start.

The Times in its first notice complained:

It became evident that faults of training or, perhaps, of temperament, were to be set off against the actress's unquestionable merits.... Parthenia was at all times more concerned with the fall of her drapery than with the effect of her speeches ... gesture, action, intonation – everything which constitutes a living individuality were in her case not so much the outcome of the feeling proper to the character, as the manifestation of diligent painstaking art which had not yet learnt to conceal itself. The gleam of the smallest spark of genius would have been a welcome relief to the monotony of talent.[11]

And other critics were using the same vocabulary. For the *Morning Post* every talent she 'cultivated to every perfection of art save one – the concealment of it'. What she lacked was

freshness, spontaneity, abandon ... of the *feu sacré* which irradiated Rachel and gives to Bernhardt splendour ineffable, Miss Anderson has not a spark. She is not inspired.[12]

The Daily Telegraph found her well-taught and trained, but:

her one great fault is insincerity, or, in other words, inability thoroughly to grasp the sympathies of the thoughtful part of her audience. She is destitute of the supreme gift of sensibility that Talma considers essential, and Diderot maintains is detrimental to the highest acting. Diderot may be right, and Talma may be wrong, but we are convinced that the art Miss Anderson has practised is, on the whole, barren and unpersuasive.... She weeps but there are no tears in her eyes....[13]

On Miss Anderson's performance in *Pygmalion and Galatea* (8 December 1883) *The Times*, the *Telegraph* and the *Morning Post* repeated their verdicts: the heart is not touched; there is no spontaneity; not a tear is shed.

Miss Bretherton was written before Miss Anderson's *Romeo and Juliet* opened on 1 November 1884. But in December the currency of Mrs Ward's concerns could only have been more striking. For the situation repeated itself, except that Miss Anderson had now a champion, with access to the highest journals. This was no less conspicuous a person than Lord Lytton, the novelist's son – as 'Owen Meredith' most determinedly a poet by vocation, a passionate amateur of the theatre, by career a diplomat – who published a minutely analytic essay in the December *Nineteenth Century*, 'Miss Anderson's Juliet'. Its highly objective tone (he makes a number of unfavourable comments) is an aspect of its polemical strategy. Lytton claims to be the 'mouthpiece' of a group of friends whose experience has belied the violent strictures of 'newspaper criticism'. He wants primarily to establish that Miss Anderson is capable of portraying passion, of moving the audience, of bringing a tear to the cheek, and that 'the gift of genius has been given'.[14]

Thus, in the Preface to the second edition of *Miss Bretherton* Mrs Ward could justifiably assert that, while her heroine's attractiveness may suggest the shadow of Mary Anderson, the book 'is the outcome, and indeed, too much the outcome, of certain critical ideas':[15]

The share in dramatic success which, in this country belongs to physical gift and personal charm; the effect of the public sensitiveness to both, upon the artist and upon art; the difference between French and English dramatic ideals; these were the various thoughts suggested by the dramatic interests of the time. They were not new, they had been brought into prominence on more than one occasion during the last few years, and in a general sense, they are common to the whole history of dramatic art. In dealing with them the problem of the story teller was twofold – on the one hand, to describe the public in its two divisions of those who know or think they know, and those whose only wish is to feel and to enjoy; and on the other hand, to draw such an artist as should embody at once all the weakness and all the strength involved in the general situation. . . .[16]

This is a fair statement, but the 'critical ideas' on which *Miss Bretherton* depends can be set out with an almost diagrammatic simplicity. Paris is art based on training and criticism, themselves based on tradition, which in turn involves a cultivated audience; Paris is a special conception of the artist as individual and in social relationships, which is shared by both artist and audience. Paris is, centrally though not exclusively, the *Théâtre français*. London is interested in personality, indifferent to art and training, without tradition. London is the city of the 'outer' and 'inner' audiences, only the latter corresponding to that of Paris. London has a wholly different conception of the artist and her role, individually and socially. London has no *Théâtre français*. Conceptions of art and artist – and these include questions of whether you expect to meet an actress at a dinner-table or not – turn on what a reviewer accurately enough called 'the relation of life to art',[17] which is in the novel a question about the relation of talent to experience. Isabel Bretherton's London critics were of course right in asserting those deficiencies in her art which had to do with training; these are rectified by lessons in Paris. But what they had not allowed for, and what her Parisian and Anglo-Parisian critics had recognized immediately, was her capacity to learn from 'mere living', from 'the accumulations of personal thought and experience'.[18]

> . . . for a creature . . . so rich in the *stuff* of life nothing is irreparable! . . . She will make a teacher out of every friend, out of every sensation.[19]

Talent and experience will come together when Isabel Bretherton triumphs in *Elvira*, when she stirs her audience into a current of feeling, 'when her extraordinary grace, her marvellous beauty were all subordinated to, forgotten almost in the supreme human passion speaking through her'.[20]

That the 'inner audience' were involved with a set of references close to and sometimes identical with Mrs Ward's is also clear from the reviews of Mary Anderson. There is the repeated insistence on 'training' and 'temperament' and 'sensibility', there is the crucial question of the actress's command of feeling, with which is linked the question of 'genius' or 'inspiration'; there are the explicit references

to French models and discussions: Rachel, Bernhardt, the *Théâtre
français*, Talma, Diderot. Or:

> a certain particular *nature d'actrice*. . . . The thing a confirmation of
> Mrs Kemble's theory . . . Rachel.

Mrs Ward's claim that her novel 'went with the dramatic interests of
the time' was also justified; and James's reflections, texts, and cases –
whether he actually talked about them or not on that June day –
would not have been new to her, or to an interested reader of the
journals of opinion.

Such references are signals pointing us to a great nexus of discussion. The texts and 'cases' are English and French.

Part of Isabel Bretherton's education in Venice is to listen to Paul
de Chateauvieux reading aloud to her 'his favourite *Paradoxe sur le
Comédien*'.[21] And, looking back in 1918 on her novel, Mrs Ward said
that 'the problem was not far removed from Diderot's problem in the
Paradoxe sur le Comédien.'[22] Topical enough. Readers of *The Theatre*
for 1 January 1884 were offered a handsome portrait-photograph
of Mary Anderson, brief gossip-column notes about her, cross-
references and lengthy discussion of her performances. On 1 March
the same readers were offered yet another unfavourable review
in terms which had become familiar – 'in no performance is there a
scintillation of genius, or a suggestion of sensibility'[23] – and this
comes just after they had read the leading article, which is a review by
William Archer of the English translation of Diderot's *Paradoxe*
which appeared in 1883 with a preface by Henry Irving. In 1883, too,
Talma's *Reflections on the Actor's Art* – which *The Theatre* had already
brought out in 1877 – was republished; and Irving also supplied a preface for this. Reviewers connect Diderot and Talma, and both with
Fanny Kemble, just as James, in 1884 and in 1893, in the memorial
essay he dedicated to this old and precious friend, was to connect her
directly with this controversy. Fanny Kemble's short pregnant essay
'On the Stage' had, after twenty years, been reprinted in 1882 for the
introduction to her *Notes of Some of Shakespeare's Plays*.[24] And
through the eighties no-one interested in acting or the theatre could
forget the terms of reference of such discussions. In 1887 it was still
worthwhile for the *Westminster Review* to publish a discussion of

Diderot.[25] In that same year a new name and a well-publicized controversy kept things going. The name is Coquelin. In 1887 Coquelin went on tour in America, and that January James, whose admiration for Coquelin was of long standing, and significant for his own life, wrote an essay about him for *Century*, presumably intended to help the actor's reception there. Coquelin could help himself. He could write about his business. *L'Art du Comédien* had come out in 1881, and now, in May, he published in *Harper's Monthly* an article on 'Actors and Acting'. In England, in *Nineteenth Century*, in June, Henry Irving answered this; in August in the *North American Review* Dion Boucicault discussed the discussion; in November, in *Harper's Weekly*, Coquelin replied to both.[26] All this hardly passed unnoticed – it was not intended to. William Archer, of course, noticed it. He, in his dogged way, was pursuing questions arising from his 1884 Diderot review: the results appeared in that very odd book *Masks or Faces? A Study in the Psychology of Acting*, in 1888.

Mrs Ward was eventually to put very succinctly what Diderot's *Paradoxe* was all about: 'What is the relation of the actor to the part represented,'[27] she says. Isabel Bretherton was quite sure (and the nature of Isabel's triumph showed Mrs Ward agreeing with her):

> But Diderot is wrong, wrong, wrong! When I could once reach the feeling of the Tybalt speech, when I could once *hate* him for killing Tybalt in the same breath in which I *loved* him for being Romeo, all was easy; I learnt them, and the thing was done.[28]

What Miss Bretherton's contemporaries thought Diderot was opposing can be defined precisely in Archer's words:

> A readiness to identify oneself mentally rather than physically with the character represented, culminating in absolute absorption in the part.[29]

'Absolute absorption' is an identification achieved through the actor's 'sensibility'. 'Sensibility' Archer and all the rest took quite rightly to be Diderot's key-word; although they did not understand its connotations. Diderot's paradox was, of course, as they received it, that the more successfully the Juliet succeeds, or thinks she succeeds, in hating and loving Romeo at that moment in the play, the worse the actress, the worse the performance. 'Sensibility' as agent of such supposed identification is a faculty the good actor does not and must not have: in order to produce the desired effect on his audience he must all the time be precisely aware of what he is doing; he must be, as Paul de Chateauvieux is made to put it, quoting some words from Diderot's text, 'the cold and tranquil spectator', 'the imitator of other men's feelings, while possessing none of his own'.[30] Isabel was arguing for the *real: real* hate, *real* love. Achieve the *real* and your audience will feel it too. The position Diderot was arguing from – with the attack on 'sensibility' it is the other pole on which his argument turns – is a traditional position: not the *real* but the *vraisemblant*, acting as one of the arts of *representation*; or, in English terms:

> Imitations produce pain or pleasure, not because they are mistaken for realities, but because they bring realities to mind.[31]

Among the French discussions two articles by the doyen of critics, Francisque Sarcey, entitled 'L'Acteur' and published in 1886,[32] should have carried an especial weight. Sarcey was concerned with the need for both 'nature' and 'étude', both 'l'instinct' and 'l'intelligence'.

> Il en est des acteurs, comme de tous les autres articles: c'est la nature qui les commence, et c'est l'étude qui les achève.[33]
> Le génie ne va pas sans intelligence. L'instinct de l'acteur s'en passe parfaitement.[34]

Sarcey had to allow for the celebrated performers who, relying on 'l'instinct' and 'les dons extérieurs', can succeed without understanding.[35] This leads back inevitably to 'sensibilité' and an absolute agreement with Diderot, predicated on a conviction of what art is and how it 'represents'.

> L'art n'est point la nature, il n'en est que l'imitation et une imitation qui enchérit sur le modèle.[36]

The actor's art is therefore most authoritatively nurtured within the ancient traditions of the *Conservatoire* and the *Théâtre français*, where the strong emphasis on formal diction and gesture preserves the agreed conventions of imitation.

Sarcey's statement was authoritative and inclusive, but the

theories about the nature of representation explicit there were not what the English arguments were about; nor, it is clear, did the English participants really grasp the point. Starting from the assumption that the great actor is 'he who powerfully affects his audiences' (that power denied to Mary Anderson),[37] from 'sensibility', they concern themselves with questions that turn on what the actor can *learn* (and how he can learn) from training (rehearsal, instruction); from observation of other people's behaviour and of his own experience; and with questions of the actor's self-consciousness; with 'genius'; with the actor's *moral* character, as private person. Talma was set as a champion of 'sensibility' against Diderot and, in professional terms, against Coquelin who had written: 'Je tiens que ce paradoxe est la vérité même.'[38] In London Archer, who sums up so much of the whole situation in *Masks or Faces?*, was passionately opposed to Diderot's definitions of 'sensibility' (as he read them) and therefore passionately on the side of the 'emotional'. But Archer offers primarily an enquiry into 'the psychology of acting' and not into the convincing 'representation' of emotion.[39] He tried to base his findings about what actors really do and feel not only on biographical records, but on the answers to a questionnaire which he devised and sent out to leading actors and actresses. Obviously such an enquiry must cover most of the points at issue already listed; and all come under Mrs Ward's rubric – the relationship of the actor to his part. On questions about a direct relationship between the actor's own private love, hate, sorrow, and his acting-out of scenes involving such emotions, Archer comes down on the side of the 'emotional' school. He notes in passing that Talma and Rachel are said to have 'consciously' noted their own 'external manifestations' of feeling with a view to 'reproducing' or 'mimicking' them on the stage.[40] Archer himself does not believe in 'cold blood'; and he suggests that those artists who claim to have noted and stored instances of 'expression' in 'life' for future use may be deceiving themselves. Yet he reports Miss Janet Achurch's answer to his question:

> It is impossible for me to help it. Everything that comes, or ever has come, into my own life, or under my observation, I find myself utilizing, and in scenes of real personal suffering I have had an under-consciousness of taking mental notes all the time. It is not a pleasant feeling.[41]

It is impossible to believe – and nowhere is it suggested – that this is what Isabel Bretherton is going to learn from her 'sensations' (or 'impressions') or from her friends; what she is going to learn from Venice, or from tutorials with Paul de Chateauvieux is, in the appropriate word, 'culture'. And this is part of what James was denying when he introduced the name of Fanny Kemble; who, niece of Sarah Siddons, a member of the great acting dynasty, spoke to him with the voices of tradition and of life so widely and curiously observed.

Her support could be used for several positions. When James said that she 'would have been a capture for the disputants who pretend that the actor's emotion must be real',[42] he refers to a moment when a friend 'addicted to the perpetual puzzle of art' asked her how much rehearsal and calculated preparation she needed for Shakespeare readings. Her contemptuous denial of any such need may, James suggests, be part of her irony, her disconcerting wilfulness, her hatred of such discussions which would have made her a dangerous recruit for any side; yet he is emphasizing the 'anomaly' of her position, her exemplification of the 'natural method', her lack of 'technical curiosity'. The point he wanted to place against Mrs Ward's reassuring Isabel is the one she makes in her one general essay and does indeed connect – 'her artistic being so vivid, yet so purely instinctive' – with what James reports of Mrs Kemble and 'the natural method'. That 'the dramatic gift is a thing in itself' is fundamental for Mrs Kemble's rather disjointed argument; that it implies 'of necessity no general superiority of mind' is a corollary. In fact Mrs Kemble's insistence on 'the natural method' or the 'purely instinctive' springs from her very clear presuppositions about what acting is. Mrs Kemble's essay is firmly based within the 'acting as representation' tradition. The theatre is not life: 'the dramatic is the *real*, of which the theatrical is the *false*.'[43] That Mrs Kemble has complicated the issue by choosing to use the term 'dramatic' – which she defines as belonging to our human nature, being its passionate, emotional, humorous element, very simple, and closely allied to our instincts – may momentarily obscure but does not conceal her reliance on the traditional formulation. What the actor has is the capacity for assuming or dissembling or 'representing' passionate emotion. This power depends on 'a specific comprehension of effect and the means of producing it'.[44] If this special capacity be united with the 'dramatic temperament', which is the power of imagining or conceiving passion and emotion, then we have the good or the great actor. From the notion of the simplicity and instructural nature of the dramatic temperament, and the combination with a quite special capacity for representing, comes Mrs Kemble's corollary. There is no connexion at all between the actor's gifts and the operation, on his actor's part, of 'analytical reasoning':

> . . . there is no reason whatever to expect that fine actors shall be necessarily profound commentators on the parts that they sustain most successfully, but rather the contrary.[45]

She instances Rachel, the Tragic Muse who had died in 1858:

> . . . I have heard, from one who knew her well, that her intellectual processes were limited to the consideration of the most purely mechanical part of her vocation.[46]

Memory (in Matthew Arnold's case, for example) still carried her great legend, supported by an uninterrupted production of books, memoirs – even, in 1884, by a sensational novel by Arsène Houssaye, *La Comédienne*, which had its English readers. William Archer was one, and Rachel figures in his pages as she must in any contemporary discussion. As a reference Rachel serves in more than one way. She who, at moments of the highest tragic intensity, knew precisely how every fold in her dress was disposed, can be a great instance of the wholly self-conscious actor, his own spectator with his divided or multiple consciousness. Mrs Kemble's point about her ignorance is related to the stories of her origins and upbringing which were part of the legend, and these fall naturally into a current and acceptable stereotype of 'genius'; and it is as 'genius', perhaps, that – except for Mrs Kemble who makes no use of this word – Rachel most characteristically figures. This reference is so taken for granted that in 1883 or 1884 a theatrical critic may use it almost as a matter of course, or a writer in *Nineteenth Century* assume without argument '. . . there is no doubt that Rachel is one of the most remarkable instances of natural genius on record'.[47]

* * *

... that the theatre, the organized theatre, will be as Matthew Arnold was in those very days announcing it, irresistible.[48]

This is the only gesture James makes in the Preface towards a document relating to the historical moment of *The Tragic Muse*, and it refers to Matthew Arnold's essay 'The French Play in London'.[49] Its occasion was the historic visit of the *Théâtre français* to London in 1879. On 12 July, the night of the last representation, James had written for *The Nation* an article on 'The *Comédie Française* in London'. James had dined in at least one distinguished house with members of the company; and at a breakfast party given by Andrew Lang he met Coquelin.

Two moments, in two cities, coalesced:

What has always counted, of course, has been the Comédie Française; it is on that, as regards this long day-dream, that I have lived. But there was an evening there that I shall long remember; it was in September 1887. I had come over from London; ... I went to see *Jean Dacier*, with Coquelin as the hero. I shall certain[ly not] forget that impression. ... He is everything in it by turns, and I don't think I ever followed an actor's creation more intently. It threw me into a great state of excitement. ... It held up a glowing light to me – seemed to point to my own path. If I could have sat down to work then I probably should not have stopped soon. But I didn't; I couldn't ... I remember how, on leaving the theatre – it was a lovely evening – I walked about a long time under the influence not so much of the piece as of Coquelin's acting of it, which had made the thing so human, so brilliant, so valuable. I was agitated with what it said to me that I might do – what I ought to attempt; I walked about the Place de la Concorde, along the Seine, up the Champs-Elysées. That was nothing, however to the state I was thrown into by meeting Coquelin at breakfast at Andrew Lang's, when the Comédie Française came to London. ... I had some talk with him which rekindled and revived all my latent ambitions. At that time, too, my hands were tied; I could do nothing, and the feeling passed away in smoke. But it stirred me to the depths. Coquelin's personality, his talk, the way the *artist* overflowed in him – all this was tremendously suggestive. I could say little to him there – not a tittle of what I wished. ... But I listened to some purpose, and I have never lost what I gained. It excited me powerfully; I shall not forget my walk, afterwards, down from South Kensington to Westminster. ... All day, and for days

afterwards, I remained under the impression. It faded away in time, and
I had to give myself to other things. But this brings it back to me; and I
may say that those two little moments were landmarks.[50]

So, in the winter of 1881–2, the coalescence was fixed and renewed
in record as James, back in America for his mother's death, attempted
in his *Notebooks* a recovery of those 'impressions' that were now part
of his life, his nature. His interrupted reverie is purposeful, mixes
memory with desire. 'In those very days': so far as the preparation
of his novel was concerned his gesture was not really imprecise either
in terms of public event or private dream. He was directing us to an
occasion that held for him meanings that would open up to involve not
only the reference of *The Tragic Muse* but much else in his art and life.

Both Arnold and James used the visit of the French company as
text for discourses on England made through comparisons with
France – or Paris. Both masters start, in tones of amusement or irony,
from the extraordinary fuss this visit stirred in the press and in
eminent dining-rooms or reception rooms; and both draw their
morals as much from the fuss as from the performances. Both were
repeating themselves.

Of the fuss there is plenty of evidence. And there was as great a
rush to draw morals for England as to find seats or offer invitations.
The company's hurried visit in 1871 had passed off with compliments
but without sensation; in 1879 the situation of the London theatre
was, as contemporaries recognized, radically changed and changing,
through the interacting work of actor, audience, critic. Only the
existence of such a sensitive situation, where issues and challenges
were already defined and areas of struggle already marked, explains
the impact of this particular visit, which offered to London not only
individual plays or players, but the spectacle of an organization, an
institution in operation.

This is what Arnold seized on. Arnold saw this visit as illustrating
and celebrating the end of the long alienation of the English middle
classes from the theatre: escaping from the prison of Puritanism
these have turned again to one of the great sources of expansion,
intellect, knowledge, beauty, social life and manners. The revolution
was needed, the needs are real, the instrument effective: 'the theatre,

therefore, is irresistible'.[51] We are not to learn from the French players that their classical drama is greater than it really is, or that their Romantic drama is great at all, or that their modern drama, so representative of modern Paris, can be transplanted to London. At this time when we are returning to the theatre we find only an English theatre 'without organization, or purpose, or dignity, and no modern English drama at all except a fantastical one'.[52] The real lesson of the *Théâtre français* is that we need in London a comparable state-subsidized institution, with controls over its repertory and with an attached training school for actors, where they are taught the arts of elocution and declamation. 'The theatre is irresistible; organize the theatre!'[53] These are Arnold's closing words – put (ironically enough) into the mouth of a visionary Bernhardt hovering over the Gaiety Theatre.

'The French Play in London' caused some stir, because it took its place in current theatrical discussion. Arnold, whether he was right in diagnosing the causes, was right in discerning a reconciliation of the middle classes to the theatre. Innovations by individual theatre managements in the seventies and eighties are a response to the needs and concerns of this class; and these needs and concerns lie behind the controversies of these decades. The call for a National Theatre was obvious and not new; nor was knowledge of the *Théâtre français*. And by 1879 the *Théâtre français* was an accepted term of comparison. The appearance in 1878 of a new series of *The Theatre* as a monthly, not for a trade audience but for a 'theatre-going' public, is sufficient indication of a change. And there is a forcible sense that this visit was itself a dramatic event, a confrontation: 'During the visit of the *Comédie française* the English stage may have been said to have been on its trial. The relative merits and shortcomings of the two schools of acting were warmly and acrimoniously discussed.'[54] In the argument about styles of acting, rather than about repertory or organization, the dominant note was, perhaps, struck by M. Got's views on the English style – as reported by *The Theatre*: 'What evidently strikes him most forcibly is our absolute lack of general cultivation of the art of elocution. . . .'[55] Or, as Arnold was to phrase this message: 'Your best and most serious actors would have been better if in their youth they had learnt elocution.'[56]

Something else, however, was happening in London. Late in 1878 Henry Irving became lessee and manager of the Lyceum and for the opening played Hamlet to Ellen Terry's Ophelia. This marks the formal beginning of Irving's long, though never undisputed, dominance in London. At the same time he was proprietor of *The Theatre* – and was to remain so until December 1879 – and the space *The Theatre* gave to questions about a national or subsidized theatre should be read in connexion with Irving's own ambitions. Briefly, Irving thought of his Lyceum as the National Theatre, with himself as director. The issue of *The Theatre* which reports M. Got's views about English actors and elocution also carries an article in praise of Irving's work, claiming that if the success of the Lyceum should continue then London will have in effect a state theatre without the need for the state to intervene. And there is no doubt that to the fury of advanced critics, both of his repertory and of his art, Irving did succeed in making his theatre into a kind of national institution which satisfied middle-class needs.

The art of elocution, however, was one of the points at which Irving was notoriously vulnerable. His success in 1879 was, for James, the most striking indication of how little this English public perceived the need for acting as art:

> ... even his most ardent admirers would probably admit that he is an altogether irregular performer, and that an artistic education has had little to do with the results that he presents to the public ... he is an actor who, in default of any help rendered him, any control offered him by the public taste, by an ideal in the public mind, has had to get himself together and keep himself together as he could. ... His starting-point is so perfectly opposed to any that I find conceivable that it would be idle to attempt to appreciate him. In the opinion of many people the basis, the prime condition, of acting is the art of finished beautiful utterance – the art of speaking, of saying, of diction, as the French call it: and such persons find it impossible to initiate themselves into any theory of the business which leaves this out of account. Mr Irving's theory eliminates it altogether, and there is perhaps a great deal to be said for his point of view.[57]

James had said as much about Irving before this, and would say as much again in the early eighties: Irving is an amateur, a man with gifts which might have come to something if he had ever been educated in his art. Irving himself was aware of his own position. He was bound in the 1880s to be on the side of Talma rather than of Diderot; and to attempt to justify an English style to set against the French.

James's articles on the London theatre written between 1873 and 1879 are of course for an American audience. He speaks as an outside observer and as one whose sole standard of excellence is the *Théâtre français*. His position has never been in doubt. He had offered his views on the *Théâtre français* to an English audience in an essay which he had included in *French Poets and Novelists* (1878). From this through the later journalism the line of argument is unbroken. But in 1879 there are new and grave preoccupations.

What James most admired about the French company, and about France, was a sense of acting as profession, or trade, or business. In that same passage on Irving he puts it like this:

> In France (as I spoke just now of France) the actor's art, like the ancient arts and trades, is still something of a 'mystery' – a thing of technical secrets, or special knowledge.[58]

It is through tradition that the nature of this is learnt, and the *Théâtre français* is important as the agent and carrier of tradition. That building in Paris is itself both emblem and carrier of the art. By 1876 or 1879 James's sense of the performance itself was deeply connected with his sense of historic continuity working through an institution, and deeply nostalgic; it is clearly and strongly connected with his early and abiding sense of the impoverishment of a society that lacked such continuing centres.

Arnold, though he laughed at the social fuss over the French visitors, was prepared to accept even 'the great ladies who are seeking for soul and have found it in Mlle Sarah Bernhardt'.[59] Although their behaviour was absurd it could be read as a sign of that hopeful reconciliation of society with the theatre. James's position has to be radically different. The members of the guild or 'mystery' are united by their possession of the technical secrets of their art; by the same token they are separated from society at large. The separation goes

with the art, the art with the separation. This is why James opens his
1879 essay on the London theatres with an attack on the contemporary English situation, where the theatre is probably worse
than it has ever been and, simultaneously, so much in fashion. Where
– 'It pervades society – it breaks down barriers.'[60] Actors are in
society and society is on the stage. For James the consequence can
only be that 'the stage has become amateurish and society has
become professional'.[61] This may be better for the world, but he
cannot hold that it is better for art and literature. This is the prelude
that leads into his account of Irving as a symptomatic case, and to the
contrast with France; and this is really the theme that dominates that
essay on the French visit which comes immediately afterwards. Even
in France there are danger signs of 'the confusion of kinds', all part
of 'the democratizing, vulgarizing movements'. James cannot believe
that the social context the French visitors found themselves in is good
for the *Théâtre français* or the English theatre. By coming to London
at all the great institution has taken a step towards the violation of the
'mystery' – and James here ranges himself with conservative French
critics who had objected to the whole enterprise. The great institution
draws its strength from Paris and the history of Paris, and to move
outside is to lose that much of strength and 'sanctity'. The 'success'
of the French company has something to do with art, but much more
to do with symptoms of a 'modernity' that James was finding deeply
disquieting. Bernhardt becomes the pivotal figure of this essay
because her success fulfils the conditions that James most disapproves:

> It has been the success of the celebrity, pure and simple, and Mlle
> Sarah Bernhardt is not, to my sense, a celebrity because she is an artist.
> She is a celebrity because, apparently, she desires with an intensity that
> has rarely been equalled to be one, and because for this end all means
> are alike to her.[62]

Bernhardt's style of acting is modern, and her social goal is very
modern. She is 'a child of her age', and the age is one of 'publicity' –
of 'reverberation'. Being a celebrity depends on advertisement and
the newspapers; and Bernhardt has the 'génie de la réclame'. Against
Bernhardt is poised Coquelin with his 'intelligence of the whole

dramatic mystery'. But 'success' is to be one of the most dangerous and powerful words in *The Tragic Muse*.

'I have seen plays and performers that have dropped as a curtain over that last aberration of the misguided Mary. I have also read a great deal of "naturalism". The distance from Paris to London is surely not hundreds, but hundreds of thousands of miles.'[63] So James wrote from Paris to Mrs Humphry Ward on 21 February 1884. Paris spoke to him as always with many voices. One is unmistakable. This visit was, as Mr Edel has shown, very deliberate: James went to Paris to meet the novelists. He arranged to see Edmond de Goncourt; he spent a remarkable evening at Daudet's with Zola, Coppée, Loti and de Goncourt. For nine years he had not sought the company of the French writers; that he should have made such an effort to do so now means that he felt a moment had arrived when he must try to come to terms with their work, which had troubled and was to trouble him so much. However wavering and ambiguous James's attitudes to 'realism' were and were to remain, there is one point about which he is perfectly decisive: he must respect the *seriousness* of these writers. To Howells he wrote:

> ... there is nothing more interesting to me now than the effort and experiment of this little group, with its truly internal intelligency of art form, manner – its intense artistic life. They do the only kind of work, today, that I respect. ...[64]

That evening at Daudet's Zola had said 'Yes, it is a sad trade – *c'est un triste métier.*' What James, in spite of all his reservations, was acknowledging was that here he was meeting a group, a society of professionals engaged, immersed, in the problems of their trade. Such a society or guild or brotherhood James could not find in London. His sense of the distance between the cities, in this respect, would be another version of the contrast between amateur and professional in the theatre.

Such contrasts obviously operate within larger comparisons between the cities, which go back to the middle of the century. In 1872 James had approved Taine's conclusion that 'the characteristic English mind is indifferent and even hostile to ideas';[65] and an essay that he published in January 1884, immediately before going to Paris, places James in a familiar, recognizable, English line. He is now writing about Matthew Arnold, to mark the occasion of Arnold's American visit; his way into Arnold's work is through the value that Arnold has always had for any stranger as guide and commentator on the English mind, and he particularly recalls 'The Function of Criticism at the Present Time' and 'The Literary Influence of Academies'. Twenty years earlier, a very young man in 1865, he had discussed these essays in a long article on *Essays in Criticism*. There, agreeing with the common view that Arnold is using France as the, standard, and agreeing with him that the English 'are singularly incapable of large, of high, of general views', he had rephrased Arnold: the business of criticism is 'to urge the claims of all things to be understood'.[66]

In 1884 Arnold still is primarily 'a representative of the critical spirit' in a society where it is

> not the success of the critical effort at large that is most striking today to the attentive outsider; it is not the flexibility of English taste, the sureness of English judgement, the faculty of reproducing in their integrity the impressions made by works of art and literature that most fixes the attention of those who look to see what the English mind is about.[67]

That astute scholar and cleric Mandell Creighton wrote to Arnold's niece, about *Miss Bretherton*, that 'it was a sketch of the possible worth of criticism in an unregenerate world'.[68] Mrs Ward's version of the contrast between Paris and London may seem too like a parody of Matthew Arnold, and of a general comparison that was now a stereotype; nor does James always escape this suspicion.

But such conversation as he heard at Daudet's, and the seriousness of the new French work, is only possible in a society where people are allowed to think general ideas important, and where it is accepted that the business of criticism is to make things understood, and where, as corollary, the artist is expected to be consciously involved in the problems of his art – which is to say that he is expected to be educated in his *métier*. The notion of professionalism depends on the assumption that there is a body of theory and practice which can be transmitted, studied, discussed.

*   *   *

As Mr Edel has pointed out, one effect of the stay in Paris upon James was to prompt him to reply to Walter Besant's lecture, 'The Art of Fiction', by writing his own essay of the same title, which was published in *Longman's Magazine* in September 1884 and later, in a revised form, in *Partial Portraits* (1888).

James could agree (and not just out of politeness) with Besant's demand for public recognition of the novelist; but essentially he exposes the *naïveté* of the 'general laws' which Besant takes as evidence of the respectability of his *métier*. They are naïve because they simplify the problem of representation and dissolve the seriousness of the *métier* in an aura of public acclaim, so that comparison of Besant and the French novelists reduplicates the London/Paris contrast in the theatre. But beyond that, both the *naïveté* of English amateurism and the mandarin 'narrowness' of the French preoccupation with style are unable to take account of the complex relationship between representation and experience.

Therefore, in 'The Art of Fiction', the argument moves easily from 'reality' to 'sensibility' to 'consciousness'.[69] Given the artist's special consciousness, he can represent through his intense, suggestive impressions what he is able to know, and not just what is known to him. For James, 'if experience consists of impressions, it may be said that impressions *are* experience. . . .'[70] Besant's word 'story' James replaces with a cluster of important words whose meanings overlap – 'idea', '*donnée*', 'subject'. And since impressions and experience are inextricable, the novel, which is a 'direct impression', cannot be thought of as other than a 'living thing'; its 'idea' pre-exists its execution only as a 'starting point'; 'in that proportion do we lose our sense of the story being a blade which may be drawn more or less out of its sheath'.[71] 'Idea' and its associate words seem to have a range of application that includes everything, from the anecdote or story first heard that inspires the resulting work, through to the final treatment, or treatments considered on the way. They are both the initial given material (subject) and what that material demands (treatment); there is always something inherent or purposive in the 'idea'.

'The Art of Fiction' allows us to see James's vocabulary in action, and reveals the way in which he justified his activity. Although extrication is difficult, perhaps impossible or, at any rate, undesirable to attempt, we can observe the grouping of terms, the overlapping of words that are almost synonymous; and we return always to a vocabulary of experience – 'impressions', 'feelings', 'ideas'.

The Tragic Muse describes a society so built that it is necessary for a man to be identified by function. These can only be verbal: the formulas of description and words meaning trade, profession or *métier*, where 'be' and 'do' are synonymous. From this situation is predicated the rhetorical *topos*: the *paragone* or comparison between the Arts.

In the novel we are offered versions of formulas in pursuit of this comparison, formulas that were to a greater or lesser extent established or familiar. 'All art is one', says Nick to Biddy, '. . . it's the same great many-headed effort' (Ch. 1). Of Thomas Wainewright, Oscar Wilde wrote, 'To him all the arts were one';[72] and in 'The True Function and Value of Criticism' he was to affirm:

> Art does not address herself to the specialist. Her claim is that she is universal, and that in all her manipulations she is one.[73]

Nick's formula is to be set against that put forward by Peter, regarding dramatic art: 'it seems to me to include all the others' (Ch. 4); again, a proposition that was known to Wilde – 'For the stage is not merely the meeting place of all the arts, but is also the return of art to life.'[74] What Peter means is still the relatively simple idea of the theatre requiring the skills of writer, painter, actor and musician which was current before revolutionary Wagnerian concepts of representation took over, although these had already started on their career in England and can be found in James's 'After the Play'.[75] Nor is it surprising to find so easily examples of these commonplaces in Wilde, one of whose undoubted talents was for the publicizing of ideas and the animation of clichés, both old and new.

The comparison of the arts, the ways in which artists may be said to do the same thing, can be extended through the consideration that what they do may be – or should be – what they are, which relates to what or how they experience. The artist, whose experience is special, uses that experience in what he produces, his representation. He may therefore be said to hold a special relationship with it, above all when his experience of other people is to be included.

In *The Tragic Muse* the central instance of representation involves the art of the actor, although there is a submerged reference to literature. In the case of the actor, the reality of expression and the reality of experience involve further considerations: which are the representation of feeling when the artist is his own material, and the reality of that feeling at the moment of representation.

This accounts for some of the difficulties of the novel: for the comparison of the arts, that traditionally essential element in theory, here includes a most problematic instance – the art of the actor – and therefore, at the same time, the other arts have been restricted. For example, painting has become portrait painting and literature is, on the surface at any rate, eliminated. This might be explained by James's growing involvement with the theatre during the previous decade, although that fated involvement only led him back to explore the problems of the art of fiction.

When Biddy announces to Lady Agnes 'The subject doesn't matter; it's the treatment, the treatment!' (Ch. 1), she is using, quite clearly, what was already a familiar formula. By 1892 it was so familiar as to be repeated, expanded, and rearranged by almost every contributor to the great nexus of discussion that centred in London on Degas's 'L'Absinthe'. By then the phrase was readily available to the leader writer of a popular newspaper: when the *Pall Mall Gazette* attacked the 'new artists', it was on the grounds that

> According to their theory 'subject' is absolutely immaterial. The 'treatment' they say, is everything; and the sole criterion of criticism should be the degree of success with which the artist has done what he tried to do. . . .'[76]

But as early as 1883 Frederick Wedmore's important article 'The Impressionists' in the *Fortnightly Review* had taken for granted the opposite point of view: 'The final basis of artistic reputation is not the subject that is treated, but the capacity to treat it.'[77]

And there were other versions: in his informative memoirs Alfred Thornton says of his friends in 1890, 'our slogan was "effects not facts" '.[78] But Biddy chooses the most frequent version, and what is noticeable is that it is applied to work about which we know very little. Nor does her brother's amusement at the remark tell us any more, for James is very careful not to commit either the narrator or Nick to a theoretical position about painting. We are given no idea what *kind* of painting he does, other than the single fact that they are portraits. Despite James's talent for evoking works of art there are no detailed descriptions. That Nick's portraits are generally acceptable is made clear when Dashwood suggests hanging those of Miriam in the foyer of his theatre, and the only surprise expressed when people see them is as to their quality.

The artist whose career James observed most closely was John Sargent, about whom he wrote an article in 1887 which contains some of his most detailed theorizing about the painter's art. Here he claimed that Sargent was in possession of his own 'style'; that his work was 'the exact "fit" of his artistic temperament'. 'Impressions' and 'style' are brought together: 'Mr Sargent simplifies, I think, but he simplifies with style, and his impression in most cases is magnificent.' The relation of 'style' to 'impression' is at the heart of the process 'by which the object seen resolves itself into the object pictured', the process about which James sometimes used the word 'translation': 'to have translated the appearance of things into the language of painting'. 'The language of painting' is 'the notation of painting' or 'the signs by which objects are represented'. This is 'a very special affair, and of the special the public at large has always a perceptible mistrust'. But it is through that special language that something is produced that is 'as generous and comprehensive as life itself'.[79] This is what the great portrait painter achieves through an understanding of the language. This is the gift that he possesses completely: 'the immediate perception of the end and of the means'.[80] We are clearly very close to 'The Art of Fiction', where the art of painting was taken, without examination, as an obvious, and in some ways more intelligible, model for the artistic process.

Sargent was something of a protégé of James, and his success posed problems.

> May not this breed [he wrote] an irresponsibility of cleverness, a
> wantonness, an irreverence – what is vulgarly termed a 'larkiness' – on

the part of the youthful genius who has, as it were, all his fortune in his pocket? Such are the possibly superfluous broodings of those who are critical, even in their warmest admirations, and who sometimes suspect that it may be better for an artist to have a certain part of his property invested in unsolved difficulties.[81]

The particular problems of translation for the portrait painter are concerned with the need to reveal the original, the subject, while at the same time making it something else. Nick attempts to do this with Miriam twice, to show her as two different things: the muse or sibyl and 'the charming woman . . . as she appears *en ville*. He fails to translate Nash, and when he finally paints Julia, Miriam at least feels sure that she knows what this will involve: '. . . paint Mrs Dallow if you wish to eradicate the last possibility of a throb' (Ch. 48). Nick has himself admitted how the act of representation can destroy or replace other kinds of relationship: 'The truth is, painting people is a very absorbing, exclusive occupation. You can't do much to them besides' (Ch. 48). What painting Julia finally demanded, of him or of her, we are not told.

It may well have to do with the conditions and dangers of success which are very regularly, if imprecisely, suggested in Nick's case. Nash is present, up until the closing moments, to remind him of them. His prophecies appear in an inconclusive piece of dialogue with Nick, who remarks of his decision to become a painter,

> . . . that the great comedy would fall very flat, the great incident would pass unnoticed.
> 'Oh, if you'll simply do your part I'll take care of the rest,' said Nash.
> 'If you mean by doing my part working like a beaver, it's all right,' Nick replied.
> 'Ah, you reprobate, you'll become a fashionable painter, a P.R.A.!' his companion groaned, getting up to go.   (Ch. 36)

Nash's connexion between work and being 'a fashionable painter' is heavily ironical. Nick himself knows (and this both qualifies his ambitions and makes him more serious as far as the reader is concerned) that he is in a more dangerous position than anyone but Nash can understand.

... the pinch, for our young man's conscience, after a few weeks had passed, was simply an acute mistrust of the superficiality of performance into which the desire to justify himself might hurry him.   (Ch. 47)

Certainly the present performance is not satisfactory, even including the two portraits of Miriam:

That they were wonderfully clever was just the detestable thing in them, so active had that cleverness been in making them seem better than they were. There were people to whom he would have been ashamed to show them, and these were the people whom it would give him most pleasure some day to please. Not only had he many an hour of disgust with his actual work, but he thought he saw, as in an ugly revelation, that nature has cursed him with an odious facility and that the lesson of his life, the sternest and wholesomest, would be to keep out of the trap it had laid for him.   (Ch. 47)

Nash has pointed out the conditions under which Nick might be successful as that word is understood by the world. Mrs Dallow, he says, will send for Nick to paint her portrait: 'she'll recapture you on that basis!' Nick will attend the country houses, paint bishops and ambassadors. 'She'll put up with the palate if you'll put up with the country house.' In brief, 'you'll have your cake and eat it'. Much of this comes true, but what that means for Nick's painting we are not told, and by then Nash has disappeared.

The structure of the early parts of the novel works through confrontation and the difficulties of placing characters in society, and their own ambitions to advance (like Mrs Rooth) or secure or consolidate (like Lady Agnes) what they precariously hold. Hesitancy or confusion about identity hovers most crucially around the disturbing presence of Gabriel Nash, although several attempts are made to label or name him by assignation to a known group or class – 'gentleman', 'aesthete' or 'writer'. Peter had tried another precise designation.

'The *raffinés* despise the theatre,' said Peter Sherringham, in the manner of a man abreast with the culture of his age and not to be captured by a surprise, '*Connu, connu!*'   (Ch. 4)

But that too has been passed by. As for Lady Agnes and Julia, they could make nothing of him at all – 'who is this extraordinary person?'

Nash delights in rejecting the labels and offers in return fanciful generalizations. Thus he claims not to live in the nineteenth century and to be only in London 'when not in Samarkand'. Such remarks preface not a personal definition but a personal doctrine, and given the failure of the characters themselves to determine Nash's place amongst them, it is extraordinarily misguided for critics to expend their energy in trying to discover a precise historical model.

False trail though it is, the problem of identification has already provoked at least one major debate, with claims made by Mr Cargill that the model was Oscar Wilde, and by Mr Powers that Nash represents aspects of James himself.[82] But this is not a novel about established or even real public identities: rather it explores the means by which people achieve identities or have them forced upon them. A proper attention to the details and vocabulary of Nash's attitudes reveals above all its range of reference.

It is certainly true that Nash has a knowledge of the theatre. Like Peter he is something of a connoisseur and knows and appreciates the French tradition. He is familiar with the repertoire – the cry '*Ah, la voix de Célimène!*' shows knowledge and may be a glancing reference to Mlle Mars, whose part this was and who continued to play it to a very late age. He is also aware of the English tradition, both past and present. But his contempt for the present state of the London theatre does not only suggest James himself (and as Cargill has pointed out, Dorriforth in 'After the Play' is not necessarily James), but also the polemicists and reformers of the late 1880s, in particular George Moore, whose sensational 'Mummer-Worship' appeared in 1888.[83]

Moore had argued with passion against recognition of the actor's art, which he dismissed as 'parasitic', requiring no intelligence; and he scathingly attacked the aspirations of the 'mummers' towards the suburban villa and the polite salon. This article was a belated and particularly violent contribution to a large discussion about the 'respectability' of actors, to which the pretensions and fears of Mrs Rooth relate.[84] Moore's culminating article about the theatre was to be 'Our Dramatists and our Literature',[85] which compared the talents and situation of the playwright unfavourably with that of the novelist in England.

Above all, in the theatre, as in the fields of painting and literature, Moore claimed to be the pioneer of French ideas in England, and his tirades against both actor and playwright derive many of their assumptions from what had been said for some time by the French *littérateurs*.

Peter's bantering challenge to Nash, 'the *raffinés* despise the theatre', refers to a stock of common attitudes, 'the culture of his age', which reappear a page later after Nash's monologue.

> 'Do you write novels, Mr Nash?' Peter demanded.
>
> 'No, but I read them when they are extraordinarily good, and I don't go to plays. I read Balzac, for instance – I encounter the magnificent portrait of Valérie Marneffe, in "La Cousine Bette".'
>
> 'And you contrast it with the poverty of Emile Augier's Séraphine in "Les Lionnes Pauvres"? I was awaiting you there. That's the *cheval de bataille* of you fellows.' (Ch. 4)

In *Le Peintre de la vie moderne* Baudelaire had given the word *raffiné* a precise social meaning:

> Que ces hommes se fassent nommer raffinés, incroyables, beaux, lions ou dandys, tous sont issus d'une même origine; tous participent du même caractère d'opposition et de révolte. . . .[86]

With modified associations it held a particular fascination for James, and he exploited its nuances on several occasions.[87]

But it is most relevant to our investigation that James should have twice applied the word to the fastidious Goncourt brothers, proud possessors of the '*tempérament aristocratique*'.

> Their culture, their imagination, their inspiration, are all Parisian; a culture sensibly limited, but very exquisite of its kind; an imagination in the highest degree ingenious and as the French say, *raffiné* – fed upon made dishes.[88]

In this they are characteristic of contemporary French culture – dilletanti – 'they are *raffinés* and they write for *raffinés*'.[89]

The application of the word to the Goncourts clearly relates to the remarks that Peter passes about Nash. For twenty-five years, between the staging of *Henriette Maréchal* at the *Comédie française* in 1865 and the belated production of *La Patrie en Danger*, written in 1867, at Antoine's *Théâtre libre* in 1889, the Goncourts had laid siege to the French theatre. In his virulent Preface to the edition of their two plays, Edmond de Goncourt expressed contempt for the Parisian stage, and argued the need for 'la fantaisie moderne', which he opposed to Zola's demands for naturalism.

But on one issue there was among the novelists considerable accord: given the conditions of a bourgeois theatre, the drama could not hope to compete against the novel:

> . . . mais, pour une recherche un peu aigue, pour une dissection poussée a l'extrême, pour la recréation de vrais et *d'illogiques* vivants, je ne vois que le roman; et j'avancerais même que si par hasard le même sujet d'analyse sérieuse était traité à la fois par un romancier et un auteur dramatique – l'auteur dramatique fut-il supérieur au romancier – le premier aurait l'avantage et le devrait peut-être aux facilités, aux commodités, aux aises du livre.[90]

Zola, although involved in his own campaign, would have agreed with that diagnosis, and wrote of the Goncourts's opinions:

> Elles sont identiques aux miennes; seulement, M. de Goncourt, après avoir raisonné comme moi, conclut à la mort prochaine du théâtre, lorsque je tâche de conclure à sa prochaine resurrection.[91]

And Zola compared Dumas Fils and Augier with Balzac, and put *Les Lionnes Pauvres* against *Madame Bovary*.[92]

At least two critics made a comparison with Balzac when *Les Lionnes Pauvres* was revived with Réjane in 1879: in the case of Barbey d'Aurevilly (unquestionably a *raffiné*) it was quite specific:

> Il le rapelle surtout par le type dominateur de la pièce, qui fait penser à l'effroyable Mme Marneffe, de la *Comédie Humaine*. La lionne pauvre du drame de M. Augier n'a pas assurément l'ampleur que la génie de Balzac a donnée à Mme Marneffe. . . .[93]

And Francisque Sarcey wrote at the same time,

> L'action du drame parait, à la lecture, devoir être très intéressante, on sent bien vaguement que Séraphine n'a pas l'enverge du Mme Marneffe, l'immortelle création de Balzac. Mais on trouve naturel qu'un écrivain

dramatique, écrivant pour la scène, ayant à compter avec les suscepti-
bilités et les pudeurs du public, ait adouci l'odieux de ce caractère et
voile l'horreur de la situation.[94]

Peter is trying to relate Nash to an established French situation in
which the cultured, or the literary, professed contempt for the theatre
as an institution and the drama as genre. Some of that frustration was
to find an outlet in the *Théâtre libre*, whose influence became
powerful in England in the late eighties, again largely through the
propaganda of George Moore. And, in passing, Peter links Nash's
style with the cultivated pose of the dandy.

Nash's attitude to the theatre may be said then to amount to a
compendium of pre-existing, but still controversial, opinions that
were French in origin but known in England. It is not surprising that
he should sometimes sound like James himself, or James's fictional
character Dorriforth.

There are further ingredients in what Mr Cargill has himself
called a 'composite'. Having already isolated his basic premises and
vocabulary, we must now consider Nash's philosophy as a 'composite
generalization' of certain topical ideas, a series of representative
statements about art and life, that together approximate to a doctrine
of experience derived from Walter Pater.

In *A Bundle of Letters* (1879) a young American writes from Paris
to a Boston friend, full of the 'French way of looking at life', and
eager for experience. He exclaims:

> The great thing is to *live*, you know – to feel, to be conscious of one's
> possibilities, not to pass through life mechanically and insensibly, like a
> letter through a post-office.[95]

He asserts a sympathy with 'the artistic temperament': 'and what is
life but an art? Pater has said that so well, somewhere.'[96]

The influence and diffusion of the doctrine, the notion that life is
'but an art', which was appropriated for many different purposes, is
notoriously complex. Vernon Lee, for example, had used Pater as a
champion for impressionist art criticism.

> The art which deals with impressions, which tries to seize the real
> relative values of colours and tints at a given moment, is what you call
> new-fangled: its doctrines and works are still subject to the reproach of

charlatanry. Yet it is the only truly realistic art, and it only, by giving you a thing as it appears at a given moment, gives it you as it really ever is; all the rest is the result of cunning abstraction. . . .[97]

Nevertheless, in the Epilogue to her *Juvenalia* (1887) she came to value the *beautiful* for its ability to ennoble and enlarge moral sympathies.

The relation of the *beautiful* (goal of the aesthetic life) to the *good*, Pater's own central difficulty, also bothered his readers and critics. Thus in Vernon Lee's *Miss Brown* Dick Brown is allowed to remark with a sneer:

> Who is it – Mr Pater, or some such great gun of yours – who says the object of the wise man is to make his life consist in as many moments of thrilling impressions as possible; that the very wise people get them out of art and song, and the less wise out of vice and philanthropy?[98]

When Mrs Humphry Ward reviewed *Marius* in *Macmillan's Magazine*, she began by referring back to the dangerous arguments of *The Renaissance*:

> The object of the book was to reproduce, as vividly as possible, certain 'special unique impressions of pleasure', made on an individual mind by various beautiful things in art and literature, to 'disengage the virtue of a picture, a landscape, a fair personality in life or in a book', so as to pass on the experience of the author to the reader intact, and as it were still warm with feeling and emotion. Such was the programme laid down in the preface to the *Studies*, while at the close of the book its general principles found still more bold and eloquent expression in sentences which were much quoted, and scandalized many to whom the rest of the book remained unknown.[99]

Mrs Ward welcomed Marius's discovery of the inadequacy of the Heraclitan doctrine of the 'subjectivity of knowledge', seeing in it an autobiographical relevance to Pater's own revised philosophy, while allowing at the same time for an essential consistency with the early aestheticism.

> But after a while the glamour of youth dies away, and a man begins to see that a system which has only the worship and pursuit of 'exquisite moments' to recommend as a rule of life, leaves three-fourths of life untouched. Mankind has never been content to spend itself on a worship

of 'moments', or in a pursuit of fugitive impressions as such. Rather, with a tenacious and pathetic faith, it has sought for continuity, for what lasts and binds and can be handed on from soul to soul. It has tried to fix and distil the essence of innumerable impressions in one great tradition – the ethical tradition – which is at once the product and the condition of human life. To live in the mere pursuit of sensations, however refined, is to live outside this tradition, so far as is possible, and therefore outside the broad stream of human history.[100]

And in order to demonstrate her disapproval of aestheticism pure, and her enthusiasm for the changed morality of the new book, she perhaps made more of Pater's modifications than was in fact justified.

Still, although the fundamental argument is really the same as that on which Mr Pater based a general view of life twelve years ago, the practical advance in position shown by the present book is considerable. . . . For, stripped of its poetical dress, the ethical argument of *Marius* is essentially utilitarian.[101]

Compared with Mrs Ward's reading, Nash, committed to the 'agreeable', the 'happy moments of our consciousness – the multiplication of those moments' (Ch. 2), expounds a restricted version of Pater, or one that Pater had himself partially superseded. The question of the actively *moral*, which after *Marius* became one of Pater's main preoccupations, is only touched upon in the conversation with Nick near Notre-Dame. And the progression from response to life to criticism of art, fruitful for Vernon Lee and Oscar Wilde for example, is obscured by Nash's virtual disappearance from the scene when Nick and Miriam begin to produce.

Much of Wilde's critical theory derives from Pater, although the ideas have often been vulgarized or systematized, and of course Nash does make remarks that are echoed in Wilde. The difference is that Wilde, in his most didactic pieces, is more concerned with art and the possible responses to it than with experience, while Nash is rarely allowed to become an effective critic.

Wilde wrote of Thomas Wainewright:

As an art critic he concerned himself primarily with the complex impressions produced by a work of art, and certainly the first step in aesthetic criticism is to realize one's own impressions.[102]

The fullest exposition of this idea is to be found in his 'The True Function and Value of Criticism'[103] – published, we cannot forget, one year after the serial appearance of *The Tragic Muse* – where the first responsibility of the critic is defined as the presentation of his own 'impressions' of the work of art. Or it can be put this way: criticism is to art as treatment is to subject. Criticism is 'the purest form of personal impression', and the sole aim of the critic is 'to chronicle his own impressions'.

Critic and artist share a special 'nature' or 'temperament', and 'a new and intense personality'. This temperament, according to Wilde, flourishes through a full and independent contemplation. Hence the denigration of action:

> It is to do nothing that the elect exist. Action is limited and relative. Unlimited and absolute is the vision of him who sits at ease and watches, who walks in loneliness and dreams. . . . We are never less free than when we try to act.

If 'the aim of art is simply to create a mood' then 'each mode of criticism is, in its highest development, simply a mood, and we are never more true to ourselves than when we are inconsistent'. The aesthetic critic, 'constant only to the principle of beauty', will 'ever be looking for fresh impressions'. Hence the primary requisite for the critic is 'a temperament exquisitely susceptible to beauty, and the various impressions that beauty gives us'.

'Temperament' and 'nature' are also important words in *The Tragic Muse*, but above all when they relate to practice. Both Nash and Wilde (through his spokesman Gilbert) have it in common that they value the *moment of being* (for Wilde the *moment of becoming*) above all else. But Nash's loathing of publicity, his fanatically pursued privacy and refusal to practise any art, distinguish him crucially from Wilde – although some superficial resemblances are undeniably present, and they share a common source in Pater. Mr Powers has claimed that Nash's emphasis on *being* relates to ultimate identity, in Nick's case as an artist; the question remains whether in *The Tragic Muse* that emphasis is shown to be related to, or even compatible with, an artist's practice.

James had apprehended a special vocabulary pertaining to a

doctrine, and he re-created it for his character: a vocabulary moulded by Pater himself from a complex range of sources and strands of ideas, and one that he had drawn on previously. There is an involvement here, a shared context that has never been adequately described, but which would surely account for so many echoes and resonances.

The significance of Nash cannot be separated from the articulation of the whole novel. He is neither the inviolate symbol of art that Mr Powers has suggested, nor Mr Cargill's satiric portrait. His 'system', composed as a synthetic topical generalization, and his 'formulas' play an important part in the counterpoint structure. Nash is a construction of ideas and associations, and his vocabulary highly individual but not unique to him, even within *The Tragic Muse* itself.

3 *Conclusion: the conditions of success*

Before commencing his second portrait of Miriam, Nick spends part of an afternoon wandering in the National Gallery. It's a moment, we are told, of reaction to having made his great decision, and may be a necessary if transient indulgence. That suggestion is to act as an important qualification, for the questions that Nick asks himself during the course of the afternoon are large and, finally, in the terms of this novel, unmanageable.

> What had happened to him, as he passed on this occasion from Titian to Rubens and from Gainsborough to Rembrandt, was that he found himself calling the whole art literally into question. What was it after all, at the best, and why had people given it so high a place? Its weakness, its narrowness appeared to him; tacitly blaspheming he looked at several world-famous performances with a lustreless eye. That is he blasphemed if it were blasphemy to say to himself that, with all respect, they were a poor business, only well enough in their small way. The force that produced them was not one of the greatest forces in human affairs; their place was inferior and their connection with the life of man casual and slight. They represented so inadequately the idea, and it was the idea that won the race, that in the long run came in first. He had incontestably been in much closer relation to the idea a few months before than he was today; it made up a great deal for the bad side of politics that they were after all a clumsy system for applying and propagating the idea. (Ch. 42)

We have drawn attention already to the frequency and obvious centrality and equally obvious equivocation of the novelist's use of the word 'idea', and now, in this passage, the word slips with very deceptive ease from one world to the other. It seems to Nick that, against the immense but immediate aspirations of the world of political *action*, the Titians and the Rubens, the Gainsboroughs and the Rembrandts, have a 'connexion with the life of man' that seems 'casual and slight'. But if the paintings represent 'so inadequately the idea', then, on the other hand, 'political as Julia was, he had not conferred with her much about the idea'. Politics, because action, are inescapably a verbal business of manipulation and strategy, of concession and dissimulation, and all that inevitably obscures or replaces the prime honest motive. And, on this one afternoon, Nick can afford to consider the artist's career as a strict parallel to that of the politician and, with self-conscious blasphemy, consider for a moment the products of the artist as in some way inferior. The eternity of a Titian is won, or triumphantly survives, only despite or through the same demands of public audience or world that the politician may recognize or, at his worst, welcome; and the force that produced the Titian is, Nick concludes, 'not one of the greatest forces in human affairs'. But the risk that Nick and the novelist take by rehearsing these speculations again, is slight. His resolve comes very promptly – 'To do the most when there would be the least to be got by it was to be most in the true spirit of production.' The solution, to attempt to 'do' Miriam again, is immediate. When Nick returns later to the National Gallery it is with an absolute conviction in the value of eternal works of art.

For Miriam the choice offered her by Peter is, as she knows and exploits, even less real. It is unnecessarily obvious to stress Miriam's enigmatic intelligence, unless it is to be shown as in itself part of the novelist's own defensive game; but when Peter proposes the role of ambassador's wife, with its attendant glories, her refusal, expressed with 'extraordinary mildness' and 'a weary tolerance that was noble in its effect' must, necessarily, fail to convince:

> It isn't to my glories that I cling; it's simply to my idea, even if it's destined to sink me into obscurity. I like it better than anything else – a thousand times better (I'm sorry to have put it in such a way) than tossing up my head as the fine lady of a little coterie. (Ch. 46)

The differences between diplomatic coterie and theatre audience may not be great; nor should we believe too readily that Miriam is seriously contemplating obscurity. By assuming that her 'idea' can be separated from her 'glories', she is skilfully suggesting that Peter is philistine, which he is not, and swiftly capitalizes:

> You say today that you hate the theatre; and do you know what has made you do it? The fact that it has too large a place in your mind to let you repudiate it and throw it over with a good conscience. It has a deep fascination for you, and yet you're not strong enough to make the concession of taking up with it publicly, in my person. You're ashamed of yourself for that, as all your constant high claims for it are on record; so you blaspheme against it, to try and cover your retreat and your treachery and straighten out your personal situation.   (Ch. 46)

Then she cruelly modifies that condemnation into flattery, by describing him as 'the best judge, the best critic, the best observer, the best *believer*, that I've ever come across'.

Miriam's failure to discriminate between artist and critic allows her to make the assumption that they are called upon to make similar sacrifices, that they lead similar lives, do the same thing. Like Nick, Miriam knows that she has to continue to practise and animate her idea, although the price that she pays in doing this is too easily admitted. Peter's protestations against the demands of the public and self-exposure are discounted, he is 'flung back against a fifth-rate world' and reduced to a dumb and helpless rage.

In the case of Nick's visit to the National Gallery, the novelist carefully informs us that his mood is temporary; so by implication are his speculations. In the case of the encounter between Peter and Miriam we are shown not a relatively simple incomprehension in the manner of the early parts of the novel, but a conversation between people who may well understand each other but, having through the course of the action consolidated their positions, will not or cannot afford to admit that they do. At no time does the novelist interfere with their assumptions other than to suggest – and this can be damning, in the case of the artists – that their talent has yet to be established and their convictions proven. The question has become, do these people fully understand what they say? – a form of irony that has been sharpened since the beginning of the story. In the language of the novel, the question might be phrased as this: do they understand their relationship to their own 'idea' now that 'idea' seems to have become their way of life and what they are?

Finally only Nick and Miriam do or can understand each other, and what they claim to have in common is a recognition of their essential solitude. But even the solitude of the artist can be treated ironically, as when Nash speaks of Miriam: '. . . it will be a merry life. Yet with its tragic passages, its distracted or its pathetic hours' (Ch. 36). Or when Nick remarks to Biddy, '. . . you cared for life, you cared for society, and you have chosen the path of solitude and concentration' (Ch. 43).

The final issues seem to be solitude and its opposite, which is success, but the novel ends with the present dubitative tense and questions about the artist's success in the future. And success is also a term which may be applied to Peter and certainly relates to Julia, Mr Carteret, Lady Agnes and their world, and even to Mrs Rooth. Money has always been basic to these, and now it would seem to be so for Miriam and Nick. We do not know how free Nick is. He may be committed to 'the real thing', but as to his future we leave him suspended with a question mark. Despite the unquestioning triviality of the political world represented by Mr Carteret that he has rejected, that world had been allowed its own possibilities, and the life of art also seems to require an alliance with society and money. And that of course is how Nash has always seen it.

We end with the unresolved issue of the conditions of success, although we have learnt, from Carré and others, that success must be connected with tradition and work. These imply an attitude to experience (in 'The Art of Fiction' James had enjoined the novice novelist to be 'someone on whom nothing is lost')[104] which presupposes the nature of the arts of representation and therefore relates to 'the real thing'. But 'the real thing' must be compared to, and in the novel continually reflects back upon, that other reality of success and money. These are, with obvious intimacy, part of the world of Dashwood. Miriam has, until her Juliet, added only three or four parts to her repertoire, and it is very clear how much she still needs Dashwood and the techniques of publicity. In the same way, when

Nick becomes involved with bishops and fashionable commissions and house-parties, it is very useful for him to have Julia, who is in her turn a kind of Dashwood. She seems to have become an impresario where once she was a political agent; her role and usefulness have hardly altered, because even as a model she ensures Nick's success. Although solitude and study and tradition are opposed to these conditions, the novel seems to suggest that in fact the terms of these lives are not going to change. The ambiguous prophecies suggest that neither Nick nor Miriam will in the end sacrifice anything, and that their schemes and lives will still be tied to the timetables of London and society. The question becomes, how can a juncture between art and the world be effected? And there would seem to be no acceptable solution to the dichotomy.

In this society it is proposed that a man in his *métier* (which is his way of making his fortune) is subject to judgement, not in terms of the effort involved but of his success: which is a social cohesion and depends on the relationship with audience. Nash can deny this but politician, actress or portrait-painter cannot – although the latter have a special relationship to truth which is denied to the former. Their *métiers* require them to convince or move their audiences, and therefore involve criticism which may become publicity. No disjunction is allowed between *métier* and success, effort and result, in a society where each person is both possessor and possessed. The artist is possessed by his nature, by how he exploits his experience, and he is in turn possessed by his audience. The politician also depends on possession (money and property), without which he cannot function ('do' or 'be'); and in this dependence he is also dependent on his audience.

For James, the theme of possession had always been crucial, and the possessed are invariably those with a special capacity for experience. Characters are defined and differentiated by an epistemological or perceptual vocabulary, by the ways in which they view or experience the world. *The Tragic Muse* has as its central concern the relation of art to experience and the processes by which the one is translated into the other, and what the artist requires to bring this about – 'ideas', 'impressions', and 'feelings'. These are to do with the 'artistic temperament', and presume a special mode of perception and potential, which James had dealt with previously. *Roderick Hudson* presents a simpler conception of the alienated artist, one firmly placed in a romantic tradition, although even there it is Roderick's ability to respond to experience that makes him, initially, so attractive to Rowland Mallet:

> The vivacity of his perceptions, the audacity of his imagination, the picturesqueness of his phrase when he was pleased – and even more when he was displeased – his abounding good humour, his candour, his unclouded frankness, his unfailing impulse to share every emotion and impression with his friend. . . .[105]

When they go to Italy the shared experience engenders different states of mind in the two men. For Rowland his impressions form a not entirely satisfactory end in themselves:

> . . . a sort of oppressive reconciliation to the present, the actual, the sensuous – to life on the terms that there offered themselves.[106]

For Roderick experience, of art as of life, must continually be referred back to the self, and what he can make of what he sees.

> I have seen enough for the present; I have reached the top of the hill. I have an indigestion of impressions; I must work them off before I go in for any more. I don't want to look at any more of other people's works for a month – not even at Nature's own. I want to look at Roderick Hudson's.[107]

As Rowland takes him up, 'watches' him, so Roderick, his speculation or 'experiment', replaces or frustrates his need to express himself. The artist can claim the whole of life, including a passion for a Princess, as material for *his* 'experimentation', for that is his 'freedom'; against the freedom works the essentially spasmodic processes of his vision.

> I haven't an idea. I think of subjects, but they remain near lifeless names. They are mere words – they are not images. What am I to do ?[108]

Given his 'artistic temperament', the essential salubrity of genius, the indulgence of emotion and experience without their translation into art, and the loss of his ideas, Roderick's bankruptcy is inevitable. And for Rowland the death of the artist means that 'his occupation was gone'.[109]

The potential for experience is what brings together many of the characters in James's fictions who are not artists of a conventional sort. In the little-known novel *Confidence* two young Americans in Europe are contrasted in terms of their attitudes to experience. Gordon Wright is practical, forthright with 'the scientific mind', and he is devoted to scientific experiment. His friend, Bernard Longueville, practises experiments of a different kind, experiments with life and with people, whom he observes and about whom he speculates. Like Nash, Bernard travels continually and cannot be fixed: he 'drops down from the moon'. Like Nash too he resists involvement:

> The charm of life is extreme. I am unacquainted with odious necessities. I object to nothing.[110]

He enjoys his intelligence for its own sake and likes to feel it at play, and cultivates impressions:

> He had moments of keen enjoyment; he laid up a great store of impressions and even a considerable sum of knowledge.[111]

This life becomes untenable only when Bernard admits to having fallen in love with the girl desired by his friend and perhaps, by having tested or 'experimented' with her feelings, betrayed him.

We can observe similar preoccupations in more major novels. Isabel Archer, Hyacinth Robinson (again one 'upon whom nothing is lost')[112] and Verena Tarrant are all examples of a rare potential for experience admired and pursued by those eager to possess them. But if we compare those various and complex instances with *The Tragic Muse* it is to realize that the artist proper is special in terms of what he does, because he alone possesses or exploits his *own* experience. It is precisely in this way that the arts create and represent. And even if in *The Tragic Muse* the artists do have their hard-won triumphs, permits of tradition, work, and their relation to the world, which are eloquently praised, still the real justification for this eloquence remains elusive. Is it solitude, sacrifice, or freedom? In terms of relationships, only Nash seems to be free, he doesn't possess people or use his experience: but is his freedom a valued thing?

Nash's mode of living is also one of possession; finally even he is not exempt, for the condition of his apparent freedom is that he should literally *not be there*. He cannot hold a real, lasting connexion with people. Although it is he who preaches that one should be present always, he is condemned precisely not to be able to endure to be present when life is at its most intense, which is when Nick is working, or doing – which is, in this novel's terms, being. Nash is himself as much possessed by his own formulas, or his little system, as are Julia or Mr Carteret by theirs. He needs something to look at, a spectacle and an audience; he denies that relationship yet he depends on it. We hear of him, although we do not see him, in solitude; but he cannot endure being an object (a portrait) standing, by himself, in a certain relationship to an observer; that is, being fixed as an object which is a representation of some sort of truth:

> He was so accustomed to living upon irony and the interpretation of things that it was strange to him to be himself interpreted, and (as a gentleman who sits for his portrait is always liable to be) interpreted ironically. From being outside of the universe he was suddenly brought into it, and from the position of a free commentator and critic, a sort of amateurish editor of the whole affair, reduced to that of humble ingredient and contributor. (Ch. 49)

Therefore, like the Cheshire Cat, he simply ceases to be and becomes a 'ghost'. The moral must be that those relationships cannot be escaped. Life cannot be confused with art, nor the artist confused with the spectator; except through his appropriate art, which is that of the critic.

Nash and Peter have it in common that they are spectators, and critical spirits. This may be permitted, but as a *métier* it must be kept to, and interference is not allowed without cost. Peter, it is clear, cannot separate his interest in Miriam's possibilities as an artist from an infatuation with her personality. He attempts release in his misguided solution – she must opt out altogether – but that for Miriam is impossible and so he ends up, inevitably, with the acquiescent Biddy, who is no artist. Peter has been duped by representation but, paradoxically, in the end it is that that saves him: '. . . he felt somehow recalled to reality by the very perfection of the representation' (Ch. 51). Recalling to reality is certainly one of the things that art can do.

If Miriam is more real on the stage than off it, then that is a testimony to a general truth about art that James had struggled with in 'The Art of Fiction' and other theoretical explorations, and was to make fiction out of elsewhere. In *The Real Thing* (1892) a painter suspects the genteel couple who offer themselves as models:

> ... I didn't easily believe in them. After all they were amateurs, and the ruling passion of my life was the detestation of the amateur. Combined with this was another perversity – an innate preference for the represented subject over the real one: the defect of the real one was so apt to be a lack of representation. I liked things that appeared; then one was sure. Whether they *were* or not was a subordinate and almost always a profitless question.[113]

At its simplest, the irony of this little story depends on the couple's inability to represent their own gentility, and this they eventually recognize for themselves:

> They had bowed their heads in bewilderment to the perverse and cruel law in virtue of which the real thing could be so much less precious than the unreal.[114]

Endowed with the ability to represent, Miriam and Nick are nevertheless in a trap, for what they represent depends absolutely upon the conditions of their experience. This accounts for the particular closed ironies of the novel, although it is a trap in which all James's artists are caught. In the short stories about artists written a little earlier, those ironies had already taken on a much more sinister tone. In *The Author of Beltraffio* (1884) and *The Lesson of the Master* (1888) the presence of an involved spectator who discovers and begins to understand truths about the artistic life imparts a sombre and serious tone which *The Tragic Muse*, with its informed and comprehensive mode of narration and reference, does not have. More than that, in the stories the practice of the art of literature is treated with a precise reverence that is largely absent from the treatments of painting and the theatre in the novel.

There is certainly no tragedy in *The Tragic Muse*, but what there is is difficult to define: irony and comedy. The deeper notes that we may feel are needed to validate the whole affair cannot in the end be allowed, and the final acknowledgement of the conditions of success excludes any consideration of the quality of art produced, or even of the love between Nick and Julia, or Peter and Biddy.

We have claimed that the method of the novel is syncretic, that it uses parabolic commentary (a verbal art) and verbal misunderstanding, which is a form of wit. Together with comparisons and identifications, these are part of an ironic strategy which sets up an apparent objectivity or distancing. Irony *is* false, it's a mask to conceal the closest involvement, a way of offering a situation and its interpretation (easy or difficult) as though it does not in the least concern oneself; and it was that enclosing irony that permitted *The Tragic Muse* to be for the novelist simultaneously both 'topical' and acutely personal.

Notes

1. All quotations are taken from the Hart-Davis edition, London, 1948. The references in 'A holiday in Paris' are contained within chapters 1–12.
2. *The Art of the Novel*, edited by R. P. Blackmur, New York, 1948, pp. 79–80.
3. Oscar Cargill, *The Novels of Henry James*, New York, 1961, pp. 182–96; Leon Edel, *Henry James: The Middle Years, 1884–94*, London, 1963, p. 192.
4. Edel, *The Middle Years*, p. 192.
5. MS letter: Houghton Library, Harvard University, Am 14 1429.
6. *Notebooks*, pp. 63–4.
7. Letter to Mrs Humphry Ward, 19 December 1884: Clifton Waller Barrett Library, University of Virginia.
8. Mary Anderson, *A Few Memories*, London, 1896, pp. 167–8.
9. George Bernard Shaw, *Our Theatres in the Nineties*, London, 1948, vol. 2, p. 88.
10. J. M. Farrar, *Mary Anderson. The story of her life and professional career*, London, 1884.
11. 3 September 1883.
12. Ibid.
13. Ibid.
14. 'Owen Meredith', 'Miss Anderson's Juliet', *Nineteenth Century*, December 1884, p. 899.
15. Mrs Humphry Ward, *Miss Bretherton*, London, 1885, preface, p. x.
16. Ibid., pp. xiii–xix.
17. Julia Wedgwood, 'Fiction', *Contemporary Review*, May 1855, p. 751.
18. Ward, *Miss Bretherton*, p. 242.
19. Ibid., p. 190.
20. Ibid., p. 237.

21. Ibid., p. 203.

22. Mrs Humphry Ward, *A Writer's Recollections*, London, 1918, p. 193.

23. *The Theatre*, March 1884, p. 144.

24. Reprinted in Brander Matthews (ed.), *Papers on Acting III : On the Stage*, Dramatic Museum of Columbia University, 1926.

25. 'Diderot and the Art of Acting', *Westminster Review*, January 1887.

26. All these articles were reprinted in Matthews (ed.), *Papers on Acting II : The Art of Acting*.

27. Ward, *A Writer's Recollections*, p. 193.

28. Ward, *Miss Bretherton*, p. 145.

29. *The Theatre*, March 1884, p. 119.

30. Ward, *Miss Bretherton*, p. 203.

31. Samuel Johnson, 'Preface to Shakespeare', 1765, reprinted in the *Yale Edition of the Works of Samuel Johnson*, London, 1968, vol. 7, p. 78.

32. *La Revue d'Art Dramatique*, 1 and 15 January 1886.

33. Ibid., 1 January 1886, p. 8.

34. Ibid., p. 9.

35. Sarcey conventionally admits that vanity is the besetting sin of actors: 'La vanité du cabotin est aussi célèbre qu'elle est insupportable. Alphonse Daudet l'a marquée d'un trait inoubliable dans sa merveilleuse création de Delobelle' (15 January 1886, p. 70). Delobelle is the actor in Daudet's popular novel *Fromont Jeune et Risler Aîné* (1874) who, although unemployed and living off the hard-earned money of his devoted wife and lame daughter, still possesses the 'aveuglement immense', and 'étrange nature' – that phrase recurs – of the 'cabotin'. So much so that, despite his genuine grief, his daughter's funeral becomes, for him and for his actor friends, another performance: 'tous maniérés et tous sincères'. He is referred to by Oscar Wilde in 'The Decay of Lying' (*Nineteenth Century*, January 1889, p. 39), and twice by James himself: first as 'the best figure in the book ... the old humbugging tragedian Delobelle – a type of which we have glimpses elsewhere' ('Alphonse Daudet', *Atlantic Monthly*, June 1882, reprinted in *Literary Reviews and Essays*, edited by A. Mordell, New York, 1957, p. 186), and then in an essay first published in *Century* (1883), where he comments that '. . . the blooming and sonorous Delobelle, ferociously selfish and fantastically vain, under the genial forms of melodrama, is a beautiful representation of a vulgarly factitious nature' (*Partial Portraits*, 1888, p. 224).

An English translation of *Fromont Jeune* was published in 1880.

36. 1 January 1886, p. 12.

37. William Archer, *Masks or Faces?*, London, 1888, p. 4.

38. Ibid., p. 2.

39. Ibid., p. 7.

40. Ibid., p. 77.

41. Ibid., pp. 101–2.
42. *Essays in London*, 1893, p. 108.
43. F. A. Kemble, *Notes on Some of Shakespeare's Plays*, London, 1882, p. 3.
44. Ibid., p. 5.
45. Ibid., p. 11.
46. Ibid., p. 13.
47. Mrs Arthur Kennard, 'Rachel', *Nineteenth Century*, December 1883, p. 1030.
48. *The Art of the Novel*, p. 94.
49. Matthew Arnold, 'The French Play in London', *Nineteenth Century*, August 1879.
50. *Notebooks*, pp. 38–9.
51. Arnold, op. cit., p. 240.
52. Ibid.
53. Ibid., p. 243.
54. *The Theatre*, August 1879, p. 41.
55. *The Theatre*, September 1879, p. 63.
56. Arnold, op. cit., p. 243.
57. Henry James, 'The *Comédie Française* in London', *The Nation*, 31 July 1890, reprinted in A. Wade (ed.), *The Scenic Art*, London, 1949, pp. 121–2.
58. Ibid., p. 121.
59. Arnold, op. cit., p. 229.
60. 'The London Theatres', *The Nation*, 12 June 1879, reprinted in Wade, op. cit., p. 119.
61. Ibid., p. 120.
62. James, 'The *Comédie Française*', p. 128.
63. Letter to Mrs Humphry Ward, 21 February 1884: Clifton Waller Barrett Library.
64. Edel, *The Middle Years*, p. 39.
65. 'Taine's Notes on England', *The Nation*, 25 January 1872, reprinted in *Literary Reviews*, p. 56.
66. 'Matthew Arnold's Essays', *North American Review*, July 1865, reprinted in Henry James, *Views and Reviews*, Boston, 1908, p. 94.
67. 'Matthew Arnold', *English Illustrated Magazine*, January 1884, reprinted in *Literary Reviews*, p. 344.
68. Ward, *A Writer's Recollections*, p. 196.
69. 'The Art of Fiction', *Longman's Magazine*, September 1884, p. 509.
70. Ibid., p. 510.
71. Ibid., p. 516.
72. Oscar Wilde, 'Pen, Pencil and Poison: A Study', *Fortnightly Review*, January 1889, p. 48.
73. Oscar Wilde, 'The True Function and Value of Criticism', *Nineteenth Century*, September 1890, p. 454.

74. Oscar Wilde, 'Shakespeare and Stage Costume', *Nineteenth Century*, May 1885, p. 807.
75. 'After the Play', *New Review*, June 1889, reprinted in Wade, op. cit.
76. 29 April 1892.
77. January 1883, p. 79.
78. *Diary of an Art Student*, London, 1939, p. 8.
79. 'John Singer Sargent', *Harper's Magazine*, October 1887, pp. 684–6.
80. Ibid., p. 691.
81. Ibid., p. 689.
82. Oscar Cargill, 'Mr James's Aesthetic Mr Nash', *Nineteenth Century Fiction*, xii, December 1957, pp. 177–87; 'Gabriel Nash – Somewhat less than Angel', *Nineteenth Century Fiction*, xiii, December 1959, pp. 231–9; *Novels of Henry James*, pp. 182–202.
    Lyall Powers, 'James's *The Tragic Muse* – Ave atque Vale', *PMLA*, lxxiii, June 1958, pp. 270–3; 'Mr James's Aesthetic Mr Nash – Again', *Nineteenth Century Fiction*, xiii, March 1959, pp. 341–9.
83. *Universal Review*, September 1888.
84. The most important group of articles appeared in 1885: F. C. Burnand, 'Behind the Scenes', *Fortnightly Review*, January 1885; Hamilton Aidé, 'An Actor's Calling', *Nineteenth Century*, March 1885; E. Lyn Linton, 'The Stage as a Profession for Women I', *National Review*, March 1885; and John Coleman, 'The Social Status of the Actor II', *National Review*, March 1885.
85. *Fortnightly Review*, November 1889.
86. 'Curiosités esthétiques, XVI IX', *Œuvres*, Bibliothèque de la Pleiade, p. 908.
87. As late as 1914 he described an early American mentor, John La Farge, from whom he gained 'the dawning perception that the arts were after all essentially one', as a *raffiné* (*Notes of a Son and Brother*, London, 1914, p. 91). Much earlier, in a review of Prosper Mérimée's letters, he had written: 'The author tells her early in the book that she has "a nature so *raffinée*" – something more than our "refined" – "as to be for him the summing up of a civilization" ' (*French Poets and Novelists*, New York, 1964 ed., p. 394). Gordon Wright in *Confidence* (1880) is chided by his friend Bernard Longueville for refusing to admit his fascination with a beautiful woman: 'If you don't want to be fascinated, what is one to say to you? "Object to being fascinated!" There's a man easy to satisfy! *Raffiné, va!*' (vol. 1, p. 128).
88. 'The Goncourts', *Galaxy Magazine*, February 1876, reprinted in *Literary Reviews*, p. 158.
89. Ibid., p. 162.
90. Edmond and Jules de Goncourt, *Théâtre*, Paris, 1879, preface, p. xviii.
91. 'Nos Auteurs Dramatiques', in H. Mitterand (ed.), *Œuvres Complètes*, Paris, 1966, vol. 11, p. 784.
92. Ibid., pp. 621–5.
93. Barbey d'Aurevilly, *Théâtre Contemporain 1870–83*, Paris, 1892, p. 119.

94. *Le Temps*, 1 December 1879.
95. *Complete Tales of Henry James*, edited by Leon Edel, London, 1962, vol. 4, p. 439.
96. Ibid., p. 441. In 1873 James had written to his brother: 'I wanted to review Pater's *Studies* but it treats of things I know nothing about' (Letter to William James, 31 May 1873: Houghton Library, Am 1094).
97. *Euphorion*, London, 1884, vol. 1, p. 10.
98. *Miss Brown*, London, 1884, vol. 2, pp. 226–7.
99. June 1885, p. 132.
100. Ibid., pp. 135–6.
101. Ibid., pp. 136–7.
102. Wilde, 'Pen, Pencil and Poison', p. 44.
103. *Nineteenth Century*, July and September 1890.
104. James, 'The Art of Fiction', p. 510.
105. *Roderick Hudson*, 1875, p. 83.
106. Ibid., p. 155. In the second (1880) edition, this reads: '. . . a sort of relaxed acceptance of the present, the actual – of life on the terms of the moment' (p. 115).
107. Ibid., p. 78.
108. Ibid., p. 135.
109. Ibid., p. 481.
110. James, *Confidence*, p. 102.
111. Ibid., p. 250.
112. *The Princess Casamassima*, 1886 (first one-volume edition), p. 165.
113. *Complete Tales of Henry James*, vol. 8, pp. 236–7.
114. Ibid., p. 258.

5

What Maisie Knew
portrait of the artist as a young girl

JULIET MITCHELL

> She wore glasses which, in humble reference to a divergent obliquity of
> vision, she called her straighteners. . . . (Ch. 4)
>
> Mrs Wix gave a sidelong look. She still had room for wonder at what
> Maisie knew. (Ch. 31)

Cross-eyed Mrs Wix looking sideways through her corrective glasses
remains – and surely the odds are against her – one of the sightless
amongst the seeing. But for the Jamesian reader, as for the Jamesian
heroine, participation in a James novel is a process of initiation into
vision. In his *Notebooks*, in his Preface and in the novel, James tells
us that the young child Maisie saw more than she understood. For
the mature Maisie, and in this precisely does her maturity consist,
seeing *is* knowing, vision and knowledge are one. What Maisie knows
is what we know, which is what the narrator knows, which is what
James knows; and that may be many things from many different
angles, but most clearly it is the knowledge that no one else in the
novel knows as much as we know about them and us.

> I am not sure that Maisie had not even a dim discernment of the queer
> law of her own life that made her educate to that sort of proficiency
> those elders with whom she was concerned. She promoted as it were,
> their development; nothing could have been more marked, for instance,
> than her success in promoting Mrs Beale's. She judged that if her whole
> history, for Mrs Wix, had been the successive stages of her knowledge,
> so the very climax of the concatenation would, in the same view, be the
> stage at which the knowledge should overflow. As she was condemned
> to know more and more, how could it logically stop before she should

know Most? It came to her in fact as they sat there on the sands that she was distinctly on the road to know Everything. . . . She looked at the pink sky with a placid foreboding that soon she should have learnt All. (Ch. 26)

The content of knowledge is important but so is the stance of the knower. The mature Maisie, of course, shows immaculate taste:

'Sure, you mean, that she'll bolt?'
Maisie knew all about bolting, but, decidedly, she *was* older, and there was something in her that could wince at the way her father made the ugly word – ugly enough at best – sound flat and low. (Ch. 19)

At the end of the novel, Maisie has certainly lost her innocence and her ignorance, but her 'knowledge' is not corrupt. To suggest, as a number of critics have done, that her final request to Sir Claude that they should leave and live together and alone is a sexual proposition, is as absurd as to suggest that James himself could have been guilty of such prostitution. Or rather, if you believe one, you have to believe the other. Maisie has learnt discretion, and in doing so she has become a discrete, an autonomous person. Like James and the required reader, having failed in participation she has gained the autonomy of the observer. But in this novel James offers us two 'observers', two viewpoints – his 'centre of consciousness', Maisie, and the governess Mrs Wix. Two views of the world: the straight and the crooked: 'Make my point of view, my *line*, the consciousness, the *dim*, scared, wondering, clinging perception of the child.'[1] 'Don't I best see the whole thing reflected in the talk, the confidences, the intercourse of Mrs Wix? . . . [she] thus serves as a sort of a *dim*, crooked little reflector of the conditions. . . .'[2] The corneal mist fades from the eyes of the growing child; the aged governess bursts through her distorting spectacles and earns the right to her cross-eyed vision: 'The straighteners . . . seemed to crack with the explosion of their wearer's honesty' (Ch. 23). Clarity, then a new dimness, the dimness of distance, can be acquired.

From reflection to reflection: the process of James's art, the history of his heroine. The pool of the self into which one gazes first to see others reflected there, then to see oneself and the others reflected, then to see that the pool is oneself: time for the thought that is no longer visual but visionary. Reflection. 'I have ever, in general, found it difficult to write of places under too immediate an impression ... the impression that prevents standing off and allows neither space nor time for perspective. The image has had for the most part to be *dim* if the reflection was to be, as is proper for a reflection, both sharp and quiet.'[3]

The mirror can be seen only as the reflection within it, or it can be seen as a mirror. Or it can be a pane of glass, looked through from either side, but the side of the viewer always dimly reflected in the glass that is being looked through. Or one can see the frame of the glass through which one is looking: the edge of the picture; the proscenium arch. In his theoretical writing James juxtaposes the pictorial and the dramatic technique: the picture and the scene. In *What Maisie Knew* they merge because both are only aspects of the dominant theme of playing with reflections. The novel is not a drama nor a painting but it is, in an important sense, a shadow-puppet show or, despite its pre-cinema imagery, a film. So is Maisie's view of her world:

> She was taken into the confidence of passions on which she fixed the stare she might have had for images bounding across the wall in the slide of a magic lantern. Her little world was phantasmagoric – strange shadows dancing on a sheet. It was as if the whole performance had been given for her – a mite of a half-scared infant in a great *dim* theatre. (Ch. 1: my italics)

In a theatre one acts plays. Children play-act, play games. Maisie and Mrs Wix don't understand children's games: 'The games were, as [Sir Claude] said, to while away the evening hour; and the evening hour indeed often passed in futile attempts on Mrs Wix's part to master what "it said" on the papers. When he asked the pair how they liked the games they always replied, "Oh immensely!" but they had earnest discussions as to whether they hadn't better appeal to him frankly for aid to understand them' (Ch. 9). But there isn't one adult in the novel whose main activity is not described as a game: 'I know your game' (Ch. 15); 'It was a game like another' (Ch. 7); 'It's her ladyship's game' (Ch. 11); 'It's a game' (Ch. 27); 'I can't make out ... what game she was playing' (Ch. 23). Maisie, in truth, is the instrument, the victim, the ball in these games. James's perception of her growing perception of it is brilliantly rendered; the balance between her metaphor and the 'facts'.

> So the sharpened sense of spectatorship as the child's main support, the long habit, from the first, of seeing herself in discussion and finding in the fury of it – she had had a glimpse of the game of football – a sort of compensation for the doom of a peculiar passivity.   (Ch. 12)

> In the course of psychotherapy with this girl, I discovered she was absorbed in a reverie of a perpetual game of tennis. Mixed doubles. Centre Court. Wimbledon. The crowd, the court, the net, the players and the ball, back and forth, back and forth, back and forth. She was all these elements but particularly, at the heart of it all, she was the ball. This ball was served, smashed, volleyed, lobbed, sometimes hit right out of court. . . .
>
> Now, when one discovered from collateral evidence the nature of her family system, it was found that this reverie was a rather accurate account, from her point of view, of her experience of the family. . . .
>
> The family set-up, under one roof, consisted of her father and mother, mother's father and father's mother – mixed doubles. They were in fact ranged against each other, father and his mother against mother and her father. She was the ball in their game, to give one instance of the accuracy of this metaphor. . . .[4]

Maisie, of course, remains sane. Indeed for James one of the chief fascinations of the original story was his notion that despite her appalling family circumstances, the child would be preserved, she would come through, triumphant. Perhaps her sanity is also achieved because, from the hints James gives us, the players at some level know they are playing a game: 'The evil they had the gift of thinking *or pretending to think* of each other they poured into her little gravely-gazing soul as into a boundless receptacle' (Ch. 2: my italics). These relationships then are the games people play.

Maisie starts as the six year old daughter of a divorced couple – Beale and Ida Farange. Her impecunious father is granted custody, but for financial considerations relinquishes her for half the time to her mother. At her mother's Maisie has a governess: Miss Overmore.

But Miss Overmore changes sides and goes over to her father. On her next visit to her mother, Maisie acquires a new governess, Mrs Wix. During her next visit to her father Maisie learns that Miss Overmore has married her father and become Mrs Beale. She also at the same time learns from the visiting Mrs Wix that her mother is to marry a handsome young aristocrat, Sir Claude. Sir Claude, her new step-father, comes to fetch Maisie from her father and meets the new Mrs Beale. Slowly, and over Maisie, they form a relationship with each other. Meanwhile Ida has a series of relationships, the main one 'on stage' being with 'The Captain' – at first taken by Sir Claude and Maisie for 'The Count'. And Beale has a number of relationships, the only one 'on stage' being with 'The Countess'. Beale takes leave of Maisie, giving up his responsibility for his daughter, pretending to be going to America. Sir Claude takes Maisie to Folkestone. Ida takes leave of Maisie, giving up her daughter to Sir Claude, and pretends that she is going to South Africa. Meanwhile Mrs Wix, infatuated with Sir Claude and scandalized by his relationship with Mrs Beale, tries to save him (and Maisie) from such an alliance. Mrs Beale tries to get Sir Claude for herself by asserting that Maisie, who is with him now in Boulogne, is her step-daughter, and her right, therefore. Maisie, after wishfully thinking that perhaps she, Mrs Wix, Sir Claude and Mrs Beale could all live together, understands the game and decides she wants to live only with Sir Claude. She asks first him and then Mrs Beale to give each other up. He is unable to and she refuses. Maisie 'loses' and goes off with Mrs Wix, back to England. This is the story: but what of the metaphorical structure?

> The litigation had seemed interminable and had in fact been com-plicated; but by the decision on the appeal the judgement of the divorce-court was confirmed as to the assignment of the child. The father . . . was . . . appointed to keep her. . . . He was unable to produce the money [he owed Ida] . . . so that after a squabble scarcely less public and scarcely more decent than the original shock of battle his only issue from his predicament was a compromise proposed by his legal advisers and finally accepted by hers.
>
> His debt was by this arrangement remitted to him and the little girl disposed of in a manner worthy of the judgement-seat of Solomon. She was divided in two and the portions tossed impartially to the disputants.

They would take her, in rotation, for six months at a time . . . the disunited couple had at last grounds for expecting a time of high activity. They girded their loins, they felt as if the quarrel had only begun. They felt indeed more married than ever, inasmuch as what marriage had mainly suggested to them was the unbroken opportunity to quarrel. There had been 'sides' before, and there were sides as much as ever; for the sider too the prospect opened out. . . . The many friends of the Faranges drew together to differ about them; contradiction grew young again over teacups and cigars.

Maisie's mother is a champion billiard-player. Three balls: two white and one red. Ida has Sir Claude; Beale, Miss Overmore: the two white balls. Maisie is the red ball which everyone uses. 'The player will not obtain an accurate aim until he has learned to keep his eye upon the object ball, and not upon the ball he is striking, especially at the actual moment of the stroke. This is a *sine quâ non* of good billiards.'[5] One can certainly see why Ida had 'so often beaten her ex-husband at billiards'. Out with the Captain in Hyde Park Ida meets her husband, Sir Claude, arm-in-arm with Maisie; she confronts Sir Claude head-on, but to hit him hard she offers a sort of side-play with Maisie: 'The next moment [Maisie] was on her mother's breast . . . only to be as suddenly ejected with a push and the brisk injunction: "Now go to the Captain!" . . . Maisie started, moved backward and, looking at Sir Claude, "Only for a moment," she signed to him in her bewilderment. But he was too angry to heed her – too angry with his wife' (Ch. 15). By the end of the novel Mrs Beale has acquired some of Ida's expertise, and Maisie finds herself once more the most important ball in the game, but not the centre of attention. Mrs Beale has mastered the art of pull and push: '. . . a push at last uncontestably maternal' (Ch. 28). 'She threw herself upon the child and, before Maisie could resist, had sunk with her upon the sofa, possessed of her, encircling her . . . [then] Maisie's back became aware of a push that vented resentment . . .' (Ch. 31). Used once more in the confrontation with Sir Claude, Maisie is again pushed aside, this time to go off with Mrs Wix as, long ago, she was pushed off to the Captain by Ida, walking with her lover in Hyde Park when she was supposed to be playing a billiards match in Brussels. In the beginning Maisie 'was divided in two'; in the end

'the child stood there again dropped and divided' (Ch. 31): the law
provides the rules of the game:

> She was still, as a result of so many parents, a daughter to somebody
> even after papa and mamma were to all intents dead. If her father's wife
> and her mother's husband, by the operation of a natural or, for all she
> knew, a legal rule, were in the shoes of their defunct partners, then Mrs
> Beale's partner was as exactly as defunct as Sir Claude's and her shoes
> the very pair to which in 'Farange *v.* Farange and Others', the divorce-
> court had given priority.   (Ch. 28)

Billiards is a sophisticated game from the point of view of the ball,
and James adds an ironic twist: the ball escapes, the winner is
defeated:

> 'Yes, my dear, I haven't given you up,' Sir Claude said to Mrs Beale at
> last, 'and if you'd like me to treat our friends here as solemn witnesses I
> don't mind giving you my word for it that I never will. There!' he
> dauntlessly exclaimed . . . Mrs Beale, *erect and alive in her defeat*, jerked
> her handsome face about. . . .   (Ch. 31: my italics)

The sets of people in the novel all use Maisie as their 'ball', but they
do this in different ways. Ida and Beale use her to toss from one to
another, first as a useful missile then as an undetonated bomb that
will hopefully go off in the other's court. Mrs Beale reifies her into a
precious ball of love, her 'love' for Maisie's fathers, first Beale then
Sir Claude: 'Mrs Beale fairly swooped upon her, and the effect of the
whole hour was to show the child how much, how quite formidably
indeed, after all, she was loved' (Ch. 14). For Mrs Wix she is an
extension of herself, to be held onto through thick and thin, a replace-
ment for the dead child, Clara Matilda, lost in a careless throw (she
was crushed beneath a hansom cab in the Edgware Road). Maisie is
caught up in a game which is confusingly the same game, and in
which the moves – constant acts of possession – seem the same and
yet are different. For they all *are* acts of possession. Even Ida and
Beale, though eventually they 'drop' her and plan to go off, never in
fact leave – they are just explicitly tired of the game: '[Beale's] was
the mildness of general indifference [to Ida]' (Ch. 19). Their 'death'
has the disturbing *presence* to it that also appertains to the 'reincar-

nated' (in Maisie) Clara Matilda, 'who was in heaven and yet, embarrassingly, also in Kensal Green, where they had been together to see her little huddled grave' (Ch. 4). James turns on its head the notion that divorce and adultery are in any sense 'desertion' of anyone. Perhaps Maisie's main deprivation as a child is that no one will leave her[6] and thus she has no conception of death until at the end when Sir Claude fails to turn up at the time expected, and James writes: 'She was yet to learn what it could be to recognize in some lapse of a sequence the proof of an extinction, and therefore remained unaware that this momentary pang was a foretaste of the experience of death' (Ch. 27).

Maisie is confused about the nature of her centrality. Is the ball the victim of the game? Or is it by its very presence the cause of the game? 'She puzzled out with imperfect signs, but with a prodigious spirit, that she had been a centre of hatred and a messenger of insult, and that everything was bad because she had been employed to make it so' (Ch. 2); '. . . the struggle she appeared to have come into the world to produce' (Ch. 7). Where does Maisie's responsibility lie? Certainly the presence of the ball *enables* the game to continue. It turns out that Maisie is not responsible where she seems to produce destruction but, alarmingly, she is responsible where apparently she introduces harmony. Her delighted refrain throughout the middle sections of the book is that she brought Mrs Beale and Sir Claude together. The irony is that harmony is chaos, and Maisie *does* divide her parents, not from each other but from their new spouses. This is the responsibility she must face, for creating for herself new parents against her old parents, not in their parental role but in their new marital roles:

> Your mother adored [Sir Claude] at first – it might have lasted. But he began too soon with Mrs Beale. As you say . . . you brought them together. (Ch. 29)

> 'Then my father [Sir Claude] and my mother [Mrs Beale] – !' But she had already faltered and Mrs Wix had already glared back: 'Ought to live together? Don't begin it *again*! She turned away with a groan, to reach the washing-stand, and Maisie could by this time recognize with a certain ease that that way verily madness did lie. (Ch. 27)

These new 'parents' she must separate if the game is to end, and sanity to triumph over madness. Failing, she leaves them to their own mad world,[7] to face themselves without her, without an excuse, without a daughter.

This is one way in which Maisie learns to decipher her role in the game, and to play it and lose it. There are others, less strategic.

A game seems to demand two or more in opposition. Opposition, polarities. The sides must be opposite each other in order to be sides. But of course they are both 'sides' and in this are disturbingly alike. At moments of intensity, Maisie instinctively glimpses that the divided world is unified. Try as they might to be opposite one another, the contestants are, after all, all contestants. Maisie has a child's knowledge of the congruity of the incongruous; she turns opposition into paradox and finally resolves it by her own *dialectical* act. The child's instincts are the metaphysical artist's formulations:

> . . . her stepmother, so changed – in the very manner of her mother. . . . (Ch. 14)

> The Captain wasn't a bit like [Sir Claude] . . . it finally made our young lady, to classify him further, say to herself that, of all the people in the world, he reminded her most insidiously of Mrs Wix. He had neither straighteners nor diadem . . . he was sunburnt and deep-voiced and smelt of cigars, yet he marvellously had more in common with her old governess than with her young stepfather. (Ch. 16)

> [Beale] gave a small laugh that in the oddest way in the world reminded her of the unique sounds she had heard emitted by Mrs Wix. (Ch. 19)

> The Countess stood smiling . . . Maisie felt herself reminded of another smile, which was not ugly . . . the kind light thrown, that day in the Park, from the clean fair face of the Captain. (Ch. 19)

and most importantly of all:

> After [Ida] had disappeared Maisie dropped upon the bench again and for some time, in the empty garden and the deeper dusk, sat and stared at the image her flight had still left standing. It had ceased to be her mother only, in the strangest way, that it might become her father, the

father of whose wish that she were dead the announcement still lingered in the air. It was a presence with vague edges – it continued to front her, to cover her. (Ch. 21)

While grasping the similiarity of the opposing sides, Maisie also tries to comprehend her position in their game. In a beautifully rendered episode, Maisie turns her doll Lisette into herself: 'Was she not herself convulsed by such innocence?' as Lisette shows. Of course she finds that she herself becomes her mother: 'she mimicked her mother's sharpness, but she was rather ashamed afterwards, though as to whether of the sharpness or of the mimicry was not quite clear' (Ch. 5). In this way Maisie learns that she does not want to become like the disputants: she is explicitly scared of being a 'low sneak', which is what her mother calls her father and her father calls her mother.

This method, by which Maisie alternates participants in the game and herself assumes other's roles and projects her own onto another, is a fundamental means of her 'knowledge' which is after all, as much as anything else, knowledge of the game. But it is, in comparison with another dimension of the struggle for knowledge, elementary. James's description of Maisie's initiation at the deepest level is profoundly bound up with his method for the whole novel, her progress so much its progress, her art his art.

Maisie's progress is from the 'unseen' centre to the 'seen' and 'seeing' observer. Her move is possible because she comes to see the game in which she is caught up. Her final knowledge is the knowledge of the expert's rejection of the game. But before she gets outside it she has to get fully into it. It is here, in tracing her development, that James's prime images achieve their deep association: the dramatic method of the novel, the drama of the story, the acting of a play, the playing of games, make-believe, the watching of the play, the looking at a picture, the spectacle, the magic-lantern, shadows, the person and his shadow, the inner and the outer self, reflections, the mirror, through the looking-glass, the meeting point of spectator and actor, playing the game, watching the play, writing the play. One could rearrange some of these points (some are parallels), but the chain is the chain of Maisie's life and the chain is the chain of the novel. Glass and shadows are the nodal point; the mirror-image – just look at the story – is crucial.

Maisie, though the centre, is also always outside. At the beginning of the novel this position is forced on her. She is the wrong side of the door:

> She had grown up among things as to which her foremost knowledge was that she was never to ask about them. . . . Everything had something behind it: life was like a long, long corridor with rows of closed doors.   (Ch. 5)

She can manœuvre her way in the dark passages: 'She had even had in the past a small smug conviction that in the domestic labyrinth she always kept the clue.' But gradually the doors change to glass, become windows, in fact. For safety's sake she still must feel she is a spectator:

> . . . the sharpened sense of spectatorship . . . gave her often an odd air of being present at her history in as separate a manner as if she could only get at experience by flattening her nose against a pane of glass.   (Ch. 12)

> She was to feel henceforth as if she were flattening her nose upon the hard window-pane of the sweetshop of knowledge.   (Ch. 15)

She becomes the window, the window as mirror: '[Ida] postured to her utmost before the last little triangle of cracked glass to which so many fractures had reduced the polished plate of filial superstition' (Ch. 21); then a two-way mirror, and the glass dissolves. What is the difference between the self and the reflection; between the self and others?

> Then she saw the straighteners all blurred with tears which after a little seemed to have sprung from her own eyes. There were tears in fact on both sides of the spectacles. . . .   (Ch. 26)

> [Maisie was] so conscious of being more frightened than she had ever been in her life that she seemed to see her whiteness as in glass. Then she knew that what she saw was Sir Claude's whiteness: he was as frightened as herself.   (Ch. 31)

Maisie has spent her childhood being a mirror for others, but the reactions she gets have a terrifying arbitrariness, particularly in the case of her mother. Ida does not reflect her child, which as a 'good' mother she would have done. This is a major deprivation and when it happens, 'the baby gets settled in to the idea that when he or she looks, what is seen is the mother's face. The mother's face is not then a mirror. So perception takes the place of apperception, takes the place of that which might have been the beginning of a significant exchange with the world, a two-way process in which self-enrichment alternates with the discovery of meaning in the world of seen things.'[8] Winnicott's terms certainly coincide with James's – Maisie is above all precociously perceptive – the mother was not the mirror she should have been. James claimed that Maisie 'by the play of her good faith' made her mother 'concrete, immense and awful';[9] and Maisie compares her mother to a wild elephant, says her movements are violent like the shutters that fall in front of a shop window. This is indeed the *perceived* mother, the mother as Other and eternally separate.

But Maisie's final relationship with Mrs Wix and with Sir Claude (the identical tears, the identical fears) reveals in its shared emotion a new 'symbiosis', a oneness characteristic of the new-born baby and its mother, from which an authentic identity can originate. Suddenly acquiring, at thirteen, the symbiotic security that should have been her birthright, Maisie can dispense with it and launch herself into an assertion of self, an understanding of others. Thought-reflection not echo-reflection:

> (Mrs Wix) 'I adore him. I adore him.' Maisie took it well in; so well that in a moment more she would have answered profoundly: 'So do I.' But before that moment passed something took place that brought other words to her lips; nothing more, very possibly, than the closer consciousness in her hand of the significance of Mrs Wix's. Their hands remained linked in unutterable sign of their union, and what Maisie at last said was simply and serenely: 'Oh I know!' (Ch. 26)

Only from the centre of the game can one get out; it is only unity that one can disrupt, only the heart of a person that one can leave. This finding of the self in others, this taking of the self from others, this is the heart of the matter:

> Now in truth she felt the coldness of her terror, and it seemed to her
> suddenly she knew, as she knew it about Sir Claude, what she was
> afraid of. She was afraid of herself.   (Ch. 30)

> She went about as sightlessly as if he had been leading her blindfold.
> If they were afraid of themselves it was themselves they would find at
> the inn.   (Ch. 31)

At last this watcher of men is sightless: in the moment of vision all is
invisible.

Most of the time even words like 'seeing' are used only 'synecdo-
chally' for total sensory and extra-sensory perception. Maisie is alive
to the entire kinesics of a person:

> [Beale] clasped her in his arms a moment and rubbed his beard against
> her cheek. Then she understood as well as if he had spoken it that what
> he wanted, hang it, was that she should let him off with all the honours.
> (Ch. 19)

> There were things Ida said that she perhaps didn't hear, and there were
> things she heard that Ida perhaps didn't say.   (Ch. 21)

Silence is the language of understanding. It is also a place of retreat
from the game, a game in which words are always hurled, a conversa-
tion-piece in which Maisie has a major part but few lines:

> Maisie felt the weight of the question; it kept her silent for a space
> during which she looked at Sir Claude. . . .
>   'Nothing,' she returned at last.
> He showed incredulity. 'Nothing?'
>   'Nothing,' Maisie repeated. . . .   (Ch. 30)

Maisie has as good a reason as Cordelia for her obstinate silence.
Silence is not only the medium in which understanding occurs, it is
its precondition – to wait and listen is as essential as to watch: 'She
would forget everything, she would repeat nothing. . . . She spoiled
their fun, but she practically added to her own. She saw more and
more; she saw too much' (Ch. 2). Maisie's technique of stupidity, her
refusal actively to participate, comfortably isolates her from the game:
'Her very silence became after this one of the largest elements of
Maisie's consciousness; it proved a warm and habitable air, into

which the child penetrated farther than she dared ever mention to her companions' (Ch. 6). This area of silence in a world of talk is a safe but lonely place: 'She had a new feeling, the feeling of danger; on which a new remedy rose to meet it, the idea of an inner self or, in other words, of concealment' (Ch. 2). An 'inner self' is, in a sense, a false self if we see 'self' as experience, and James, although he tells us that for Maisie concealment is not deception, betrays his own fears that it is, by his reiterated use of the term. The 'self' that Maisie attains at the end is the assertive, active self in which 'inner' and 'outer' selves are seen to be just her equivalent polarities to those polarities which were the 'siders' in the game. Like the 'opponents', they are merged in her new knowledge.

At the end, Maisie finds her 'discretion' 'shabby'. She starts to ask the taboo questions, both on her own behalf and on behalf of Sir Claude. She also makes her demands: 'She had never yet in her life made any claim for herself, but she hoped that this time, frankly, what she was doing would somehow be counted to her' (Ch. 24). 'What helped the child was that she knew what she wanted. All her learning and learning had made her at last learn that' (Ch. 31). What she wants is Sir Claude, what she gets is Mrs Wix. Why?

Maisie, like everyone else, is enchanted by the fair, young Sir Claude. Among a group of extraordinarily handsome people, he is someone always to be looked at. He is the 'Prince' of the fantasies Mrs Wix relates to Maisie. But all that glitters is not true, and in an inoffensive way Sir Claude lies, evades and 'funks' it. 'His 'princely' qualities show a tarnish in their irresponsible extravagance that Maisie learns to recognize, but that she also learns to love. The most interesting thing about Sir Claude is that his position is strangely analogous to Maisie's own. Like her he is possessed rather than possessing; he plays a part in the game, but it is a reluctant one – he is always trying to 'get out' of it.

Sir Claude and Maisie have a real companionship. He shows not 'a deceitful descent to her years [but] a real indifference to them' (Ch. 10). A delicate homosexuality is established as he calls her 'dear boy', 'chap', 'old man'. Hand-in-hand they share a terrible fear of women. Neither are scared of Beale or his associates, but both are terrified of Ida and Mrs Beale, and theirs. Sir Claude is quite explicit about the cause of his fear:

> 'Why, then, did you marry her?'
> 'Just because I *was* afraid.'
> 'Even when she loved you?'
> 'That made her the more alarming. . . . Fear, unfortunately, is a very big thing, and there's a great variety of kinds.'
> She took this in with complete intelligence. 'Then I think I've got them all. . . . I'm awfully afraid of Mrs Beale.' . . .
> 'I *am* in the same state.'
> 'Oh but she likes you so!' Maisie promptly pleaded.
> Sir Claude literally coloured. 'That has something to do with it.'
> Maisie wondered again. 'Being liked with being afraid?'   (Ch. 13)

He is not afraid of Maisie because her love is not possessive, and she is too young to class as a 'woman'. He flirts but he shies away from the adoration he consequently receives.

Apart from his obvious methods of evasion, he has one means of escape that again makes him an interesting parallel to Maisie. He has the child's relationship to reality through fantasy. Treated by others as a 'Fairy Prince', he decides to act the part and refashion the world accordingly. Hyde Park and his adulterous wife are to him the Forest of Arden and fair Rosalind, until Maisie insists on the facts. He 'plays' with Maisie: '. . . if he was to have the credit of perverting the innocent child he might also at least have the amusement' (Ch. 11). Poverty-stricken, he cannot give up his luxuries any more than he can give up 'the women'; benign humour covers the dire choices of life, or the dire failure to make choices:

> His fear at all events was there; his fear was sweet to her, beautiful and tender to her, was having coffee and buttered rolls and talk and laughter that were no talk and laughter at all with her; his fear was in his jesting postponing perverting voice; it was just in this make-believe way he had brought her out to imitate the old London playtimes, to imitate indeed a relation that had wholly changed. . . .   (Ch. 30)

Sir Claude is in no sense 'childish', but his role is definitely that of a child to a series of grabbing 'mothers'. James uses the same term of

him as he uses of the children in *The Turn of the Screw* – 'plastic' –
'poor plastic and dependent male' (Ch. 24).

Most interestingly from my point of view Sir Claude's relation to
the glass-mirror-spectacle image series bears analogies with Maisie's
own. He is introduced as a photograph haggled over (as he is, again,
at the end) by Maisie, Mrs Wix and Mrs Beale. Maisie gets the
photograph and she keeps hold of this perspective of him. He is
always 'showman of the spectacle'; he is 'like the single, the sovereign
window-square of a great dim disproportioned room' (Ch. 17). He is
her light in the world and on the world, the lens of the magic lantern,
and will take her on his travels. He is an object to be looked at, but
also an object to look through. More importantly, in him can she
occasionally see herself:

> . . . 'All the same, if you hadn't had the fatal gift of beauty – !'
> 'Well, what?' Maisie asked, wondering why he paused.
> It was the first time she had heard of her beauty.   (Ch. 14)

Because he offers her a mirror, it is with him that she can identify
herself, and find herself, at the end. Sir Claude is the childhood
companion whom Maisie outgrows and whom she wants to save and
comfort. Sir Claude can only be happy in her release. Maisie gets
free of the game in the way that Sir Claude cannot. The refrain
'you're free' echoes throughout the book. To Ida, Beale and Mrs
Beale it means they are released from a marital contract only, ironically, to re-endorse the terms of their captivity. A chaos of 'freedoms'
litters the last chapters: to Sir Claude 'to be free' means to escape:

> 'Let her go!' Sir Claude more intensely repeated.
> He was looking at Mrs Beale and there was something in his voice.
> Maisie knew from a loosening of arms that she had become conscious
> of what it was; she slowly rose from the sofa, and the child stood there
> again dropped and divided.
> 'You're free – you're free,' Sir Claude went on. . . .   (Ch. 31)

For Mrs Wix 'freedom' is immorality:

> 'Why not, if now she's free?'
> 'Free? Are you imitating *him*? Well, if Sir Claude's old enough to

know better, upon my word I think it's right to treat you as if you also were. . . .'

. . . Maisie could guess that she herself had never appeared so wanton. . . . Her wantonness meanwhile continued to work upon her friend, who caught again, on the rebound, the sound of deepest provocation.

'Free, free, free? If she's as free as *you* are, my dear, she's free enough, to be sure!' (Ch. 25)

I find the majority of critical reactions to Mrs Wix staggering: to Gale she is 'a homely, good woman', to Edmund Wilson 'the ridiculous old governess', and to Andreas she is, unlike Sir Claude or Mrs Beale, 'complete'. Leavis rebukes Bewley for his derogation of her with the statement that if she is ugly she is very respectable – she only adores Sir Claude in the sexless way that Maisie does; she is also kind, muddled and conventional and thus will always be so – 'and perhaps – may we not reflect? – it is as well that Maisie, after a childhood that has provided us with James's comedy, should enter adolescence under that kind of respectable tutelage.'[10] Mrs Wix is quite simply one of James's nastiest characterizations. That she is pathetic in no way detracts from this. It is partly a question of tone: 'She had had a little girl quite of her own, and the little girl had been killed on the spot. She had had absolutely nothing else in all the world, and her affliction had broken her heart. It was comfortably established between them that Mrs Wix's heart was broken' (Ch. 4); 'Everyone knew the straighteners; everyone knew the diadem and the button, the scallops and satin bands; everyone, though Maisie had never betrayed her, knew even Clara Matilda' (Ch. 4). There is no gap between James and the mean-minded 'everyone'. This is really dirty writing. When James is explicit he is less nasty, but no less damning: 'the old-fashioned conscience, the dingy decencies, of Maisie's simple instructress' (Ch. 9). 'She seemed to sit in her new dress and brood over her lost delicacy, which had become almost as doleful a memory as that of poor Clara Matilda' (Ch. 11). When she tells Sir Claude of Ida's lover it is an 'ugly honesty' (Ch. 23) – ugly is syntactically ambiguous. One of the high peaks of what Leavis has called her sexless adoration of Sir Claude is surpassingly unpleasant. Sir Claude has just asked why she is so pleased he is 'free':

Mrs Wix met this challenge first with silence, then with a demonstration the most extraordinary, the most unexpected. Maisie could scarcely believe her eyes as she saw the good lady, with whom she had associated no faintest shade of any art of provocation, actually, after an upward grimace, gave Sir Claude a great giggling insinuating naughty slap. 'You wretch – you *know* why!' And she turned away. (Ch. 24)

Mrs Wix is the ultra-possessive mother and Maisie's awareness of this is expressed in extravagant metaphors. When she is first separated from her she feels as if she has been 'embedded in Mrs Wix's nature as her tooth had been socketed in her gum' (Ch. 5). Mrs Wix penetrates into Maisie's most remote silence, even in her absence. 'Somewhere in the depths of it the dim straighteners were fixed upon her; somewhere out of the troubled little current Mrs Wix intensely waited' (Ch. 6). Clara Matilda is turned into Maisie's sister with whom Maisie feels as involved as does the child in Wordsworth's 'We are Seven'. Even Sir Claude plays with the notion of Mrs Wix as his mother: 'I don't love *her* . . . she's not my daughter – come, old chap! She's not even my mother, though I daresay it would have been better for me if she had been . . .' (Ch. 30). The end of the novel is predictable in her first introduction: 'Mrs Wix took her and, Maisie felt the next day, would never let her go' (Ch. 4). But if Mrs Wix is possessive, and others are not so much an extension of self as a filling-up of the self,[11] she also requires to be possessed: for example, at one stage she says to Sir Claude

You stay here with Maisie, with the carriage and the larks and the luxury; then I'll return to you and we'll go off together – we'll live together without a cloud. Take me, take me. (Ch. 24)

The cry of the desperate virgin. Virgin Mother? '[Mr Wix] had been remarkably absent from his wife's career, and Maisie was never taken to see his grave' (Ch. 4). This aspect of Mrs Wix prefigures a series of images and notions which James suddenly employs late in the novel. In Boulogne, the long colloquies and the intensest moments that Mrs Wix and Maisie experience take place whilst they are awaiting Sir Claude in a square dominated by a view of a huge gilt Virgin Mary. This symbol is repeated: it picks up previous references to Mrs Wix as a 'prophetess' and 'ardent priestess' to '[her] deep, narrow passion', and it looks forward to her own 'confession' to Maisie that she had 'probably made a fatal mistake early in life in not being a Catholic' (Ch. 25) – a gaudy religiousity which in its turn connects up with her 'moral sense' and with her romantic fantasies.

When Sir Claude evades through 'make-believe', Mrs Wix compensates for ugliness and poverty by romance. Both make-believe and romantic tales have an appeal to a young child – Mrs Wix makes for Maisie a version of life wondrous 'beyond magic or monsters' (Ch. 4). She *is* a good companion for a child in a sense, just as in a sense she is, with her possessiveness, a good mother; despite her 'ugliness and her poverty, she was peculiarly and soothingly safe; safer than anyone in the world' (Ch. 4). Of course James ironizes even this safety – she is as 'safe' as the dead Clara Matilda: she is a permanent feature of the landscape, taken care of, impersonalized; as Maisie comes to say, 'Oh, you're nobody' (Ch. 28).

Mrs Wix is also safe because she is firmly part of the world (her fantasizing confirms, not denies, this). She has 'sidled and ducked through life' and knows the game. Indeed she teaches it to Maisie:

> There were hours when Mrs Wix sighingly testified to the scruples she surmounted, seemed to ask what other line one *could* take with a young person whose experience had been, as it were, so peculiar. 'It isn't as if you didn't already know everything, is it, love?' and 'I can't make you any worse than you *are*, can I, darling?' (Ch. 9)

A large aspect of her romantic story-telling about the 'princely' Sir Claude is clearly salacious gossip, as pathetic as that of an aspirant's to a part in this play must be. (Anyone can win her over to their side by kindness.) She initiates Maisie into what she calls a 'moral sense', and this consists precisely in making her understand all the most immoral details of the adults' relationships. In a sequence rich in innuendo, in the middle of Chapter 26, just after Maisie has realized that she must know 'Everything', Mrs Wix completes her enlightenment. The episode runs over two pages and is too long to quote, but a few selections should make the nature of Mrs Wix's action beyond dispute:

> . . . she was visibly at a loss how to make up to such a victim for such contaminations: appealing, as to what she had done and was doing, in

bewilderment, in explanation, in supplication, for reassurance, for pardon and even outright for pity.

'I don't know what I've said to you, my own: I don't know what I'm saying or what the turn you've given my life has rendered me, heaven forgive me, capable of saying. Have I lost all delicacy, all decency, all measure of how far and how bad? . . . What I did lose patience at this morning was at how it was that without your seeming to condemn – for you didn't, you remember! – you yet did seem to *know*. Thank God, in his mercy, at last, *if* you do!'

Maisie tries to put on this 'moral sense' which should go with knowledge of the game. She responds to Mrs Wix's prescription.

> (Mrs Wix) 'Has it never occurred to you to be jealous of [Mrs Beale]?' It never had in the least. . . .
> (Maisie) 'If I thought she was unkind to him – I don't know *what* I should do!'
> Mrs Wix dropped one of her squints; she even confirmed it by a wild grunt. 'I know what *I* should!'
> Maisie at this felt that she lagged. 'Well, I can think of *one* thing.'
> Mrs Wix more directly challenged her. 'What is it, then?'
> Maisie met her expression as if it were a game with forfeits for winking. 'I'd *kill* her!' That at least, she hoped . . . would guarantee her moral sense. (Ch. 26)

> 'Why shouldn't I? *You've* come out. Mrs Beale has come out. We each have our turn!' And Maisie threw off the most extraordinary little laugh that had ever passed her young lips. (Ch. 28)

Maisie of course tries her hand and gives it up; the tears that she finally sheds lie too deep for a 'moral sense': her knowledge is pure, her freedom complete. 'Mrs Wix spoke not only as if Maisie were not a woman, but as if she would never be one' (Ch. 29). As far as the women of the novel are concerned, she never will be one of them.

Critical reactions that make Mrs Wix a latter-day Juliet's nurse or a Mrs Micawber (though marginally preferable to those which see her as an 'old dear'), fall far short of the point. But the point is, of course, a confusing one. It is not only that James evokes sympathy from the reader for Mrs Wix, though this he indeed does: 'Even to the hard heart of childhood there was something tragic in such elation at such humanities' (Ch. 9). It is also that she *is* his viewpoint. She

acts to desperation a role that places herself as object – 'The straighteners, she explained to Maisie, were put on for the sake of others,
whom, as she believed, they helped to recognize the bearing, otherwise doubtful, of her regard' (Ch. 4); but she is also, as gossip, commentator and translator, a window on the world. This wished-for
'looked at' and in fact 'looked with' perspective is an ironic parody on
the parallelism of her and Sir Claude, of her and Maisie. It is also a
fundamental aspect of James's art.

> The formula from the frump at the end of V *facilitates* my making the
> child witness the phenomenon in question – prepares the mirror, the
> plate, on which it is represented as reflected.[12]

Mrs Wix wears glasses to be seen, to see through and as a screen on
which the world is reflected, for Maisie and for the readers. If one
perspective is innocent (Maisie) and one pornographic (Mrs Wix),
what does this make of the novel?

Maisie doesn't give us an innocent view and Mrs Wix a corrupt one:
nothing so simple. The wide-eyed guileless child can be a literary
'peeping-Tom' device. When the relationship is growing up between
Beale and Miss Overmore we are looking at them and Maisie from
the position of a passer-by staring into their carriage; but our viewpoint is also from Maisie, who is seeing the scene in which she is
involved reflected in the stare of a passer-by; and then there is
James's own window on the scene. This three-way mirror system
deeply corrupts the very language of innocence:

> 'Did papa like you just the same while I was gone?' she inquired – full
> of the sense of how markedly his favour had been established in her
> absence. . . . Papa, on whose knee she sat, burst into one of those loud
> laughs of his. . . . 'Why, you little donkey, when you're away what have
> I left to do but just to love her?' Miss Overmore hereupon immediately
> took her from him, and they had a merry little scrimmage over her of
> which Maisie caught the surprised perception in the white stare of an
> old lady who passed in a victoria. (Ch. 5)

Alternatively, in the scene where Mrs Wix fully enlightens Maisie,
James shows us only her hysterical feelings about doing so. He doesn't
tell us what she tells her: that 'corrupt' knowledge is assumed on the

behalf of the reader. As Maisie learns, we have to admit that we already know – but what do we know, or rather what *is* there to know? Because James gives us Mrs Wix's horrid horror of it, it assumes those grand proportions of mystery that James felt were the essence of life, and that he was always wanting to portray. Doubtless the Lady of Shalott found Sir Bedivere mysterious as well as handsome; if you look through too many windows and at too many mirrors, or through a telescope, or through corrective glasses, then a clear sense of obscurity is inevitable. Maisie learns, and *What Maisie Knew* is about this lucid vision of obscurity. The mirrors complicate but the vision of multiple reflections is knowledge. But knowledge is also Mrs Wix's gossip. Pornography and vision co-exist – they use the same means. First as the child Maisie, then as the man, Henry James looks through a glass dimly in order that the reflection should be 'sharp' and 'quiet'. Too much light darkens the mind.

Notes

1. *Notebooks*, p. 236.
2. Ibid., p. 258.
3. *The Art of the Novel*, edited by R. P. Blackmur, New York, 1934, p. 27 (my italics).
4. R. D. Laing, 'Family and Interpersonal Structures' in P. Lomas (ed.), *The Predicament of the Family*, London, 1967, p. 122.
5. *Harmsworth Encyclopaedia*, vol. 1, p. 730.
6. Maisie's reactions confirm her wish to be left alone. Mrs Beale tells Maisie that Ida has given up her own daughter – Sir Claude is to: ' "Take the whole bother and burden of you and never let her hear of you again. It's a regular signed contract." "Why that's lovely of her!" Maisie cried' (Ch. 28).
7. Maisie also foresaw for her departing mother 'madness and desolation' (Ch. 21).
8. D. Winnicott, 'Mirror-Role of Mother and Family' in Lomas, op. cit., p. 298.
9. Preface to *What Maisie Knew*.
10. F. R. Leavis, '*What Maisie Knew*, A Disagreement', in M. Bewley, *The Complex Fate*, London, 1952, p. 131.
11. This ingestive technique is made evident a number of times, where Maisie and Mrs Wix become one body: 'Shrink together as they might they couldn't help, Maisie felt, being a very large lumpish image of what Mrs Wix required of [Sir Claude's] slim fineness' (Ch. 12).
12. *Notebooks*, p. 239.

6

Keeping the place tidy
for the young female mind
The Awkward Age

MARGARET WALTERS

1 *The awkward nineties*

The Awkward Age is very much a novel of the nineties; it shares
themes and techniques with those other problematic stories written
in the years after James's abortive efforts for the stage. It is a comedy
of manners, its range deliberately limited. James concentrates with
exclusive intensity on English drawing-room life, on a social world
refined to the last degree of self-conscious sophistication. Taste and
tact are the touchstones of this world; morals have become manners.
His characters are wholly social beings, who live in terms of a network of conventions, elaborately and exclusively articulated, a whole
'envelope of circumstances'. They resemble Madame Merle in *The
Portrait of a Lady* who believes that 'one's house, one's furniture,
one's garments, the books one reads, the company one keeps – these
things are all expressive' (Ch. 19). In these later novels, and particularly in *The Awkward Age*, James confronts the complex problem of
just what they *do* express. He accepts the world of manners as his
novelistic *donnée* and works almost wholly within its limits. The very
form of the book derives from fashionable stage plays; presented as a
series of self-contained conversation pieces, its structure is as enclosed, as circular as the conversations it imitates.

Not trying to present more than surfaces, James gives us those in
careful detail. The characters are carefully placed, not simply in
their immediate 'envelope of circumstances', but in terms of income,

occupation and status, their roles in a larger world. They include the Brookenhams, living as much on her wit and charm as on the Civil Service job (Rivers and Lakes) that she secured for him; the charming, well-bred but impecunious Vanderbank, another Civil Servant; the unattractive Mitchy who lives off a vast inherited fortune (bootmaking and building speculations); Lord Petherton, who lives off Mitchy, and his sister, the expensively erring wife of a wealthy but vulgar M.P.; and the Duchess – carefully placed as a 'foreign' one. The old-fashioned and country-bred newcomer Mr Longdon, who has preserved at Beccles his values and expectations, along with his memories of their mothers, throws their 'modernity' into sharp relief. It consists at least partly in their rootless, anomalous nature *as* a group. Van always claims pressure of work, but his job is marginal to his life; he seems as functionless as the rest of this 'collection of affinities', who exist in and for personal relationships. In various and subtle ways, James indicates that this very individual group is typical at least of 'London life' in the nineties.[1]

Moreover, in his 1908 Preface, James stressed not only his realism, but the 'current actuality' of his story, which reflects 'the difference made in certain friendly houses and to certain flourishing mothers by the sometimes dreaded, often delayed, but never fully arrested coming to the forefront of some vague slip of a daughter'. The action is trivial enough, and James apologized for its inordinate growth from a small idea. Mrs Brook's daughter Nanda comes down into the adult world; Mr Longdon, moved by her startling physical resemblance to her grandmother, and seeing how awkwardly she is situated in her mother's circle, informs Van that he will settle a fortune on Nanda when she marries. Nanda persuades Mitchy to marry the Duchess's niece, the impossibly innocent Aggie; but Van, the curiously absent centre of the novel, continues to hesitate. In the end, Nanda and Mr Longdon, 'fearfully battered and bruised' by their exposure, withdraw to Suffolk, leaving Mrs Brook in possession of Van and a reconstituted circle. Yet she and her friends have been deeply shaken. For all their efforts to reduce the problem to triviality ('keeping the place tidy . . . for the young female mind'), Nanda's presence calls in question all the social fictions by which they live. During that brief period of tension, the 'awkward age', the confused attempts to deal with the 'awkwardness' that Nanda represents brings to light the contradictions of a whole society.

And James extends the implications of his drawing-room comedy in other directions as well. The very completeness of his immersion in the particular develops, through his contemplation of their claims to be 'modern', into an *historical* awareness. The nineties themselves come to figure as an awkward age, a period in which the forms of the past are less and less relevant to present realities. Yet because social status is divorced from social function, style from meaning, morality from convention, the outer forms and codes of social behaviour are more and more elaborately articulated. They take on a kind of life of their own, in which appearance is everything. So many scenes depend for their impact on our recognizing just what it means, say, for a girl to smoke, or to visit a man alone, or to read French novels. And we have to discern further the meaning of that meaning; the fact that in this wholly exploitative society, callous and promiscuous, manners determine respectability.

The more alert of the characters occasionally realize that they are living out a fiction (and marriage is shown to be the most meaningless fiction of all); that their lives are wholly determined by *la règle du jeu*. But neither James nor they see any possibility of escape. The social being *is* the self, and all that anyone can achieve is a tragic knowledge of his role in the comedy.

But if knowledge, or knowing, is a key to *The Awkward Age* – as to the other novels of this period – it's an ambiguous one. The word echoes curiously through their pages, pointing us in various and conflicting directions. The whole of *What Maisie Knew* is an explication of the multiple significances of the title; all the central passages of *The Awkward Age* are about what Nanda knew, and about what that knowing means; while James teases us all through the labyrinth of *The Sacred Fount* with what the narrator did – or did not – know. In each case he leaves us with questions that radiate beyond the particular action. What is knowledge? Is the knowing mind capable of anything more than a plausible interpretation, a consistent fiction?

James had of course always been less interested in events than in the perception of events. The Preface to *The Portrait of a Lady* provides the clearest definition of his concerns, as he describes a key scene as 'a representation simply of her motionlessly *seeing*, and an attempt to make the mere still lucidity of her act as "interesting" as the surprise of a caravan or the identification of a pirate'.[2] But this lucidity becomes more difficult to achieve, for the novelist as for his characters.

The very fact that James twice uses a child as the centre of his fiction is a sign of his new stress on the problematic nature of knowing. For Nanda, as for Maisie, the word denotes a deceptive, even dangerous relationship with the bewildering adult world; it implies the struggle to understand, to puzzle out, to piece together hints of meaning, while maintaining a blank and unruffled surface. For the adults at once encourage and deny their efforts. They are caught in an intolerable double bind. The ideal is that a child knows nothing, for knowing (knowing the adult world) is corruption; the third possibility – an evasion rather than a solution of the contradiction – is for a child to be 'knowing', to adopt the forms of adult knowing in a comic precocity that's regarded as a sign of innocence. For the adults too are caught up in a series of elaborate social games in which knower takes all. What one knows is what one is; it's the basis of all conversation (or gossip) and all action (or manipulation of others for one's own ends). Social life is a series of gambles based on one's reading of oneself and others, predictions of what others may know, as well as of what they may do. ('She knows I know she knows'; 'I know you know what I've known'.) Mrs Brook is the supreme 'knower' in this tangled and inward-turning world, where the other sense of knowing – the imaginative struggle for lucidity, the discovery of oneself and of the outer world in the fullest consciousness – can only imply a tragic recognition of defeat.

For the hypocrisies and riddles of the outer world are matched by the deceptions of the knowing mind itself. Each is a product of the other; each reflects and distorts the other. When James uses a central consciousness in the nineties, it's never to be taken for granted; the Governess in *The Turn of the Screw* is only the clearest of many examples. Maisie is just a child, Fleda in *The Spoils of Poynton* is trapped between duty and desire, while the narrator of *The Sacred Fount*, who certainly uses his 'knowing' as a substitute for living, may even have gone crazy in his fine-spun world. James is interested in the relationship between the mind and the outer world, which can never be accurately determined. For knowledge is power and impotence, creation and destruction. Knowing is the process by which a mind and a world come to life; and by which a mind and a world are corrupted and destroyed. Nanda's repeated assertion 'I know everything' takes on more and more of these connotations as the labyrinth that is social life is revealed to her and to us.

In the end the complexities focused on the word even threaten to undermine the possibility of fiction. At the end of the nineties, *The Sacred Fount* seems to stand as a fable-like representation of one fearful potentiality in James's fiction. Knowing becomes almost wholly negative – it is linked with obsession, impotence, madness, destruction; but it is also seen as *art*. Even the narrator's refusal to be told anything, his determination to create what he knows from arbitrarily set terms, point us back to consider the very nature of fiction. Our efforts to 'know' the book are baffled, just as the narrator is baffled; and if he is exposed, then so is James, and so are we. A nightmare lurking in all James's work, in all fiction, is brought to light and – perhaps – exorcized.

2 *Floundering in a deep warm jungle*

Predictably, there are very different interpretations of *The Awkward Age*. It's sometimes read merely as a virtuoso piece, with dazzling and rigorous techniques deployed on an unimportant theme. This, according to one's critical orientation, can be praise or blame. But even those who insist on the novel's seriousness, and on the indivisibility of its form and content, come up with conflicting accounts.

Thus on the one hand F. W. Dupee plausibly describes the book as a celebration of social values in which 'the world scores a distinct victory over innocence become stiff-necked and grotesque'. For him Mrs Brook is the undoubted heroine, as against her bleak and graceless daughter, who indulges in the 'unfashionable romanticism of high virtue and unrequited love'. Mrs Brook represents society which 'for all its vices is seen to be the human medium; the source of amiability, proportion, beauty, wit'. In complete contrast Ian Gregor reads the novel as a revelation of the 'depravity and sterility' of Mrs Brook and her intimates. He demonstrates very persuasively how James carefully and subtly plots the circle's self-exposure through talk. Their vaunted wit divorces words from values, and depends on treating people as objects to be enjoyed or exploited. All relationships in the novel, however refined the terms in which they're presented, rest on crude material calculations. Only Nanda, Mr Longdon and the unhappy Mitchy manage in the end to speak to each other with real love and friendship.[3]

Part of the difficulty of the book is that both readings are possible, are part of our final response. There seems to me no doubt at all that James feels all the charm of this life, or that he values charm pretty highly. Critics like Gregor tend to be embarrassed by the tone of the Preface; they discount its connoisseur's interest in the suffering caused by the English tendency to muddle through, and read ironically its loving description of those circles where

> the wide glow was bright, was favourable to 'real' talk, to play of mind, to an explicit interest in life, a due demonstration of the interest by persons qualified to feel it: all of which meant frankness and ease, the perfection, almost, as it were, of intercourse, and a tone as far as possible removed from that of the nursery and the schoolroom – as far as possible removed even, no doubt, in its appealing 'modernity', from that of supposedly privileged scenes of conversation twenty years ago. The charm was, with a hundred other things, in the freedom – the freedom menaced by the inevitable irruption of the ingenuous mind; whereby, if the freedom should be sacrificed, what would truly *become* of the charm?

The dramatization of this freedom and charm certainly reveals that the words are more equivocal than James is here prepared to admit. But the book is mimetic; its speculating, wide-ranging, detached talk is the soil from which James's fiction grows. The limits of this talk, this social world, are the limits of James's novels. The coolness, the detached knowingness that can so easily destroy the less socially adept; the concern with appearance; the juggling with reticence and frankness – all these are elements in James as well as his characters. Does the coyly vulgar tone in which he describes Carrie's make-up or Tishy's undress belong to James or to them? Is the refusal to define the relationship between Mrs Brook and Van a reticence on the part of James or of his characters? In his essay 'The Future of the Novel' (1899), James attacked the absurdity of a literature that limited itself to what was acceptable fare for children, and foresaw a time when women and children, the repositories of hypocritical morality, would themselves demand a more genuine realism. But though he parodies Mrs Brook's double standards towards French novels (not in front of the children), and though he shows Nanda reading and evaluating them, he himself stays well within the bounds of propriety. If he attacked Hardy's *Tess of the D'Urbervilles* on the grounds that 'the pretence of "sexuality" is only equalled by the absence of it', isn't he perhaps open to the same charge?[4] Indeed, occasionally he almost seems to endorse sexlessness as a positive virtue. The most crucial problem raised by the novel is how deeply James himself is involved in the equivocations which he explores so brilliantly.

Both the critics quoted oversimplify the novel. If Mrs Brook's ease and artificiality are virtues as well as dangers, so Nanda and Mr Longdon are disturbing as well as sympathetic – the more disturbing *because* they're sympathetic. Edmund Wilson is one of the few critics to have grasped how odd the novel is; he long ago pointed out the sexual implications, quite clearly indicated by James but not often by critics, of the final relationship between these two.[5] (Mrs Brook, for example, asks Nanda if she would marry the old man; while Mitchy's joking references to their departure use the imagery of an elopement.) In fact this pair, who are good, honest, and 'conscious' in the full Jamesian sense of the word, together bring to a focus all the hints of perversity and sterility that shadow the novel. Their 'marriage' is representative – in its sterility, even in the disparity of their ages – of all the novel's marriages.

One of the paradoxes of *The Awkward Age* is that, in spite of its insistent concentration on outward behaviour, it continually hints at all kinds of disturbing psychological possibilities. The idealized but surely perverse relationship between Mr Longdon and Nanda is only one example; there are continual suggestions of intense sexual jealousy between mother and daughter, of sexual attraction (and hostility) across generations, of impotence masking itself either as promiscuity or as morality, of the barrenness of any conceivable marriage, of weak homosexual links between men, of the masochistic basis of heroism – and all this to an extent that's comparatively new in James. An interesting contemporary review described James as the 'artistic outcome of our national habit of repression. He has learned how to make repression a factor of art instead of an impediment.'[6] There are moments in this novel when we're tempted to consider *only* the darker patterns underlying its glittering surface structures, to read it wholly in terms of the repressed, the submerged world.

Richard Poirier's argument about *The Portrait of a Lady* is perhaps relevant here. He claims convincingly that in *Portrait* a complex network of barely conscious fears underlies Isabel's idealism and her choices; but that because James's interest is primarily moral, 'ideological', he fails to develop the connexion between the two. This he does, however, in *The Bostonians*, with its exploration of the twisted roots of militant feminism.[7] But it seems to me that the women, comically objectified, make too easy targets; that although the book is magnificently successful within its chosen terms, it doesn't involve James in any serious questioning of his *own* idealism, the basis of all his fiction. The pervasive ambiguities in the novels written during the nineties derive partly from a new and subversive recognition of the curious and tangled sources of morality, of all civilized values, of art itself; and a consequent awareness of the psychological and social *functions* of art or morality, their relative and not their absolute value.

There is yet another dimension to these receding ambiguities. James sees his role as writer as that of a spectator. He is 'infinitely addicted' to noticing, possesses 'a liberally amused and beguiled, a richly sophisticated, view of relations and a fine inquisitive sense for them' which condemns him at times to 'flounder in a deep warm jungle'. James means his phrase in a technical sense; it takes on a more problematic meaning when we consider that the subject of all this speculation is the corruption of the young. He takes, with Nanda as with Maisie, a connoisseur's pleasure in the violation of her innocence, the 'death of her childhood';[8] a pleasure detached, voyeuristic, almost pornographic. And so do we. For the peculiar techniques by which James at one and the same time involves and distances the reader, turn us into voyeurs, in a way that immensely complicates judgement, and leaves us wondering whether judgement is possible at all. It can prove very difficult to find our bearings in the jungle of James's fiction; we are all too likely to be left floundering.

3 *The ingenious observer*

As James pointed out in his Preface, *The Awkward Age* was conceived in theatrical terms. Its books correspond to 'the successive Acts of a Play': we are left to work out connexions for ourselves, 'shut up wholly to cross-relations, relations all within the action itself'. Those cross-relations multiply into an incredibly complicated web. James chooses to do without the usual novelistic techniques of 'going behind' the surface. Scenes are presented mostly in dialogue, with movement, gesture, position in a room as carefully plotted as in any stage scenario.

Sometimes this works fairly simply, as in the scene in the billiard room at Mertle where Mr Longdon makes his offer to Van, and at a crucial point the two change places. The scene between Mitchy and Van at Beccles is more subtle; Mitchy's restlessness and Van's stillness in fact counterpoint Van's embarrassed evasions and Mitchy's steady strength. Even within a single paragraph, James can achieve very complex effects:

> '. . . never give up a friend for anything anyone says!' It was Mitchy who rang out with this lively wisdom, the action of which on Mr Longdon – unless indeed it was the action of something else – was to make that personage, in a manner that held the others watching him in slight suspense, suddenly spring to his feet again, put down his tea-cup carefully on a table near and then without a word, as if no one had been present, quietly wander away and disappear through the door left open on Vanderbank's entrance. It opened into a second, a smaller sitting-room, into which the eyes of his companions followed him. (Bk. 3, Ch. 2)

Gesture reveals emotion; the commentary indicates the source of the feeling but, by qualifying itself, insists that we work out for ourselves why Mitchy's innocent remark should prove so disturbing. (We make, presumably, a connexion with Mr Longdon's earlier emotion at Nanda's resemblance to Lady Julia; to his earlier defence of friendship to Van; and to the fact that her defence of her friends suggests a frightening knowledge of the world.) Moreover, our reading of Mr Longdon's response echoes, mimics, that of his companions. We watch as they watch him move away; his physical retreat gives concrete form to our growing sense of the novel's receding dimensions.

There's a similar complexity in a crucial fragment in the key scene of the novel – the party at Tishy Grendon's when Mrs Brook, demanding that Nanda be returned home, and by making clear to everyone the extent at least of Nanda's reading, in fact destroys her own circle. We watch (as if at a play) as the Duchess and Mr Longdon watch (as if at a play):

> Separated from them by the width of the room, Mrs Brook was, though placed in profile, fully presented; the satisfaction with which she had lately sunk upon a light gilt chair marked itself as superficial and was moreover visibly not confirmed by the fact that Vanderbank's high-perched head, arrested before her in a general survey of opportunity, kept her eyes too far above the level of talk. Their companions were dispersed, some in the other room, and for the occupants of the Duchess's sofa they made, as a couple in communion, a picture, framed and detached, vaguely reduplicated in the high polish of the French floor. (Bk. 8, Ch. 2)

This carefully framed glimpse is, we assume, relevant to the subsequent action. The Duchess reads one meaning into it – that Mrs Brook, losing her hold on Van, is about to take her revenge by 'working' him so that Nanda will lose him too. We see with her amused eyes – she, after all, has got what she wants – but also with Mr Longdon's baffled hatred. He at least is no mere spectator. But we also see them seeing, and as a result the inner scene retains its oddly elusive precision. As so often in the novel, the composition of details is quite clear, but not their significance.

James praised the 'guarded objectivity' of this theatrical technique. In passages like these he uses it rather to involve us, though to involve us not with the characters but with the game of interpretation. It's a game played by James as well as his characters.

The effect is further intensified by the constant self-qualification,

the hesitations and suspensions of the narrating voice. James continually reminds us that he is only offering a plausible interpretation
of appearances. Sometimes he presents us with alternative interpretations: 'turning her eyes about the room as if from the extremity
of martyrdom or the wistfulness of some deep thought' (Bk. 2, Ch. 1);
sometimes he interrupts with a teasing reminder that he is setting
himself arbitrary limits: 'his chronicler takes advantage of the fact
not to pretend to a greater intelligence – to limit himself on the
contrary to the simple statement that they produced in Mr Van's
cheek a flush just discernible' (Bk. 5, Ch. 1). The spectator lurking
behind these stylistic tricks is often evoked explicitly: 'nothing for a
spectator could have been so odd . . .'; 'a person who knew him well
would if present at the scene . . . such an analyst would furthermore
have noticed . . .'; 'the acute observer we are constantly taking for
granted would perhaps have detected in her . . .'; and so on. This
ghostly figure, tireless in his ingenuity, sometimes seems to be the
novel's main character.

Another paragraph shows the effect at its most involuted:

> An observer at all initiated would, at this juncture fairly have hung upon
> his lips, and there was in fact on Vanderbank's part quite the look of the
> man – though it lasted but just while we seize it – in suspense about
> himself. The most initiated observer of all would have been poor Mr
> Longdon, in that case destined, however, to be also the most defeated,
> with the sign of his tension a smothered 'Ah if he doesn't do it *now*!'
> (Bk. 7, Ch. 1)

The extraordinary suspensions of this sentence mimic the suspense
of an observer following the signs of Van's suspense. The imagined
observer finds a momentary – hypothetical – incarnation in Mr
Longdon; intellectual curiosity is assimilated to Mr Longdon's pre-
sumed reaction, which might betray his urgent emotional concern
with Van's answer. We as readers are simultaneously distanced and
involved by the style; if we take the trouble to follow it – and some
readers might argue that it's hardly worth it – we *become* the passionately ingenious spectator.

And so many scenes in the novel demand this same passionate
ingenuity before they yield any meaning. Speech and gesture are

brilliantly defined, but the intentions behind them remain in shadow – a shadow all the darker for the fact that each character is only too ready to offer interpretations of his own and other people's actions. We are never sure, for example, of Nanda's motives in asking Mitchy to marry Aggie; while Nanda's mother is always an enigma. We can disentangle her various motives, but never assess the exact blend of impulse and calculation behind, say, her first apparently clumsy appeal to Mr Longdon. We never know 'whether as she went on she thought she bettered her case or she simply lost her head' (Bk. 4, Ch. 3). Or what is the full significance of her climactic exposure – of Nanda? of herself? – at Tishy's party? That James never intends us to 'know' her in any simple way becomes obvious in the following scenes, where Mrs Brook, with her husband, with Van and with Mitchy, discusses her action and motives. She herself puts forward an apparently straightforward and rather altruistic reason to Edward: by revealing herself and her circle in their worst light, she hoped to arouse Mr Longdon's pity to the point where he would accept complete responsibility for Nanda. This is qualified but not altogether negated by Mitchy's half-admiring, half-condemning account of her 'perfect policy' which he seems to imply succeeded in its object of keeping Van away from her daughter. While Van sees it as a calculated act of destruction, and self-destruction:

> It was a wonderful performance. You pulled us all down – just closing with each of the great columns in its turn – as Samson pulled down the temple. I was at the time more or less bruised and buried and I didn't in the agitation and confusion fully understand what had happened. But I understand now. (Bk. 9, Ch. 1)

His present confident understanding springs, he explains, from sleepless and solitary nights spent trying to 'puzzle it out'. But his initial assurance seeps away, for within a few lines he is questioning her, and a few pages later he admits 'I understand less than ever your unforgettable explosion'.

The effect of the novel's stylistic and structural complexities is to demand that we, like Van and the other characters, should 'puzzle it out'; and that at the end we, like them, should achieve only the equivocal knowledge possible in social intercourse. When we open the novel we are in a position not unlike that of Mr Longdon when he is described as 'a stranger at an Eastern court – comically helpless without his interpreter' (Bk. 4, Ch. 3). If we continue to read, we, like Mr Longdon, have to learn the game, accept the novel's terms. We have to learn to follow its rapid shifts, its allusions and omissions; to become as subtle as James and his characters. We are seduced into accepting their style; otherwise, neither particular conversations nor the novel as a whole make any sense, and we are left, like Tishy, always one step in the rear. Our effort in reading mimics their activities; we observe them observing, analyse their analyses, speculate on their speculations. And our complicity with their style, with James's style, is a complicity with their values, with James's values.

4 *Mere talk*

The other aspect of the novel's 'theatrical' form – its unusual dependence on dialogue – is another source of its ambiguity. As I suggested, the form of the book echoes the form of its characters' lives; talk is their medium, as it is James's. And talk is his main theme, as it is theirs; they talk about talking, their conversations are almost all self-reflecting. Almost every important development in the novel is established through a comment on language. James explores the function of talk, of language, in a highly sophisticated society.

The dilemma posed by the adolescent Nanda is seen almost exclusively in linguistic terms: will her presence inhibit the free charm of their worldly intercourse, or conversely, will her exposure to their talk corrupt her, make her unmarriageable? By the end she is certainly unmarriageable in their terms, though the unacknowledged contradiction in the assumption that civilized talk will corrupt a child has also been 'exposed' along with the false values on which marriage is based. But Nanda *is* corrupted, and not just in their sense. James presents neither her nor Maisie as images of innocence remaining inviolate. Nanda, unlike Maisie, learns to judge the world to which she's exposed, partly through her friendship with Mr Longdon, whose very different vision helps her to achieve a different perspective on herself. But the terms by which she judges are fatally compromised, riddled with the same moral confusion, the same double thinking, that besets her elders. She sees some things more clearly than they; but what she sees is her own involvement. She sees that she is injured mainly by their evasion of the truth that 'girls understand now'; and that the adults hide, in words, from the reality of their own feelings and of her situation. And she also sees that what's damaging is not what is said, but how it's said – or not said. In order not to compromise her social innocence she has had to 'unlearn' surprise, to understand so as to appear not to understand, to interpret silence silently. As she explains, 'what's so awfully unutterable is just what we notice most.' For a hypocritical censorship is more harmful to her than what her mother sees as corrupting talk with the unhappily married Tishy. Tishy, Nanda insists to the embarrassed Van, 'is natural; we just talk.'

The talk at Buckingham Crescent is anything but 'natural'. In one of the most complex scenes of the book, Mrs Brook warns her friends not to see 'too tremendous things, even in each other', and describes her own speech as 'natural' and 'sincere' (Bk. 6, Ch. 2). The words echo ironically through her elaborate web of ambiguities. The dramatic context, placing her claims as yet another move in a calculated and dangerous game, draws our attention to the equivocal functions of honesty itself.

Her 'temple of analysis' sometimes sounds like a mutual admiration society. Even the Duchess pays malicious tribute to its charm:

> The men, the young and the clever ones, find it a house – and Heaven knows they're right – with intellectual elbow room, with freedom of talk. Most English talk is a quadrille in a sentry box. (Bk. 5, Ch. 4)

But this cleverness is mainly exercised on themselves. Talk is a calculated and complex performance; all the characters watch themselves playing, take pleasure in their own skill. They take a positive pride in being able to match a daring, a subtly surprising phrase, or in following, without spoiling explanations, the most delicate analogies, the most obscure transitions. Discussion of an experience is more important than the experience, which – as Mitchy finds when he visits Beccles – is hardly real until it's discussed. They're less interested, for example, in Aggie or Lady Fanny than in their own perceptions and analyses. Even when their own feelings are concerned, they're preoccupied with working out their significance, weaving them into an elaborate verbal fabric. Thus Van, half ironic, half afraid of the game breaking down, explains to Mr Longdon:

> We hate and we love – the latter especially; but to tell each other why is to break that little tacit rule of finding out for ourselves which is the delight of our lives and the source of our triumphs. (Bk. 8, Ch. 3)

When Cashmore tells Mrs Brook that he is no longer pursuing Carrie Donner, she is as disappointed as if 'a fabric had crumbled'. But she soon finds a new interest in speculating on his relationship with her own daughter, just as she later placidly accepts her son's relations with Lady Fanny as a further twist in the saga of that lady's adulteries. All her creative energy goes into gossip; content is almost irrelevant, and moral judgement completely beside the point.

James is of course fully aware of the extent to which their verbal brilliance depends on the divorce of language from morals. The point is made quickly and effectively in the opening scenes, where Mr Longdon and Van take the difference in talk as the focus for their discussion of changing manners. As he leaves, Mr Longdon rejects the superficial response of being shocked at their freedom; instead, he gravely insists 'I think I was rather frightened'. We come to understand what he fears, and all the more sharply because it emerges through the comedy of his bewilderment and Van's slightly patronizing amusement. Van's brilliant analysis of the commercial basis of marriage is undermined when he goes on to explain how, for Nanda, everything depends on her looks; Mr Longdon pinpoints the double-thinking of which Van isn't fully aware, and which is to prove the source of Nanda's tragedy:

> '. . . What, once more, do you mean by everything?'
> 'Why, naturally her marrying, above all her marrying early.'
> Mr Longdon stood before the sofa. 'What do you mean by early?'
> 'Well, we do doubtless get up later than at Beccles; but that gives us, you see, shorter days. I mean in a couple of seasons. Soon enough,' Vanderbank developed, 'to limit the strain –!' He broke down in gaiety at his friend's expression.
> 'What do you mean by the strain?'
> 'Well, the complication of her being there.'

'Being where?'
'You do put one through!' (Bk. 1, Ch. 2)

Mr Longdon struggles to 'maintain' the full value of words like 'friendship', 'love', the 'home circle', against Van's admission that these haven't perhaps the meaning in London that they have at Beccles. It will prove increasingly difficult for Mr Longdon to maintain his sense of those values as he becomes more deeply involved with Buckingham Crescent; but in the early stages of the book at least, his naïvely literal queries serve as pertinent reminders of the extent to which its wit ignores both emotion and moral considerations.

But the novel is more than a simple 'exposure' of this immediately established point. Mr Longdon himself has to revise his comparatively simple strictures, as he comes to love Mitchy (who is 'all right' although his speech, his life, is 'all wrong') as well as Nanda. He comes to see – as we do – that Mitchy is subtly differentiated from the others. If he too plays games with language – adopting a clown-like *persona*, turning his unhappiness into farce, evaporating his emotions in strings of fantastic ironies and self-punishing caricatures – he plays with a difference. For Mitchy is always aware that he's pretending; his word-play springs from a conscious effort to master his pain and come to terms with his handicaps. The difference between his games and those played by Van or Mrs Brook is crystallized when they impose a fine on his 'cheap paradox'. Mitchy is struggling to contain emotion; they are using arbitrary rules to disparage and diminish the pressure of real feeling. His detachment, which Nanda notes so acutely, is a subtle acknowledgement that he has no choice but to live out an absurd fiction and accept the role in which he's cast. He privately counters their callous exploitation of his indifferent generosity *by* his indifference; his game is to name their game, his amusement 'to see us believe what he says'.

Similarly, Mr Longdon learns to accept Nanda by understanding and accepting her 'slangy' modern speech – the speech of Buckingham Crescent, the only speech she knows. James subtly parallels and distinguishes her speech from her mother's. There is 'something in the girl that would always make for lucidity', but a lucidity inevitably clouded by the words she must use. Her struggles to communicate honestly are both like and unlike her mother's stupefying ability to expose the truth; though with Mrs Brook exposure is usually a counter in some obscure manœuvre, and she often speaks truth simply in order to discount it. But Nanda too, of urgent necessity, comes to hide behind words, using language to conceal as well as to reveal. Even her reiterated 'I know everything' sounds at moments like a verbal smokescreen thrown up to protect herself from further discussion. It is not only Van who sees her as her mother's daughter; so does Mitchy, for example, when at the end of the book he looks forward to the luxury of always going to the bottom of things with her. His terms exactly recall the pleasure with which he'd earlier spoken of Buckingham Crescent, and we are forced, for a moment, to see and hear her as her mother. The tragedy for Nanda and Mitchy alike is that they are confined to the language that's available to them, and no amount of clarity or self awareness will enable them to transcend its limits. The words in which feeling is expressed also define, determine, the nature of that feeling. In more senses than one, they are what they say.

The situation is further complicated by the fact that Mrs Brook is at least partly aware of all this, aware of how her life depends on maintaining a verbal fiction, on juggling with social and moral meaning.

> 'Good talk: you know – no one dear Van, should know better – what part for me, that plays. Therefore when one has deliberately to make one's talk bad –!'
> ' "Bad"?' Vanderbank, in his amusement, fell back in his chair, 'Dear Mrs. Brook, you're too delightful!'
> 'You know what I mean – stupid, flat, fourth-rate.' (Bk. 6, Ch. 1)

Her enjoyment of her own epigrammatic skill is shadowed by a tired recognition that she too is caught in a linguistic trap, divided between convention and morality, appearance and truth. This is explored most fully in the scenes in Book 6 between Mrs Brook and Van, and then Mitchy, when the three discuss Mr Longdon's offer to Van. They are at their most characteristic, superbly witty and self aware, but their incessant comments on their own conversation betray an increasing weariness, an irritation threatening to erode their civilized poise. Each is under stress – Mrs Brook is jealous, Van panics under the pressure of other people's desires and demands, Mitchy has to struggle with the fact of his own unattractiveness, compared with the magnetic Van. 'None of the inner circle at Buckingham Crescent was ever angry', but it's increasingly clear, as each picks up and queries the other's words, and therefore threatens to expose the other's game, that their game can no longer contain their impatience and frustration. Under cover of praising their style, Van comes close to subverting all their pretences; typically, he shys away from the implications of his own words, fails to make anything of their un-acknowledged contradictions:

> ... what stupefies me a little ... is the extraordinary critical freedom – or we may call it if we like the high intellectual detachment – with which we discuss a question touching you, dear Mrs Brook, so nearly and engaging so your most private and most sacred sentiments. What are we playing with, after all, but the idea of Nanda's happiness? (Bk. 6, Ch. 2)

They seem trapped in that very skill with words on which they've always prided themselves, imprisoned in their own preoccupation with *style*. Nanda is not the only victim of their 'playing'. For it has become clear by now that if their talk corrupts, it's not because the glittering surface hides anything very dreadful; it's because the surface is everything, there's nothing *to* hide. James may be obscure about how much real promiscuity there is in this society; but talk is clearly its only real passion. Intercourse is only verbal, gossip more exciting than sexuality; only in their *talk* do these people discover, express and renew their vitality. But because their talk is self-referring, self-sustaining, the illusion finally shivers. They are left at least temporarily stranded in a waste of words.

> 'And yet to think that after all it has been mere *talk*.' Something in her tone again made her hearers laugh out; so it was still with the air of good humour that Vanderbank answered: 'Mere, mere, mere. But perhaps its exactly the "mere" that has made us range so wide.' Mrs Brook's intelligence abounded. 'You mean that we haven't had the excuse of passion?' Her companions once more gave way to merriment, but 'There you are!' Vanderbank said, after an instant, less sociably. With it too he held out his hand. (Bk. 6, Ch. 2)

Yet even as she names their illness, she perpetuates it. The context places her abounding intelligence as a retreat from real understanding. Once again, we are reminded that to articulate a dilemma is not to transcend it; once again, the novel's mimetic form suggests that the dilemma is crucial for James as well as for the society which engages him so deeply.

5 *Comrades in obliquity*

Mrs Brook and Van are the most completely *social* beings in the novel, and James explores all the ambiguities of the word in his account of their sophisticated amorality.

Their long standing relationship seems to have wearied itself out by the time the book begins, at least for Van. Sadly recognizing their separation after Tishy's party, Mrs Brook recalls

> 'There was a time, in fact, wasn't there? when we rather enjoyed each other's dim depths. If I wanted to fawn on you,' she went on, 'I might say that with such a comrade in obliquity to wind and double about with, I'd risk losing myself in the mine.' (Bk. 9, Ch. 1)

The exact nature of their relationship remains as obscurely allusive as this sentence. We're faced again and again with the difficulty of interpreting even an apparently straightforward statement, given the complex games played with language. We, like Mr Longdon, are puzzled by an 'alliance that would be difficult to explain at Beccles', and presumably different from his own chaste loyalty to Lady Julia; on the other hand the Duchess later informs him – but how reliably? – that they 'haven't done, as it's called, anything wrong'. How much weight are we to give, for example, to Mrs Brook's breathy reminder to the distracted Van of the 'ways' in which she'd like to show her love; to her condescending explanation to her husband that 'we were in love with him'; or to her graceful mockery of the possibility that she could possibly want Van for herself, or that she could feel anything so '*bête*' as jealousy? There are indications of real passion in Mrs Brook at least; though Van, pulling away from an old loyalty grown tedious, seems as remote from her as from anyone else. But as the essence of her social grace is to play, even with her own feelings, as she's so totally a creature of tact and delicacy – or 'duplicity' – we're never sure whether she's to be excused by her passion, or whether she's lost touch with feeling and is simply acting up to an image. James's elusiveness about the sexual basis of their relationship may reflect an impotence beneath their charm, the discontent that seems to be the price they pay for their high civilization.

Their real bond is their curious likeness – a likeness that emerges the more clearly because of the difference in their presentation. Van is first seen at his most charming. We are swayed partly by Mr Longdon's response to his self-deprecating irony and social grace, and prepared to believe that he may indeed possess 'that sort of fulcrum for salvation which consists at least in a deep consciousness and the absence of a rag of illusion'. But – as various critics have pointed out – each following scene only reveals more clearly what's implicit, potential, from the start – his egoism and his shallow evasiveness. By the close of the book, it is he and not Mr Longdon who is placed as lacking perception. In a revealing little incident at Tishy Grendon's, he retreats in horror from the reflection of himself in Harold's crudeness, and chooses instead to identify himself with Mr Longdon. But as Nanda comes to recognize, he's more old-fashioned than Longdon. Like Mrs Brook, he has his moments of introspective honesty, when he can name his calculating superficiality and even glimpse its social significance; but these remain arid because they're purely of the mind. His admission that he fears Nanda's 'conscience' is the final statement, and proof, of the inadequacy of 'consciousness' divorced from value and feeling. The presentation of Mrs Brook, on the other hand, almost reverses this pattern. In one sense the book has nothing to add to the first exposure of the hard materialistic calculations, the indifference even to her own children, that underlie, support, her decorative grace. As the book proceeds, we're forced to an unsettling recognition of the inextricable links between her intelligent charm and her calculating worldliness. We sympathize with her awareness that she reflects the confusions of her 'mixed' world; with her superb inventiveness, with the verve and sharpness of her wit. No simple reading of the novel as an exposure of depravity can do justice to the way James balances these two complex figures in their complex world.

But the different presentation only emphasizes how alike they are in their total dependence on the social medium. If Mrs Brook is active, if she invents, manipulates, controls, she's also wholly dependent for life on those whom she governs. Their admiring devotion is a continuing confirmation of her own wit and vitality; it's the source of her creativity. 'Mrs Brook became as wonderful as if she saw in her friend's face some admiring reflection of the fine freedom of mind that . . . she could always show' (Bk. 4, Ch. 2). Without that reflection, she hardly exists. Her 'despair' when Nanda's presence threatens her circle is probably as genuine as anything she ever says; in the end she's prepared to gamble on destroying herself and her world – they're one and the same thing – rather than take second place. Nanda, by the end, sees how pathetic her mother is, 'so often nowadays practically alone', though Mitchy is more realistic when he predicts that her salon will continue, if with a different personnel. It corresponds, he explains, to a 'deep human need'; he hardly needs to point out that that need is perhaps primarily Mrs Brook's.

If she is active, Van is passively dependent. Just as the other characters pay tribute to her charm, so almost everyone in the book is in love with Van. Mr Longdon's offer is as much for Van's sake as for Nanda's, and he's barely to be comforted in his frustrated 'dream of benevolence', his painful 'personal wound'. Mitchy, equally, wants to 'do something' for Van; his self-sacrificing marriage to Aggie is offered to Van as much as to Nanda. He finds in Van the image of everything he would wish to be, sees him as the source of a 'sacred terror', a great case of 'privilege', who goes through life 'guaranteed' by his charm, by his power to attract people's fantasies:

> You'll walk in magnificent mystery 'later on' not a bit less than you do today; you'll continue to have the benefit of everything our imagination, perpetually engaged, often baffled and never fatigued, will continue to bedeck you with.   (Bk. 6, Ch. 2)

Even the Duchess pays him rather patronizing tribute; she describes him as a beautiful object to be enjoyed, everyone's 'property'. For once the reification sounds as a statement of fact and not simply as an exposure of the speaker's attitudes. For Van's charismatic charm derives from his narcissism. His existence, too, is a reflected one. His image is endlessly refracted back from the devotion of his friends, who in their turn project on to him some dream of their own. He can sustain their imaginings because he never really engages with anyone. He's less interested in Mr Longdon, for example, than in his own self reflected back from so novel a screen – he tries to shock him – and he later admits to the danger of boredom with the old man. To Nanda's almost violent clarity he opposes a muffling 'kindness'. The word echoes through their conversations, as James brilliantly dramatizes how corrupt kindness can be. It's a way of diminishing people, controlling them by insisting on a one-sided relationship; but it's also a defence, an effort to preserve his emotional virginity, to protect his inviolate – and hence sterile – self. If he's for a moment 'in suspense' about himself, he soon falls back on his 'niceness', which 'instantly converted everything to its image'.

> Kindness, therefore, becomes for us, by a quick turn of the glass that reflects the whole scene, the high pitch of the concert – a kindness that almost immediately filled the place, to the exclusion of everything else, with a familiar friendly voice, a brightness of good looks and good intentions, a constant though perhaps sometimes misapplied laugh, a superabundance almost of interest, inattention and movement. (Bk. 10, Ch. 1)

We come to realize, I think, that if Mrs Brook's prediction that he'll never offer for Nanda is self-fulfilling, it's also based on a deeper recognition that he wants 'nothing at all'. Van is locked into himself, his gentlemanly self image; for all his flashes of self mockery, and his admission that he trades on his charm, he's ultimately its victim. (It's perhaps significant that in our one glimpse of him alone, he first reacts uneasily to the sight of his own name written in Nanda's hand on the French novel, then looks in the mirror.) He betrays uneasiness whenever his separateness is threatened, his poised and perfected image shaken in any way. When Nanda and Mrs Brook challenge him (in different ways, for perhaps similar reasons), he instantly withdraws. James continually and subtly indicates his efforts to *demonstrate* his ease, *show* his 'good humoured detachment', *prove* his gaiety. His restlessness and his compulsive talking suggest how he's over-playing, over-projecting his part.

At their final meeting, Nanda finally abandons any attempt to penetrate his defences, recognizing that 'to force on him an awkwardness was like forcing a disfigurement or a hurt'. She offers herself up to preserve his image, perhaps partly because she can't face the nervous terror and emptiness just below his surface:

> ... what that she could ever do for him would really be so beautiful as this present chance to smooth his confusion and add as much as possible to that refined satisfaction with himself that would proceed from his having dealt with a difficult hour in a gallant and delicate way? (Bk. 10, Ch. 1)

Yet her perceptions give her a kind of strength, a mastery of the situation that she's never had before:

> she arrived at the appearance of having changed places with him and of their being together precisely in order that he – not she – should be let down easily. (Bk. 10, Ch. 1)

Van can only 'bargain' with her; his final act in the novel is the conclusive proof of his emptiness. He asks, in return for his care of her mother, that Nanda should care for his 'character as a gentleman'. It's the final unacknowledged acknowledgment that he *is* his reputation, and that, his reputation lying in the power of others, he is impotent.

At the end of *The Awkward Age*, Van and Mrs Brook are tied together by their static quality. James's techniques insist that while our understanding of them changes, they do not. The social masks which they sustain with so much effort allow no possibility of growth; they become, in the end, death masks. When Nanda confronts them with the personal problems of ageing, as well as the wider problems of a changing society, their very claims to youth and modernity trap them. Imperviousness to time implies resistance to change and therefore to any possibility of development. It finally means living death. At the end Van is far more 'fussy' and 'ancient' than Mr Longdon, who in his own curious way has developed. Mrs Brook's often praised youthfulness comes to seem more and more ambiguous – though all the ambiguities flow from that first description:

> She had about her the pure light of youth – would always have it; her head, her figure, her flexibility, her flickering colour, her lovely, silly

eyes, her natural, quavering tone, all played together towards this effect by some trick that had never yet been exposed. (Bk. 2, Ch. 1)

James does indicate, as we see her in action, how her 'trick' operates; he also suggests how her determined youthfulness conceals a terror of old age, a resentment at 'giving up the stage' to her daughter even before she recognizes her as a rival, a determination to 'live a little yet' at no matter whose cost. When Nanda finally appeals to Van, it's because her mother is so 'fearfully young'. The phrase crystallizes the gathering ambiguities of the whole novel. And Van's uneasily optimistic response 'She's youth. She's *my* youth – she *was* mine . . . if she *really* wants to know, she's booked for my old age', hints at the pathos and sterility of a relationship (and a society) that, having failed to change or develop, is condemned to an endless and nostalgic repetition of a pattern that's empty of significance.

6 *The death of childhood*

If Van and Mrs Brook are finally the victims of time, this is even more painfully true for the children. *The Awkward Age*, like *What Maisie Knew*, is about growing up; but about growing up in a society where growth is impossible, and where adolescence is simply an awkward gap between childhood and adulthood.

James explores ironically the complicated but apparently necessary fiction by which children are viewed as blank innocents, yet at the same time immensely capable of depravity. Aggie is a comic (and tragic) embodiment of the contradiction. Part of the irony springs from the fact that she's formed to a foreign ideal, and one so old-fashioned that even Mr Longdon finds it new. Yet the very exaggeration of the Duchess's care is an accurate enough comment on the English scene. Aggie's 'emphasized virginity' is a consumer product, geared very successfully to the demands of the marriage market. Moreover, the need to maintain moral values and social ideals, more and more difficult in the practice of a materialistic society, is projected onto children, particularly girls; *their* blatant purity is the necessary other face of confusion and immorality. 'Aggie, don't you see? is the Duchess's morality, her virtue; which, by having it that way, outside of you, as one may say, you can make a much better thing of . . . There it is – to show' (Bk. 6, Ch. 2). Mrs Brook suggests half mockingly that, partly because she's less of a hypocrite than her friend, Nanda embodies her 'vice', her 'immorality'. She recognizes that Nanda is 'exposed' to her own mother, but though she impatiently dismisses 'the preposterous fiction of Nanda's blankness of mind', she uses that fiction for her own ends. For all her claims to enlightenment, her life depends on maintaining social fictions, and throughout the book, it is she who in various ways, crude and subtle, publicizes Nanda's 'knowledge', the extent to which she falls short of the ideal. Only Mitchy, of all this group, can see that the ideal young girl is a 'pious fraud', and genuinely accept 'the modern girl, the product of our hard London facts, and of her inevitable consciousness of them'. He recognizes, with a full and painful acceptance of responsibility, that Nanda is what they've made her; for his understanding springs from the fact that he, like Nanda, is a 'monster' who doesn't fit into any social category, and who has no choice but to 'smash' traditions. Ironically, Mitchy finds himself unhappily married, not to Nanda whom he loves and understands, but to Aggie.

In this world, children become adults overnight. Their childhood is violated and destroyed. When we first see Harold, as his mother pushes him out to fend for himself, he has the voice and the clothes of a man of forty. We're hardly surprised when he later takes his full adult status as Lady Fanny's lover. Throughout, his crude precocity and openness about sex and money serve as an effective commentary on the more gracefully disguised motives of the adults from whom he has learned. Aggie, again, 'the other day was about six, is now practically about forty'. Nanda tries to comfort Mitchy by explaining that Aggie is only trying to find out 'what sort of person she is. How can she ever have known? It was carefully, elaborately hidden from her – kept so obscure that she could make out nothing' (Bk. 10, Ch. 3). But precipitated as she is into adult society, Aggie can only become the kind of person she sees around her. Her seduction of her aunt's lover is fearfully predictable.

Aggie and Harold throw light on Nanda's more complex tragedy. Her first eagerly childish identification with her mother's circle, before she comes down, proliferates with ironies:

We discuss everything and everyone – we're always discussing each other. I think we must be rather celebrated for it, and its a kind of trick – isn't it? – that's catching. . . . Mother says we haven't any prejudices. (Bk. 3, Ch. 3)

This comic assumption of adult poise soon becomes a trap from which she can't escape. Her growing friendship with Mr Longdon helps to clarify for her what it really means to be part of this circle; and helps her to maintain the courage to face the facts and to 'brazen it out' as herself, whatever the cost. Van's uneasiness rapidly indicates what that cost will be. He will never marry her because she is too much her mother's daughter, too much 'one of us'. She confronts him directly with his modesty:

'I can't help it any more than you can, can I?' So she appeared to put it to him, with something in her lucidity that would have been infinitely touching; a strange, grave, calm consciousness of their common doom and of what in especial in it would be worst for herself. (Bk. 7, Ch. 1)

But he retreats because Nanda (unlike Aggie, whom he ought to have married) makes him see too clearly what *he* is.

Because of her awareness, because of the seriousness with which she nerves herself to confront the adult world, Nanda becomes, overnight, the oldest person in the book. She treats Mr Longdon with the tenderness due to a sick child; at the end, it's she who is the parent, and Van and her mother the terrifying impervious children. (Van as usual sees the fact but not its significance: 'You're indeed, as she herself used to say, the modern daughter! It takes that type to wish to make a career for her parents': Bk. 10, Ch. 2). And as an adult, she can only act in terms of the world she knows. She adopts their mode, not only verbally. She begins to manipulate others when she 'works' Mitchy, with disastrous consequences; and Mitchy is not just joking when he sees her at the end as complementing her mother's activities by looking after the unhappy husbands.

Paradoxically, the only person in the novel who seems to go through a process of developing growth is Mr Longdon; the stress on his age, the nearness of death, is a sad and limiting counterpoint. Nanda elucidates her own situation with tragic accuracy:

I shall never change – I shall be always just the same. The same old, mannered, modern, slangy hack . . . what I am I must remain. I haven't what's called a principle of growth.   (Bk. 5, Ch. 1)

Her story is a negation of the idea of growth; in this she resembles the much younger Maisie. We are simultaneously aware of Maisie as both child and adult. The adults exploit both her innocence and the knowingness she needs to survive, until by the end they have destroyed the child. She speaks for the first time wholly as an adult, with adult understanding, as she makes her ineffective but oddly sexual bid for Sir Claude; then goes off in charge of the pathetic Mrs Wix, older in her knowledge than anyone else in the novel. For what Maisie knows, and what Nanda knows, is her own violation, her own corruption. And what we come to know through them is the corruption of a whole society.

There's a further dimension suggested with Nanda. For if she achieves an uncompromising recognition of her own compromised identity, even this is qualified by the divorce of that knowledge from what she feels. Nanda's tragedy is that she *shares* Van's old-fashioned ideals, that she can accept her modernity with her intelligence but not her emotions. She is unable to love the truly sympathetic Mitchy precisely because he *can* accept her, because he doesn't share those 'hereditary prejudices' that pervade this supposedly prejudice-free circle. Nanda could only love an old-fashioned 'gentleman' just as Van could only love a 'lady'. And just as Van represents to Mitchy everything he is not, so Nanda mourns that lost golden innocence which she thinks she sees in Aggie. The sudden strained ugliness of her mannered language – 'Doesn't one become a sort of a little drain-pipe with everything flowing through?' – suggests a terrified and barely controlled revulsion from everything she is. And this division of feeling from intelligence can only issue in a perverse masochism, a cherishing of frustration. Recognizing that Mitchy too has chosen martyrdom, she gives a grave and considered 'yes' to his question, 'Do you positively like to love in vain?'

The only comfort the novel proffers is a kind of historical awareness; an awareness achieved only by the misfits, those who're forced, by their sense of dislocation, to a wider understanding. Mitchy, for example, seems to reach it through a recognition of his own anomalous position, 'handicapped almost to death' by his birth and his looks, but accepted everywhere because of his money. Mr Longdon simply by virtue of his age has the 'long backward vision' that enables him to recognize, and partly understand the significance of that transitory house party Mitchy gives in the great rented house, Mertle; or that leads him to speculate as to whether Petherton lowers his position, his class, or whether it was 'the position that let down the man'. Mr Longdon (and at moments James as well) idealizes the past; yet the beautiful loyalty to Lady Julia is surely the issue of impotence. Mr Longdon even sees that she probably enjoyed his hopeless love, and that he was only capable of attracting 'that dreadful consolatory liking' which is what Nanda gives Mitchy. He comes to revalue past as well as present as he slowly and painfully becomes part of the London circle and, like Nanda, is forced to play its manipulatory games; and as he learns to reject the old-fashioned Van and accept the thoroughly modern Nanda. He is 'indoctrinated' by Nanda who understands that she is divided because she is of her time. 'We can't help it . . . . There's so much else that's extraordinary that if we're in it all so much *we* must naturally be' (Bk. 10, Ch. 4). She sees that she cannot be Lady Julia, but nor can she – how could she? – discover in the modern world any forms or conventions that correspond to what she is. Nanda is the victim of history.

This is not to suggest that James describes anything as simple as the individual oppressed by society, the self crushed by convention. He no longer tries to envisage a non-social self; as is made clear in that single startling moment when Nanda breaks down under the dammed-up pressure of her never-expressed passion for Van:

> It burst from her, flaring up, in a queer quaver that ended in something queerer still – in her abrupt collapse, on the spot, into the nearest chair, where she choked with a torrent of tears. Her buried face could only after a moment give way to the flood, and she sobbed in a passion as sharp and brief as the flurry of a wild thing for an instant uncaged. (Bk. 10, Ch. 4)

But that 'wild' emotion, which might, indeed, break down the whole social fabric, is seen as sub-human, primitive, animal. (Nanda, the

Duchess earlier remarked unaware, is 'as sick as a little cat with her passion'.) The passion can have no place in Nanda's life, for to live it out, even to express it fully, would amount to *self* destruction. We recall that Mrs Brook was described as wild in her moment of self-destruction; and that Nanda labels Mitchy as 'wild' when he playfully hints at the painful self-immolation that's the only possible expression of his love for Nanda. It's not that Nanda is caged: she herself *is* the cage. Convention has been internalized, can issue only in the masochism of her perversely willed heroism. She and Mr Longdon take the social world with them into their Suffolk Arcadia. They disturb and move us because, as they reject society, their strange relationship – father and daughter, mother and child, husband and wife – serves, in its half-sublimated sexuality, its sad but loving sterility, as the book's most complete image of social living.

Notes

* In some modern editions, such as the Penguin, the chapters are numbered consecutively: those of Book 2 are numbered 4–9; Book 3, 10–12; Book 4, 13–15; Book 5, 16–20; Book 6, 21–3; Book 7, 24–6; Book 8, 27–30; Book 9, 31–4 and Book 10, 35–8.

1. See the illuminating discussion by Elizabeth Owen, '*The Awkward Age* and the Contemporary English Scene', *Victorian Studies*, xi, 1967, pp. 63–82.

2. *The Art of the Novel*, edited by R. P. Blackmur, New York, 1934, p. 57.

3. F. W. Dupee, *Henry James*, New York, 1956, pp. 164–76. Ian Gregor and Brian Nicholas, *The Moral and the Story*, London, 1962, pp. 151–84.

4. Letter of February 1893, in Janet Adam Smith (ed.), *Henry James and Robert Louis Stevenson*, London, 1948, p. 221.

5. 'The Ambiguity of Henry James' in *The Triple Thinkers*, London, 1952, esp. pp. 126–7 and 146–7.

6. Unsigned review in *Academy*, May 1899, reprinted in Roger Gard (ed.), *Henry James, The Critical Heritage*, London, 1968, p. 286.

7. Richard Poirier, *The Comic Sense of Henry James*, London, 1960, esp. the conclusion, pp. 247–55.

8. *The Art of the Novel*, p. 146.

7

The Ambassadors and *The Sacred Fount* the artist *manqué*

BERNARD RICHARDS

The title of *The Sacred Fount* suggests that its ostensible theme is the ability of people to drain away the life forces of others. The title of *The Ambassadors* draws attention to the ambassadorial mission to naughty Paris. Yet the two novels have an extraordinary number of similarities, especially in their respective heroes. A study based on a comparison of the heroes will focus attention on other basic similarities of theme and method.

The fictional method is not identical. *The Sacred Fount* is autobiographical, whereas *The Ambassadors*, being a longer work, avoids what James called 'the terrible *fluidity* of self-revelation' in the form.[1] We know from the Preface that the germ of *The Ambassadors* was Strether's anguish at his missed opportunities, and his exhortation to little Bilham to 'live'. The Preface stresses the importance of the fact that the drama matters only in so far as it concerns Strether and his inner life. There is no preface to *The Sacred Fount*. It was not included in the New York edition of the works – perhaps because it was too perverse. But I suspect that if James had written a preface, it would have drawn interest away from the mysterious and dark subject of emotional cannibalism and psychic vampirism, and the reader's interest would have been directed to the problem of the consciousness of the narrator. The entries in the *Notebooks* do not concentrate on the theme of subjectivity, and this is a case where the preliminary notes should not be used as the main pointer to the achieved work. When one reviews the two works, it can be seen that a dominant theme running through them is the way in which a healthy life depends upon a regulation of the observation and interpretation of one's self, one's society and one's relation to it. It is in fact the traditional theme of 'appearance and reality'. Traditional as the theme was by 1900, James had something new to offer to its development. He makes himself as a novel writer, his characters and his readers share in the problem of the reception, the analysis and the expansion of data. Strether and the unnamed narrator of *The Sacred Fount* (whom I will call the Narrator from now on) both have a characteristic in common: that of making wilful assumptions about life, and trusting too much in the truth of these assumptions before they have really had time to test them. Strether is perhaps less blameworthy than the Narrator, because he develops his own theories, whereas the Narrator accepts his basic hypothesis from someone else – someone, moreover, who does not take the idea very seriously, and would not place as much reliance on it. This same quality of fanciful inventiveness is invariably shared by James himself, whose prefaces contain many references to the expansion of tiny ideas dropped in conversation. The Preface to *The Ambassadors* contains a long discourse on the process of the amplification and exploration of a *donnée*. What distinguishes James from many authors, however, is his particular pride in being able to point to very slight and trivial sources for his novels. The smaller the seed, the prouder he seems of the plant. We know that he stopped dinner-table stories when he thought he had collected enough for his purpose. In writing *The Ambassadors* James's first concern was to cut off the story from its originator: William Dean Howells. This was only right and proper. He then goes on to describe how he explored the possibilities in the phrase so casually dropped. Here, he gives the impression of dealing with something almost magical, and having an objective existence:

> It being thus the respectable hint that I had with such avidity picked up, what would be the story to which it would most inevitably form the centre? It is part of the charm attendant on such questions that the 'story', with the omens true, as I say, puts on from this stage the authenticity of concrete existence. It then *is*, essentially – it begins to be, though it may more or less obscurely lurk. . . .[2]

James suggests that there comes a point in creation when one does not so much 'invent' but 'discover'. As far as writing a work of fiction is concerned, there need not be anything wrong with starting from small beginnings, and spinning out facts from one's entrails like Swift's spider. In any case, the novelist does not rely entirely on such a slender basis: one cannot create from 'nothing', and *The Ambassadors* does not only grow from a chance remark in a garden, but from a lifetime of experience and observation. No one who has lived has ever had the chance to check up on the validity of the multifarious assumptions, both major and minor, on which he bases his life; but many people at least make the attempt, and do not hold up a finger at the dinner-table of life to say 'I have enough facts now, thank-you'. If one does, there is a danger of retreating into a private world, and perhaps even becoming paranoiac. James was always anxious to stress the relations between life and art, and often recommended that they should mutually sustain each other. If he took this seriously, he may have had slight, or even acute guilt feelings about his fictional method, and *The Sacred Fount* may well be a self-admonitory fable, with applications to life and art. It could be that the maturing James felt that his works were less and less related to the way people actually live, and decided to put his misgivings on record in this whimsical and self-abusing fable. Robert Perlongo, who holds this view, quotes from James's letter to the Duchess of Sutherland, in which James refers to *The Sacred Fount* as a 'profitless labyrinth',[3] and perhaps there is strong self-irony in the work. James employs a common rhetoric of the growing seed, the elaborately fabricated building, the woven tapestry, the pursuing bloodhound, the flashing light of revelation and the cunning detective to describe his own artistic activity, as well as the imaginative activity of the Narrator of *The Sacred Fount* and Lambert Strether.

The 'parable' of *The Sacred Fount* is admonitory in that it refers not only to the author, but also to the readers. James was well informed of the habits of his readers. The Preface to *The Ambassadors* shows that he always bore in mind the potential for dimness and insensitivity in the bulk of his readers. All of James's later works have a treacherous surface to trap readers who are dim, imperceptive, over-confident or careless. Over-confident and imperceptive readers will think that they have guessed the 'secret' of *The Sacred Fount*. The

perceptive readers will see that there is no 'secret' to learn, because
the deluded witness is the sole purveyor of information, and his
evidence is not enough to go on in framing an absolute picture of the
state of affairs at Newmarch. If one does construct elaborate theories
of relationships in the novel, one will be trapped into the same
situation as the hero – of building castles in air. This is by no means
the first time that the reader has been exploited in the novel. In
Emma, Jane Austen employs match-making 'habits' which she knows
are common in real life, and in the reading of fiction. This partly
explains why the reader is sympathetic to Emma: both are on the
look-out for marriageable pairs and satisfying symmetrical patterns.
With Jane Fairfax, or the omniscient narrator at the centre of consciousness, the situation would be different. James knew that the
reader shares in the activities of characters in the novel to a very
intimate degree, and perhaps there is something in Parker Tyler's
thesis that Mrs Brissenden is 'a symbol of James's own readers'.[4] *The
Ambassadors* does not exploit the dim readers as cruelly as *The Sacred
Fount*, but James is aware of their presence – as the Preface shows,
when he says that many of them will fall for that old *ficelle* Maria
Gostrey.[5] He is aware of readers even as he is telling his story –
though he refers to them in a more discreet fashion than Sterne,
Thackeray and Trollope.

From the technical point of view, the big difference between *The
Sacred Fount* and *The Ambassadors* is that the former is an autobiography and the latter has an omniscient narrator who presents
events from the point of view of the hero. The narrator stands behind
Strether's shoulder and shares more of the limitations of his limited
view than the narrator of *Emma*. The narrator of *Emma* is allowed a
varied make-up, with room for spite, generosity, narrow judgement
and tolerance, whereas the narrator of *The Ambassadors* is rather
colourless and self-effacing. The narrator of *The Ambassadors* does
not entirely restrict himself to Strether's viewpoint. We sometimes
feel that the narrator is running in a kind of three-legged race with
the hero, strapped onto his leg like a mute, but recording, witness. If
he shares Strether's consciousness, there is not much point in having
him there. If he does not share it, then he is a different person, and if
he is a different person, one wants to know something of his own

basis for judgement, understanding and sympathy. Clearly, the narrator here *is* a different person: one who is always making unobtrusive little value judgements. (Indeed, it is impossible to choose words without making a value judgement.) If he makes a value judgement at one point, one feels he ought to be capable of making it at another. The reader is at a particular disadvantage, as he is denied means of checking up on almost everything that happens in the novel. In real life, and in the theatre, we have some basis for judgement of others by observing facial expression and listening to their tone of voice. But by virtue of the nature of this novel, and novels in general, we are deprived of this useful adjunct, and are in a sense blindfold spectators of the three-legged race. James was aware of this problem, as his Preface shows. One of the important questions in the novel is 'Has Chad changed?' We are not even sure whether or not he has had a startling physical change. And because he has not been presented to us in his transatlantic state, we are in no position to judge. One feels that if the omniscient narrator could tell us so many other things, he could tell us that, but he confines himself, and us, to Strether's consciousness. The whole situation of the novel exists in a kind of moral vacuum. This method of presentation did represent a big sacrifice for James, as one can see in the following passage:

> The true inwardness of this may be at bottom but that one of the suffered treacheries has consisted precisely, for Chad's whole figure and presence, of a direct presentability diminished and compromised – despoiled, that is, of its proportional advantage.[6]

What is gained, on the other hand, is the fact that the reader can distance himself from Strether more than he could if he were seeing events entirely through Strether's eyes, and gain a more composite and scenic picture of what is going on. The narrator is never violently disapproving of Strether, but the style sometimes conveys an evanescent impression of amused criticism in its poise, restraint and discrimination. The tone of the opening page is typical of what is to come:

> The same secret principle, however, that had prompted Strether not absolutely to desire Waymarsh's presence at the dock, that had led him

thus to postpone for a few hours his enjoyment of it, now operated to make him feel he could still wait without disappointment. (Bk. 1, Ch. 1)

Nevertheless, it is only when we wander into James's letters and essays that we can form an impression of how much he would disapprove of a real-life Strether, if he met him.

Strether is a very full fictional character, though it is only when we have finished the novel that we can begin to see how much we know about him. As we are actually reading, he seems to be a little flat and empty, almost another John Marcher – a man to whom nothing has ever happened. Of course, an irony lurks in the phrase 'a man to whom nothing has ever happened'. No one can go through life without something happening. Turgenev reveals this in the ironical work *The Diary of a Superfluous Man* – a man who turns out to have been far from 'superfluous'. However, Strether is like the Narrator of *The Sacred Fount* and several other Jamesian heroes – a man distinguished for his contemplative life rather than for his active one. Strether is a man who is timid, self-centred, ungenerous, over-diplomatic, untrustworthy and on many occasions untrusting. These qualities he shares with the Narrator of *The Sacred Fount* and with several other heroes of James's later novels. James does not offer exhaustive reasons why Strether should be like this, and the financial and cultural poverty of his American upbringing could only ever go a small way towards explaining why he has this make-up. James would probably have to say 'He is as he is'. Strether changed as a character as the novel grew under James's hands. As originally conceived, he had a stauncher set of Puritan attitudes. The *Notebook* entry reads: 'He has never really enjoyed – he has lived only for Duty and conscience – his conception of them; for pure appearances and daily tasks – lived for effort, for surrender, abstention, sacrifice.'[7] The Strether we know from the completed work is still a Puritan in the American tradition, but shorn of transcendental beliefs and moral rigidity, so that a Puritan temperament remains, but little more. The facets of effort, surrender and abstention remain, but subservient to a private goal rather than a social and religious one. The life of abstention and withdrawal means that one is forced to develop inner resources and, to some extent, create 'countries of the mind'. To an outsider, such a life could seem the product of earnest effort, and a gloriously perverse act of assertive triumph. I do not think that in Strether's case we are faced with a disinterested practice of aesthetic belief. His attitudes are more defensive, and are concerned with avoiding too close a contact with life and involvement in it. He is a non-creative artist, in that he is more concerned with self-cultivation than in fabricating artefacts. The mainspring of his character seems to be timidity rather than the desire for artistic beauty. If we were not told that he had a son, it would not be unlikely to guess that he is virginal. He fears being made a fool of. In the last chapter he tells Maria Gostrey that this is one of the reasons why he is going back to New England – because he is less likely to appear silly there. It is not unlikely that he will be just as big a fool. All through the novel he has been building up Mrs Newsome's ghostly presence. Unless he makes the adjustment to her actual and changed presence on his return, he is likely to begin the cycle of deluded initiation all over again. In the course of the novel he has lived a life too inward, and too nurtured on art. Art has helped him to prepare for Europe, as it prepared Isabel Archer and other of James's characters, but Strether is less self-critical of this feature of himself than most of the others. He feels that if he had been brought up in Europe he would have been more content with his surroundings, and would have found less pretext for retreating into the green covers of his Review. When Strether is wandering in the countryside, he finds it so accordant with his prepared vision that he is tempted to imagine that European life would have brought him out of his shell more:

> Not a single one of his observations but somehow fell into a place in it; not a breath of the cooler evening that wasn't somehow a syllable of the text. The text was simply, when condensed, that in *these* places such things were, and that if it was in them one elected to move about one had to make one's account with what one lighted on.   (Bk. 11, Ch. 3)

He has a passion for 'symmetry' (Bk. 5, Ch. 2), and for 'the picturesque' (Bk. 11, Ch. 1). And when taken to the theatre in London by Maria Gostrey, he thinks he sees drama on the stage and on the audience's side of the curtain. I stress the fact that Strether 'thinks' he sees resemblances between ordered art and ordered life, because the novel's incidents give no sustained suggestion that European life would ultimately satisfy Strether's yearnings for order and beauty. The 'international situation' is not an essential part of Strether's dilemma. One feels that he has personal inadequacies which would involve him in defeat and humiliation anywhere in the world, including his home State. The Narrator of *The Sacred Fount* goes through *his* crisis in his native habitat, though it is hard to guess what class he comes from as he has been out of the Newmarch circle for some time. Hints abound in *The Ambassadors* that Strether has already made the mistake, back in America, of expecting life to conform to his dreams: there is the case of his dim little boy – though perhaps he would have been less dim if Strether had devoted more attention to him. The 'international situation' serves the purpose of making Strether's mistakes a little more excusable. He is in Paris for less than a year, and anyone can make mistakes of judgement in a strange country in that short time. Also, there is the fact alluded to in the Preface of Paris being the traditional setting for one's second 'Fall'. James was anxious to dissociate himself from the vulgar treatment of 'the dreadful little old tradition . . . that people's moral scheme *does* break down in Paris', but the fact remains that he could use this tradition – even if only negatively: 'The *likely* place had the great merit of sparing me preparations. . . .'[8]

The world picture shared by Strether and the Narrator perhaps gives them a fairly good reason for being timid of life. They see a world of the menacing and the menaced. Strether thinks he sees in Europe a host of social booby traps lurking in the different manners and forms. He imagines he is always on the point of setting off a spring in the social machine that will reveal him as gauche and un-initiated. He wants to *know* about life before he commits himself to living it, but he does not want to find out either by participating or by snooping in keyholes. He wants to find out in the discreet and much more artistically satisfying way of *watching* the people who indulge in social intercourse, and *guessing* from gestures, facial expressions and tone of voice what kind of people they are. Obert in *The Sacred Fount* expresses a similar view, with which the Narrator concurs:

Resting on the *kind* of signs that the game takes account of when fairly played – resting on psychologic signs alone, it's a high application of intelligence. What's ignoble is the detective and the keyhole.   (Ch. 4)

Strether and the Narrator both possess the rather primitive belief that the inner man draws the outward man 'to suffer all alike'. They both hide their ignorance and proceed to play the game of duplicity which they assume everyone else is playing. In both novels the game of pretending to be in possession of knowledge, while at the same time fishing for facts, is played by the device of the incomplete sentence: the sentence which one person leaves hanging, and the second person either rushes to complete, or is forced to complete. There are hundreds of examples in both works. I cite just one from a chapter dense with them: Chapter I of Book 10. The scene is Chad's big party, where Strether looks particularly like a child at a grown-up feast. After an unproductive conversation with little Bilham, he has another one with Miss Barrace. He is horrified to find himself regarded as the 'hero' of the piece, especially as that could mean his being called upon to *do* something. He tries to divert attention by pointing to 'the heroine'. The reader probably assumes that Strether has Sarah Pocock in mind, as he says 'I haven't been near her. I haven't looked at her.' This ties in with the comment a little earlier: 'Those eyes during the wonderful dinner itself he hadn't once met; having confessedly – perhaps a little pusillanimously – arranged with Chad that he should be on the same side of the table.' It is difficult for the reader to know how much reliance to put on phrase echoes like these. However, Miss Barrace thinks he is treating Madame de Vionnet as the heroine, and that he is pointing to some kind of liaison between her and Jim Pocock. Miss Barrace thinks that Strether has the missing links and the 'connexions unnamed', and Strether thinks that Miss Barrace has them. There is a sort of Emperor's new clothes situation, with both sides too proud to admit that actually they know nothing. It is in situations such as these that slander and calumny thrive. What delays Strether from coming to a state of self-knowledge earlier is that other people are prepared to play the game with him, just as the guests at Newmarch are prepared to be sparring partners for the Narrator. Miss Barrace and Maria Gostrey are both guilty of it. Little Bilham is a more sceptical, direct and dry individual, as far as one can see from his speech. Strether knows, or thinks he knows, that other people spin out visionary worlds, and live a good part of their lives in them. He attributes the facility to Mamie Pocock when he finds her on her balcony staring into the Rue de Rivoli:

> It came to him indeed the next thing that there was perhaps almost an excess of refinement in having left Mamie in such weather up there alone; however she might in fact have extemporized, under the charm of the Rue de Rivoli, a little makeshift Paris of wonder and fancy. (Bk. 9, Ch. 3)

And yet he does not make enough allowance for the deceit and pretence which this must involve, especially when on a fact-finding mission, though he over-allows for deceit and pretence when he should be engaging in action, confessing to ignorance, offering sympathy and trying to form a workable impression of friends and enemies. He alienates and isolates himself. His alienation is not as extreme or as noticeable as that of the Narrator of *The Sacred Fount*, who has to suffer direct and humiliating rebukes on this account, but it is significant that Strether does not make any new friendships during the course of the novel that will continue when he has returned to America, and he does not reinforce any of his old ones. As far as Maria Gostrey is concerned, he will join the ranks of the 'repatriated' referred to at the outset (Bk. 1, Ch. 3).

I have mentioned 'the social machine' that Strether and the Narrator fear. Perhaps James believed that the social machine of Europe could administer more crushing blows that the American one of the period. The American machine could be exclusive and influential, but the European one had a greater capacity, by virtue of its self-confidence, cohesiveness and stability, to be humiliating as well as exclusive. But this is not all that makes the heroes seem 'timid' in the two novels under review, as well as self-centred and passionless. They both have a view of human relationships that would make anyone quiver in his boots. One could apply various labels to the type of relationships which the heroes think they can detect in life – moral vampirism, emotional cannibalism and so on. As they see it, the partners in an intimate and amorous relationship sustain losses or reap gains of a physical and psychomatic kind. In a close relationship, one of the partners grows younger and more vigorous at the expense of the other, who grows older and emotionally depleted. This is the theme that gives *The Sacred Fount* its title. The Narrator goes to the country house believing that one of a pair of secret lovers is draining away the fount of life of the other, and gaining all the benefits. The irony is that the Narrator is, in a sense, guilty of the crime he is looking for. He is drinking at the fount of life, and living off the experiences of others, and putting nothing into the lives of those around him – at least nothing that could pass as sympathy or understanding. And perhaps one of the characters we meet is in love with him. Many critics who have written on the novel favour Mrs Server as a possible candidate. Mrs Brissenden encourages the Narrator in his theory at first – no critics have really suggested why. There can be no final answer, but it seems not unlikely that the reason why Mrs Briss supports the Narrator is that she really is having an affair with Long, and the vampirism theme is being used as a fire-screen. So long as the Narrator and his allies are looking for contrasting halves in the relationship, they will miss Mrs Briss and Long, who are both happy and blooming. Mrs Briss and Long *do* travel together. Guy Brissenden has acquiesced either willingly or unwillingly in his wife's affair, and is installed in the bachelor wing at Newmarch. Mrs Briss is perhaps at the end of her affair with Long, and feels the need not only to tell the truth about him, but also to shatter the Narrator's world in such a way that he will never be able to guess the truth about her. Mrs Briss exhibits a certainty about Long's stupidity which *could* betray a close relationship. For Mrs Briss to encourage the Narrator in his primitive philosophical view that people in love leave 'a sufficient show of tell-tale traces' (Ch. 2) on each other, is to guarantee the surest form of protection, because she has put the Narrator onto the scent of pairs who are in give-take relationships, whereas *her* relationship with Long is one of mutual giving and taking. If *The Sacred Fount* is to be read as a comedy of manners, and I believe it is, then an interpretation of this kind, though not necessarily *this* interpretation exactly, is what is needed.

Strether has a similar faith in external signs, and if it were well-founded it *would* enable him to learn secrets in life without revealing his ignorance, or being involved in vulgar snooping. We see traces of

The Sacred Fount philosophy in *The Ambassadors*. There is an undercurrent of suggestion all the way through that Madame de Vionnet,
has been draining Chad, as well as assisting in his development: that
she has become young and that he has become old. Strether keeps
playing with the idea that it is *he* who is the young and innocent man,
and Chad who is the old man. It is only when Strether thinks that
Chad has broken free from Madame de Vionnet that he can begin to
see him as a young man again:

> Strether met his eyes with a sense of multiplying thoughts. What was it
> that made him at present, late at night and after journeys, so renewedly,
> so substantially young? Strether saw in a moment what it was – it was
> that he was younger again than Madame de Vionnet.   (Bk. 12, Ch. 4)

Conversely, Madame de Vionnet seems older when Strether sees her
for the last time: 'she was older for him tonight, visibly less exempt
from the touch of time' (Bk. 12, Ch. 2). Madame de Vionnet, in this
interview, does in a sense confess to the emotional vampirism, so at
least the reader has more basis for believing that this is how some
people in love view themselves than he was offered in *The Sacred
Fount*:

> What I hate is myself – when I think that one has to take so much, to be
> happy, out of the lives of others, and that one isn't happy even then.
> One does it to cheat one's self and to stop one's mouth – but that's only
> at the best for a little. The wretched self is always there, always making
> one somehow a fresh anxiety. What it comes to is that it's not, that it's
> never, a happiness, any happiness, at all, to *take*. The only safe thing is
> to give. It's what plays you least false.   (Bk. 12, Ch. 2)

Attitudes such as these need to be learned at first hand, however, and
Strether is really only at the beginning of wisdom at the end of the
novel, with still a long way to go. He has treated Maria Gostrey as a
'fount' but even there he has sipped rather than gulped, and as Maria
is herself rather timid, withdrawing and selfish, the astute reader has
never had any serious hopes of a 'match' between her and Strether.
Here is the rhetoric of *The Sacred Fount* used to describe Strether's
cooling relationship with Maria Gostrey:

> . . . the time seemed already far off when he had held out his small
> thirsty cup to the spout of her pail. Her pail was scarce touched now,

and other fountains had flowed for him; she fell into her place as but one of his tributaries; and there was a strange sweetness – a melancholy mildness that touched him – in her acceptance of the altered order. (Bk. 7, Ch. 3)

Strether is living off others, even as the Narrator of *The Sacred Fount* does. He fails to 'give' partly because he is not sure who he wants to bestow his gifts on, and partly because he thinks the act of giving will reveal the paucity of his gifts.

I do not know how James felt himself about the views of love held by Strether and the Narrator. One would like to think he dissociated himself from them, and had a sense of his own distancing from the pernicious doctrines, and realized that, in the happiest relationships, both parties grow more rich by giving. If James *did* think that this mutual growth and destruction was an essential feature of love, and even milder relationships, then he would allow a greater degree of excuse for Strether's highly elaborate and well-developed defence mechanisms. There is some suggestion that he did think in similar terms of his own love for Minny Temple. In a letter to his brother after her death, he described 'the gradual change and reversal of our relations: I slowly crawling from weakness and inaction and suffering into strength and health and hope: she sinking out of brightness and youth into decline and death. It's almost as if she had passed away – as far as I am concerned – from having served her purpose, that of standing well within the world, inviting and inviting me onward by all the bright intensity of her example.'[9] However, James makes views of this kind subjective in the novels, and protects himself from criticism.

The dependence on external signs and the evidence of the eyes also involves Strether in a passion for symmetry and picturesqueness. The Narrator of *The Sacred Fount* suffers from this too. He has a habit of reading too much significance into groups of people striking him as being 'pictorial', or 'balanced'. Any spasms of self-deprecation are quickly overcome:

These opposed couples balanced like bronze groups at the two ends of a chimney-piece, and the most I could say to myself in lucid deprecation of my thought was that I mustn't take them equally for granted merely *because* they balanced. Things in the real had a way of not balancing; it was all an affair, this fine symmetry, of artificial proportion. Yet even while I kept my eyes away from Mrs Briss and Long it was vivid to me that, 'composing' there beautifully, they could scarce help playing a part in my exhibition.   (Ch. 9)

One feels that, in more fortunate circumstances, Strether and the Narrator could have been creative artists. The existence of the first person narrative attests to the Narrator's skill, and we get the impression that he will use the document called *The Sacred Fount* as an instrument to formulate new theories of what went on during his stay at Newmarch. In the *Notebooks*, James played with the idea of making Strether into a novelist. I said earlier that timidity rather than an irrepressible aesthetic instinct was probably the mainspring of Strether's character, but it would be unfair to deny entirely a well-developed aesthetic sense in Strether. His responses to Paris and the French countryside are those of an especially sensitive and visually trained man. Many of the perceptions attributed to him are almost indistinguishable from James's own travel writings. There is however an undercurrent of a rather sinister kind – that Strether both subverts artistic productions for the basis of his own wayward romancing, and uses the patterns of art as a convenient paradigm for the patterns of life. He is often searching in life for the regularity and predictability which one finds in works of art. It is when he finds life consonant with art that he can feel most secure and in control. Life for him is something that can be poured into moulds, or fitted into a neat form – a square frame for America and an oblong frame for Europe. His alarm grows when life threatens to overflow the moulds or break out of the frame. The Narrator of *The Sacred Fount* suffers from the same illusions of 'control'. He likes to see himself as a Providential figure and, 'under the appeal of phantasmagoric life' (Ch. 9), almost believes that people act out roles he has judged to be appropriate for them.

The famous boat episode in *The Ambassadors* exemplifies Strether's view of art and life better than almost any other scene, but similar principles have been operating all through the novel. Towards the end of his mission, Strether goes out in the country for a day's relaxation, to escape from the present and try to relive an experience he had years ago in Boston: that of seeing France through a picture in a gallery. One of the big regrets of Strether's life is that he did not *buy* the picture, yet one feels that the initial intensity of vision was not really affected by his failed bid at possession. On the trip Strether is lucky. It is a fine day, the countryside has not been ruined by the creeping mildew of subtopia, and all the scenes are exactly right. It reminds him of literary works, as well as the picture he saw in Boston by Lambinet. Emile C. Lambinet was a minor member of the Barbizon School, the group of painters which included Troyon, Daubigny and Rousseau, 'and which summed up for the American collector and in the New York and Boston markets the idea of the modern in the masterly'.[10] A beautiful Lambinet, 'Fishing on the Banks of the Seine', was acquired by the Boston Museum of Fine Arts in 1872, the same year that James visited Doll and Richard's gallery and wrote his appreciative essay 'French Pictures in Boston' for the *Atlantic Monthly*. As John L. Sweeney points out in *The Painter's Eye*, the exhibition rooms of Doll and Richards were in Tremont Street.[11] Perhaps the reference in the novel enshrines a memory and a lost opportunity for James himself. It certainly helps to give one of the many realistic touches of local colour. It would have been possible for Strether to buy a Lambinet, and by refusing to name a famous painting by Corot or Daubigny, James is keeping the sense of realism alive, and avoiding the distraction which can be created when a famous work of art is referred to in a novel. Strether wanders into the painting, but he does not become a figure in the painting: he is only aware of himself as a pair of eyes looking on, and still drawing an imaginary frame around what he sees:

> The oblong gilt frame disposed its enclosing lines: the poplars and willows, the reeds and river – a river of which he didn't know, and didn't want to know, the name – fell into a composition, full of felicity, within them; the sky was silver and turquoise and varnish; the village on the left was white and the church on the right was grey; it was all there, in short – it was what he wanted: it was Tremont Street, it was France, it was Lambinet. (Bk. 11, Ch. 3)

So far so good. Dealing with landscape, Strether does not find it difficult to have the illusion of having an aesthetic experience. But when he encounters the human element he runs into trouble. He has an expectation that he will find a picturesque carriage driver, when his day is done, 'who naturally wouldn't fail of a stiff clean blouse, of a knitted nightcap and of the genius of response – who, in fine, would sit on the shafts, tell him what the French people were thinking, and remind him, as indeed the whole episode would incidentally do, of Maupassant' (Bk. 11, Ch. 3). As it happens, things do not arrange themselves so conveniently for him, and 'the liberties with which his fancy played' remain fancies. When he meets the rustics they strike him 'perhaps a little more as men of the world than he had expected', and the journey to the station turns out to be a 'somewhat tedious progress' in the company of Chad and Madame de Vionnet, so that he forgets to see whether the driver's blouse is clean. When Strether first sees the couple rowing on the river, he can fit them into his picture, and they enhance it:

> What he saw was exactly the right thing – a boat advancing round the bend containing a man who held the paddles and a lady, at the stern with a pink parasol. It was suddenly as if these figures, or something like them, had been wanted in the picture, had been wanted more or less all day, and had now drifted into sight, with the slow current, on purpose to fill up the measure. (Bk. 11, Ch. 4)

So long as the figures are distanced and picturesque, they remain 'idyllic' and within the frame; but when it turns out that they are Strether's friends, and in an awkward situation, they break from the frame and menace his ideal world. Now he has to face what he has been trying not to face for months and months – that the liaison is illicit. The picture in Tremont Street has been altered. Strether has tried to enter it, but in doing so has changed the nature of this crystalline world of artistic perfection. He has come to the fountainhead of Lambinet's vision, but is *further* from 'buying' or 'possessing' the visionary world than he was in Boston years before.

This episode does not cure Strether of imagining himself and the rest of society in a 'scene' or a 'picture'. In his final interview with Madame de Vionnet in her house in the Rue de Bellechase, he keeps her at a distance by retaining his aesthetic attitude. The apartments are magnificent First Empire rooms. In Strether's eyes they are signally representative of the noble and turbulent period, and he thinks he can catch the distant sound of ancestral voices prophesying war. He assumes that Madame de Vionnet has a close identity with the setting. It may be that she has, but she has inherited her surroundings, and she *could* feel out of key with them. Her environment is not to be compared with Maria Gostrey's little nook, which is almost an extension of her clothing – just as Poynton is for Mrs Gereth. Maria Gostrey has lovingly scraped together what she has got. In the following passage, the narrator seems to be more than half inviting criticism of Strether's response:

> Her noble old apartment offered a succession of three, the first two of which indeed, on entering, smaller than the last, but each with its faded and formal air, enlarged the office of the antechamber and enriched the sense of approach. Strether fancied them, liked them, and, passing through them with her more slowly now, met a sharp renewal of his original impression. He stopped, he looked back; the whole thing made a vista, which he found high melancholy and sweet – full, once more, of dim historic shades, of the faint far-away cannon-roar of the great Empire. It was doubtless half the projection of his mind, but his mind was a thing that, among old waxed parquets, pale shades of pink and green, pseudo-classic candelabra, he had always needfully to reckon with. They could easily make him irrelevant. The oddity, the originality, the poetry – he didn't know what to call it – of Chad's connexion reaffirmed for him its romantic side.   (Bk. 9, Ch. 1)

He is reading surface data, and almost converting the present into a historical novel. James's letters show that he would not endorse this habit of mind. James shows Strether as he makes the assumption that Madame de Vionnet lives in a world vastly different from his own, and attempts to deduce her character from her surroundings. In his last interview with Madame de Vionnet, the old spell of the picturesque continues to work and, once again, Strether is lucky, as there is a thunderstorm outside, and his hostess is dressed in black and white – reminiscent of Madame Roland on the scaffold. In the scene there *is* a strong symbolic sense of visual appropriateness, which one could call 'the pathetic fallacy' in an ungenerous moment, but what remains important is that Strether is aware of the visual melodrama, and this helps him to remain distanced from Madame de Vionnet.

Despite the setting (or perhaps because of it) Madame de Vionnet still manages to be natural, simple and rather touching. Strether's fancy is at work even before he gets into the house: 'Strether had all along been subject to sudden gusts of fancy in connexion with such matters as these – odd starts of the historic sense, suppositions and divinations with no warrant but their intensity' (Bk. 12, Ch. 1). And when he meets his hostess, the mystic images grow to satisfy his fancy: 'the associations of the place, all felt again; the gleam here and there, in the subdued light, of glass and gilt and parquet, with the quietness of her own note as the centre – these things were at first as delicate as if they had been ghostly. . . .' (Bk. 12, Ch. 1). Strether partakes in the scene as a spectator might at a play. He is already looking forward to the time when the events will be enshrined in memory for the fancy to play with, and as he absorbs the scene it is 'with pleasing thoughts that in this moment there is life and food for future years': 'he should soon be going to where such things were not, and it would be a small mercy for memory, for fancy, to have, in that stress, a loaf on the shelf' (Bk. 12, Ch. 1). The glamour and brilliance of the scene could prove overwhelming in a play or a film, but in the novel the loneliness and resignation of the middle-aged woman forms just as big an impression, an impression which Strether does not seem to register as clearly as the more melodramatic aspects.

A final example from an earlier point in the novel will show how normal it is for Strether to have amounts 'of experience out of any proportion to his adventures', and perhaps this example is the most extreme in the novel. He goes to a Sunday party at Gloriani's and invents a makeshift mythology of Gloriani's incredible powers of perception, and of the predatory nature of the society surrounding him. Speaking of Strether's vision of Gloriani's eyes, the narrator writes:

> He wasn't soon to forget them, was to think of them, all unconscious, unintending, preoccupied though they were, as the source of the deepest intellectual sounding to which he had ever been exposed. He was in fact quite to cherish his vision of it, to play with it in idle hours; only speaking of it to no one and quite aware he couldn't have spoken without appearing to talk nonsense. (Bk. 8, Ch. 1)

And he thinks he sees a 'terrible life' behind the sculptor's eyes. The vision intensifies when Strether sees Gloriani talking to the Duchess, whom he has made out to be knowing and insolent; yet he has no more basis for believing that what he has seen is true than his quick interpretation of a fleeting impression. Even so, 'trifles light as air are to jealous confirmations strong as proofs of holy writ'. Strether asks himself:

> Were they, this pair, of the 'great world'? – and was he himself, for the moment and thus related to them by his observation, *in* it? Then there was something in the great world covertly tigerish, which came to him across the lawn and in the charming air as a waft from the jungle. Yet it made him admire most of the two, made him envy, the glossy male tiger, magnificently marked. These absurdities of the stirred sense, fruits of suggestion ripening on the instant, were all reflected in his next words to little Bilham. 'I know – if we talk of that – whom *I* should enjoy being like!'   (Bk. 5, Ch. 2)

Then follows one of those incomplete sentences which abound in the novel, to be completed by a second person. Strether is about to say 'Gloriani', but in the gap of talk 'another impression had been superimposed'. The new impression is of Chad and Jeanne de Vionnet; and this picture of the innocence of youth, which he thinks he sees as the obverse of the age and corruption of Gloriani, makes him change his mind. He answers 'Oh, Chad!' (Bk. 5, Ch. 2). The Jamesian conceit 'fruits of suggestion' describes very aptly Strether's thought processes. They are growths and to him seem as natural and as preordained as the growth of a plant. James frequently uses the analogy of plant growth to describe his own modes of composing. This is not to say that Strether's habits of thought are being endorsed. A further extension of the conceit shows Strether in a more unsatisfactory light. At Chad's party, after little Bilham has proved gently but persistently obtuse,

> ... Strether relapsed into the sense – which had for him in these days most of comfort – that he was free to believe in anything that from hour to hour kept him going. He had positively motions and flutters of this conscious hour-to-hour kind, temporary surrender to irony, to fancy, frequent instinctive snatches at the growing rose of observation, constantly stronger for him, as he felt, in scent and colour, and in which he could bury his nose even to wantonness.   (Bk. 10, Ch. 1)

In the Jamesian family of images, burying one's nose in the rose is an emblem of indulgence in decadent experience. An example from *English Hours*, describing lunch in pre-Reform All Souls will suffice:

> Pending these righteous changes, one would like while one is about it . . . to attach one's self to the abuse, to bury one's nostrils in the rose before it is plucked.[12]

The Narrator of *The Sacred Fount* also uses images of growth to describe his developing hypotheses. We read of him 'cherishing the fruit of the seed dropped' (Ch. 6), picking 'the full-blown flower of my theory' (Ch. 9) and making a 'woven wreath' (Ch. 12). The flowers of fancy cultivated by Strether and the Narrator are not to be cherished, but discarded as rank weeds.

Connected with images of the growth of plants in descriptions of imaginative activity are images of the growth of buildings. Images from architecture are particularly appropriate for visionary activity, as buildings have a pre-existence in an architect's brain to a much greater extent than paintings and literary works do. The Narrator refers to 'the edifice of my precautions' (Ch. 7), to 'the whole airy structure I had erected' (Ch. 8), to his 'great glittering Crystal palace' (Ch. 10) and to his 'perfect palace of thought' (Ch. 14). Mrs Brissenden is less impressed with his structure and prefers to see it as a house 'of cards' (Ch. 12), or as a glass house from which stones should not be thrown (Ch. 14). In *The Ambassadors* Strether refers to a theory he had had about Mamie Pocock as a 'tall house of cards' (Bk. 10, Ch. 1). Near the end of the novel Coleridge's 'caverns measureless to man' are invoked, and there is a hint that the poem 'Kubla Khan' is being offered as an analogue of Strether's return to America (Bk. 12, Ch. 3). The imaginative stream of Strether's imagination is to flow underground, like the sacred river Alph, to rise again in America. In Woollett, there will be no real 'stately pleasure-dome', but there will be the consolation of the 'shadow of the dome of pleasure' which can be revived in the mind's eye, if need be:

> It faced him, the reckoning, over the shoulder of much interposing experience – which also faced him; and one would float to it doubtless duly through these caverns of Kubla Khan. It was really behind every-

thing; it hadn't merged in what he had done; his final appreciation of what he had done – his appreciation on the spot – would provide it with its main sharpness. The spot so focussed was of course Woollett, and he was to see, at the best, what Woollett would be with everything there changed for him.   (Bk. 12, Ch. 3)

What Strether and the Narrator of *The Sacred Fount* gain from treating life in the artistic fashion that they do is not only a satisfying sense of distance from life, but also an illusion that treating life in this way gives them some sort of control over it. Quentin Anderson's description of the Narrator of *The Sacred Fount* as a 'kind of futile Mephistopheles' is very apt.[13] If life is analogous to fanciful and artistic creations, then it is ordered and predictable, and one can move in it with more assurance. In both novels, the real world is continually being put into the shade by the power of phantasmagoric activity, and finally the good or bad nature of the world seems to matter very little, as these parallel passages show: 'Light or darkness, my imagination rides me' (*The Sacred Fount*, Ch. 13); 'Ugly or beautiful – it doesn't matter what we call them – you were getting on without them, and that's where we're detestable' (*The Ambassadors*, Bk. 12, Ch. 2). The works of art most appropriate to the analogy of the controlled and predictable life are works of art which are themselves tightly ordered, predictable and even primitive, rather than ones which are diffuse, realistic and impressed with the chaotic and intractable quality of life. This explains why both of the characters under review see their situations in fairy-tale terms. A revealing passage in Chapter 8 of *The Sacred Fount* shows that the Narrator has still not escaped from the appeals and the illusions of childish fairy-tales:

> I scarce know what odd consciousness I had of roaming at close of day in the grounds of some castle of enchantment. I had positively encountered nothing to compare with this since the days of fairy-tales and of childish imagination of the impossible. *Then* I used to circle round enchanted castles, for then I moved in a world in which the strange 'came true'. It was the coming true that was the proof of the enchantment, which, moreover, was naturally never so great as when such coming was, to such a degree and by the most romantic stroke of all, the fruit of one's own wizardry.

Primitive myths of transformation dominate the novel. Lady John is 'the sorceress by whose wand [Long] had been touched' (Ch. 2), and later the Narrator imagines that Long has 'changed back' (Ch. 10). The story of Cinderella is cleverly used throughout the novel. Perhaps there is an undercurrent of suggestion that the glass slipper represents a transparently empty theory, and that the fanciful elements will resolve themselves back into pumpkins after midnight. The Narrator's glass palace is shattered after midnight. Perhaps a deeper analogy is suggested to the reader, but missed by the Narrator. In the story of Cinderella, the glass slipper *survived* when the rest of the illusion vanished, suggesting that there was some validity in the experience of Cinderella, and when one discarded the paraphernalia of the ball, an actual human relationship still existed. Strether thinks of a fairy-story too. He casts himself and Maria Gostrey as 'the Babes in the Wood' after the drama has passed them by (Bk. 12, Ch. 3).

If the Narrator of *The Sacred Fount* is a 'futile Mephistopheles', then Strether is one too. The desire to manipulate people is the most terrifying symptom of the artist *manqué* and illustrates a collapse of the necessary boundaries between life and aesthetics. Strether manipulates people as a protective device against being manipulated himself. This is one of the paradoxes of his character, as he is passive too. The crucial party scene, to which I have alluded twice already, contains examples of his bid for manipulation: to give birth to an idea, and 'make it fill the cradle right'. He tries to persuade little Bilham to marry Mamie Pocock. This is the outgrowth of an idea he jumped at when he saw Mamie on the balcony, that she might love little Bilham. Little Bilham will have none of it of course:

> Little Bilham laughed out. 'Why it was only the other night, in this very place, that you were proposing to me a different union altogether.'
> 'Mademoiselle de Vionnet ?' Well, Strether easily confessed it. 'That, I admit, was a vain image. *This* is practical politics. I want to do something good for both of you – I wish you each so well; and you can see in a moment the trouble it will save me to polish you off by the same stroke.' (Bk. 10, Ch. 1)

Strether is distressed when Chad seems to manipulate Jeanne de Vionnet's marriage. Organized marriage is one of the 'crimes' of

Europe, in James's eyes, not only in this novel, but in many others, especially *The American* and *The Portrait of a Lady*; and yet here is Strether trying to accomplish the same thing. He is like Jane Austen's Emma, revealing a fear of and a withdrawal from life in the activity of match-making. He does not have social or financial aggrandisement to gain from the activity – neither does Emma – but he does stand to gain inner satisfaction, which is equally as sinister. In the same conversation, Strether tells little Bilham,

> I've been sacrificing so to strange gods that I feel I want to put on record, somehow, my fidelity – fundamentally unchanged after all – to our own. I feel as if my hands were imbrued with the blood of monstrous alien altars – of another faith altogether.   (Bk. 10, Ch. 1)

But the plan he has for little Bilham, far from being 'expiatory', represents the same type of sacrifice that Strether has just been deploring – though in a different guise.

A lot of harsh things have been said about Strether and the Narrator. Strether is probably not as ignoble as the earlier hero. In both works James was very much in control of his effects, and most readers should be able to recognize that the heroes are not offered as patterns of virtue. At the end of both works the characters seem to have come to some state of self-knowledge – though there is a chance that the Narrator of *The Sacred Fount* will try out his 'method' elsewhere, and has not finally learnt his lesson. He remains amusing but mad, rather like the notorious Ludwig of Bavaria, to whom he refers on one occasion (Ch. 13).[14] The end of *The Ambassadors* is a shade more enigmatic. Maria Gostrey hints that Chad has also had an affair in London: 'And is your idea,' Miss Gostrey asked, 'that there was some other woman in London?' 'Yes. No. That is I *have* no ideas. I'm afraid of them. I've done with them' (Bk. 12, Ch. 5). This all seems very proper. And he also renounces the chance to establish a close relationship with Maria Gostrey because he feels that to have gained anything tangible from his ignominious progress would be a kind of treachery. That is probably very proper too. But the reader should not be lulled into a false sense of security on the last page. Strether thinks he sees an offer of 'exquisite service' and 'lightened care' from Maria Gostrey, but she is probably an old *ficelle* to the last, and there is no reason for believing that Strether could find a niche in her little temple. He is very likely 'renouncing' a niche that is not even offered for his occupation. The last two pages of *The Ambassadors* are a hornet's nest of ambivalent and ironical sentences. Strether is still not at the state of complete knowledge. He has still not entirely learnt about the treachery of words. Maria Gostrey perhaps thinks that he is going to continue his habits of fanciful dreaming and with-drawal in America. She asks:

> 'To what do you go home?'
> 'I don't know. There will always be something.'
> 'To a great difference,' she said as she kept his hand.
> 'A great difference – no doubt. Yet I shall see what I can make of it.'
> 'Shall you make anything so good –?' But, as if remembering what
> Mrs Newsome had done, it was as far as she went.   (Bk. 12, Ch. 5)

By the vagueness of their use of words, the characters reveal the possibility that Strether's 'making' is going to be an extension of the fanciful fabricating that he has been indulging in during his European mission. At the end of the novel he is less satisfied, but more en-lightened than the Narrator at the end of *The Sacred Fount*. One feels that the remainder of his life is going to be filled with more of the self-recrimination and disappointment that he expressed in Gloriani's garden, unless he resorts to the Jamesian technique of routing his aggressors, of turning defeat into victory and crystallizing in his memory the Paris experience as the beautiful late Romance of his declining years. Much as we know about Strether's mental processes, the moral instability in the novel and our constant uncertainty about events generates very little of the kind of knowledge that could take us with confidence even a little way beyond the closing pages. It is always impossible to give detailed psychological accounts of literary characters, as one never has enough facts to go on, and one cannot use the question and answer method. One has to be content with what is on the page. As we do not know enough about Strether's youth, it is impossible to give a confident account of what has led him to adopt the defence mechanism of treating life as a spectacle to be looked at, but not participated in. The ambassadorial experience in Europe remains isolated, so that all attention is concentrated on it, rather than on the past and the future. Perhaps the lack of firm ground is a deliberate part of the novel's effect. It should make us suspicious of any elaborate moral interpretations of the work, for in such readings most of the morality is imported by the critic, and is not inherent in the work. All that is inherent at a moral level is the perilous nature of trying to live true to one's impressions. I should hesitate to describe Strether's actions as good or bad: the most that can be said is that they are necessary and inevitable, considering what he is.

To the last, the play on the words 'right' and 'wrong' continues. The finality of judgement which James has been avoiding all through the novel is avoided to the very end. Strether's last words 'Then there we are!' are bound to make the reader ask 'Where?'

Notes

* In some modern editions of *The Ambassadors*, such as the Signet Classic, the chapters are numbered consecutively: those of Book 2 are numbered 4–5; Book 3, 6–7; Book 4, 8–9; Book 5, 10–12; Book 6, 13–15; Book 7, 16–17; Book 8, 18–21; Book 9, 22–4; Book 10, 25–8; Book 11, 29–31 and Book 12, 32–6.

1. *The Art of the Novel*, edited by R. P. Blackmur, New York, 1947, p. 321.
2. Ibid., pp. 311–12.
3. R. Perlongo, '*The Sacred Fount*: Labyrinth or Parable', *Kenyon Review*, xxii, 1960, p. 635.
4. Parker Tyler, '*The Sacred Fount*: "The Actuality Pretentious and Vain" vs "The Case Rich and Edifying"', *Modern Fiction Studies*, xi, 1963–4, p. 12.
5. *The Art of the Novel*, pp. 323–4.
6. Ibid., p. 325.
7. *Notebooks*, p. 226.
8. *The Art of the Novel*, p. 316.
9. *The Sacred Fount*, edited by Leon Edel, London, 1959, introduction, p. 10.
10. *Henry James's Autobiography*, edited by F. W. Dupee, London, 1956, p. 193.
11. *The Painter's Eye*, London, 1956, p. 43.
12. *English Hours*, London, 1905, p. 184.
13. Quentin Anderson, *The American Henry James*, New Brunswick, 1957, p. 120.
14. For a systematic comparison of the Narrator and Ludwig of Bavaria see Jean Frantz Blackall, *Jamesian Ambiguity and 'The Sacred Fount'*, New York, 1965.

8

The pervasive mystery of style
The Wings of the Dove

JOHN GOODE

1 *Lifestyles and eyestyles*

'She died for you in order that you might understand her.'[1] Nothing seems clearer than the parabolic direction of *The Wings of the Dove*. Although it seems arbitrary to limit it to Swedenborg, we shall find it difficult to dissent from Quentin Anderson's general account of the plot of the novel. Structurally at least, Densher is certainly used as an Everyman whose character is unformed at the beginning of the novel, and Kate relates to him as an object of his earthly love which drives him towards mercenary gain. The dove's wings, victims of human rapacity, finally touch him with a transcendental grace, which brings him to an awareness of his guilt, Kate's limited nature, and the possibilities of redemption. Unable to bring himself to read Milly's letter, Densher is left wondering not about its intention but about the turn she would have given her act:

> This turn had possibilities that, somehow, by wondering about them, his imagination had extraordinarily filled out and refined. It had made of them a revelation the loss of which was like the sight of a priceless pearl cast before his eyes – his pledge given not to save it – into the fathomless sea, or rather even it was like the sacrifice of something sentient and throbbing, something that, for the spiritual ear, might have been audible as a faint far wail.   (Bk. 10, Ch. 6)

'Died for you', 'pearl cast before his eyes', 'faint far wail' – it is no wonder that the joys of Kate's body are forsaken for the consecrated splendours of Brompton Oratory. Of course, the Christian imagery is used rather than affirmed for its own sake, and we are conscious above all of a variety of religious experience. The language never quite coincides. The substitution of 'understand' for 'save', and the theatricalization of 'still, small voice' into 'faint far wail' scale the experience down for the confines of human awareness and allow for its possibly overstated subjectivity. But it isn't completely humanized, as in George Eliot, because it seems to have no reference to secular values. We are not shown that Densher becomes a morally better person – only that his wasted passion divides him inexorably from Kate. It simply has to do with the affirmation of a level of reality beyond the phenomenal. The situation at the end of the novel is most closely paralleled by James's warmest praise of his father's ideas: 'it would absolutely not have been possible to us, in the measure of our sensibility, to breathe more the air of the reference to an order of goodness and power greater than any this world by itself can show which we understand as the religious spirit.'[2] Milly's triumph is the development of Densher's plastic consciousness to the point at which it acknowledges the 'religious spirit'. It is a concept which, precisely because of its syncretism and vagueness, dissolves many contradictions; and since it is one which, in a number of forms, as Brian Lee and Richard Poirier, among others, have shown, pervades American literature, we are missing the point if we ask for precise identification. In any case, if William James, with his philosophical training, can get no closer to explaining it than by the lugubrious image of the vivisected dog offered comfort because his suffering is of value to a higher level of life,[3] it is perhaps less dangerous for the suspension of our disbelief, that the novelist should give us no more than a solvent – a mild, dove-diffused air.

So if the moral fable is simple, it is also vague, and there doesn't seem to be much room for varying interpretations. The problem for the critic is very much one of evaluation, and that is going to depend not on the fable but on its realization. For with this novel more than most, we are aware, I think, that accounts of its structure do not coincide with our experience of the book, because the book is so much an expansion from a simple plan. If it has value, the value will reside in the significance and effectiveness of the texture which the frame holds. And the most difficult problem here is, of course, Milly. It is essential not to oversimplify. On the one hand, the novel is not about Milly. Two-thirds of it are concerned with the development of Densher's consciousness, and she is absent from both the beginning and the end. The title indicates her structural role – it is not a story about a dove but about its wings, wings which act as an agent of evaluation for the other characters in the novel. In this respect, Milly is James's most important *ficelle*. On the other hand, we cannot go to the other extreme and say that the dove stands mute at the centre, the focus of other, foreground relationships,[4] since the middle of the book is concerned with her registration of English society. Neither is she a victim of a dehumanizing transformation, since we are only aware of her as discontented before she has elected to accept the sacrificial dove image. To treat her as a catalyst would be to ignore the centre of the novel, but since the novel isn't about her in the way *The Portrait of a Lady* is about Isabel, we are not given anything like the complexity necessary to dramatize her suffering and development. Milly has to be, as Lee has remarked, an insubstantial type.[5] And since she is to be an agent of Densher's metamorphosis, she cannot be presented with the 'satiric penalties'[6] which attend the line of Jamesian heroines, of which she is a late flower. We can imagine a *tale* in which Milly might be an inexplicable force ambiguously alienating Densher from Kate. But the novel is too extended, Milly too visible for her to remain a mystery, and the way she changes Densher is too fully explored for it to remain ambiguous. On the face of it, there are no ironic shadows thrown by the lights of Brompton Oratory, and critics who find Milly 'an irritating sentimentality'[7] cannot be facilely dismissed. On the other hand, I think that if we are as articulate as possible about the solidity of specification in the novel, words such as 'irony' and 'sentimentality' become difficult to use. The moral patterning is highly romantic, and, like William James's comfort for the dog, nauseating, but what is impressive about it is the detailed working of the prose, and the complexity of experience which the detail embodies.

   The Wings of the Dove is the most panoramic of the three international novels at the turn of the century. *The Ambassadors* is Strether's novel, and its theme is his encounter with his own identity in the context of a liberated, fully subjective consciousness. *The*

Golden Bowl is Amerigo's and Maggie's and its theme is marriage. *The Wings of the Dove* has four centres of consciousness, and its theme is social relations. It is striking how much of the novel is dominated by triangular relationships: at the centre, of course, there is the triangle of Kate, Milly and Densher, but there are others – Densher, Kate, Mrs Lowder; Densher, Lord Mark, Milly; Milly, Susan, Mrs Lowder; Densher, Sir Luke, Eugenio, and so on. The plot depends on the tensions in such relationships in which two people struggle for a third, or combine against a third, or in which the third struggles to square the other two. Moreover, the talk tends to be triangular – Lord Mark and Milly discuss mainly Kate, as do Mrs Lowder and Milly; Kate and Milly carefully don't discuss Densher, which comes to the same thing, and Milly and Densher, who come closest to a self-contained dialogue tend to discuss a fictional, all-American Milly. And much of the seeing in the novel follows the same tendency to refer both to an object of vision and a third referent which is invoked by mutual relationships. The most obvious case is the way in which Milly learns to see Kate as she imagines Densher might do; but also Densher learns about his relationship with Milly by seeing Lord Mark in Florians, and Milly learns the truth about herself by seeing Susan's face after the interview with Sir Luke. This triangularity emphasizes the social concern of the novel: it is not the other person which most matters, it is the other person's relationship to someone who is related to you, and the ultimate concern of the novel is the way in which one person's geometry squares with everybody else's.

We can also group the characters statically on a triangular classification of which the most important distinction is between plasticity and force – we think of Densher as opposed to Kate and Mrs Lowder, Susan as opposed to Milly and Maud, Lionel and Marion as opposed to Kate. Secondly, there is an opposition between the kinds of relationship with experience that the various characters have. Many of them occupy fixed positions in the social scene and have distinctive lifestyles – obviously Mrs Lowder has with her florid expressive furniture, but so has Sir Luke with his surgery. And many of the others are felt to be sharply defined by the social position they occupy: 'His type', Milly feels of Lord Mark, 'somehow, as by a life, a need, an intention of its own, took all care for vividness off his hands' (Bk. 4, Ch. 1); and even the deliquescent Lionel Croy has been met halfway by life 'placing a hand in his arm and fondly leaving him to choose the pace' (Bk. 1, Ch. 1). All these characters, however forceful or passive they may be, play a distinctive role as a group in the novel, constituting a world in relation to which the main characters have to discover or invent the values by which they are to live, and the styles through which they are to express themselves. The novel's narrators don't have a distinctive lifestyle: neither Kate nor Densher have enough status to occupy a definite role; Susie has forsaken her previous role as lady author to watch Milly; Milly has only a decadent inherited lifestyle, symbolized by her expensive but obscuring dress, which is at odds with her desire to see life. But precisely because they don't have a distinctive lifestyle, they each have an individual way of looking at the 'world'. The complex texture of the novel is built up from the competing attempts of these 'eyestyles' to cope with and square the threatening lifestyles of the world.

2 *The art of seeing things as they are*

The most assured moment in the presentation of Milly comes early in Book 5, when she has been confronted with the image of how the English see her – as the dead woman of the Bronzino portrait. James has built up throughout the previous chapter both the sense of 'a high-water mark of imagination' – the rich, colourful social world – and at the same time its lurking ambiguities. These focus sharply as she is led by Lord Mark to the picture, made to run the gauntlet of the world's pity, and finally left to the mercy of Kate:

> A minute or two later the situation had changed, and she knew it after-wards to have been by the subtle operation of Kate. She was herself saying that she was afraid she must go now if Susie could be found; but she was sitting down on the nearest seat to say it. The prospect, through opened doors, stretched before her into other rooms, down the vista of which Lord Mark was strolling with Lady Aldershaw, who, close to him and much intent, seemed to show from behind as peculiarly expert. Lord Aldershaw, for his part, had been left in the middle of the room,

while Kate, with her back to him, was standing before her with much sweetness of manner. The sweetness was all for *her*; she had the sense of the poor gentleman's having somehow been handled as Lord Mark had handled his wife. He dangled there, he shambled a little; then he bethought himself of the Bronzino, before which, with his eye-glass, he hovered. It drew from him an odd vague sound, not wholly distinct from a grunt, and a 'Humph – most remarkable!' which lighted Kate's face with amusement. The next moment he had creaked away over polished floors after the others and Milly was feeling as if *she* had been rude. But Lord Aldershaw was in every way a detail and Kate was saying to her that she hoped she wasn't ill.   (Bk. 5, Ch. 2)

James clearly uses the imperfect here to register a critical immediacy of consciousness. Milly only becomes aware of what she is saying and doing as she is doing it, and if it is the Aldershaws who are handled in the most obvious way, Milly's sympathy for them clearly arises from her own sense of vulnerability and exposure. Meanwhile all the social poise has become a threat; consideration becomes an index of one person's power over another. 'Pity would be no more/If we did not make somebody poor.'

That it should be Kate who is standing there, controlling a situation which for Milly has become such an exposure, is apt not only because the plot demands that Kate have special insights, but because it is Kate above all who understands the exploitative nature of society, and it is Kate from whom Milly is to learn about the way society works. Aunt Maud's patronage is the impress of wealth upon deprivation – her kindness merely making of Kate a 'sensible value' which is 'chalk marked for the auction'. The tension we feel before the Bronzino is derived from the comparisons we are bound to be making between the vulnerability of Milly's wealth and the vulnerability of Kate's poverty, as well as the contrast between the healths of the two women. The tension is very encompassing because by giving us, in the opening two books, such a full account of Kate's dilemma, we are bound to sense here not merely Milly's danger but also Kate's opportunity. And more than that: by giving the opening book to Kate's consciousness, James creates a moral world in which the most lucid values are treachery and exploitation ('the moral of which moreover of course was that the more one gave oneself the less of one was left'). From this moment, Kate begins to acquire a peculiar authority for Milly – but it is an authority which we already recognize. James establishes Kate's and Densher's situation so carefully that it is impossible to see whatever they do in the remainder of the novel as anything but a response to values deeply embedded in the human world.

Our starting point is her predicament and our initial perspective is one she provides. It establishes as the major criterion in the novel the success of a style, not its rightness in absolute terms. We are told, for example, that 'She saw, as she had never seen before how material things spoke to her' (Bk. 1, Ch. 2), but since we have just been given her father's house in Chirk Street and Marian's in Chelsea, we are unable to see this as a limitation. For James does more than enumerate the items of the hole she is trying to avoid collapsing into; he seems to insist on its utterly irredeemable quality by making what are normally positive attributes seem nauseating. Thus 'the small homely hum of Chirk Street' linked with the shabby sun and the cry of the costermonger becomes oppressive precisely because it is homely. So too, the worst feature of the dead Condrip seems to be his saintly profile, and his fatuousness seems to have been decisively demonstrated by his earthly death. In this deprived world, all the values become values of oppression or escape. Father and sister turn moral concepts into instruments marking her for the auction: 'duty', 'the bond of blood', become major threats to personality. The keyword is 'mark'. Mrs Lowder openly uses the reductive terminology which endorses Kate's estranged relationship to her world:

> . . . Kate's presence, by good fortune, I marked early. Kate's presence – unluckily for *you* – is everything I could possibly wish. Kate's presence is, in short, as fine as you know, and I've been keeping it for the comfort of my declining years. I've watched it long; I've been saving it up and letting it, as you say of investments, appreciate; and you may judge whether, now it has begun to pay so, I'm likely to consent to treat for it with any but a high bidder. I can do the best with her, and I've my idea of the best.   (Bk. 2, Ch. 2)

But it's not only Mrs Lowder who talks in these terms – Lord Mark does too. There is nothing in fact to suggest that social relationships are ever to be seen in any other terms. Kate is, in the context she finds herself in, right to see life as she sees it: 'life at present turned to her view from week to week more and more the face of a striking and distinguished stranger' (Bk. 1, Ch. 2). It pays its respects to what the wealthy social world has to offer – but it recognizes too that there can be no compact between the markers and the marked.

I am not trying to exonerate Kate – she doesn't need it, for she tries to be open with Milly ('oh you may very well loathe me yet') and Milly is not really deceived by Kate's pity ('She had felt herself alone with a creature who paced like a panther'). Milly accepts Kate's view of her as a dove because she sees a prospect of triumph in it. Kate's role is not so much to stand for a particular group of values as to embody a way of seeing life which is, on the face of it, an art of seeing things as they are. Nowhere else in the novel do we get the same density and sharpness of realization that we do in the opening chapter, and there is a clear reason for this. 'It was a medium, a setting, and to that extent, after all, a dreadful sign of life' – such phrasing, and the embodiment of its assumptions in the concrete creation of a medium for her father, remind us above all of Auerbach's analysis of Balzac: 'What confronts us, then, is the unity of a particular milieu, felt as a total concept of a demonic-organic nature.'[8] Lionel Croy is not realized simply as a pathetic old man but as a force, 'the force of his particular type' (Bk. 1, Ch. 1). The word, which is used about other characters too, seems to have a specific frame of reference. Taine, for example, wrote of Balzac: 'l'homme n'est point une raison indépendante supérieure, saine par elle même, capable d'atteindre par son seul effort la vérité et la vertu, mais une simple force, du même ordre que les autres, recevant des circonstances son degré et sa direction.'[9] Kate is, of course, a Balzacian character, a female Rastignac who throws down her gauntlet to society at the opening of the novel. But much more she is a Balzacian seer: her mode is the mode of consciousness of the *Comédie Humaine* itself. The image of society which she gives Milly is one in which everyone is working everyone else, and what she most fully acknowledges as a source of power is money (we might recall *Gobseck* in which the miser gains an artist's hold over the lives of his characters by their debts to him). She habitually sees individuals as types, 'espèces', which demonstrate the significance of forces and the milieux they take shape in (I'm thinking here particularly of her feelings about the Misses Condrip and Aunt Maud). More specifically, her habitual mode of imagery is from natural history: 'and she compared herself to a trembling kid, kept apart a day or two till her turn should come, but sure sooner or later to be introduced into the cage of the lioness' (Bk. 1, Ch. 2). And, of course, it is she who provides the title image of the novel, out of this naturalistic world view. Kate mediates our vision of the London scene as she mediates Densher's and, later, Milly's. The art of seeing things as they are is the art of understanding a social jungle.

However, of course, James certainly didn't regard Balzac as a novelist who could see things as they really are, and Kate's world view is as limited as that of the naturalist writer. Like Balzac, Kate has an obsession with things which derives from a money-orientated attitude to society. If life confronts Kate as a stranger, it is because her own force demands of the milieu she finds herself in that she should be able to work it without being worked by it: 'What she felt was that, whatever might happen, she must keep them, must make them most completely her possession, and it was already strange enough that she reasoned, or at all events began to act, as if she might work them in with other and alien things, privately cherish them, and yet, as regards the rigour of it, pay no price' (Bk. 2, Ch. 1). Possession without price here means without sacrifice, and the only way to achieve this is through the transcendent power of money. It doesn't take long for Milly to realize that it is money that Kate mainly sees in her:

> It was a fact – it became one at the end of three days – that Milly actually began to borrow from the handsome girl a sort of view of her state; the handsome girl's impression of it was clearly so sincere. This impression was a tribute, a tribute positively to power, power the source of which was the last thing Kate treated as a mystery. (Bk. 4, Ch. 2)

What is odd about this passage, however, is not that Milly should realize this fact, but that she should see it in Kate especially, whereas it is clear that everyone else, from Lord Mark to Susan Stringham, sees her wealth as the most important thing about her. The key phrase is surely 'tribute to power': it is the creative agency of money in Milly that Kate is so responsive to. It should be linked with the clearly Darwinian sense of her own vitality that makes Kate exercise it in pursuit of this power: 'She looked at him now a moment as for the selfish gladness of their young immunities' (Bk. 6, Ch. 4). One way in which the structure of the novel can be described is that of an attempt by a superior vitality to survive the unfit and usurp her inherited power: the upstart tries to overreach the final flower of a dying race. But something else is going on in the passage quoted above. Milly is borrowing a view of her own state, which means that she defines that view, and definition means limitation: she can assimilate Kate's vision of herself, and that enables her to scale the vision down. The art of seeing things as they are takes on a curious kind of *naïveté*.

In his first essay on Balzac, in 1879, James makes it clear that he regards Balzac's concern with money a limitation of his 'realism':

> There is something pitiful in the contrast between this meagre personal budget and his lifelong visions of wealth, and of the ways of amassing wealth, his jovial sensual colossal enjoyment of luxury, and the great monetary architecture, as it were, of the *Comédie Humaine*. Money is the most general element of Balzac's novels; other things come and go, but money is always there.[10]

The social observation is seen to be underwritten by a naïve obsession with the protagonistic potentiality of money, explained as the distortion made by the impact of great wealth on underprivilege. Kate's mode of vision is, for all its shrewd understanding, that of one to whom life presents itself as a distinguished stranger. The distortion is not incompatible with Milly's sense of the accuracy of Kate's view of London society. The point is that there are other societies (the international theme), and that the art of seeing things as they are has no real sense of the art of making things as they should be. In his later essay, of 1902, James speaks of the artist in the *Comédie Humaine* being half smothered by the historian, and goes on to say that 'the reporter, however philosophic, has one law, and the originator, however substantially fed, has another'.[11] Kate's predicament is that the art of seeing things as they are has to be squared with her desire for possession without price, and she has no way of relating the two except through the highly intangible power of great wealth. Her feelings for Densher are, by her own term, 'romantic', but the romance has to remain within the 'real', the material world which speaks so eloquently to her. Given Lionel and Marian, Lancaster Gate and what it stands for cannot simply be placed – as it is by Densher's more plastic imagination – as a negation of the world of thought: it speaks too clearly of resolved contradictions, of a place in the social world which is neither on the counter nor in the shop window. Again we are reminded of James's criticism of Balzac:

> The romantic side of him has the extent of all the others; it represents, in the oddest manner, his escape from the walled and roofed structure into which he had built himself – his longing for the vaguely felt outside and as much as might be of the rest of the globe. But it is characteristic of him that the most he could do for this relief was to bring the fantastic into the circle and fit it somehow to the conditions.[12]

What is 'pitiful' about Kate is that the only way she has of escaping from the cage is by the pursuit of what has built the cage in the first place. The novel is to create an alternative vision, but the alternative is stated, rather sentimentally, in the 1902 essay:

> 'Things' for him are francs and centimes more than any others, and I give up as inscrutable, unfathomable, the nature, the peculiar avidity of his interest in them. It makes us wonder again and again what then is the use on Balzac's scale of the divine faculty. The imagination, as we all know, may be employed up to a certain point in inventing uses for money; but its office beyond that point is surely to make us forget that anything so odious exists.[13]

The Wings of the Dove is concerned above all with exploring the point beyond which imagination and money become mutually exclusive (it ends, after all, with Densher giving up money). But the difference between the essay of 1902 and the novel is that the novel traces, rather than asserts, that point. And it traces it primarily by the assimilation of the Balzacian art of seeing things as they are into a larger, more encompassing vision. In terms of the novel's central image, we are witnessing the movement from a creatural view of social identity (oh you're a dove) to a pragmatic symbolist one ('It gave her straightaway the measure of the success she could have as a dove'). The movement is complex and I think it is fully realized. Its starting point is an alternative view of money, and its pervasive irony is that the best way to escape the Balzacian limitation of the use of the divine faculty is to have so much money that you no longer have to think about it.

3 *The real thing, the romantic life itself*

Although she accepts Kate's image, Milly is immediately able to qualify it:

> 'Because you're a dove.' With which she felt herself ever so delicately, so considerately, embraced; not with familiarity or as a liberty taken, but almost ceremoniously and in the manner of an *accolade*; partly as if, though a dove who could perch on a finger, one were also a princess with whom forms were to be observed.   (Bk. 5, Ch. 6)

The immediate context is obviously ironic. It makes it worse that Kate's humiliating image should be presented with so much apparent respect. But by the end of the scene Milly is to recognize the possibilities of success in it: and one of the reasons is that by this stage in the book there is already an alternative set of images made available for her, which she is able to take up and use later. The most important is the image of the princess who has it in her to command consideration. And the princess image is the most characteristic metaphor in the style of vision offered straightforwardly as an alternative to Kate's: that of the New England author, Susan Shepherd Stringham.

Susie is not easy to define in terms of a single aesthetic in the way that Kate is, partly because she represents a whole tradition that James knew intimately as a tradition, and which cannot therefore be disentangled without distortion; partly because she is a writer and therefore conscious of the sources of her imagery; but mainly because her enlightenment is one which enables her to assimilate fashionable writers – notably Maeterlinck and Pater – to a vision which is primarily transcendentalist rather than symbolist. Much of the third book, it is true, is taken up with the register of 'impressions', but the impressions have ultimately to take a secondary place to the significance that she places on them, and above all on her impression of Milly:

> She moved, the admirable Mrs Stringham, in a fine cloud of observation and suspicion; she was in the position, as she believed, of knowing much more about Milly Theale than Milly herself knew, and yet of having to darken her knowledge as well as make it active. The woman in the world least formed by nature, as she was quite aware, for duplicities and labyrinths, she found herself dedicated to personal subtlety by a new set of circumstances, above all by a new personal relation. . . . (Bk. 3, Ch. 1)

It is surely a very New England predicament, having to darken knowledge of labyrinths – the predicament of the allegorist confronted with evil. Yet the allegorization, for all the disingenuous disclaimers, is not reluctantly undertaken, for the naked eyeball sees primarily to a world beyond the forms it registers. Through an accumulation of words such as 'real' and 'romantic' – a hyperbolic vocabulary of the enrapt imagination – and a tissue of potently dangerous illusion, James registers the fine cloud of observation as the thick veil of an obsession:

> This was poetry – it was also history – Mrs Stringham thought, to a finer tune even than Maeterlinck and Pater, than Marbot and Gregorovius. She appointed occasions for the reading of these authors with her hostess, rather perhaps than actually achieved great spans; but what they managed and what they missed speedily sank for her into the dim depths of the merely relative, so quickly, so strongly had she clutched her central clue. (Bk. 3, Ch. 1)

The breathless, absurdly discursive syntax places Susie's eyestyle very firmly. But the fact that it is funny shouldn't detract from the fact that it is also very dangerous and destructive. The central clue she clings to is as reductive as Kate's art of seeing things as they are. The difference is that her typology is 'representative' in an Emersonian sense, rather than naturalistic. Like Kate, she attempts to possess through knowledge, and possession means defining the human as creatural, created not creative: 'the charm of the creature was positively in the creature's greatness' (Bk. 3, Ch. 1). 'Merely relative' defines the limits of her plasticity. Like Kate, she governs her vision by an absolute, and like her the absolute turns out to be money: 'it prevailed even as a *truth of truths* that the girl couldn't get away from her wealth' (Bk. 3, Ch. 1: my italics).

Matthiessen argues that Susie's 'literary' view of Milly is saved from being 'silly' because it is endorsed by Densher.[14] The logic of this is not apparent: surely we have to judge Susan's vision as it is given us, and our verdict will necessarily influence our final judgement on Densher. However, by the time Densher does endorse it, it has become transformed by the events of the novel. Like Kate, Susie offers Milly a metaphoric supply which she can assimilate into her own ultimate lifestyle. But also like Kate, the initial impact constitutes a clear threat to Milly: it is only not silly because it is so dangerous, and it is dangerous because, like Kate's imagery it is exploitative. Thus at the beginning Susan, even through her own exaggerated self-humiliation, reduces Milly: if she makes of Milly a great new steamer to whom she is as a little boat in the slipstream, she can become a tug pulling the new American miracle into London as a 'trophy'. The trophy is a way of overcoming the unmediated relationship between herself and Maud, which is one in which she is otherwise 'patronizingly pitied'. To be pitied is the novel's major criterion of failure. In taking her to London, Mrs Stringham makes Milly a function of her own relationships. And, for all her strident sympathy, this never really changes. She participates in the deceit of Milly at the end of the novel, and if it is through kindness, it only makes it worse. The significance of her middle name, Shepherd, has often been pointed out, but what is more significant is her real surname – and Stringham goes all too well with Manningham. But it is not just a question of 'plot' – the whole hyperbolic sycophancy of the texture of Susan's prose sets Milly up as a set of 'strong marks'. In the first three books, the terms of war are set out: if you don't wish to be marked, first mark the markers.

It would be quite wrong, however, to see Susan's vision as simply a parallel threat to that of Kate's. If both reduce Milly to the product of her wealth and try to exploit her on that basis, Susan Stringham's way of doing it offers much more opportunity to Milly for counter-exploitation. In the first place, whereas Kate's tribute to the power of money is entirely secular (it's the last thing she regards as a mystery), Susan's is mediated by a mystifying vocabulary which gives money a symbolic status. The fact of Milly's wealth is an absolute, the truth of truths, and her existence is the real thing, the romantic life itself. The juxtaposition of the two apparently contradictory adjectives is meaningful because the 'romance of wealth' is one of the clichés used about the New York millionaires who became such talking points in the last years of the century. 'There is a rich mine of romance, as well as solid reality,' wrote Walter Barrett, 'in the history of the merchants of the old time.'[15] And what is chiefly romantic about it is that it can supply for the United States an equivalent for the life of royalty: 'there is no nobility in this country. There is a class of princes, and they are the highest in the city . . . princes of commerce.' James is never very clear about the kind of wealth Milly has, but though it is more likely to be akin to the real estate fortune of the Astors than the wealth of the Vanderbilts or Rockefellers, even this was hardly very deep-rooted. Nevertheless, as Gustavus Myers, a hostile historian, wrote, the tributes paid them were monarchical: 'the people were assiduously taught in many open and subtle ways to look up to the inviolability of property, just as in the old days they had been taught to look humbly up to the majesty of the king'.[16] Such regality is modified only by the tendency of such wealth to belong to families who are doomed to live, and decline, fast: 'For this country,' Barrett writes, 'the continued existence of one house for fifty-four years is a long time.'[17] When Susan thinks of Milly's story as 'a New York history' she is imposing an order which is both more metaphoric and more local.

Her most potent metaphor is, of course, from an English text, but in its context this is equally apt. When she thinks of Milly as the 'potential heiress of all the ages', she is thinking also of Tennyson:

Mated with squalid savage – what to me were sun or clime?
I, the heir of all the ages in the foremost ranks of time.

What is important here is the way in which she adopts (and adapts) the image. Later, James writes of Susan's mother, using another famous phrase from the same poem: 'She had given her daughters the five years in Switzerland and Germany that were to leave them ever afterwards a standard of comparison for all cycles of Cathay'

(Bk. 3, Ch. 1). At least Tennyson thought the ratio fifty years to one cycle. It points out the sharpness of James's irony in his presentation of Susan's consciousness: she has a mind that grabs at anything around to stick it into the discursive flow (it's an essayist's style, a debased echo of Emerson's omnivorous vigour), to inflate the moment and dissolve it into a generality identifiable only by its capacity to provoke ecstasy. It must make us wonder about the potential heiress of all the ages. On one level, it is a highly romanticized use of Tennyson's rather crudely racist and undiscriminating embrace of Western progress (the lack of discrimination is indicated by the fact he retained the image of 'ringing grooves of change' even when he learned that it was not accurate). Susan sublimates Milly's potential, but it is an acquisitive potential nonetheless: 'She was looking down on the kingdoms of the earth. . . . Was she choosing among them or did she want them all?' We wonder whether 'taking full in the face the whole assault of life' is anything more than the commitment Tennyson's hero makes to the mighty wind of social progress. If it is, it is because Susan does more than romanticize Tennyson – she updates it, and Americanizes it. For Tennyson's hero is talking about involvement with the foremost ranks of time, but Susan sees Milly as the potential possessor of the kingdoms of the earth. The morality of self-help is replaced by the power of the corporation; the decision to move on is here a decision to continue the tour. Milly is an heiress of all the ages because she is the heiress of New York millions. From an assertion, however crude, of cultural values, we have moved to an assertion of a single value – money. But, on the other hand, money has in the process been raised above time by a symbolizing imagination. The romantic life itself is possible because money is meaningful. And in making this claim, and making it available to Milly, Susan is being deeply responsive to an American tradition.

4 *What it was to be really rich*

James could hardly have ignored Howells's review of Veblen, 'An Opportunity for American Fiction'. Passages of it are so close to the novel that we cannot doubt that James is partly, in his own way, making a contribution to one of the major debates of the American nineties – the debate about 'plutocracy'. Howells claims that 'the flower of the American leisure class does not fruit in its native air, and perhaps cannot yet perpetuate itself on our soil.'[18] Milly is, of course, the final flower of her race and her career is close in many ways to the typical career for wealthy Americans defined in the article:

They are only representations on a wider stage of the perpetual and universal drama of our daily life. The man who makes money in a small town goes to the nearest large town to spend it – that is, to waste it; waste in some form or other being the corollary of wealth; and he seeks to marry his children there into rich and old families. He does this from the instinct of self preservation which is as strong in classes as individuals; if he has made his money in a large town, he goes to some such inland metropolis as Chicago to waste his wealth and to marry his children above him. The Chicago, and San Francisco, and St Louis, and Cleveland millionaires come to New York with the same ambitions and purposes.

But these are all intermediate stages in the evolution of the American magnate. At every step he discovers that he is less and less in his own country, that he is living in a provisional exile, and that his true home is in monarchical conditions, where his future establishes itself often without his willing it, and sometimes against his willing it. The American life is the life of labour, and he is now of the life of leisure, or if he is not, his wife is, his daughters and his sons are. The logic of their existence, which they cannot struggle against, and on which all the fatuous invective of pseudo public spirit lavishes itself effectlessly, is inter-marriage with the European aristocracies, and residence abroad. Short of this there is no rest, and can be none for the American leisure class. This may not be its ideal, but it is its destiny.

It is by far the most dramatic social fact of our time, and if some man of creative imagination were to seize upon it he would find in it the material of that great American novel which after so much travail has not yet seen the light. It is, above all our other facts synthetic; it sums up and includes in itself the whole American story: the relentless will, the tireless force, the vague ideal, the inexorable destiny, the often bewildered acquiescence.

Were it not for the fact that he had touched on the theme so often before, James might almost seem to have taken up the challenge of that last paragraph in this novel. Certainly the logic of Milly's existence, at least for Susan and at first for Kate, is European marriage and residence abroad, and what drives the novel forward is her restlessness, her capacity to use up kingdoms of earth. Certainly the true home of a princess is in monarchical conditions, and tireless force, vague ideal and inexorable destiny sum up our first impressions of her. But if the novel shares some of Howells's sociological insights, its direction is completely opposite, of course. Howells's phrase 'bewildered acquiescence' is very close to Susan Stringham's phrase 'consenting bewilderment' except that Susan is using it about the effect Milly has on her associates. It implies a potentially positive role in opposition to Howells's wryly sympathetic portrayal of futile *naïveté*. *The Wings of the Dove* might be said to be a novel about conspicuous waste – except that it isn't certain that the waste is wasted (though the novel ends with Densher clinging to his 'wasted passion'). The novel's major paradox is that consenting bewilderment, the reversal of Howells's final note of failure, is achieved by taking the Howellsian process a step further – Chicago, New York, Europe and beyond that death. The inexorable destiny of American wealth is its transcendent immortality, which it achieves by its secret working on the plastic human soul. It is a paradox made possible by turning a dramatic social fact into a style. Even before they confront the dangerously considerate world of London, Susan implicitly recognizes that Milly only exacts consenting bewilderment as perceived object exposed to knowledge: 'She worked – and seemingly quite *without design* – upon the *sympathy*, the *curiosity*, the *fancy* of her associates . . .' (Bk. 3, Ch. 1: my italics). By the end of the novel, the consenting bewilderment Milly exacts is a highly-wrought aesthetic and moral system. What she does essentially is to make Susan's romance of wealth (which she doesn't at first share, thinking of herself as belonging only to 'the fashion'), and the traditional view of money which it assumes, come 'true'.

Like those in the psalm, the wings of this dove are covered in silver and gold. Rahv says that James is too immersed in personal relations to have any historical sense; but a full enough awareness of the role of Milly's money reveals, in this novel at least, a remarkable sense of the historical implications of the personal relationships, and the ways in which they are expressed. We cannot hope to understand the way in which Milly achieves a lifestyle which will leave her free of the objectifying process of pity, unless we first recognize fully the potentialities and obstacles involved in being the heiress of all the progressive Western ages.

One of the obvious contexts is Emerson's essay 'Wealth' in *The Conduct of Life*. Its most important point is that wealth cannot be severed from the human energies and skills which possession of it signifies: 'money is representative'.[19] It is so because making money is a part of the individual's self-manifestation:

> Man was born to be rich, or, inevitably grows rich by the use of his faculties; by the union of thought with nature. Property is an intellectual production.

But not only is it a valid representation of self, it is also a valid analogy for personal relations. With what James called that 'ripe unconsciousness of evil', he goes on to say:

> He is the rich man who can avail himself of all men's faculties. He is the richest man who knows how to draw a benefit from the labours of the greatest number of men, of men in distant countries, and in past times.

The Wings of the Dove seems to me to operate within these definitions and their assumptions. The wings vindicate the dove, and elevate her from the object of pity to the successful demander of consenting bewilderment. In a queer way she even gets everyone, Aunt Maud and Kate included, to work for her, to teach her and to act on her behalf for the gaining of Densher's soul. James also said of Emerson that 'he had a particular faculty . . . for speaking to the soul in a voice of direction and authority . . . it seems to go back to the roots of our feelings, to where conduct and manhood begin',[20] and this is the way in which Milly, and Milly's transcendent power, finally speak to Densher. This is not to say that the novel offers a simple affirmation of Emerson's bland *naïveté*. But neither, in the end, does it ironize or reject. It reassesses, in a concrete situation (one that reflects in some ways Emerson's other, and very different, essay on wealth in *English Traits*), Emerson's claims for the moral significance of money, and reformulates them in an historical situation, so that nothing is affirmed without attendant ambivalence. In *Notes of a Son and Brother*, James quotes his father's brilliantly accurate comment on Emerson, 'Oh you man without a handle', adding that the philosopher's answer always 'seemed to anticipate everything but the unaccommodating individual case'.[21] *The Wings of the Dove* offers an *accommodating* individual case, changing the details in the process and creating something more solid, if not more attractive, than that wide-eyed verbosity.

One of the reasons that he is able to do this is because the novel tacitly takes account of a changed social situation. Emerson was not of James's generation and his bewildering vagueness was felt not by him but by 'the passionately living of the earlier time'. The later time sees two developments, both of which give the novel opportunity to put a handle to Emerson. One is that in the world of cases there is a vastly increased possibility of wealth, and wealth becomes linked with a wide range of human activities – Morgan in Europe buying up paintings, the Astors coming to Cliveden. American wealth, as 'Covering End' programmatically demonstrates, is great enough to be able to underwrite European history. Secondly, the Emersonian view of wealth is under direct and extensive attack in the decade preceding the novel, so that any realization has a definite polemical base.

Throughout the eighties and nineties, much social writing concentrated on the influence, mainly evil, of 'plutocracy'. Henry Demorest Lloyd radically challenged the Emersonian structure of thought by insisting that wealth must be considered as an active and not representative phenomenon: 'Liberty produces wealth, and wealth destroys liberty.'[22] And in 1899 the attack reached its climax in Veblen's great book, *The Theory of the Leisure Class*. He relates the pursuit of wealth not to any moral self-fulfilment but to the most primitive of urges, invidious comparison which sees leisure as an index of superior prowess. Since, in a sophisticated society, it is necessary to push the acquisition of wealth to ever greater heights, the comparison tends to base itself on conspicuous waste and vicarious leisure, so that the primitive urge from which the pursuit of wealth derives is seen to pervade every manifestation of a society's culture. Within the shadow of such concepts everything, from professional football to institutions for the study of liberal arts, becomes a function of invidious comparison. Even the intellectual whose role is partly to criticize the accretions of wealth is a sign of conspicuous waste. What is explicit in Veblen had long been implicit in Howells.

James praised *A Hazard of New Fortunes* in terms at once so excessive and so carefully angled that we must regard his attitude to it as highly ambiguous. 'As a triumph of *communication*,' he writes in a letter to Howells, 'I hold the *Hazard* so rare and strong.'[23] The italicization of 'communication' sums up the care with which James makes his praise an exercise in critical *disponibilité*: 'the novelist is a particular *window*. . . .' It is hardly the sort of praise the novel is looking for – what is most characteristic of Howells's window is its claim to be plain glass looking on the world from an objective viewpoint, and it is clearly to evade the issue not to take up the sharp challenge the novel offers to the reader's political and social intelligence:

> 'Such people as the Dryfoos are the raw material of good society. It isn't made up of refined or meritorious people. . . . All the fashionable people there tonight were like the Dryfoos a generation or two ago. I dare say the material works up faster now, and in a season or two you won't know the Dryfoos from the other plutocrats.'[24]

This may be one of the characters talking, but it is a statement about actuality, not about the world of the novel: there is no qualitative difference, this is saying, between the Rockefellers and the Vanderbilts, and the more established 'fashion' – the Astors and perhaps the Jameses. 'Plutocrat' is the keyword: it suggests that money itself does the ruling. It isn't representative but active, and what it purchases in the way of culture and refinements of civilization is a very minor function of its hegemony. The Dryfoos, after all, without the refinements, run the novel's intellectual and cultural world. James is clearly as far from the social viewpoint of Howells as it is possible to be. Whatever the ambiguities of money, its potentialities are essentially good. The only really squalid and irredeemable people in *The Wings of the Dove* are Lionel and Marian – who are relatively poor.

But *A Hazard of New Fortunes* is especially important because, like James's novel, its primary concern is not with wealth in itself but with the role of the intellectual in relation to wealth. Howells's story is above all that of March's problematic relationship with his commercial masters, and its complexity foreshadows in a general way the complex relationship Densher has with the wealth he confronts – a relationship which veers between satiric criticism and consenting bewilderment. The best moments of *Hazard* present this issue squarely and unsentimentally:

> 'I think,' said Mrs March, 'that city girls, brought up as she must have been, are often the most innocent of all. They never imagine the wickedness of the world, and if they marry happily they go through life as innocent as children. Everything combines to keep them so; the very hollowness of society shields them. They are the loveliest of the human race. But perhaps the rest have to pay too much for them.'
> 'For such an exquisite creature as Miss Vance,' said March, 'we couldn't pay too much.'
> A wild, laughing cry suddenly broke upon the air at the street crossing in front of them. A girl's voice called out 'Run, run Jan! The copper is after you.' A woman's figure rushed stumbling across the way, and into the shadow of the houses, pursued by a burly policeman.
> 'Ah, but if that's part of the price. . . .'[25]

Milly too is a wealthy city girl brought up free of the wickedness of the world, and March's attitude is basically that of James himself, for whom the flower of a civilization is its just measure. But March's consenting bewilderment is undermined by the cry of guilt on which such innocence is raised, and by the superior intelligence of his wife. The intellectual who tries to make some compact with the plutocracy is made to seem expediently sentimental. In *The Wings of the Dove*, James sets out to realize an unsentimental acceptance of the price of innocence by regranting money its mystery and its representativeness, by creating for the intellectual a relation to it which is not that of contract but of consent, as to a power greater than any this world by itself can show. In Regents Park, Milly feels herself at one with the poor because she too has her rent to pay: it is as though Miss Vance and the laughing girl have been reunited in a single vision. Milly is the final flower of New York millions, but she has her own price to pay for it – flowers are the end point of a plant's growth; they are there to die. By making herself take on the suffering of guilt while remaining innocent, Milly replaces Howells's Manichean social vision with atonement. The result is a novel much more conservative, but also more profound, for James's realization is of the interpenetration of economic and metaphysical values. In spite of its occasional dry light, Howell's novel is finally dissolved in a cloud of milk and water socialism; whereas, for all its informing admiration for money and disease, *The Wings of the Dove* remains a convincing comedy about the ultimate mystification of the intellectual.

5 *A working view of the general case*

What I have been trying to suggest is that the novel is concerned with the connexions between ways of seeing and modes of relationship, in the context of the social role of money in general and large accretions of money in particular; and that in its concern it embodies highly representative visions and attitudes which are relevant to the historical situation out of which the novel grows. None of this, of course, resolves the problem of Milly's sentimentality, though it should help us to mark out that sentimentality which is being realized as part of the novel's texture.

The clearest statement is Bewley's: 'The guilt of the past,' he writes, 'so largely European, is revealed in all its musty squalor by the contrasting purity of a young girl who being American, has no part in that heritage of crime and misery that belongs in the old world.'[26] It is true, I think, that Bewley sees *The Wings of the Dove* too narrowly in terms of *The Marble Faun*, and in this statement fails to take full account of the connexion made in James's novel between being American and being rich. Nor does it take account of what ironies are there, such as the fact that the young girl's heritage is one which matches the squalor of Europe, and that if Milly remains innocent, she only manages it by being very clever. But some kinds of irony can be sentimental too, and elaborating the novel's many paradoxes doesn't answer Bewley's basic point. I don't think it will do, in the end, for example, to say that Milly adopts the dove image as a disguise under which her 'fullblown consciousness' is concealed for the remainder of the action: this assumes, in a very simplified manner, that 'you' can be different from the role you play, and although there are Jamesian protagonists who make that assumption (above all Isabel Archer), it is placed as an illusion.[27] And it only makes matters worse to suggest that James is trying to get away with making the dove image operate ironically on a social level and symbolically on an 'intuitional' one. Nor will it do to say that Milly is not allowed to strike through the pasteboard mask she adopts – since in that case we have no way of knowing that it is a mask.[28] The only hope for the novel's coherence is to resist injecting irony into the process of transformation just because it may be objectionable to humane sensibilities. Milly copes with the fact of her own disease and the destructive perception of it by the Europeans by cultivating an image supplied for her by those perceptions. And the image becomes a reality by operating on the consciousness of Densher and others: Milly, in other words, apotheosizes herself, conquering death by the impression she makes. The problem seems to me not that it is objectionable but simply that apotheoses don't happen: Bewley's point is important because it resists being palmed off with a simplifying fable. My argument is that we are given more – the whole process and conditions by which Milly can achieve her success.

Kate uses the dove image, as we have seen, as a creatural reduction. If she is thinking of any of its allusive referents, it must be those in Leviticus, where the dove is a sacrificial object used as a substitute for a lamb (Kate thinks of herself as a trembling kid). Milly receives the image as something that identifies what is wrong with her – the odd way people see her and judge her. It is only when she has felt that her exchange with Mrs Lowder is like dove cooing to dove that she sees the possibilities of success in the image. Mrs Lowder, of course, has money, and doves have wings. In Psalm 68, the dove's wings are used as a metaphor of triumph over humiliation: 'Though ye have lien among the pots, yet shall ye be as the wings of a dove covered with silver, and her feathers with yellow gold'; and in Psalm 55 they become the agents of flight from malicious tongues and are linked, as Sandeen has noted, with faith in God's revenging power.[29] Milly has turned the objectifying image she has been offered into an image of triumph and revenge, into a basis for subjective vision and detachment. It works at this point because of the multiple possibilities of the metaphor. But making a cliché viable in the face of complexity is not what makes a great novel; what happens to the image merely reflects the changing structure of relationships. What is asserted theatrically in the penultimate chapter of Book 5 is worked out in the novel's actuality in the chapter which follows it.

Throughout the book, Milly is coming to terms with exposure. The agent of exposure is pity: 'and when pity held up its tell-tale face like a head on a pike, in a French revolution, bobbing before a window, what was the inference but that the patient was bad?' (Bk. 5, Ch. 3). Just as specifically Christian virtues, such as Condrip's saintliness or Marian's turning the other cheek or even the homeliness of Chirk Street (which clearly has to do with humility) are part of the abyss that Kate has to escape from, so for Milly even the disinterested consideration of Sir Luke becomes a threat. It is true that she is sick, but she is also James's choice to register the impact of moral virtue. The effect of making Milly ill is to dramatize more acutely the potentiality of her wealth: she will overcome death itself. She can do this, however, only because she can embrace life in a very special way. After her visit to Sir Luke, she wanders through London confronted with a simple, existential either/or. On the face of it, it is a moral centre from which an embrace of being will radiate; but standing in the middle of Regents Park, Milly seems to be in a remarkably empty world compared with Strether's. The reason, I think, is because Milly's concern is less with life than with the impression she can make on life – with 'success':

> Wonderments in truth, Milly felt, even now attended her steps: it was quite as if she saw in people's eyes the reflection of her appearance and pace. She found herself moving at times in regions visibly not haunted by odd-looking girls from New York, duskily draped, sable-plumed, all but incongrously shod and gazing about them with extravagance; she might, from the curiosity she clearly excited in by-ways, in side-streets peopled with grimy children and costermongers' carts, which she hoped were slums, literally have had her musket on her shoulder, have announced herself as freshly on the war-path. But for the fear of *overdoing the character* she would here and there have begun conversation. . . .   (Bk. 5, Ch. 4: my italics)

The casual subjectivity of 'which she hoped were slums' both draws attention to the nature of the affirmative experience, which has little to do with actuality, and places it within the limits of Milly's wealthy experience. But the ironies are not only James's. Milly is quite conscious of acting out a character: the wonderments are not hers but those of the people who see her. 'Regions visibly not haunted by odd-looking girls from New York' is about as anti-impressionistic as it is possible to be. Lebowitz speaks of the struggle in this novel of the object to become subject, but we see in a passage such as this how inadequate such a description is. Milly's struggle is to become the subject of those to whom she is object, and to control what they see. Her self-irony is a part of this control. It has none of Strether's bemused self-questioning. 'Literally have had her musket on her shoulder' comically exaggerates, since she is only going for a walk, but with an intended 'charm' which we are supposed to admire – 'plucky little girl, able to admit her oddity and still go on walking'. Furthermore, the metaphor is clearly linked with the tell-tale pike. Milly is walking out to defend her regality: her musket is harnessed to a counter-revolutionary struggle against the levelling-down process effected by the great leveller, death. If she feels herself to be like a poor girl with her rent to pay, she will obtain magnificent lodgings in return and, in the meantime, no local colour is going to outshine her sable plumes. Sir Luke speaks of Milly as having a great rare chance, and this seems odd since he is only offering her the common chance. But it is another tribute to her wealth. Dying will not matter. Already she is able to invade and assimilate the consciousness of others, recognizing Susan Stringham's 'positive need' to treat her as a princess, seeing that the way Kate looks sometimes 'was the peculiar property of someone else's vision'. Milly is able to create a lifestyle which is also a mode of vision, in which object and subject coalesce, and distinctions between life and death cease to matter.

The final chapter of Book 5 carries these potentialities of consciousness into the realms of actual relationships.

> She should have been a lady-copyist – it met so the case. The case was the case of escape, of living under water, of being at once impersonal and firm. There it was before one – one had only to stick and stick. (Bk. 5, Ch. 7)

Milly is escaping from two encounters – one with Susie and another with Sir Luke – by conflating them and withdrawing. She is allowing them to build their own image of her while she gets lost in the National Gallery. But she is not running away from difficulties – only from the sense of the unknown which she confronts when she becomes aware of 'the margin always allowed her' by others. She is opting for the known by becoming the oddity others are trying not to reveal they think of her. Rather than have an unknown margin, she fills it up according to Susie's image of her – 'and the proposal now made her – what was it in short but Byzantine'. Sir Luke, too, is deployed on the basis of her knowledge of what he will want – 'she knew him to desire just now. . . .' Anticipating others' knowledge, she can attain a kind of impersonality even in her very exposure. She can do it too because she can rely on the exposure being limited by human reticence and embarrassment: 'The worst would be that he was in love and that he needed a confidante to work it.' Nobody makes such sick jokes as Milly does about herself: it grants her a kind of firmness by overreaching the softness of others' pity. Ultimately, of course, it will not involve living under water (which I take to be an image of being submerged in anonymity) but quite the contrary, living high in the air; and only vicariously will she stick and stick – in personal terms she will take flight. But the lady copyists supply an initial image of retreat into adopted style.

The lady copyists serve two other functions. They link Milly with Densher – if she can't talk to them she can fall in love with one of their sons. But locally they serve as a distraction from the Titians and the Turners, and in this they are very important. Many critics speak of Milly's tendency to become a work of art; but the trouble is that people just don't become works of art, and James is not writing a fairy tale (or not one that can't come true). Milly begins her triumph in the National Gallery, and this is certainly a world of art which she chooses as a refuge from the vulnerability of personal relationships, with the positive motive of 'overtaking' some of the great moments of history 'among the Titians and the Turners'. The utterly undiscriminating alliteration should put us on our guard.[30] Milly is not capable of aesthetic rapture, and is not to be overwhelmed – as Strether is – by the resolution of reality into the consciousness which reproduces it. She finds herself too weak for the Titians and the Turners, but this is not merely because of her fatigue. The fatigue itself is the product of the motive. 'Pictures and things' are one of her 'general heads' connected with 'the continental tour'. She is less concerned with appreciation than getting her 'schools' right. For the purposes of this novel, the National Gallery is only secondarily the world of art: primarily it is the centre of tourism. Tourism and aesthetic appreciation are close in many ways, but you can be a tourist in a way you can't be a work of art. Milly's apotheosis is achieved not by becoming a picture, but by becoming a consummate tourist.

Tourism is, of course, one of the major themes of the chapter. Milly spends her time counting Baedekers until the American mother and daughter discuss Densher. Later, to help Densher over his embarrassment, Milly offers her 'unused margin as an American girl', and Densher is made to talk about his own tour of the States. The chapter ends with Milly metaphorically clinging to the Rockies to avoid the personal exposure of her forthcoming interview with Susan. The general theme mediates the dramatic changes of relationship which take place, and so socializes any subsequent triumph Milly has. Moreover it supplies an epistemological system in itself which destroys the dualistic subject/object relationship which makes Milly so vulnerable.

In the recognition paragraph, Milly studying the mother and her daughters becomes subject of their subjectivity. They are looking at Densher, she watches them looking, and later becomes aware that Kate has been watching her watch them. But what is important is the way in which such knowledge is expressed. The American's knowledge of Densher is generic, 'in the English style', so much so that Milly thinks they are talking of a picture until she realizes that the description doesn't correspond with her knowledge of the styles of the pictures in front of her. Her knowledge of them, in turn, is in the same mode, for she sees at this point with less of her usual extravagant gaze and more of Kate's lucidity: 'She *knew* the three, generically, as easily as a schoolboy with a crib in his lap would know the answer in class.' The crib is, of course, herself – she later resents the fact that they don't know her. The tourists are seen as tourists by a tourist who herself, as she is recognized (that is, seen by

Kate and Densher to be watching him), makes herself so much the
tourist (the American girl) that she becomes, knowingly, the object of
his tourism: 'She became as spontaneous as possible and as American
as it might conveniently appeal to Mr Densher, *after his travels*, to
find her' (Bk. 5, Ch. 7: my italics). Throughout Book 5, Milly has
been escaping from her own objectification by understanding, knowing the subjectivity of others – knowing, that is, about the way they
know her. The National Gallery creates the terms of reference by
which she can make this not a painful and sporadic vision, but a
successful system to cope with the undeniable objective facts of her
existence – her wealth and her illness. The system is a style, and style
closes itself against the contingent.

Already, by the end of the chapter, Milly is working out a system
of transcendence in two ways. In the first place, she reduces the
relationship between Kate and Densher in her own mind to a
romance of unrequited love: she stylizes it, even without being convinced by her own explanation. More importantly, she comes to
terms with her own image by watching others watch it and learning
to control it:

> Whatever he did or he didn't, Milly knew she should still like him –
> there was no alternative to that; but her heart could none the less sink
> a little on feeling how much his view of her was destined to have in
> common with – as she now sighed over it – *the* view. She could have
> dreamed of his not having *the* view, of his having something or other,
> if need be quite viewless, of his own; but he might have what he could
> with least trouble, and *the* view wouldn't be after all a positive bar to
> her seeing him. The defect of it in general – if she might so ungraciously
> criticize – was that, by its sweet universality, it made relations rather
> prosaically a matter of course. It anticipated and superseded the –
> likewise sweet – operation of real affinities. It was this that was doubtless
> marked in her power to keep him now – this and her glassy lustre of
> attention to his pleasantness about the scenery in the Rockies. She was
> in truth a little measuring her success in detaining him by Kate's
> success in 'standing' Susan. It wouldn't be, if she could help it, Mr
> Densher who should first break down.   (Bk. 5, Ch. 7)

Everybody in this scene is playing the 'lively line', and Densher's
way of playing it is to talk about his trip and neglect to talk about

Milly. He is being 'kind' and this, as we have already seen, is the most destructive relationship. The crux is, of course, that Milly accepts it and remains detached at the same time, so that by the end of the passage she is positively using the Rockies, and the careful inattention to her they imply, to compete with Kate's self-control. From this point on, the novel will not be about the betrayal of Milly, but about competing lies. 'Glassy lustre of attention' emphasizes how much her capture of Densher will be a matter of role-playing. By allowing him his style of decent pity, she can offer him her pity, pretending to herself (and getting him to pretend to her) that he needs it. And a mutual pity will overreach the selfish gladness of young immunities.

What is important is that these paradoxes are growing out of specific contexts in a social comedy. We haven't suddenly entered some mysterious aesthetic realm. The possibilities for a stylized transformation of the relationships in the novel are thrown up by Milly's manipulation of the awkward social situation: the accidental personal encounter creates an opportunity for being impersonal and firm. Milly has her rent fixed: she cannot rescue Densher from the general view but she can, by accepting the general view, learn to keep him with her; and this will enable her to compete with Kate's manipulations, and, as the second half of the paragraph explicitly states, hold herself at a convenient distance from the inevitable confrontation with the facts that make the general view unavoidable. The effects on the language of this distancing are clear in the passage quoted: 'The defect of it in general – if she might so ungraciously criticize – was that, by its sweet universality, it made relations rather prosaically a matter of course. It anticipated and superseded the – likewise sweet – operation of real affinities.' The irony is hers, and again is self-admiring (how nice I'm being), and what it does is to flatten the comparison of the actual and the possible relationship by making sure that either way it will be sweet. Through a mannered verbalization, Milly has found a way to make his love, her disease and the real substance of their relationship irrelevant: 'I'll make it charming for you' she later tells Susan, and she does, beguiling all the forms of her relationships of any reality. The language in the chapters immediately before Venice has a strange rococo excess of flourish. 'Beautiful and good', 'the most charming person', 'a lovely acquaintance', 'a sight for the gods' – such phrases are uttered by Milly with a sickening glibness which is clearly her strongest shield against pity. Susie is 'wonder-struck', and this becomes the word to describe the effectiveness of Milly's strategy for the rest of the novel. It is a strategy which defies mere truth – she says, for example, that Kate has been 'gentle and nice' (Bk. 7, Ch. 1). Awareness and recognition become the major forfeits in an involved game of let's pretend: 'It put them again face to face, but it had wound Mrs Stringham up. . . . She had risen by Milly's aid to a certain command of what was before them' (Bk. 7, Ch. 1). The charm also involves an accommodation of everybody else's vision. 'What was before them' turns out to be nothing more than a new idea which emerges from the gloom like a Maeterlinckian star. Sir Luke, too, is assisted in his need to offer kindness to his patient, and this isn't seen as just an aspect of Milly's love, but as a deft game: she has to be careful not to 'embarrass his exercise of a kindness that, no doubt, rather constituted for him a high method' (Bk. 7, Ch. 1). And the effect of this accommodation is a reversal process: 'the pledge of protection and support was all the younger woman's own' (Bk. 7, Ch. 1); 'what *was* he in fact but patient, what was she but physician' (Bk. 7, Ch. 1). Sweetness, accommodation, reversal – all add up to a sustained *trompe-l'œil*.

The proper perspective in which to see this transformation is offered by the apparently irrelevant scene between Susie and Mrs Lowder inserted in the middle of these pre-flight chapters. Aunt Maud is a butt for much of the satire in the novel; but this is only one of its finer ironies, for in the end she, more than anyone, gets what she wants – she parts Kate and Densher, and in some ways gets Densher for herself ('I like him for myself'). Her real dramatic value is to offer a brutal but comic commentary on the sentimental ambience being generated at this point in the novel: 'I might be crying now,' she says, 'if I weren't writing letters' (Bk. 7, Ch. 1). The remark, however revealing of her own philistinism, puts in its place Susie's ridiculous declaration 'I'm to be with her regularly sublime'. She sits like an earringed matron, knees apart at a market stall, while Susie tosses the 'truths' of the situation into her lap. It is an image which includes Susie as well, and it suggests the primitive nature of all the relations which are being struck up. All the sublimity, the benevolence, the consenting bewilderment would be nothing if it weren't that Mrs Lowder sees her own interest in the plan to get Densher for Milly – in this way she might 'handle' Kate. Milly has been making a takeover bid for the truths of those who threaten her with a personal relationship, but the bid only succeeds because the American millionairess has a common interest with Britannia in the Market-place. Suitably, then, it is Aunt Maud who sums up the whole situation at this point in the novel:

'I lie well, thank God,' Mrs Lowder almost snorted, 'when, as sometimes will happen, there's nothing else so good. One must always do the best. But without lies then,' she went on, 'perhaps we can work it out. (Bk. 7, Ch. 1)

'Work it out' is a key phrase in this section of the novel (cf. 'the account of their situation that most showed it as workable', 'what would now make working for Milly such a general upward tug', 'though tactfully working', 'a working view of the general case', 'since she was to be worked for'), and it enables us to distinguish between the sentimental surface and its tough-minded base. Susie is sentimental, to be sure, and her symbolizing and sublimating style is being worked for all it is worth to create what Sir Luke later defines as a beautiful show. But Mrs Lowder accepts here that lies won't do, and we have already discovered this to be the case with Milly: lies imply truths. What she has to create is something which can assimilate both lies and truths, which has its own inner logic and is immune to the law of natural selection which Kate is seeking to operate. The clue is offered by the National Gallery – recognition and awareness can be controlled by the all-embracing, subject/object conflation of the tourist. Tourism has to become a style, and its natural style is spatial totality and impenetrable representativeness. Milly has to become not merely a symbolist like Susie, but a symbol; and a symbol that, unlike Susie's romances, cannot be challenged by the lucidity of realism.

6 *How to be a symbol without really dying*

'Venice has been painted and described many thousands of times, and of all the cities of the world is the easiest to visit without going there.'[31] For the tourist, the image takes precedence over its actual source. In suddenly switching to Venice, Milly is able to 'become' the images the others have created for her, without being exposed thereby to their control. She can do this because Venice is the symbolic city where even the misery is part of the spectacle. Susan's metaphoric excesses can be taken over and given their own reality. But this is possible only because in moving to Venice herself, Milly brings everybody else onto its stage to act out their lifestyles around her, and because although she is in Venice, she has little to do with it. The palazzo is central and detached. She is not exposed to everybody else because they too become their images, and on the symbolic stage Milly is above them, watching. It is important to stress that James isn't suddenly writing a symbolic novel: we have seen that Milly's flight is carefully prepared within the terms of social comedy set up in the first six books. It is simply that she moves to a situation in which the symbolic life can triumph over the 'real', Darwinian world by affirming 'the religious spirit' – that level of human awareness that Balzac failed to do justice to, and that James never pretended was dissociated from the liberating effect of great wealth.

What most emphasizes the way in which symbolism is chosen as a mode to meet the modes Milly has found hostile, is the conventionality of her situation and the way in which she manipulates it. There are many possible references in the last part of the book, but two are actually named by James – not because they are exclusively right, but as reminder that a highly literary style is being wrought to 'compete with life'. 'Our consciousness,' Maeterlinck wrote, 'is our home, our refuge from the caprice of fate, our centre of happiness and strength';[32] and in her fortress above the dramatic world of the city, Milly finds that refuge in becoming in many ways like one of what Maeterlinck defined as 'the predestined'. The predestined are those who seem from the first marked out for an early death, and who appear at once completely innocent and strangely knowing: 'Why do they come to us like the bee to the hive, like the dove to the cote . . .?'[33] The

postulated answer is that they leave us 'the sadder and the more
gentle' because they bring to mind something deeper and more
obscure than human understanding normally encompasses:

> It is as though they were on life's further shore, and the feeling rushes
> in upon us that now, at last, the hour has come for affirming that which
> is graver, deeper, more human, more real than friendship, pity or love;
> for saying the thing that is piteously flapping its wings at the back of our
> throat, and craving for utterance – the thing that our ignorance crushes,
> that we have never said, that we shall never say, for so many lives are
> spent apart in silence.

Both the remoteness and the affinity are what Milly sets out to achieve
and does dying so meaningfully in her palace. The whole purpose of
Wisdom and Destiny is to affirm consciousness as a way of overcoming
the illusion of fate. Milly will overcome her fast-approaching doom
by living on in the consciousness of Densher: 'There were times
when they seemed to be looking down upon us from a lofty tower;
and for all that we were the stronger, we dared not molest them.' The
plot has faint echoes of *Pelléas et Mélisande* and *Aglavaine et Selysette*,
and Susan recognizes the dim, symbolic atmosphere of Milly's
Venetian home as a Maeterlinckian scenario. Moreover, Maeterlinck
was very appreciative of Emerson, and Arthur Symons had stressed
the connexion. His deliberately mystifying moral framework bridges
the distance between European ambiguity and American innocence.
Of course, Maeterlinck's dramas were very expensive to put on.

The other invoked presence is Pater who is also, of course, concerned with the primacy of consciousness. The Palazzo Leporelli
recalls in several ways the house of Cecilia (the mystical German
writer again makes the connexions with the older forms of tran-
scendentalism that Susie inherits):

> 'The house in which she lives,' says that mystical German writer quoted
> once before, 'is for the orderly soul which does not live on blindly
> before her, but is ever out of her passing experiences, building and
> adorning the parts of a many-roomed abode for herself, only an
> expansion of the body; as the body, according to the philosophy of
> Swedenborg, is but a process, an expansion of the soul. For such an
> orderly soul, as life proceeds, all sorts of delicate affinities establish

themselves between herself and the doors and passage-ways, the lights and shadows, of her outward dwelling-place, until she may seem incorporate with it: until at last, in the entire expressiveness of what is outward, there is for her, to speak properly, between outward and inward no longer any distinction at all; and the light which creeps at a particular hour on a particular picture or space upon the wall, the scent of flowers in the air at a particular window, become to her, not so much apprehended objects, as themselves powers of apprehension, and doorways to things beyond – the germ or rudiment of certain new faculties, by which she dimly yet surely apprehends a matter, lying beyond her actually attained capacities of spirit and sense.'[34]

Milly becomes, of course, an orderly soul in a house 'all toned with time' where light reflects and flickers and where she can move 'aloft in the divine, dustless air'. Like Pater's Sebastian Van Storck, who is also wealthy, clever, detached and consumptive, she retreats to a room high above the contentious world, and in her death rescues another from it as Sebastian rescues the child from the flood.

Holland has noted that there are two rhythms in the novel – one of engagement and one of withdrawal. I think that really they are part of the same rhythm, the systole and diastole of the heart-throb which has to be pitted or preserved against the terminating drive of Kate's plot. Engagement and withdrawal come together, for example, in Sir Luke's room: 'She had come forth to see the world, and this then was to be the world's light, the rich dusk of a London "back", these the world's walls, those the world's curtains and carpet' (Bk. 5, Ch. 3). Pater's Sebastian manifests the same potentiality for 'going forth' before he finally retreats:

> There have been dispositions in which that abstract theorem has only induced a renewed value for the finite interest around and within us. Centre of heat and light, truly nothing has seemed to lie beyond the touch of its perpetual summer. . . . Sebastian Van Storck, on the contrary, was determined perhaps by some inherited satiety or fatigue in his nature, to the opposite issue of the practical dilemma. For him that one abstract being was as the pallid sun, disclosing itself over the dead level of a glacial, a barren and absolutely lonely sea.[35]

But Sebastian has had the first possibility – his tutor fancies that his power of determination means that 'his ultimate destination may be the military life'. Milly too, as we have seen, thinks of herself as a soldier when she walks out of the surgery to conquer life. In the Palazzo Leporelli she is tacitly recognizing that the abstract is in opposition to the phenomenal, but not merely to die but also to make a more systematic conquest. Just as Sebastian's detachment makes him strangely attractive to his fellow beings, so Milly in her retreat pervades more fully the consciousness of those around her. Like Poe's telltale heart, she will throb on long after she has retreated from the body.

But if we recall the affirmations of Pater's portrait in what happens to Milly in the Palazzo, we should note too its ironies. Sebastian dies for another, but an unevaluated comment by a physician suggests that this is a possibly meaningless gesture: he would have died anyway 'of a disease then coming into the world; disease begotten by the fogs of that country – waters, he observed, not in their place, "above the firmament" – on people grown somewhat overdelicate in their nature by the effects of modern luxury'. It reminds us that Milly was going to die anyway: living high above the flood, she cannot avoid the fogs which keep her under water, cannot avoid the ultimate depersonalization of the impersonal firm. And she is especially prone to them because, like Sebastian, she is overdelicate. Making herself into a symbol so metaphysically abstract that the borders between life and death cease to have meaning, she is only making a virtue of necessity. At the same time, she goes one better than Sebastian. Far from escaping from her wealth, she makes it the preservative of her everthrobbing heart. She might offer a lesson to Sebastian in how to become a symbol without *really* dying.

It depends on her moving into the city where she is not an object viewed by others, but where all are tourists viewing one another. Venice is an extremely complex literary image and I can only hope to indicate some of its features. The most important is that it is a city of defiant appearances. Thus Ruskin:

> Well might it seem that such a city had owed its existence rather to the rod of the enchanter, than the fear of the fugitive; that the waters which encircled her had been chosen for the mirror of her state, rather than the shelter of her nakedness; and that all which in nature was wild or merciless – Time and Decay, as well as the waves and the tempests – had been won to adorn her instead of to destroy.[36]

He goes on, it is true, to dismiss this as impotent romance and to describe the geological realities, but this is only to affirm God's miraculous and non-human wisdom. In this respect, as in the novel, Venice is the antithesis of England – a world of beautiful appearances and light, rather than one of dark ambiguity:

> Between that grim cathedral of England and this, what an interval! There is a type of it in the very birds that haunt them; for instead of the restless crowd, hoarse voice and sable-winged, drifting on the bleak upper air, the St Mark's perches are full of doves, that nestle among the marble foliage, and mingle the soft iridescence of their living plumes, changing at every notion, with the tints, hardly less lovely that have stood unchanged for seven hundred years.

But again, the analogy with what goes on in the novel is more exact. For if Venice contrasts with England in that it has doves and not restless ravens, it doesn't mean that it is a contrasting paradise. On the contrary, the stones of Venice need saving, like its glory; for under the arches where the doves nestle, the hurly burly of daily life, with its cheapjack traders, its idle middle classes and its Austrian occupiers, ignores the city's splendour. The doves link it with the past, but below them throats hoarse with cursing recall the ravens of England, archetype of the modern world. Below the dove-like Milly, Kate and Densher, Lord Mark and Mrs Lowder act out their shabby realities.

Ruskin makes a brief explicit comparison with England, but it is Gibbon, another of Susan's set authors, who makes possible an extensive analogy:

> The policy of Venice was marked by the avarice of a trading and the insolence of a maritime power, yet her ambition was prudent; nor did she often forget that if armed galleys were the effect and safeguard, merchant vessels were the cause and supply of her greatness. In her religion she avoided the schism of the Greeks, without yielding a servile obedience to the Roman pontiff, and a free intercourse with the infidels of every clime appears to have allayed betimes the fever of superstition. Her primitive government was a loose mixture of democracy and monarchy. . . . The twelfth century produced the first rudiments of the wise and jealous aristocracy which has reduced the doge to a pageant, and the people to a cypher.[37]

Avarice, insolence, prudence, compromise, mixed constitution concealing an effective oligarchy – these surely define the features of the
London Milly meets. This passage comes from a chapter describing
the ransack of Byzantium. Milly is, of course, a Byzantine princess.

Venice then offers an ideal, lighted version of the London scene.
Milly's viewers are themselves caught in a symbolic drama in which,
for example, the secret love of Kate and Densher becomes a highly
melodramatic sexual encounter, arranged at first as they stand highlighted in the Square of St Mark. Even the weather comes to symbolize the changing drama. And if it is all consummated in a Veronese
scenario, it is worth recalling that Symonds, who also stressed the
independence of Venice, wrote: 'Veronese was precisely the painter
suited to a nation of merchants, in whom the associations of the
counting house and the exchange mingled with the responsibilities
and the passions of Princes.'[38] A city of mercantile integrity, built on
swamps, destroying Byzantium, in which the doves express its true
spirit presiding above the petty trading and hoarse aspiration – Milly
could find no better symbol for the way in which her silver and gold
could suffuse uncontaminated the dark world which is staring her
out of life. And if it should seem incredible that a girl should become
a dove, Pater has Socrates tell the story of the Halcyon and remind
his pupils of a storm and calm and ask: 'Which do you think the
greater and more difficult thing to do: to exchange the disorder of
that irresistible whirlwind to a clarity like this, and becalm the whole
world again, or to refashion the form of a woman into that of a
bird?'[39] In the symbolist metaphysic, even metereology is a supreme
fiction – so it is not unconvincing that Densher after the storm should
accept the dove.

I have dwelt on these references to emphasize how much, by just
going to Venice and living and dying in a palace, Milly is adopting a
style, a style in which the merely phenomenal world becomes a tran-
scendable manifestation of hidden moralities. I don't think James is
ironizing Milly, but I don't think either that he ever forgets that the
ultimate symbol is money:

> She was now playing with the thought that Eugenio might *inclusively*
> assist her: he had brought home to her, and always by remarks that
> were really quite soundless, the conception, hitherto ungrasped, of

some complete use of her wealth as a counter-move to fate. It had passed between them as preposterous that with so much money she should just stupidly and awkwardly *want* – any more want a life, a career, a consciousness, than want a house, a carriage or a cook. It was as if she had had from him a kind of expert professional measure of what he was in a position, at a stretch, to undertake for her; the thoroughness of which, for that matter, she could closely compare with a looseness on Sir Luke Strett's part that – at least in Palazzo Leporelli when mornings were fine – showed as almost amateurish. Sir Luke hadn't said to her 'Pay enough money and leave the rest to *me*' – which was distinctly what Eugenio did say. . . . She was more prepared than ever to pay enough, and quite as much as ever to pay too much. What else – if such were points at which your most trusted servant failed – was the use of being, as the dear Susies of earth called you, a princess in a palace?   (Bk. 7, Ch. 3)

Eugenio, the servant who is too old to make love but not to make money, is the only person in the novel with whom Milly has anything like a trusting relationship, and we see the significance of this in the texture of the prose. Living is reduced to a metaphor based on money, because Milly has endless resources of money and no resources of life. Of course, her plucky little self-irony is at work again here, but what she actually does is to use her money as a counter-move to fate – both in the sense that she lives in a palace where all appears beautiful, and in the sense that, by creating an image of herself that overwhelms Densher, she can avoid the fate of being used to provide a means by which Kate's strength may express itself. She gets from Eugenio a metaphoric world, a world in which money replaces biological reality as the courier replaces the healer. Money makes for fiduciary relationships. In this sense, she really is a princess in a palace who can look down on the Susies of earth, play the game of sincerity with Kate, and pity Lord Mark for his failure to cope with her and her 'sinister light of tragedy'. And climactically, of course, she is able to purchase a Veronese party at which she appears transfigured, suited 'down to the earth' by a string of pearls. She purchases a 'perpetually charmed vision' because all are included in the 'candour of her smile, the lustre of her pearls, the value of her life, the essence of her wealth'. Innocence and wealth are completely fused in such an image, and together they are powerful. Her smile accepts her dove-like nature, but only so that it can precipitate the ravens of England towards their melodrama of lust and guilt in the 'drawing-room of Europe'. The Emersonian concept of money is triumphantly restored. Money is moral, representative. But what has restored it is the high sublime of the tourist lifestyle, and that is built on the *actual* value of money.

7 *The circle of petticoats*

The register of the high sublime is, of course, Densher, and our final estimate of the novel must depend on how we see his role in the novel, and how we judge James's success in portraying it. For if Milly is objectively dazzling the whole of society, her dazzling of Densher is the more intense because he is looking for a confrontation with the unknown. He has met, on his arrival in Venice, an atmosphere of stale familiarity generated by the cockneys of all climes, the tourists who pervade the respectable quarters of the city. He looks for more Bohemian lodgings, trying without success to lose his way. Initially the Palazzo is included in this ennui. Milly is after all the tourist of tourists, and the back-street lodgings are to serve to give privacy to his relationship with Kate. And yet, before he has actually got Kate into bed, his mind is paying tribute to the impression Milly can make, and soon he is to find the unknown, not in Kate's body but in the pervasive mystery of Milly's style. And this is going to appear to him as a superior knowledge: aware of how much Kate is 'under the impression of the element of wealth in her', he is able to see also that the pearls 'would uncommonly suit' Kate. Later, he is to give pearls the metaphoric sense they have in the Bible. Seeing what Kate sees he is able to see also what she doesn't: that Milly's wealth is dove-like 'only so far as one remembered that doves have wings and wondrous flights'. Milly, and Milly's power, is already becoming, quite strictly speaking, an objective correlative for Densher's pursuit of the unknown. Paradoxically it is precisely what Densher despises most at the outset, wealth and tourism, that becomes the medium in which he learns to love Milly. In fact, this most important of the novel's triangles simply gets turned on its head: a movement from pity to love is paralleled in the relationship with Kate by a movement from love to pity. In other terms, this is a movement from the admiration of lucidity to the admiration of mystery. This inversion is not difficult to perceive. The problem is that if we take it straight, it seems both incredible and sickening – the fairy princess with the thumping bank account, by dying decently (which really means not smelling of drugs) and forgiving all (which means being kind to a failed attempt to get some of the millions to whose excess her life is forfeit), obliterates the beautiful woman with the strength to live. If we take it ironically, which means seeing Densher as a super-subtle fool (like the narrator of *The Sacred Fount* or John Marcher), the novel becomes a terribly inflated authorial joke, exposing a mode of consciousness so specialized and ingrown that, for all its intelligence, it cannot see that it is being used by Kate to defeat Aunt Maud, Milly to defeat Kate, and in turn by Aunt Maud to defeat everybody. If the texture of the novel has the value I am claiming for it, Densher's experience has to have representative value. I think that it has, though its presentation is full of ironies, some of them satirically directed against him; but the most important *dramatic* ironies are features of the novel's universe manifested through him.

James is definite and specific about the kind of consciousness Densher has. Densher himself feels 'plasticity, within limits, to be a *mode of life* like another' (Bk. 8, Ch. 1: my italics). Plasticity is a formal commitment to a world of thought, of which the positive life-style of Mrs Lowder, with its 'immense expression of her signs and symbols' (Bk. 2, Ch. 2), is a 'portentous negation'. It negates because it speaks with a fixed and unimpressionable 'language' – '*solid* forms', 'wasted *finish*', 'general *attestation* of morality and money' (Bk. 2, Ch. 2: my italics) – so that plasticity is positively a mode of consciousness seeking another language than that of fixed signification. And seeking it, plasticity must necessarily be without objective identity: Densher is a citizen of the world, 'too probably spoiled for native, for insular use' (Bk. 2, Ch. 2). The ingenious discriminator, the *disponible*, Densher is an Everyman figure only to the extent that, in this novel, a particular world view is made a universal one. Significantly, he is contemplating an article when he is thinking of Mrs Lowder's furniture, for he has, above all, what St Beuve defined as the 'génie critique' in his essay on Bayle. Densher's critical ability is very different from Kate's, however. We can see this most clearly when he is using a similar kind of imagery to Kate:

> The huddled herd had drifted to her blindly – it might as blindly have drifted away. There had been of course a signal, but the great reason was probably the absence at the moment of a larger lion. (Bk. 6, Ch. 3)

There is nothing naturalistic about the use of animal imagery here – herd and lion are stock literary metaphors used for purely moralistic distinctions. If Kate's vision is the aesthetic of estrangement, Densher's is the aesthetic of detachment – there is an overlap which draws them together, but a distinction which is destined to part them. Vision for vision, Densher's has more universality because it is not kinetic.

However, James is chiefly concerned to explore, in his portrayal of Densher, the 'mode of life' such vision implies. At the core of Densher's 'mode' is a fear of his own non-existence. Plasticity replaces doing with thinking ('his strength merely for thought'), and Densher contrasts 'life' with 'thought' so that it has to be a special mode of thought as well. The two marks on Densher's forehead (which he significantly thinks of as smudges) are impecuniousness and the facile verbalization of experience. The first is a negation – it makes him, in Mrs Lowder's eyes mediated through his understanding, 'a very small quantity' – and the second leaves him dependent not only on vicarious experience but on vicarious understanding. Both are present in terms of his own vocabulary when he senses that he has got beyond the 'reflux of the first emotion' of returning home:

> His full parenthesis was closed, and he was once more but a sentence, of a sort, in the general text, the text that, from his momentary street-corner, showed as a great grey page of print that somehow managed to be crowded without being 'fine'. (Bk. 6, Ch. 1)

'Parenthesis' links Densher even at this stage with Milly, who has in the previous book felt the 'short parenthesis' of the crowded imagination close after her sense of Aunt Maud 'keeping the day'. It isolates, for each a moment of full consciousness, but is not a matter of mere subjectivity. Milly's parenthesis had begun with Lord Mark telling her that she was a 'success' – giving her, that is, the possibility of an unexploited objective existence. Densher's parenthesis closes when he feels that he himself is a sentence in the general text – when he is nothing but a purveyor of a predetermined structure of words. A little later, he feels himself '*relegated* to mere spectatorship' (Bk. 6, Ch. 3: my italics). In fact what most *threatens* Densher is mere subjectivity, because it also implies lack of will. He admires Kate because her intelligence is at one with her passion, and because she reveals 'a note of character that belittled his own incapacity for action'. It means that she not only mediates his relationship to the active world, but becomes the guide of his awareness – 'Kate's multiplied lights led him on and on'. To maintain that very plasticity which is his subjective mode, Densher has to try to achieve an objective existence.

In his attempts to achieve this, surely the ironies are heavily loaded against Densher. The attempt is self-contradictory, since it involves both an attempt to erect plasticity into a code and an attempt to overcome its will-lessness. Once he is involved in Kate's scheme, Densher becomes comically obsessed with 'how a gentleman would behave':

> He had never known himself so generally merciful. It was a footing, at all events, whatever accounted for it, on which he should surely be rather a muff not to manage by one turn or another to escape disobliging. (Bk. 6, Ch. 5)

'Muff' gets exactly the right note of gentlemanly slang, a calculated minimizing of questions of moral integrity; and the proliferation of negatives and auxiliaries ('not to manage . . . to escape disobliging') measures the passivity, the other-directedness of behaviour which is, with only mild irony, the subject for such self-congratulation. Henceforward, the key words of moral discrimination have to do with awkwardness, tact and delicacy. It reaches its climax in Book 9 when we get a sentence such as 'so that he best kept everything in place by not hesitating or fearing, as it were, to let himself go – go in the direction, that is to say, of staying' (Ch. 2). By escaping disobliging and not hesitating to hesitate, Densher constructs a whole ethical system which includes, as the high point of complacency, feeling righteous indignation against Lord Mark because he has told Milly the truth:

> Densher had indeed drifted by the next morning to the reflection –
> which he positively, with occasion, might have brought straight out –
> that the only delicate and honourable way of treating a person in such
> a state was to treat her as *he*, Merton Densher, did. (Bk. 9, Ch. 2)

As it turns out, of course, he is in many ways, from Milly's point of view, right; but only because she has carefully prepared for every-body a web of illusion. From his own point of view, of the man attempting to create a mode of life from plasticity, Densher is placed as absurd: 'drifted' in the first clause, which is indicative in mood, is contrasted wryly with the determination of 'positively' and 'straight' of the subjunctive parenthesis. Not being a muff, as Densher sporadi-cally realizes, means standing quietly in a circle of petticoats.

The second way in which he tries to achieve objectivity is the very opposite – not the extension of plasticity as a mode of life, but a de-marcation of it from immateriality through the assertion of will. We should not sentimentalize the sexual relationship in the novel simply because it seems refreshingly physical in a world pervaded by the 'spiritual'. Kate's and Densher's young immunity is seen primarily in Darwinian terms: it is what they have to oppose Aunt Maud with in the struggle for survival. And that struggle is, in the last analysis, an individual one. The relationship is never something in itself, separate from its protagonists. Each uses the other to mediate a relationship with life; each sees the other as supplying a lack in the self; each seeks to possess the other. Kate feels of his long looks – which stand for the world of 'mind' – that she 'must make them most completely her possession' (Bk. 2, Ch. 1). Densher too has a completely acquisi-tive attitude towards Kate:

> Having so often concluded on the fact of his weakness, as he called it,
> for life – his strength merely for thought – life, he logically opined,
> was what he must somehow arrange to annex and possess. (Bk. 2,
> Ch. 1)

We should note too that although Densher is recognizing here the dependence of life on thought, the use of a word such as 'annex' keeps them apart. Life is to be possessed so that thought shall not suffocate in its withdrawal from the general text. It's a way of keeping the parenthesis open. The problem is that it is *life*, with its integrity of passion and intelligence, that is to annex him by the time he finds himself in Venice. Again, he reacts to his 'so extremely manipulated state' with a metaphor bringing his literary profession to bear on his impecuniousness:

> There were things enough, goodness knew – for it was the moral of his plight – that he couldn't afford; but what had had a charm for him if not the notion of living handsomely, to make up for it, in another way? of not at all events reading the romance of his existence in a cheap edition. (Bk. 8, Ch. 1)

The final limitation of Densher's world view is surely clear in this: the facts of life have to be met with the fictions of thought. And if this means primarily squaring his conscience with his passivity ('he hadn't come all the way from England to be a brute'), it also means that he has to stop himself from feeling silly: 'There's nothing for me possible but to feel that I'm not a fool' (Bk. 8, Ch. 2). Foolishness becomes with awkwardness a major discriminating concept in Book 9. The sexual consummation is a 'test' on Kate of whether he has a will left at all, and of whether their contract entails obligations on her part as well.

It is also an episode in the struggle for epistemological survival. What spurs him on is that his plan is something that Kate can't see: 'It wound him up a turn or two further, none the less, to impute to her now a *weakness of vision* by which he could himself feel the stronger' (Bk. 8, Ch. 1: my italics). It is significant that not only does Densher gain strength from feeling that he is duping Kate, but also that he doesn't absolutely feel this but chooses to because it makes him feel better. Densher is a seer who has to see himself given definition within the picture. The definition he requires is that of the *bon prince*, capable of exerting a will and being seen to. In the significantly highlighted Piazza he makes his demand explicit for the first time, and James's prose registers precisely the nature of the demand and its determinations: 'For the knowledge of what she was he had absolutely to *see* her now, incapable of refuge, stand there for

him in all the light of day and of his admirable merciless meaning'
(Bk. 8, Ch. 2). There is a note of sadism, but it is essentially directed
towards *exposure*. 'Merciless' echoes the 'merciful' of his feelings
about obliging the circle of petticoats. Plasticity as a mode of life
depends on an underworld in which the petticoats can be torn aside.
Or at least seen to be torn aside: later Densher is struck by 'the
vividness with which he saw himself master in the conflict'. The
reflexive verb sums up the whole affair – we are concerned with a
relationship of competing visions. Specifically this is the invasion of
'life' by thought – 'the fact of the idea as directly applied, as converted from a luminous conception into an historic truth' (Bk. 9,
Ch. 1). The vocabulary in relation to the situation is almost
Schopenhauerian. Getting Kate into bed is a triumph of idea over will.

The sex act is thus aptly only visionary – it exists only as future
and past, as concept and percept. It is an act, not an entry into a new
phase – they meet only once, and we know of it only as an 'arch of
associations'. And it is precisely because of this that Densher moves
so swiftly towards Milly. The opening chapter of Book 9, particularly
the second and third paragraphs, carefully track down Densher's
development: the move from his feeling 'possessed' by the value of
Kate's gesture, to his feeling taken up by Milly's imagination. The
memory of the act is described first of all as something so intense that
it is renewed for Densher each time that he unlocks the door; and
because of this, by a deceptively natural transition, it is transcendent:
'it was in view as nothing of the moment, nothing begotten of time
or of chance could be or ever would.' Once out of time, it becomes
comparable to art – the act becomes the scene, and Densher who
witnesses the scene again and again, occupies an ambiguous role
between actor and audience, becoming like one of the 'fiddlers': 'He
remained thus, in his own theatre, in his single person, perpetual
orchestra to the ordered drama, the confirmed "run"; playing low
and slow, moreover, in the regular way, for the situations of most
importance.' It is a pornographic way to relate to one's sex life: the
act, by its very intensity, has become distanced and stylized (ordered),
and Densher has become a voyeur of his own past. Or rather, his sex
life consists of nobody but Kate, who has performed *for* rather than
with him. And if he feels a renewal of his fidelity as a result, the terms

in which he feels it are highly significant: 'The force of the engagement, the quantity of the article to be supplied, the special solidity of
the contract, the way, above all, as a service for which the price named
for him had been magnificently paid, his equivalent office was to take
effect – such items might well fill his consciousness when there was
nothing from outside to interfere.' Article, contract, price – they are
terms in which Milly is more likely to win than Kate. The forms of
appreciation available to Densher (and I don't think there is any
relevance in saying that James is just being old-maidish about sex
here: Kate's gesture was objectively a price paid for a service) –
timeless memory, faithful admiration – conspire in themselves to
reduce the act to a *condominium* of aesthetics and economics which is
actually the realm of tourism.

By the end of that paragraph, the intensity of impression is
defeated not only because it creates no kinetic response, but because
it fails aesthetically too – the vividness of the memory and the loyalty it
inspires deprives it of 'the warmth of the element of mystery'. What is
finally to defeat Kate is her lucidity. From this point on, Densher
is more and more drawn towards the inscrutable and the oblique.
The final turn of the screw is that the memory, being timeless,
becomes so fixed in space that, from feeling that the act renews itself
whenever he opens the door, Densher begins to feel that closing the
door of his room is closing it on the memory too: so that 'before he
reached the palace, much more after hearing at his heels the bang of
the greater *portone*, he felt free enough not to know his position as
oppressively false'. That composite verb, 'felt free enough not to
know', brilliantly encapsulates both what Densher is and the way in
which he fits with the general themes of the novel. The *portone* of the
palace liberates him from knowledge, and liberation from knowledge
is liberation from the oppression of falsity – not by emancipation into
truth but by emancipation from real false dichotomies. So by the end
of the paragraph he can feel that Milly's imagination purges the
relationship of its guilt. 'Worse things than being duped,' wrote
William James, 'may happen to a man in this world.'[40] The inscrutable has dissolved the lucid: 'Something incalculable wrought for
them – for him and Kate; something outside, beyond, above themselves, and doubtless ever so much better than they.' That 'doubtless'

fixes the terms of the novel – the moral superiority of Milly's imagination is chucked in as an asserted afterthought because it doesn't finally matter. What matters is that she wins, and the extent of her triumph is to be measured by the comic rout of Kate's memory – by the arrival at Densher's lodgings of New England Susie in a wet waterproof.

Densher's conversion can be usefully set in a context provided by Susie's eyestyle as well. In 'The Tragical in Daily Life', Maeterlinck writes:

> Its province is rather to reveal to us how truly wonderful is the mere act of living, and to throw light upon the existence of the soul, self-contained in the midst of ever restless immensities; to hush the discourse of reason and sentiment, so that above the tumult may be heard the solemn, uninterrupted whisperings of man and his destiny.[41]

Densher gets from Milly above all the metaphysical justification of his stillness, 'creating studiously the minimum of vibration'. When he finally leaves Kate it is to seek in his rooms not a memory but a stillness, 'so that it might prevail there till the inevitable sounds of life, once more, comparatively coarse and harsh, should smother and deaden it'. The wings of the dove hush the discourse of reason and sentiment – that is of the intelligence and passion, the personal life offered with chill lucidity by Kate.

What it is replaced by is realized with a prose style hovering brilliantly on the border between comedy of manners and divine allegory:

> When one went on tiptoe one could turn off for retreat without betraying the manœuvre. Perfect tact – the necessity for which he had from the first, as we know, happily recognized – was to keep all intercourse in the key of the absolutely settled. It was settled thus for instance that they were indissoluble good friends, and settled as well that her being the American girl was, just in time and for the relation they found themselves concerned in, a boon inappreciable. If, at least, as the days went on, she was to fall short of her prerogative of the great national, the great maidenly ease, if she didn't diviningly and responsively desire and labour to record herself as possessed of it, this wouldn't have been for want of Densher's keeping her, with his idea, well up to it – wouldn't have been in fine for want of his encouragement and reminder. He

didn't perhaps in so many words speak to her of the quantity itself as of the thing she was least to intermit; but he talked of it, freely, in what he flattered himself was an impersonal way, and this held it there before her – since he was careful also to talk pleasantly. It was at once their idea, when all was said, and the most marked of their conveniences. The type was so elastic that it could be stretched to almost anything; and yet, not stretched, it kept down, remained normal, remained properly within bounds. And he *had* meanwhile, thank goodness, without being too much disconcerted, the sense, for the girl's part of the business, of the queerest conscious compliance, of her doing very much what he wanted, even though without her quite seeing why. She fairly touched this once in saying: 'Oh yes, you like us to be as we are because it's a kind of facilitation to you that we don't quite measure: I think one would have to be English to measure it!' – and that too, strangely enough, without prejudice to her good nature. She might have been conceived as doing – that is of being – what he liked in order perhaps only to judge where it would take them. They really as it went on *saw* each other at the game; she knowing he tried to keep her in tune with his conception, and he knowing she thus knew it. Add that he again knew she knew, and yet that nothing was spoiled by it, and we get a fair impression of the line they found most completely workable. The strangest fact of all for us must be that the success he himself thus promoted was precisely what figured to his gratitude as the something above and beyond him, above and beyond Kate, that made for daily decency. There would scarce have been felicity – certainly too little of the right lubricant – had not the national character so invoked been, not less inscrutably than entirely, in Milly's chords. It made up her unity and was the one thing he could unlimitedly take for granted.   (Bk. 9, Ch. 2)

So many of the themes of the novel are brought together here. The opening sentences pick up the theme of what a gentleman would do, but we notice also that Milly can match his plasticity with an elasticity of role: without him having to assert himself, she is doing, being what he wants. She too achieves that impersonality she has desired from the time of her visit to the National Gallery. The conditions of this achievement are precise. Intercourse is to be in the key of the absolutely settled, and the musical metaphor is picked up again with 'keep her in tune' and 'Milly's chords', and echoed in

'without being too much disconcerted'. They are not having intercourse so much as playing together in concert, and James emphasizes
this by the reflective self-consciousness of the game ('Add that he,
again, knew she knew . . .' – it is the epistemological equivalent of a
French farce) and, startlingly by bringing 'us' – 'the strangest fact for
us' – into the prose as audience to admire their performance. The
theatricality is not reductive because it is precisely what they are
aiming at – producing between them a fiction which will not be spoiled
by the fact that they know it is. What Kate's act becomes inevitably in
Densher's mind is what Milly's style voluntarily is, in this sense. On
the other hand, it survives because it offers not a lucidity, but a
'workable' line: a line which makes for decency rather than truth, and
in making for it reaches a higher, vaguer, more obscure truth – a
'something beyond'. But, of course, the line itself is very precise – it
grows out of the tourist role Milly is prepared to adopt, 'the great
maidenly ease'. The metaphor at the end is important – the national
character is a lubricant, and in the following paragraph a 'non-
conductor' (i.e. an insulator). Both images are from mechanical
contexts and have to do with the repression of forces (friction or
electricity) in order to keep the machine going. James hasn't
abandoned the ironies of that first sentence by the end, but he has
certainly redirected them; so that instead of Densher rationalizing
his malleability and tacit hypocrisy, we have Kate outmanœuvred by
a machinery for eliminating the clash of interests in an innocent game
of types, fact outmanœuvred by fiction, Milly's bewildered acquiescence transformed to our consenting bewilderment. James transcends
his own ironies without losing their penumbral interrogations.
Following Densher into the dark warmth of the element of mystery,
we carry shreds of his satiric light.

8 *The mere money of her, the darling*

If then, Densher's conversion is to be seen as the intercourse between
his flawed plastic consciousness and Milly's stylistic power (which is
her wealth), it is also to be seen as an initiation into a vision which
really overreaches the art of seeing things as they are, exposing it as a
distortion capable of mere lucidity. There seems to be no system of

values outside the grand alliance of Susie, Milly and Densher, who oppose their styles against Kate's. Densher occasionally recognizes that outside his circle of petticoats there are male witnesses – Sir Luke, Lord Mark, Eugenio – who might see the absurdity of his postures. But they do not represent an ideal other case, a potential male *ransome* of human vitality, because each of them is in some way on hire to the circle of petticoats. Eugenio has lost the ability to make love, though not to make money; Sir Luke is concerned only with a beautiful show of life, and gives tacit approval to the pretences of the Palazzo; and Lord Mark is merely an effect without being a cause, and his irruption of reality is merely destructive. The male witnesses are not male enough, because in this novel there is only one real source of power which is impersonal and firm, and that is hard cash. The final irony of the novel is that the satiric ironies, which are allowed full play in local details, are made to look ridiculous as we witness the power of Milly to survive, and exact, in death, even more consenting bewilderment.

This is emphasized, as is the transcendent power of wealth, by the fact that Densher's conversion is completed not by Milly herself, but by the two agents of her love who were most the butts of his satiric mind, Susie and Aunt Maud (if he had felt sorrow for the first, and hatred for the second, it is merely because of their relative force). We have seen how much Susie contributes to the lifestyle Milly acquires, and how it is she, grotesque parody of pity like a naked new-born babe, who dissolves the lucidity of Kate's act. Densher finally speaks of her as 'a person who does see' (Bk. 10, Ch. 1). And, of course, for all her strident hyperbole, she does: for she sees the romantic potential of money, and the realization of that potential is what the novel is about. But the fact that Densher is saying this to Kate would make it one of the best jokes in the novel, if it weren't that the best jokes come from Susie's better half.

Mrs Lowder, as I have already suggested, offers brutally simple perspectives on the mystifying events of the novel, and these are too valuable to allow us to see her only as a comic butt. In the last book of the novel she is granted a positive dramatic role which is only hinted at earlier. The high mark of imagination that Milly has at Matcham is her awareness of Mrs Lowder's 'spiritual ebriety' – it is the climax of what turns out to be a parenthesis in which she enjoys a simple, unworked-for success as a veritable young lioness. When she loses this and is made a mere dove, it is Mrs Lowder who enters and is like dove cooing to dove, who gives Milly the idea of the success she can achieve after the lionizing has stopped. She is deeply bound up with Milly's triumph both in practical and thematic terms. With her nauseating amalgam of uninhibited avarice and sanctimonious sentimentality, she becomes the earthly spokesman of an unearthly power:

> What most deeply stirred her was the way the poor girl must have wanted to live.
>
> 'Ah yes indeed – she did, she did: why in pity shouldn't she, with everything to fill her world? The mere *money* of her, the darling, if it isn't too disgusting at such a time to mention that –!'
>
> Aunt Maud mentioned it – and Densher quite understood – but as fairly giving poetry to the life Milly clung to: a view of the 'might have been' before which the good lady was hushed anew to tears.   (Bk. 10, Ch. 2)

Given the earlier placing of Aunt Maud, we cannot but turn the irony on Densher too, and yet it is only to acquiesce in the bizarre reality – the mere money is what gives her poetry. A poor girl dying wouldn't 'matter' in this way. And although Densher tries to dissociate himself from Mrs Lowder's sentimentality, he comes to feel more free with her than in 'the strange chill' of Kate's brightness. He dresses, on Christmas morning, 'quite as if for church', but it is Mrs Lowder who sends him there. She has become Milly's vicar, ensuring that the mere money continues to speak of the 'solemn, uninterrupted whisperings of man and his destiny'. The 'commendable fictions' of Susie, 'the wealth of sentiment' of Aunt Maud, and his own 'wasted passion' constitute a moral surplus generating a large gap between actual value and psychological value, which is what the world of thought lives off. The gap can be measured by Densher's adoption of Milly's counter-revolutionary image; during his reflections on Mrs Lowder's evocation of the mere money, 'Milly had held with passion to her dream of a future, and she was separated from it, not shrieking indeed, but grimly, awfully silent, as one might imagine some noble victim of the scaffold, in the French Revolution, separated at the

prison-door from some object clutched for resistance' (Bk. 10, Ch. 2).
It is a highly sentimental image, since Milly died in luxury from
natural causes, able to afford the most expensive surgeon, the most
lavish apartments (which were the very opposite of prison), and
bathed in a decent vagueness. But above all it is Milly's image – her
style, invoked by Britannia in the Market-place. As though to make
quite sure we don't miss it, James goes on in the next paragraph to
describe Densher's feelings about Lancaster Gate: 'Before the fire in
the great room that was all arabesques and cherubs, all gaiety and
gilt, and that was warm at that hour too with a wealth of autumn sun,
the state in question had been maintained. . . .' The state in question
is the princely state in which Densher, responding to Susie's princess
image, describes himself as having been received by Milly. The
Palazzo is thus maintained at Lancaster Gate, and 'warm' places it
firmly on Milly's side against Kate. But what is most striking is that
we are witnessing a complete reassessment of Aunt Maud's 'medium'
by Densher. It has the same vulgarity, but vulgarity is no longer a
negation of thought. And the remainder of the paragraph describes
him as playing a part for the sake of Lancaster Gate gossip, seeing its
sentimental exaggerations, and accepting them. We almost have an
image at the end of Mrs Lowder and Densher holding hands and
gazing at the wonderful romance they have constructed. Certainly
Mrs Lowder's most witty remark, 'I want him for myself', has been
realized by the end of the novel. The liberal imagination, the world
of thought, the plastic consciousness has come to rest in the ample
bosom of the mercantile matron. I was going to add 'and all on
American capital' but, of course, it is finally without Milly's money,
only with her credit. The will to believe keeps the churches full and
the stock exchanges afloat.

I haven't, obviously, given a complete account of the novel's texture
or of the contexts it invokes, but I hope that I have said enough to
show that the deceptively simple, and simplifying plot is elaborated
to become a coherent and wide-ranging study of the relationships
between aesthetic and epistemological ideals and social relationships
(specifically in a world which is becoming a plutocracy ruled by the
corporation), and the trust which reinforces the establishment, not
personally but in the ultimate impersonality of death. A right evalu-

ation of the novel depends on seeing it, to the end, as comedy, instead of sentimentalizing it, as most critics do, as tragedy. The effects of Milly's death are very funny. More strictly, in the end the social world re-forms, and only the *idiotes*, Kate, the stranger who has tried to subvert it, is banished. I don't think necessarily that James made moral judgments on the world he was depicting, unless it was to endorse its structure by seeing in it the potential of aesthetic contemplation. What I claim is that his understanding of the dramatic relations between great wealth and the world of thought is deep enough for him to bring out all the complexities involved in experiencing those connexions. The simplicity of the plot not only permits the spatial presentation of these complexities, it is the direct reflection of the connexion: for money and language both seek to compose relationships into commendable fictions.

To demonstrate once more how great it is, we should put *The Wings of the Dove* into one final context, which is that of the fictional treatment of the millionaire. If we contrast, for example, Dickens's presentation of Merdle with Trollope's of Melmotte eighteen years later, we can see a significant development which corresponds historically to the increasing importance of large concentrations of capital, and a changing relationship of novelist to public. Dickens makes us sorry for Merdle – despite his iniquity he remains a pathetic old man, insignificant in all his personal relations. Trollope is even more morally indignant against Melmotte, who is seen as a crude, sadistic father, as well as an unscrupulous businessman in a world of unscrupulous fools. And yet Trollope obviously has terrific admiration for him as an artist. Most of the other characters are presented from a very cool, clinical distance unless, like Roger Carbury, they are woodenly idealistic. But he moves closer and closer to Melmotte; the scenes in the House of Commons, up to his death, are presented dramatically from inside Melmotte's consciousness. Clearly this is because, despite his moral fervour (which seems fairly routine anyway), Trollope can identify more easily with this crook than with any other character; and the reason for this is equally obvious. There are no other values realized in the novel than the ones Melmotte perpetrates – Carbury is not only fictionally dead, but his only substantial objection to Melmotte is that he is an upstart. Melmotte is close to the novelist because he is creative – his money and his morality determine the world of the novel as the novelist determines it also. What seems contradictory in Trollope is made explicit in Meredith's *One of Our Conquerors*: not only is the mind of Victor Radnor the centre of consciousness in the novel, it is also the entangled hiding-place of the transforming 'idea' which generates all vitality in the world of the book. The comic climax of the novel happens when Radnor is conducting the whole of high society as his orchestra at Lakelands. It is comic because of its incongruity: the financial whizz-kid has society in his hands, and this is a verdict on society; but on the other hand, the radical outsider has transformed society into a work of art. Meredith goes a long way towards making articulate the links between the millionaire and the artist: both aliens in the social world, they transform their perceptions into modes of life which assimilate other modes. For the financier, as for the novelist, there can be no self-realization which doesn't include the orchestration of all the other powers in the world. To go from Trollope to Meredith is to go from a secret, guilty complicity based on contempt of the rest of society, to a sophisticated attempt to sort out the artist's role in relation to the hegemonic consciousness.

But, finally, Meredith seems to shy away from his theme. Committed to a vitalistic liberalism, which in the later work is not sharply distinct from crude imperialism and racism, he scales Radnor down, limiting his mind to a flawed response to respectability; and *One of Our Conquerors* becomes an increasingly simple tale about the conflict between social and sexual interests. The conqueror does not, as he promises to do, conquer our imagination. But it is the conquest of imagination by accretions of money so large that they liberate the mind, both from money itself and from the shame of the lack of it, that underlies our culture. The illusion that there is a world of mind or a realm of art apart from the *merde* of the Merdles is the concern of *The Wings of the Dove*. 'The romantic stands, on the other hand, for the things that, with all the facilities in the world, all the wealth and all the courage and all the wit and all the adventure, we never can directly know; the things that can reach us only through the beautiful circuit and subterfuge of our thought and our desire.'[42] Wealth, no – but money? What operates a circuit if it is not currency? In his novels at least, James finds something so different from *merde* in the coffers of the millionaire that it becomes, in effect, the root of innocence and the flower of imagination. We meet the real, 'the things we cannot possibly *not* know'[43] with the lies we see by, and no other novel in English seems to me so honest, so dramatic about what purchases the lens.

Notes

* In some modern editions, such as the Penguin, the chapters are numbered consecutively: those of Book 2 are numbered 3 and 4; Book 3, 5 and 6; Book 4, 7–9; Book 5, 10–16; Book 6, 17–21; Book 7, 22–5; Book 8, 26–8; Book 9, 29–32 and Book 10, 33–8.

1. Quentin Anderson, *The American Henry James*, New Brunswick, 1957, pp. 233–80.
2. *Henry James's Autobiography*, edited by F. W. Dupee, London, 1956, p. 335.
3. William James, *The Will to Believe and Other Essays in Popular Philosophy*, New York, 1899, p. 58.
4. S. Koch, 'Transcendence in *The Wings of the Dove*', *Modern Fiction Studies*, xii, Spring 1966, p. 94.
5. B. Lee, 'Henry James's "divine consensus"', *Renaissance and Modern Studies*, vi, 1962, pp. 5–24.
6. M. Bewley, *The Complex Fate*, London, 1952, p. 41.
7. F. R. Leavis, *The Great Tradition*, London, 1962, p. 175.
8. E. Auerbach, *Mimesis: The Representation of Reality in Western Literature*, New York, 1957, p. 416.
9. H. A. Taine, *Nouveaux Essais de Critique et d'Histoire*, 8th ed., Paris, 1905, vol. 3, p. 48.
10. *French Poets and Novelists*, Leipzig, 1883, p. 71.
11. Henry James, *Notes on Novelists, with some other notes*, London, 1914, p. 91.
12. Ibid., p. 110.
13. Ibid., p. 95.
14. F. O. Matthiessen, *Henry James: The Major Phase*, New York, 1963, p. 74.
15. 'Walter Barrett' (pseud. Joseph A. Scoville), *The Old Merchants of New York City*, New York, 1870, vol. 2, p. 115.
16. *A History of the Great American Fortunes*, Chicago, 1910, vol. 1, p. 187.
17. 'Barrett', op. cit., vol. 2, p. 126.
18. C. M. Kirk and R. Kirk (eds.), *Criticism and Fiction, and other essays*, New York, 1959 ed., p. 340. In 1903, Howells was to write warmly and acutely about *The Wings of the Dove* itself: see 'Mr Henry James's later work' in F. W. Dupee (ed.), *The Question of Henry James*, London, 1947, pp. 26–39.

19. *The Complete Prose Works of R. W. Emerson*, edited by G. T. Bettany, London, 1889, p. 517.

20. *Partial Portraits*, London, 1911, p. 32.

21. *Henry James's Autobiography*, p. 347.

22. *Wealth against Commonwealth*, New York, 1894, p. 2.

23. *Letters*, vol. 1, pp. 166–9.

24. W. D. Howells, *A Hazard of New Fortunes*, New York, 1965, p. 248.

25. Ibid., p. 223.

26. Bewley, op. cit., p. 53.

27. J. Kimball, 'The Abyss and *The Wings of the Dove*', in T. Tanner (ed.), *Henry James: Modern Judgements*, London, 1968, p. 279.

28. Naomi Lebowitz, *The Imagination of Loving: Henry James's legacy to the novel*, Detroit, 1965, p. 76.

29. E. Sandeen, '*The Wings of the Dove* and *The Portrait of a Lady*: a study of Henry James's later phase', *PMLA*, lxix, 1954, p. 1078.

30. The phrase, like that other joke epithet 'Britannia of the Market', comes in Ruskin (*A Joy for Ever* and *The Crown of Wild Olive* respectively). But that context is one of the 'accumulation' and 'distribution' of art.

31. Henry James, *The Art of Travel*, New York, 1958, p. 384.

32. M. Maeterlinck, *Wisdom and Destiny*, London, 1898, p. 26.

33. M. Maeterlinck, *The Treasure of the Humble*, London, 1909, pp. 45–58.

34. W. H. Pater, *Marius the Epicurean*, 2 vols., London, 1892, pp. 99–100. Stuart Sherman in 'The Aesthetic Idealism of Henry James' (1917) emphasized the connexion with Pater in such a way as to yield some of the insights which the present essay explores – notably the importance of 'style' (Dupee, op. cit., pp. 86–106).

35. W. H. Pater, *Imaginary Portraits*, London, 1890, pp. 124–5. Subsequent quotations are taken from this edition, pp. 91–133.

36. *Complete Works*, London, 1902–12, vol. 10, pp. 6–7.

37. *The Decline and Fall of the Roman Empire*, London, 1898, vol. 6, p. 382.

38. *The Renaissance in Italy*, vol. 3 of *The Fine Arts*, London, 1899, p. 273. See also L. B. Holland, *The Expense of Vision, Essays on the craft of Henry James*, Princeton, 1964, p. 306. Holland is generally very informative about James's use of the visual arts in this novel.

39. *Marius the Epicurean*, vol. 2, pp. 89–90.

40. *The Will to Believe*, p. 19.

41. Maeterlinck, *The Treasure of the Humble*, pp. 97–8.

42. *The Art of the Novel*, edited by R. P. Blackmur, New York, 1960, pp. 31–2.

43. Ibid.

9

The novel to end all novels
The Golden Bowl

GABRIEL PEARSON

In my reading, *The Golden Bowl* represents James's ultimate attempt to salvage imaginatively the ideals of a civilization that his deepest instincts warned him was doomed. It is written heroically against the pull of the abyss which undermines it and the moral abscesses that draw its strength. ' "Wait!" It was the word of his own distress and entreaty, the word for both of them, all they had left, their plank now on the great sea' (Pt. 6, Ch. 2).[1] Given the syntactical elaboration of the late style, this wretched huddle of simple clauses indicates that the statement is something more than a baroque flourish. It is rather in the nature of a vision of catastrophe that has accumulated from a whole sequence of images of voyage, shipwreck and immersion. It strikes the note of isolation and departure that sounds through the concluding pages of the novel. We are surely in the presence of James's final things; if it is not a noisy apocalypse, the novel's last phrase evokes, with almost ritual stress, the tragic emotions of 'pity and dread'. The Prince's remark that 'everything's terrible, *cara* – in the heart of man' may be no more than a rather hollow, sententious response to Maggie's upwelling of pity for herself and Charlotte: 'It's terrible . . . I see it's *always* terrible for women' (Pt. 6, Ch. 2). But the Prince's remark has the feel of direct authorial sponsorship. The hesitation between dramatized and general statement is one local instance of James's acrobatic suspension on the hair's breadth that separates appearances and the collapse they are maintained against. We catch the novelist poised between the buoyant relativism involved in his dramatic method and direct report of his own sense of the world.

The Prince's remark has a Conradian ring. It is instructive to cite Conrad at this juncture as a novelist chronologically adjacent to James and technically sympathetic to him, who is yet operating through and beyond the illusions of the civilization that James's practice upholds. For Conrad, bourgeois civilization is sustained by power and protected by lies. To the initiate into its underlying realities, it is a hollow cheat, one which it is, however deviously, the main impulse of his fiction to confess. The lie in James is sanctified by what it salvages and the disaster it postpones. The action of *The Golden Bowl* turns upon a whole series of lies, duplicities, casuistries and silent suppressions. These do not of themselves create panic and guilt, whereas in Conrad – and his narrative indirections measure the resistance – the lie presses insistently towards revelation. The use of Marlow as narrator involves essentially a mode of confession – 'After such knowledge, what forgiveness?' The dense night in which Marlow aboard the *Nellie* describes to his invisible audience his knowledge of the atavisms that impel civilizing ideals is like the darkness of a confessional. Indeed, the word civilization in Conrad cannot be sounded without an inaudible festoon of ironic quotation marks. Marlow seeks absolution and attempts to re-establish community on the basis of shared guilt. The world he depicts is that of after-the-deluge. His characters experience and live out the catastrophe. There has always been an explosion, a murder, a suicide, some definitive act of betrayal and separation. Certainly, Conrad's analytic and reconstitutive techniques muffle the impact of these collapses; their artistic reassembly, despite the hysteria latent in Conrad's irony, reasserts control. Of course, he frequently lacks the courage of his own insight and relapses into a characteristic romantic and rhetorical melodrama. Yet fundamentally the crust of appearance has been broken: Conrad consciously inhabits a world of ruins and desolations.

This is what makes Conrad, in contrast to James and despite his proximity to him, essentially a modern writer, even a modernist, who has entered fully into the condition of twentieth-century man. He has, however unwillingly, acknowledged a new epoch of social experience: the collapse of sustaining ideals of civilization and a disenchanted encounter with the forces that support it and may now be destroying it – imperialism, open class struggle, the deep connexion between surface and depth, the involvement of the exotic with the domestic. Admittedly, awareness of this kind was available to some of the great nineteenth-century realists, perhaps most of all to Dickens; which is why, both for Conrad and indeed James, the precedent of Dickens is so important. But James essentially survives from a period of late bourgeois supremacy and security. His one attempt, in *The Princess Casamassima*, to deal directly with the forces of the abyss remains, by general consent, a brilliant guess. With desperate casuistry, James made his disabling ignorance central to his treatment, or at least that is how he came to justify it in his Preface:

> My theme called for the suggested nearness (to all our apparently ordered life) of some sinister anarchic underworld, heaving in its pain, its power and its hate; a presentation not of sharp particulars, but of loose appearances, vague motions, and sounds and symptoms, just perceptible presences and general looming possibilities.[2]

Of course, this is the James of 1908 or thereabouts, and it is also the James of *The Golden Bowl* who has become habituated to using abstractions concretely, demonically, to describe absent presences. More usually quoted in this connexion is the passage where James makes a specific virtue out of his ignorance:

> ... the value I wished most to render and the effect I wished most to produce were precisely those of our not knowing, but only guessing and suspecting and trying to ignore, what 'goes on' irreconcilably, subversively, beneath the vast smug surface[.] I couldn't deal with that positive quantity for myself ... but I might perhaps show the social ear as on occasion applied to the ground, or catch some gust of the hot breath that I had at many an hour seemed to see escape and hover.[3]

James typically casts his ignorance in metaphors of adventure. He puts his ear to the ground like an Indian scout and 'the gust of hot breath' seems both volcanic and zoological. Hyacinth Robinson, the hero of *The Princess Casamassima*, is really a lower-class James, whose dualisms mirror James's own, torn between the values of 'civilization' and 'democracy'; his suicide, because the social issues are so explicit, is by the same measure the most explicit of those negative deeds that are the centre and culmination of action in James. They 'save' the contradiction that value rests upon the expropriated lives of others. Maggie's battle not to sacrifice anyone – ironically quite unsuccessful – makes her the last in a sequence of heroes and heroines who resolve this contradiction by electing an extreme negative consciousness. They become scapegoats, and their self-abnegation a way of expiating the original sin of all culture, that it expropriates of the lives of many in order to fulfil those of a few.

But if, as the supreme culmination of such a culture, there can be found those who will deny themselves its fruits, consciously and disinterestedly, then that culture, as against the upwelling of anarchy involved in its collapse, can still be humanly justified. This I think was the unstated reason for James's conservatism. It would of course be possible to read his tragedies of self-negation at other levels, religious, metaphysical or more diffusely experiential. James himself, however, seeking to remain a novelist in the Balzacian tradition, invites us to think of him in social terms, even when these involve mostly negation, the anxiety of not knowing, which amounts to a kind of exclusion from social experience. James, I think, senses from studying the naturalists that to render the lower depths meant treating human lives from the outside, and hence abdicating to the forces of depersonalization. His refusal to know involves then a kind of integrity, but one for which, like his own heroes, he has to pay dear.

The self-ensnared heroines like Isobel Archer (whose fall is all the greater for her sensuous and moral vitality) and Fleda Vetch can be viewed as redeeming their culture by consciously denying themselves its opportunities for individual self-aggrandisement. James's pre-Conradian security depends upon acts of extreme self-abnegation. If these are no longer possible or available, if grossness prevails and there are no fine, complex self-destroying heroes to pay the price, then the cultural order to which James felt himself to belong is humanly indefensible. This is the nightmare that haunts his later fiction. His own artist's dedication is itself a model act of self-sacrifice. Within his art, the quest for redemptive, self-negating heroes, and the ambiguities of that quest, become increasingly his theme.

The self-negating heroine recovers in consciousness the raw vitality of social and sexual existence that she loses in fact. Consciousness is nonetheless, finally, negation. You can possess only what you have lost, which of course would make *The Golden Bowl* a queer case if read as Maggie's success story in worldly terms. She does indeed get the Prince back – but on the terms, I would argue, of his surrendered manhood, the free, elusive, almost unconscious play of life that the first book so beautifully enacts. What she does gain is the imagination of him, which she exchanges for her infatuation. *The Spoils of Poynton* is the classic instance for it involves the sacrifice both of desirable objects and a desirable young man. The flames that consume the spoils are the flames of the redeeming consciousness in which they can live on as negations. The correlative of these is the neglected furniture of the spinster aunt with which Fleda restocks her house of consciousness.[4] James's entire art rests upon a metaphysic of loss – loss of the actual, the sexual, the carnal, the power-giving – which only gross souls can enjoy, in their unconsciousness. It is for this reason that Charlotte, who at the beginning of the novel has, like Fleda Vetch, nothing, having committed the original sin of getting and possessing, disappears into a gross materiality, a matter of splendid dresses and superb hats, becoming a kind of Lamia, a gilt and enamelled snake. Only as she begins to lose confidence in her possession of the Prince, and so in her carnal identity, does she become accessible again: not as a demon, but as another consciousness to Maggie. That seems to me to be what happens; whether one imaginatively, or morally for that matter, endorses this is another question.

Notoriously, James's own practice as an artist is continually conspicuous in the shape of every paragraph, the architecture of every sentence, the suspension of every parenthesis, the placing of every period. Punctuation in late James is just that, the intrusion of incessant crises and cruxes of choice, into the flow of language. Language in the gross becomes a kind of analogy of raw life itself, which is then processed, reconstituted, innoculated with consciousness. James is there in all his bulky, breathing, punctilious selfhood. Never for one moment does style lapse into the dim unconsciousness of mere prose. The efforts of his heroes are one with his own – they live out an epic of attentiveness analogous to that of his composition of them. This is why the late novels, at every level of style and form, are noisily and unanonymously James's own, and yet can continue to be about real characters, whose world – which is of course a body of metaphor for their conscious possession of it – is their own. The climax of a late James novel occurs when one of the characters' consciousness – Strether's, Merton Densher's, Maggie's – fuses, as it were, with James's own: this gives James's consciousness a kind of social endorsement and extension, suggesting the possibility – which it is most difficult for a novelist, of all kinds of writers, to do without – of some spiritual community with others, even if those others are his own fictitious creations. In those intricate but infinitely solacing interviews between Maggie and her father, and perhaps Fanny and her husband, we come close to fictional enactments of such spiritual communities. They stand in, as it were, for the relationship between novelist and reader, the existence of which, one senses, James, in moments of panic towards the end of his career, must have sometimes doubted. The habit of postulating these spiritual communities and the fear of utter isolation, which leads to some rather groping irony – as though James were literally trying to use his syntax as a blind man uses his finger-tips, to feel out the dimensions of a stranger's face – come together beautifully in a long sentence from the close of his lecture 'The Lesson of Balzac' (1905):

> It will strike you perhaps that I speak as if we all, as if you all, without exception were novelists, haunting the back shop, the laboratory, or, more nobly expressed, the inner shrine of the temple; but such assumptions, in this age of print – if I may not say this age of poetry – are perhaps never too wide of the mark, and I have at any rate taken your interest sufficiently for granted to ask you to close up with me for an hour at the feet of the master of us all.[5]

'The master of us all' is of course Balzac: James conducts his audience of acolyte quasi-novelists from the shop to the shrine via the laboratory, taking in the realms of commerce, science and religion in that order. The fact that Balzac is encountered finally 'in the sacred grove, as our towering idol . . . gilded thick with so much gold – plated and burnished and bright, in the manner of towering idols'[6] is a trifle disconcerting: James seems to acknowledge the petrification of a living force into a dead icon.

For James, material social reality is really a shadow, or metaphor or perhaps embryo of consciousness. This has to be said, despite John Bayley's eloquent claim that, in *The Golden Bowl*, 'the physical nature of life is recorded with unique emphasis':

> The characters have baths, use latch-keys, get their clothes wet, smoke and drink, feel hungry, and experience sexual desire. A male gesture 'tests the growth of the beard against the back of the hand'; a female voice sounds 'a high coerced quaver. . . .' The grotesqueness – endearing or otherwise – is admirably and constantly conveyed, and this unobtrusive documentation extends to every kind of relevance. We are made very familiar with nationality and background. . . .[7]

This makes late James sound like Tolstoy. Yet a marked fact about James's fiction is the way in which his concentration on scenic representation precludes any real operation of his facts, objects and backgrounds on the formation of his characters' fates. Backgrounds are at best occasions, when they are not merely back-drops. Their tendency is to disappear into the interiority of metaphor, or purely mental action. It is hard to say which is the more real – the ivory pagoda image at the opening of the second book, which is a metaphor for Maggie's consciousness of her exclusion from the life which Charlotte and the Prince have arranged for her; or Fawns, the country house through whose rooms, terraces and gardens Charlotte and Maggie pursue and retreat from each other, as through some entirely internal, mental architecture. Given James's emphasis on economy of form, the tendency of the late fictions is towards symbolic equivalents of the designing act of composition itself; hence their repression of design. A raw crassness of contingency is required if we are to have a sense of *out-there* against which any *in-here* can manifest itself. And much of the information James does give us remains unused, except in a purely opportunistic and illusionist way. The fact that Maggie and Charlotte were school-fellows, for example, is never really brought to bear on their relationship. One weakness of *The Golden Bowl* is a curious failure of interplay between Maggie and Charlotte until adultery is sensed and they are connected through the

circuit of the shared body of Maggie's husband. Background only
operates if it is felt to do so by the characters. Beyond the character's
own awareness of one, there is really no world. The heights and
depths, securities and perils of contingent existence remain essentially
metaphors of consciousness for James.

I suspect that we find this state of affairs less surprising than we
might, because we effect a kind of inversion as we read. We take the
metaphorical expression of consciousness as being its origin or basis.
This smothers what is in fact a position of what was in James something very close to realism in the philosophical sense, that is, idealism.
James could not be a whole-hearted idealist: one would suspect that
to be so and to be a novelist involves at least a practical contradiction.
Still, one senses an increasing pressure and presence behind his
fiction and his critical theory of a variety of circumambient philosophical idealisms – transcendentalist, Swedenborgian, Hegelian. But
perhaps this implicit idealism is something his fiction discovers rather
than inherits. It comes out for example in his metaphors of sublima-
tion and transmutation, which remain distinctly alchemical rather
than chemical. In James's scheme, crude matter strives through art
to become a conscious and hence 'real' representation of itself. Art is
the highest form of transmutation, but what saves James from a
purely *symboliste* and anti-realist position (in the literary-historical
sense of the term) is some underlying hunger for reality which
operates in terms of analogy. The metaphorical sequence in the
'Lesson of Balzac' example is instructive: the shop, the laboratory,
the temple are certainly a kind of hierarchy, but they are also a
structure of analogy involving a kind of theoretical identity. Transmutation operates at every level and – at least up to the time of *The
Golden Bowl* – James is not prepared to write off even the crudest
productive activities as being possibly lower forms of the transmuta-
tional operation. The relevance of this to Adam Verver hardly needs
stressing. James himself – after all – owes his own career as an artist,
his independent consciousness, to a 'sufficient fortune from commercial sources' (as J. I. M. Stewart charmingly puts it).[8] Removed
from these sources by one generation, they were liable to appear
alchemical, almost magical. The Jameses, more than most, seem to
have removed themselves with unusual rapidity from the milieux in

which money was made. Not of course, that James is ignorant or heedless, at any stage in his career, about the general way in which modern fortunes were generated. He knew that value was produced grossly and at an enormous cost in waste and suffering. One could almost regard his art as propitiatory. Art is, as it were, industry without loss – and also without, as it turned out, in a material sense, much gain. Perhaps it was his own exclusion from reward and power that led James to identify himself with Hyacinth Robinson, when he came to write the Preface to *The Princess Casamassima*, while half guiltily acknowledging the ludicrous disproportion of their fates:

> To find [Hyacinth's] possible adventure interesting I had only to conceive his watching the same public show, the same innumerable appearances, I had watched myself, and of his watching very much as I had watched; save indeed for one little difference. This difference would be that so far as all the swarming facts should speak of freedom and ease, knowledge and power, money, opportunity and satiety, he should be able to revolve around them but at the most respectful of distances and with every door of approach shut in his face. For one's self, all conveniently, there had been doors that opened – opened into light and warmth and cheer, into good and charming relations; and if the place as a whole lay heavy on one's consciousness there was yet always for relief this implication of one's own lucky share of the freedom and ease. . . .[9]

One is almost tempted to wonder whether 'lay on one's consciousness' isn't a mistake for 'lay on one's conscience'! It is certainly fascinating to watch James fencing uneasily with what he calls his 'luck'; in the shared identity of watcher, one senses the play of James's own sense of exclusion, despite his 'one little difference' – an exclusion which comes partly from his being an American in England and an Englishman in America. Yet there is also a certain identifiably American confidence in James's estimate of what the novel was and what it could do. It can, in his estimate, measure up to the productive forces that have produced bourgeois society. Indeed, he assumed that it could transcend and redeem the grossness of the system. But it was at least adequate, the only art form that was. No clearer statement of this confidence can be found than in the 1903 essay on Zola:

What has most come home to me in reading [Zola] over is that a scheme of fiction is in fact a capacious vessel. It can carry anything – with art and force in the stowage; nothing in this case will sink it. And it is the only form for which such a claim can be made. All others have to confess to a smaller scope – to selection, to exclusion, to the danger of distortion, explosion, combustion. The novel has nothing to fear but sailing too light. It will take aboard all that we bring in good faith to the dock.[10]

The mercantile metaphor seems not only confident but ironic. For implicit in James's whole career is the sacrifice of the selfishness of gross participation in social goods to the ideal order that consecrates modern civilization. The line that separates James's vaunting analogy for the importance of his art and the Flaubertian or *symboliste* disgust with quotidian reality is obviously a very fine one, as fine as the thickness that separates the two sides of the dialectical coin of naturalism and symbolism. James is neither naturalist nor symbolist or perhaps he is both at once, but the area in which the realist can operate has shrunk to the dimensions of his own craft (the pun can usefully stand).

This familiar story makes the late James of the Prefaces and the last novels modally a contemporary of the younger Thomas Mann and of Proust. All three obviously derive in some sense from Flaubert, in whom James saw with such sharp percipience a realism which operates as the notation of the disease of Flaubert's own romanticism.[11] Flaubert was both a naturalist and *symboliste*, or rather both tendencies were in him, resolved not in his works, but in the story of his lifelong dedication to art. Similarly, James, Mann and Proust reconstructed the dislocated dialectic of symbolism and naturalism, idea and fact, only in their activity as artists and fictional accounts of that activity. James's case is complicated by his being an American, as also by the extraordinary length of his career. His origins are in a rather different, more native and naïve kind of romance – and these romance antecedents provide him with his later symbolic plots, rather as the Goethian *Bildungsroman* provides Mann with his. The subject of artists as heroes is explicit but fairly marginal in James's fiction. In his later phase, it is almost wholly implicit, though nonetheless central for that; arguably, the Prefaces to the New York edition can be read not only as a continuous critical treatise but as a Portrait of the Artist and a Research of Lost Time.

Their deployment of a hypertactic prose is what all three novelists have in common. It is as though the world of experience could only be unified through the conscious exercise of syntax. This syntax looks superficially like the formal syntax of earlier epochs, and part of its symbolic meaning is that it should do so. This is least true of James, where the development of the late style seems to be a correlative of the tightening of his forms, so that what is jettisoned in action can be redeemed in the prose. Basically, in all three cases it is arbitrary and willed, and yet it wears the look of having been generated out of the compulsions of an external reality. In this it is unlike a modernist, synthetic prose, whose arbitrariness is its meaning. Hypertactic prose of the late James kind manifests as fully as possible the artist's conscious operations, witnesses his presence and stresses the chaos against and out of which continuous meaning has to be established. Incidentally, such prose permits a very full articulation of individual, psychic life, either the narrator's or his characters', though this, on inspection, turns out always to be something of an illusion. Certainly there is greater closeness of coverage, more attentiveness, more anxious ingenuity of elaboration, but this is because the conventions, and the generalized social consciousness which gives rise to them, have lost their viability; which is another way of suggesting that the audience is unknown, distanced and fragmented; and it is the prose itself which has to re-establish the illusion of community. The unravelled world has to be conscientiously, femininely woven afresh; it is no accident that the hypertactic mode is also a highly feminine one. All three writers, in varying degrees, seem concerned with women, feminized men, and above all with literary art, their own included, as a feminizing activity. James characteristically puts the consciousness of women or of feminized men at the centre of his novels, until, in *The Golden Bowl*, Maggie ceases to be in any traditional sense a heroine, and becomes the hero of her book: her roles of daughter, wife, mother become issues and aspects of an entirely individual and non-generic struggle for identity. So much seems declared in the very architecture of the book: we progress from the solid block of inherited and assumed masculinity represented by The Prince to the subjective domain and dominance created for herself by The Princess.

Writing in the hypertactic mode is a response to naturalism – a response which is both a challenge and defence: for naturalism itself is a complex attempt to discover an artistic method appropriate to new conditions, one that could both give scope to, and participate in the energies of the increasingly abstract and technological charact:r of social life. James himself remained a sensitive observer and commentator on naturalism and its English derivatives. He was certainly influenced by it in the writing of *The Bostonians*, as John Goode has suggested.[12] At the same time, his critical position and artistic practice involves a repudiation of naturalism, most obviously at the stylistic level. Naturalist writing should in principle have abolished the problem of style. Since it was to be the systematic registration of objective reality which organized meaning, style should have become no more than a kind of subjective colouration of an ideally neutral transparency. The issue is at root that of the possibility of a value-free social science, but the deep absurdity as well as pathos of the inherent contradiction of such an enterprise was liable to be immediately and painfully obvious in the attempt to apply procedures analogous to those of the laboratory or observatory to literature, the most subjective of activities, even granting that the novel, with its dissolution of pre-existent genres and its adoption of plain, middle diction, was the most objective-looking form of literature. James, in contrast to the prevailing English practice, saw naturalism as at least serious, and in a misguided way as an immensely flattering estimate of the importance of literature. Yet he spotted the internal contradictoriness of the whole enterprise remarkably early, without getting too distracted by the spurious 'moral' issue. His essays on Zola are rich with the paradox of how the whole naturalist enterprise is the expression of a titanic and, in its own terms, inexplicable moral commitment on the part of its practitioners. Moreover, though perhaps only by implication, he saw that naturalism is involved with insuperable problems of style. If style arises from discrimination, and discrimination is at bottom an exercise in freedom, then James's criticism of Zola is at once a criticism of his stylistic incoherence and of his abdication to abstract, anonymous power, which becomes the counterpart of a kind of obsessive titanism. The case is beautifully put in the 1880 review of *Nana*, which does bear some of the marks of the moralistic climate in which James as a critic had to operate. The point is that he at least had a rationale for his accusations of gratuitous coarseness in Zola:

> M. Zola's attempt is an extremely fine one; it deserves a great deal of respect and deference, and though his theory is constantly at odds with itself, we could, at a pinch, go a long way with it without quarrelling. What we quarrel with is his application of it – is the fact that he presents us with his decoction of 'nature' in a vessel unfit for the purpose, a receptacle lamentably, fatally in need of scouring. . . .[13]

The metaphor is perhaps a little unsure, and the younger James of 1880 is still wavering between moralistic and more sophisticated criteria. The concept of 'taste' which he goes on to employ is perhaps ambiguous; but the ambiguity, whether calculated or not, is an attempt to hold together some notion of public interest and individual discrimination, suggesting that these may participate in a common world:

> Reality is the object of M. Zola's efforts, and it is because we agree with him in appreciating it highly that we protest against its being discredited. In a time when literary taste has turned, to a regrettable degree, to the vulgar and the insipid, it is of high importance that realism should not be compromised. Nothing tends more to compromise it than to represent it as naturally allied to the impure. That the pure and the impure are for M. Zola, as conditions of taste, vain words, and exploded ideas, only proves that his advocacy does more to injure an excellent cause than to serve it. It takes a very good cause to carry a *Nana* on its back, and if realism breaks down, and the conventional comes in again with a rush, we may know the reason why. The real has not a single shade more affinity with an unclean vessel than with a clean one, and M. Zola's system, carried to its utmost expression, can dispense as little with taste and tact as the floweriest mannerism of a less analytic age.[14]

For 'taste and tact' we could read style and decorum, which are their stylistic counterparts. Peculiarly impressive is the conceptual confidence of James's handling of the terms realism and naturalism. He avoids constricting definitions of realism: but his basic position in 1880 at least is critical, humanist and moralist – certainly not narrowly technical and aesthetic. By 1905 – the year of publication of *The Golden Bowl* – while his confidence in the novel remained unshaken, one feels that a deepening sense of the disappearance of any possible public world has driven him much further in the direction of an idealism whose artistic result is the increasing addiction to the alchemy of metaphor and reticulation of reality in syntax. Yet this in itself is a reflex of an abiding humanism, one which the 1880 review states quite unambiguously:

> Go as far as we will, so long as we abide in literature, the thing remains always a question of taste and we can never leave taste behind without leaving behind, by the same stroke, the very grounds on which we appeal, the whole human side of the business. Taste, in its intellectual application, is the most human faculty we possess, and as the novel may be said to be the most human form of art, it is a poor speculation to put the two things out of conceit with each other. Calling it naturalism will never make it profitable.[15]

Naturalism wore many faces and was many things. For the hypertactic sensibility, it becomes the art of the domain of death, of crude anonymity, uniformity, the cheerful, sometimes cocky selling-out to sheer success, a misguided scientism devoted to the destruction of the prerogatives and dignities of individual consciousness. It is slightly saddening to watch James's dogged attempt to give credit and do business with the various English followers of naturalism. Though Wells of course is not a classical naturalist, nonetheless the dialogue between James and Wells represents, at least on James's part, a persistent attempt to keep a line open, against the grain of his own developed aesthetic, to what he saw as the vitality and responsiveness of post-naturalist literature. As I have suggested however, his real and growing affinity was with Conrad. Indeed, placing James, and particularly late James, is a matter of tracing an extremely fine network of affiliations and lines of distinction. In one aspect, naturalism itself was, in practice, a protest against the very forces whose aid, at other levels, it enlisted. It is frequently a number registration of the forces which were eroding personality and history. It sometimes involves an effort to wrest individual lives from mass suffering, as Zola does those of Nana or Gervaise and the heroines of *Germinal* and

La Terre. Naturalism characteristically deals in heroines: perhaps specifically heroines rather than female heroes. There is a long line stretching from Emma Bovary to Esther Waters and Crane's Maggie which would include examples as diverse as the Goncourts' *Woman of Paris* and Hardy's Tess. In this perspective, heroines are not so much saving consciousnesses as consecrated victims, passive sufferers of brutal process. The reasons why this is so are obviously ramifying and complex. And within this lineage the position of an Anna Karenina broken under the wheels of a train, or indeed of Miss Julie and of Hedda Gabler, is as difficult to define as the connexion is to deny. Within this framework, Maggie's outburst – 'I see it's always terrible for women'– has clear contemporary resonance. Through their portraits of women, novelists in this period seem to focus a double sense of human nature as the passive victim and the active embodiment of compulsive, carnal forces. Maggie's vision of terror seems to derive from passionate insight into that dualism, embodied for her in the wretchedness of Charlotte's fate. To avoid Charlotte's abjection means a terrifying assumption of unremitting, conscious awareness. The forces that would reduce human nature to automatism are not merely outside but in the very biology of being female. One even finds Maggie using similar imagery to that James had used of Emma Bovary in his 1902 essay on Flaubert. Here is Maggie on Charlotte:

> ... Maggie's sense meanwhile [was] open as to the sight of gilt wires and bruised wings, the spacious but suspended cage, the home of eternal unrest. ... (Pt. 5, Ch. 1)

Emma too is seen by James as caged and suspended, though with less room to struggle in:

> Then the setting, the medium in which she struggles ... the tiny world in which she revolves, the contracted cage in which she flutters, is hung out in space for her. ...[16]

The contrast of size, within the similarity of image, suggests the scope of James's anti-naturalism. Emma Bovary's abjection is too small an affair. By contrast, Charlotte's case exhibits a zeal on James's part to give tragic and mythic glamour to his fallen woman. But despite this marked difference, I would argue that in *The Golden Bowl*, as in *The*

Wings of the Dove and *The Ambassadors*, James's abject women, driven by sensual passion, are one with the women victims of naturalism. Their own carnality is essentially of the same substance as the other impersonal forces that render down and demonically possess free will and consciousness. The carnal in James's work becomes a representation moreover of what in naturalist novels is the domineering force of pure environment. Sex, in James, to put the matter brutally, equals poverty, and consciousness is not only the privilege of wealth but analogically wealth itself, the true gold, the novelist's own resources of creative power, the mental substance that gilds the idol of Balzac. In late James anyway the carnal is twice associated with (very relatively) moneyless girls trying to get themselves out of the (very relative) mire. Perhaps the oddest illustration of this is the Prince's response to Charlotte when he meets her again on the eve of his marriage:

> He knew above all the extraordinary fineness of her flexible waist, the stem of an expanded flower, which gave her a likeness also to some long loose silk purse, well filled with gold pieces, but having been passed empty through a finger-ring that held it together. It was as if, before she turned to him, he had weighed the whole thing in his open palm and even heard a little the chink of the metal. When she did turn to him it was to recognize with her eyes what he might have been doing. (Pt. 1, Ch. 3)

To know Charlotte in this way is apparently already to have handled her, and the fact that James has the Prince immediately seeing her as a filled and clinking, but also empty, silk purse establishes a complicated series of connexions between sex and money: money as what you buy if you have it, and money as what you desire if you do not. The glance that Charlotte bestows on the Prince is one of complicity in having been made the passive object of his inventory of what James has the Prince think of as 'the perfect working of all her main attachments'. Maggie's struggle is precisely to avoid becoming this kind of knowing, collusive object, not only of another's fancying gaze but of her own passion. She has actively to struggle to avoid becoming a victim-heroine, of the kind which Charlotte makes herself, in her passage in Hyde Park with the Prince when she claims her eternal moment. How we are to judge Charlotte's action is difficult to determine. Seemingly, she is trying to turn the very completeness of her abasement into a kind of freedom. Had she been able to live with that, James seems to be suggesting, then she might be a heroine indeed. At least the reader thinks so, and it is this impression that makes the subsequent diminishment of Charlotte seem shabby. Looking back on *The Spoils of Poynton* and the two stories published with it in the New York edition, James touched both retrospectively and prophetically on the type of woman who was to feature in his fiction:

> They are each – and truly there are more of such to come – 'stories about women', very young women, who affected with a certain high lucidity, thereby become characters; in consequence of which their doings, their sufferings or whatever, take on, I assume, an importance. Laura Wing, in *A London Life*, has, like Fleda Vetch, acuteness and intensity, reflection and passion, has above all a contributive and participant view of her situation; just as Rose Tramore, in *The Chaperon*, rejoices, almost to insolence, very much in the same cluster of attributes and advantages. They are thus of a family – which shall have also for us, we seem forewarned, more members, and of each sex.[17]

This account shows how James's *point of view* ('a contributive and participant view') is related primarily to women of a certain kind whom James thought of as constituting a family, and how far *point of view* is connected with 'doings' and 'sufferings'. Maggie is surely the head and consummation of this family, for in her case the beauty of her high lucidity is that we see it growing beneath our eyes, participate in its deepening penetration, and discover that it embraces the obscurity of her own passion – in a way in which Laura Wing's, for example, does not – losing itself in confusion, fever and terror. There is a marvellous moment at the end of *A London Life*, where Laura suddenly sees herself as seen by her brother-in-law, behaving in exactly the same way that her abandoned and runagate sister, whom Laura herself so much despises, has behaved. Laura has threatened to kill herself unless the brother-in-law reveals the whereabouts of her sister, and in a brilliant analytic paragraph James probes, without perhaps fully exploring, the identity of the apparently good and 'American' with the bad and 'European' sister:

Later on, however, she saw very well that it was not her threat that had acted, and even at the moment she had a sense from the way he returned the light of her eyes, that this was in no manner the first time that a baffled woman had told him she would kill herself. He had always accepted his kinship with her, but even in her trouble it was part of her consciousness that he now lumped her with a mixed group of female figures, a little wavering and dim, who were associated in his memory with scenes of violence, with importunities and ultimatums. It is apt to be the disadvantage of women, on occasions of measuring their strength with men, that they may feel in the man a larger experience, and feel their own precious substance, their general 'side', alas, as part of that resource. It is doubtless as a provision against such emergencies that nature has opened to them operations of the mind quite independent of experience.[18]

This is a young, passionate girl waking to the experience of seeing herself a member of a sex and one that moreover is experienced as a class, a generic category, by men. *A London Life* never really explores this insight: though its crisis, an apparent proposal by Laura to a young American, precipitated by her fear that she has become un-marriageable (because of her sister's scandalous conduct and the light in which it has placed her), centres upon a choice as to whether to think of herself as a woman to whom respectability is necessary because of her close, in this case familial, proximity to a 'bad' woman, or whether there are any independent grounds in terms of which she can exist to herself as a person. Her frantic flight to try to 'save' her sister, her refusal of the young American and her own panic retreat to America all suggest that there is no such identity; or one so lonely, strange and eccentric as to be unthinkable.

In *The Golden Bowl* Maggie's adventure consists partly in freeing herself from the generic category of woman, despite her married status and despite her own 'abjection', without having to opt for a lonely, eccentric exclusion from ordinary life. One could regard this as an evasion of the tragic necessity at the heart of even a relatively lightweight story like *A London Life*, let alone *The Portrait of a Lady* or *The Awkward Age*. It is important that James should be able to show the completeness of Maggie's own abjection, and show it as essentially not different in principle from Charlotte's. James's rendering of Maggie's feelings for the Prince, and the heroic negative act required from her in resisting her enthralment, depends a good deal on establishing the depth of her conjugal surrender. This is one of the successes of the novel. He is good at tendering the Prince's amused recall of the flirtatious intimacy of the engaged pair:

> One of the most comfortable things between the husband and the wife meanwhile – one of these easy certitudes they could be merely gay about – was that she never admired him so much, or so found him heart-breakingly handsome, clever, irresistible, in the very degree in which he had originally and fatally dawned upon her, as when she saw other women reduced to the same passive pulp that had then begun, once and for all, to constitute *her* substance. There was really nothing they had talked of together with more intimate and familiar pleasantry than of the licence and privilege, the boundless happy margin, thus established for each: she going so far as to put it that, even should he some day get drunk and beat her, the spectacle of him with hated rivals would, after no matter what extremity, always, for the sovereign charm of it, charm of it in itself and as the exhibition of him that most deeply moved her, suffice to bring her round. What would therefore be more open to him than to keep her in love with him? He agreed . . . he knew but one way with the fair. They had to be fair – and he was fastidious and particular, his standard was high; but when once this was the case what relation with them was conceivable, what relation was decent, rudimentary, properly human, but that of plain interest in the fairness? His interest, she always answered, happened not to be 'plain'. . . . (Pt. 2, Ch. 3)

This hyperbolic jokiness doubtless conceals a certain sexual brutality on the part of the Prince (there are plenty of other hints) and exhibits on Maggie's part both a trace of hysteria as well as a certain confidence, not so much in her own sexuality as in the security of her legal enjoyment of his. Doubtless too the stereotype of the passionate Italian and the repressed but avid Anglo-Saxon is at play, and perhaps one of the suggestions of 'fair'. But while Maggie in some respects surpasses Charlotte in helpless abjection, she rises above it by her power to stand away from her passion and become conscious of it. Charlotte, even in her diplomacy, is always driven upon the current of her instinctual life. Consciousness in her is a matter of superb performance. In Maggie there is a barrier between instinct and its expression – we continually experience her as simultaneously present and absent to herself, even in her most passionate moments. This is partly due to the way her consciousness is dramatized; but it is equally an important fact about Charlotte that she cannot be dramatized. She is already dramatic – she loses her self in her performances. Maggie has always to be slightly absent from her performance, distanced and watching it. Perhaps we are to understand that the undramatized, tranquil Maggie of Part 1 is in fact deeply enthralled and self-abandoned. Certainly, she claims the privilege of a total passion to her father, implying that her kind of abandonment is all the more complete for involving the conscious abdication of consciousness itself:

> My idea is this, that when you only love a little you're naturally not jealous – or are only jealous also a little, so that it doesn't matter. But when you love in a deeper and intenser way, then you're in the very same proportion jealous; your jealousy has intensity and, no doubt, ferocity. When however you love in the most abysmal and unutterable way of all – why then you're beyond everything, and nothing can pull you down. (Pt. 5, Ch. 3)

This comes late in the novel when Maggie is asking Adam Verver in effect to sacrifice himself in the interest of her marriage by removing with Charlotte. Adam's sense of Maggie – and we cannot be sure how far this is a dramatized fact about Adam and how far it is endorsed by James – is that she magically manages an innocent mastery of passionate depths. Of course, Adam's sense of Maggie is by no means identical with Maggie's of herself. One of the disconcerting depths in this novel is the sharp gap that seems to open between the self as perceived by others and as experienced by itself. It may be the word 'love' that describes the bridging of this gulf or its simple acceptance. Yet James – as Adam's mental response shows – is fully aware of how those who love also project their own needs and lacks upon the beloved:

> The mere fine pulse of passion in it, the suggestion as of a creature consciously floating and shining in a warm summer sea, some element of dazzling sapphire and silver, a creature cradled upon depths, buoyant among dangers, in which fear or folly or sinking otherwise than in play

was impossible – something of all this might have been making once more present to him, with his discreet, his half-shy assent to it, her probable enjoyment of a rapture that he in his day had presumably convinced no great number of persons either of his giving or his receiving. (Pt. 5, Ch. 3)

Actually, this does not seem a particularly pertinent response to Maggie's account of her love. Adam's tortuous disclaimers of 'rapture' (and the word, the longer you look at it, seems to accumulate ironic shades) presumably enacts his constitutionally self-deprecating way of thinking about himself. But does it imply, despite the beautiful play of imagery, some deprecation of Maggie too, turning her at best into an almost Wordsworthian child 'cradled upon depths' whose conversational intensities may also be a form of gush? It is true that she says that 'nothing can pull her down', but the translation of this brave assertion into 'consciously floating and shining in a warm summer sea' is a strange one. Moreover, Maggie's actual behaviour hardly consorts with this vision of playful security within passion. It suggests that we are in the presence of a Jamesian epiphany, hearing the children sporting by the shore. And, as so often in late James, the epiphany is a matter of metaphor and syntax – here the floating subjects of this immense sentence suspend themselves, dizzyingly, but with an ultimate syntactical assurance, over a long series of phrases and clauses, before subsiding into the full close of their predicate. Despite these doubts and qualifications, it is clear enough what is being claimed for Maggie – that while subject to the final abjection, she does not relapse into automatism. She retains a mastery, which is very much like that which James himself experiences in the formation of his vast, dangerous sentences. She is no naturalist heroine-victim, though she takes the full force of those inner and outer compulsions that make Charlotte one. Analogously, James himself, while he takes the force and seriousness of the naturalist response to brute process, still asserts the brave freedom of style. I would conjecture that *as* Adam Verver, James watches himself at play with some benevolent reservations.

It is loving 'in the most abysmal and unutterable way of all' that gives retrospective and prospective meaning to her reaction to the Prince's adultery. At the core of her passion is not only abandonment, but resistance in full consciousness of what deeply draws her. We have to bear in mind her sense of being 'reduced to . . . passive pulp' by the Prince to weigh the full heroism of her withdrawal from him. The crucial occasion occurs early in the second book when the Prince and Princess return home in their carriage from Eaton Square, the Ververs' house, where entertainment has been given to the Castlemains. Maggie has suddenly acted up, begun to manage the situation on her own account and reduced the Prince and Charlotte to a palpable complicity of alarmed silence. On the way home, the Prince tries to overwhelm her and reduce her to consenting submission by bringing to bear on her the full weight of his sexual charm, seeking to arouse a response that will be a tacit submission. It is a form of bullying, whose terror lies in the fact that it is inflicted by one 'abysmally' loved. It is an extraordinarily impressive piece of writing and repays attention:

> She had, in her compressed state, another pause, and it made her feel as if she were immensely resisting. Strange enough was this sense for her, and altogether new, the sense of possessing, by miraculous help, some advantage that, absolutely then and there, in the carriage, as they rolled, she might either give up or keep. Strange, inexpressibly strange – so distinctly she saw that if she did give it up she would somehow give up everything for ever. And what her husband's grasp really meant, as her very bones registered, was that she *should* give it up: it was exactly for this that he had resorted to unfailing magic. He *knew how* to resort to it – he could be on occasion, as she had lately more than ever learned, so munificent a lover. . . . She should have but to lay her head back on his shoulder with a certain movement to make it definite for him that she didn't resist. To this as they went every throb of her consciousness prompted her – every throb, that is, but one, the throb of her deeper need to know where she 'really' was.   (Pt. 4, Ch. 3)

James's success consists here in literally *embodying* Maggie's conscious resistance to the Prince's pressure. The word 'feel' takes on the full double force of sensation and thought, translating one into the other, as the physical 'throb' becomes a motion of consciousness. Her husband's 'grasp' *means*; her 'bones' *register* – both his grasp and her resistance. The Prince's amatory 'know-how' is felt to be brutal and, as it were, technological. There is a marvellous sense of the movement of the carriage being also the fatal motion of a physical compulsion. The Princess is evidently, in normal circumstances, tinder to the Prince's touch: so her heroic refusal to take fire, or simply settle for the habitual responses of intimacy, is to enter the realm of consciousness, of the strange and the new. The 'attempted capture and achieved escape' of the carriage scene represents almost the first of Maggie's many negations and abnegations. Indeed, *The Golden Bowl* is an epic of a selfhood achieved and disengaged from such raw coercions of carnality. Given her great wealth, Maggie's poverty has to be the weakness and need of her flesh.

Maggie's prolonged abstention from outrage and outcry and also submission is analogous to the novelist's own abstention from raw living in order to refine it, the kind of abstention that in his own life Flaubert, or Mann's fictional representation of the artist in *Death in Venice*, Aschenbach, practised. In Mann, the carnal life – though an active possibility of the nature that sacrifices it – is apt to take its revenge, becoming, as negated matter, a form of evil, with a parodic spiritual life of its own. One could view the Prince in the carriage as likewise embodying the seductive force of negated life. Mann of course was ostensibly concerned to show how abstaining spirit and demonic flesh are mutually sustaining opposites within one reality. James, at least consciously, opted for the spiritual side of the dualism, and his awareness of the other side is much more a matter of a latent life burning in the body of his language. Indeed, the very sophistication of the late novels sometimes strikes one as protecting a fundamental innocence and *pudeur* of James's own. The intricate structure, in which so much of the purely developmental logic of the story is attenuated and diffused, creates a kind of space in which contradictory insights can coexist without collision. Perhaps this helps to explain the curious duality of Maggie's sexual nature, as being both a form of innocence and a condition of slavish doting, a pure child to her father and an enthralled wife to her husband. On the level of the story, part of what seems to happen is that initially Maggie regresses increasingly into being a daughter. One has the impression that James himself takes a much kinder view of this withdrawal of Maggie and her father into a nursery world than we can. The Assinghams comment on this precious community of father with daughter as simply a *donné* of the situation, and Mrs Assingham links it to a specifically American innocence:

> '. . . But it's his innocence, above all,' Mrs Assingham added, 'that will pull them through.'
>
> Her companion, at this, focused again Mr Verver's innocence. 'It's awfully quaint.'
>
> 'Of course it's awfully quaint! That it's awfully quaint, that the pair are awfully quaint, quaint with all *our* dear old quaintness – by which I don't mean yours and mine, but that of my own sweet country-people, from whom I've so deplorably degenerated – that,' Mrs Assingham declared, 'was originally the head and front of their appeal to me and of my interest in them. . . .'
>
> '. . . You believe so in Mr Verver's innocence after two years of Charlotte?'
>
> She stared. 'But the whole point is just that two years of Charlotte are what he hasn't really – or what you may call undividedly – had.'
>
> 'Any more than Maggie by your theory, eh, has "really or un-dividedly", had four of the Prince? It takes all she hasn't had,' the Colonel conceded, 'to account for the innocence that in her too so leaves us in admiration.'
>
> So far as it might be ribald again she let his pass. 'It takes a great many things to account for Maggie. . . .'   (Pt. 3, Ch. 11)

The speculation here, as always with the Assinghams, seems to tremble on the verge of an indecency, which comes out in such ambiguities as that on the word 'had'. This ambiguity in the Assing-hams' conversation seems to parallel the ambiguity in James himself about the exact status of Maggie's and Adam's innocence. The knowingness of Fanny Assingham, which still manages just to contain the Colonel's indecorum, seems to be one with her conviction that 'forms . . . are two-thirds of conduct' (Pt. 3, Ch. 11); and this in turn reflects interestingly on James's own cultivation of form as one instance of the general preservation of 'forms', a kind of extreme literary good manners grown so elaborate that it leers palpably in the direction of the lurid facts it is meant to mask. Ultimately, Maggie is as much a mystery to Fanny as she is to the reader. It takes a great many things 'to account for' her – and her freedom lies in that un-accountability. This unaccountability, as Fanny sees it developing just before the close of the first book, may well take the form of consummate deceit:

> I like the idea of Maggie audacious and impudent – learning to be so to gloss things over. She could – she even will, yet, I believe – learn it, for that sacred purpose, consummately, diabolically. (Pt. 3, Ch. 11)

James wants us to enter Maggie's book with that 'diabolically' ringing in our ears. The possibility that innocence may be 'diabolical' is one that lurks in the implications of Maggie's success. The Prince, as we are given his state of mind at Matcham, finds the innocent compact of father and daughter mainly an irritation and aspersion on his worldliness. And Fanny too appears not to be without a certain relish at the prospect of Maggie's innocence being despoiled:

> '. . . Maggie was the creature in the world to whom a wrong thing could least be communicated. It was as if her imagination had been closed to it, her sense altogether sealed. That therefore', Fanny continued, 'is what will now *have* to happen. Her sense will have to open.'
>
> 'I see.' He nodded. 'To the wrong.' He nodded again almost cheerfully – as if he had been keeping the peace with a baby or a lunatic. 'To the very, *very* wrong.'
>
> But his wife's spirit, after its effort of wing, was able to remain higher. 'To what's called Evil – with a very big E: for the first time in her life. To the discovery of it, to the knowledge of it, to the crude experience of it.' And she gave, for the possibility, the largest measure. 'To the harsh bewildering brush, the daily chilling breath of it . . . unless indeed, as yet (so far as she has come, and if she comes no further), simply to the suspicion and the dread. What we shall see is whether that mere dose of alarm will be enough.'
>
> He considered. 'But enough for what then, dear – if not enough to break her heart?'
>
> 'Enough to give her a shaking!' Mrs Assingham rather oddly replied. 'To give her, I mean, the right one. The right one won't break her heart. It will make her,' she explained – 'well, it will make her, by way of a change, understand one or two things in the world.'
>
> 'But isn't it a pity,' the Colonel asked, 'that they should happen to be the one or two that will be the most disagreeable to her?'
>
> 'Oh "disagreeable" – ? They'll have *had* to be disagreeable – to show her a little where she is. They'll have had to be disagreeable to make her

sit up. They'll have had to be disagreeable to make her decide to live.'
(Pt. 3, Ch. 11)

At this point the critic of late James is liable to complain of an excess
of interpretation more subtle than his own can be, and operating with
an intimacy with the central situation that he cannot rival. He may
also feel the presence of a certain short-circuiting opportunism in the
casual introduction of big concepts – like 'Evil – with a very big E'.
Hasn't the novel ceased to exist at such moments and become instead
the conversation of intent commentators, practically creating what
they annotate? Or can we still, just, go on reading even these inter-
preters dramatically, viewing Fanny's remarks about Maggie as a
revelation of a latent hostility, or at least irritation, which would make
some of her later conduct to Maggie even more duplicitous than anything involved in the one or two downright fibs she does commit
herself to?

All those who reflect on Maggie and Adam in the book seem agreed
that the Verver father and daughter create, almost force, the adultery
to come about, as a product of their blind, innocent absorption in
each other. True, neither knows about the previous relationship
between Charlotte and the Prince, but even that apparently would
have affected nothing if the Ververs had not behaved in the way they
did. Yet I cannot remember one instance of Maggie's acknowledging
that her attitude towards her marriage may have been responsible for
the situation in which the adultery occurred. Nor does she quite confront the submerged – but one would think inescapable – influence of
the Prince's adultery with Charlotte upon her own sexual awareness.
And, in any case, Evil – even with a capital E – is not just a state she
is shaken into. She incorporates it right from the start in the fact of
being part, indeed at the apogee, of a system of power relationships.
The selfhood that she gradually disengages from naïve, sensual
enthralment to the Prince and childish dependence on Adam Verver
is forged at the expense of almost everyone: of Charlotte most of all,
whom she dooms to museum management in an American hick town,
married to an impotent old man, who yearns only for his lost daughter.
Again, are we to take as an illustration of Maggie's monomania the
curious inversion by which we are invited to see Adam as the real

victim who pays all; one which even goes out of its way to dismiss
the idea of Charlotte 'as paying for his daughter's bliss?' 'What have
you ever done, that hasn't been *for* me?' Maggie asks of her father,
who replies:

> 'Many things; more than I can tell you – things you've only to think
> of for yourself. What do you make of all that I've done for myself?'
> ' "Yourself?" ' – She brightened out with derision.
> 'What do you make of what I've done for American City?'
> It took her but a moment to say. 'I'm not talking of you as a public
> character – I'm talking of you on your personal side.'
> 'Well, American City – if "personalities" can do it – has given me a
> pretty personal side. What do you make,' he went on, 'of what I've done
> for my reputation?'
> 'Your reputation *there*? You've given it up to them, the awful
> people, for less than nothing; you've given it up to them to tear to
> pieces, to make their horrible vulgar jokes against you with.'
> 'Ah my dear I don't care for their horrible vulgar jokes,' Adam almost
> artlessly urged.
> 'Then there exactly you are!' she triumphed. 'Everything that
> touches you, everything that surrounds you, goes on – by your splendid
> indifference and incredible permission–at your expense.'   (Pt. 5, Ch. 3)

We readers are to be included among the vulgar detractors of vast
munificence, one supposes, and Adam himself, early in the novel, has
indicated a silent awareness of 'public detraction' and 'local vulgarity'.
Still, it is hard not to see detraction involved on James's own part in
the very designation of American City. Is this, then, Maggie again
illustrating a naïve confusion between filial piety and rich man's
propaganda and, by derivation, a startling ignorance of her real
standing in the power game involving the four protagonists? What
are we to make of the scenes that have so repelled most critics of *The
Golden Bowl*, where father and daughter meet in an unspoken complicity over the torture of Charlotte:

> Charlotte hung behind with emphasized attention; she stopped when
> her husband stopped, but at the distance of a case or two, or of whatever
> other succession of objects; and the likeness of their connexion wouldn't
> have been wrongly figured if he had been thought of as holding in one
> of his pocketed hands the end of a long silken halter looped around her

beautiful neck. He didn't twitch it, yet it was there; he didn't drag her, but she came; and those betrayals that I have described the Princess as finding irresistible in him were two or three mute facial intimations which his wife's presence didn't prevent his addressing his daughter – nor prevent his daughter, as she passed, it was doubtless to be added, from flushing a little at the receipt of. They amounted perhaps only to a wordless, wordless smile, but the smile was the soft shake of the twisted silken rope. . . . (Pt. 5, Ch. 4)

It is almost like some allegory – 'beauty led by the neck'; or 'the proletariat in the chains of Capital'. If the dramatizing method logically held up, then characters should be responsible for what they behold. It could be that Maggie simply triumphs in a vision which bears no relationship to what her father is actually doing. But I think we read such a passage as James's own narrative. James does not blush to show us the father intimating wordless complicities in victory to his daughter over their fallen foe. This is registered faintly as an enormity – Maggie's flush almost turns the tethered Charlotte into a kind of love-gift from father to daughter – and yet it is not really built, as a tragic paradox, into the moral scheme of the novel. It never occurs to Maggie to reflect that the original purchase of Charlotte and this subsequent punishment of her follows directly from the power of her father's money-bags.

Against this it would be urged that such a view is in fact sentimental, that this is a novel that accepts without question the right of some to own and others to be owned. It is true that this is an obvious premise of the story. At a deeper level, the metaphorical, James shows a very active awareness of the human underworld that sustains the privileges of wealth. Charlotte, it should be noted, never herself doubts that her position as Adam's wife is a solid good. She is represented as having a peculiar talent for high and splendid living. In a sense, there is no other vocation for her but to be charming and wear a tiara. Moreover, Adam is almost totally idealized by Maggie in a way which suggests, despite the reservations of Fanny and the Colonel, that this is in fact the measure of his real worth. By the time Maggie has her final vision of her father, we have really no independent criteria for judging him. Still, his calculated subjection of Charlotte, particularly when we bear in mind the additionally unpleasant implications that accrue from his sexual impotence, remains an element of contradiction – an example of the mutually subversive understandings that hang in suspension in the depths of the novel, and whose potential collision is sensed as a latent ambiguity, if not as an immediate issue. For James seems to allow for the possibility that Adam's 'wordless, wordless smile' smacks of a kind of indecency – it comes out for Maggie 'only, as if it might be overheard when some door was closed behind her'. Its savouring seems to demand an almost guilty privacy; and only then can Maggie begin breathlessly to decode it:

> Yes, you see – I lead her now by the neck, I lead her to her doom, and she doesn't so much as know what it is, though she has a fear in her heart which, if you had the chances to apply your ear there that I, as a husband, have, you would hear thump and thump and thump. She thinks it *may* be her doom, the awful place over there – awful for *her*; but she's afraid to ask, don't you see? just as she's afraid of not asking; just as she's afraid of so many other things that she sees multiplied all about her now as perils and portents.[19] She'll know however – when she does know. (Pt. 5, Ch. 4)

Metaphor stands here in rather uneasy proximity to the realm of fact. Adam does literally, one supposes, have opportunities 'as her husband' to monitor the thump of Charlotte's heart. And what, in any case, is Maggie up to, imagining such intimacies, even if only in metaphor. The words Maggie extracts from that 'wordless, wordless smile' have an odious, gloating, purring quality that could well suit a triumph over the kind of 'hated rival' that Maggie denies she considers Charlotte to be. So that we have to face the insistent questions whether the only lies Maggie perpetrates are the conscious deceits she glories in. James's next paragraph ostentatiously suppresses any such question. It turns away with 'Charlotte's one opportunity, meanwhile, for the air of confidence . . . that agreed so well with her firm and charming type . . . was the presence of visitors.' This to my mind is a rather clumsy, forced transition, which prematurely terminates the stream of Maggie's reflection. True, a little later we are told that Charlotte's voice 'sounded, for our young woman, like the shriek of a soul in pain'; and, with another mute look, she asks her father 'Can't she be stopped? Hasn't she done it enough?' (Pt. 5, Ch. 4) This comes somewhere near to admitting that Maggie's success is Charlotte's ruin. Her father strikes her 'as confessing with strange tears in his own eyes, to a sharp identity of emotion'. But why 'strange' one wonders – because he does not usually weep? Or because the whole mute complicity between Maggie and her father strikes even James – perhaps even Maggie herself – as indeed strange. This is as close as we come to a tragic estimate of the cost of the Ververs' joint, silent subjugation of the rebellion in their domestic realm. But the focus is not kept sharp and rapidly weakens. True, again Adam is caught blushing at 'the shame, the pity, the better knowledge, the smothered protest, the divined action': but not so much, apparently, at any sense of the relevance of these to Charlotte as at Maggie's detection of them – and they seem a rather abstract set of reactions – in his mute passage with her. It is this 'snatched communion' that seems the important thing, and that is shown as having 'lifted Maggie as on air'. Again she comes close to admitting a tragic sense of Charlotte's fate when she reflects that 'there was, honestly, an awful mixture in things. . . .' But this is quickly qualified, in a way which makes one look askance at the word *honestly*, by the further reflection 'that the deepest depth of all, in a perceived penalty, was that you couldn't be sure whether some of your compunctions and contortions wouldn't show for ridiculous'. I suppose we are to assume that tough, competent Charlotte can take even American City in her stride. But if this is so, wherein then lie the terror and the pity, where lies the true action of the second half of the novel? James comes very near here to destroying the elements of illusion which are still absolutely necessary to the viability of this novel – namely, that feelings are real and fierce and authentic – by turning it into a kind of grotesque comedy. He comes dangerously close to the kind of current scepticism which calls the reality of all such feelings into question. Or it could call embarrassing attention to elements of unacknowledged ruthlessness in Maggie – as the true daughter of American capitalism – and in Adam himself. They wield, in tacit combination, a terrifying degree of power.

Yet this is only part of the story, one not really integrated into the overall meaning of the novel: Maggie *does* experience imaginatively the depth of pain in Charlotte's plight, as if it were her own. The vacuum in which the Prince leaves Charlotte gropingly suspended when he has learnt what Maggie knows, is not so different from that experienced by Maggie herself after her resistance in the carriage. She can even half glimpse the tyranny of her father's undemonstrative, meagre control, from Charlotte's point of view. Yet this sympathy of Maggie both for the Prince and for Charlotte does not strike one as simply honourable. Ought not something more to follow from these 'fantastic flights of divination?' Perhaps the sympathy involves a measure of participation which is only half acknowledged, not merely in Charlotte's plight, but in the outraged vengeance that persecutes her:

> What retarded evolution, she asked herself in these hours, mightn't poor Charlotte all unwittingly have precipitated? She was thus poor Charlotte again for Maggie even while Maggie's own head was bowed, and the reason for this kept coming back to our young woman in the conception of what would secretly have passed. She saw her, face to face with the Prince, take from him the chill of his stiffest admonition, with the possibilities of deeper difficulty that it represented for each. She heard her ask, irritated and sombre, what tone – in God's name – since her bravery didn't suit him – she *was* then to adopt; and by way of a fantastic flight of divination she heard Amerigo reply, in a voice of which every fine note, familiar and admirable, came home to her, that one must really manage such prudences a little for one's self. It was positive in the Princess that for this she breathed Charlotte's cold air – turned away from him in it with her, turned with her, in growing compassion, this way and that, hovered behind her while she felt her ask herself where then she should rest. Marvellous the manner in which, under such imaginations, Maggie thus circled and lingered – quite as if she were, materially, following her unseen, counting every step she helplessly wasted, noting every hindrance that brought her to a pause. (Pt. 5, Ch. 4)

Even granted her compassion, isn't Maggie experiencing the penalties and exultations of carnal life, at second hand? It is something to do with the imagery of turning, circling, hovering, lingering, counting, and noting. This feeds into the impression that James's own hold on life is a matter of the illusionistic virtuosity of his language.

James's prose is not shaped by what it describes; rather, as at a magician's flourish of his wand, it creates it. Maggie is fully enlisted in these syntactical conjurings. If her sympathy is not especially sympathetic at such moments, the reason may be her privileged collusion in James's own illusionistic facility. It is difficult not to view Maggie's sympathy as impertinent, another more effective exercise of power and control, a silken noose round Charlotte's neck. It has in fact no practical outcome. It does allow Charlotte to retain some dignity, but this is as much a convenience to the Ververs as a consolation for Charlotte. This occult sympathy for Charlotte seems really another way of experiencing the Prince in his dealings with other women, and her sharp imperatives and snubs in the last chapter could be construed as a kind of revenge for the feminine abjection that sympathy with Charlotte allows her to experience at second remove.

But of course Maggie's sympathy cannot have any outcome; to expect it to is to question the premises of the novel. It is worth noting, however, how often one is tempted to do just that. As a structure it trembles on the verge of certain absurdities and artificialities, and James's talk has to be fast and rich and deep to stop it crumbling away. How can so much conscientiousness be lavished in some respects, and such worldly brutality be unquestioningly assumed in others?[20] For an element in the excitement the novel generates is its quality of power struggle, the sheer tussle over beautiful bodies and beautiful things. It is not a physically substantial novel, as Bayley claims, but it is a worldly novel, involving what is, as Maggie calls her silent struggle with the Prince, a 'high fight'. Spoils – in this case the sumptuous person of the Prince – are at stake, as surely as the furniture of Poynton or some schemed for and haggled over inheritance in Balzac. But if in *The Spoils of Poynton* we are to account failure the only true success, then Maggie's success ought to count as failure. I think it does, but yes or no here may arise from the reader's application of his own ethical criteria, rather than from any positive conclusion of the book. Obviously, if there is failure then it is of a very subtle kind, for on the face of it not only appearances are saved, but the very forms that stand for civilized amenity. Within these forms, it might be argued, lies the resolution of the novel's extreme worldliness and extreme conscientiousness. This would justify the Prince's mercenary marriage and the Ververs' romantic indulgence of their unlimited power of purchase. James seems to be offering, at least as a kind of hypothesis, as a viable arrangement, the alliance of American industry and old world culture. The novel could then be regarded as an exploration of this possibility and, again, whether it was judged a success or failure would be a question of interpretation. Actually, it seems to me that such a scheme is only one of several with which the novel operates. James could have felt that such an alliance, in spite of the duplicity and cross-purposes involved, was superior to such a plainly barbarous and gross arrangement as the British Empire. This seems to be the Prince's sense when, at the beginning of the novel, he contemplates 'the vast machineries and facilities' that the Ververs have at their disposal. So, after all, that scheme may figure rather in the opinions and sensibilities of the characters, than in James's own.

The same perhaps goes for the museum, or collector's theme. Inevitably this rapidly develops ironic overtones, which James to some extent neutralizes by making it a theme also of his characters' conversational playfulness. In Maggie's conversation with her husband-to-be – amusedly, even lovingly recalled by the restless Amerigo on the eve of his marriage – we find her explaining:

'You're at any rate a part of [Adam Verver's] collection . . . one of the things that can only be got over here. You're a rarity, an object of beauty, an object of price. You're not perhaps absolutely unique, but you're so curious and eminent that there are very few others like you – you belong to a class about which everything is known. You're what they call a *morceau de musée*.'

'I see. I have the great sign of it,' he had risked – 'that I cost a lot of money.'

'I haven't the least idea,' she had gravely answered, 'what you cost' – and he had quite adored for the moment her way of saying it. He had felt even for the moment vulgar. But he had made the best of that.

'Wouldn't you find out if it were a question of parting with me? My value would in that case be estimated.' She had covered him with her charming eyes, as if his value were well before her. 'Yes, if you mean that I'd pay rather than lose you.' (Pt. 1, Ch. 1)

Obviously, if a Prince risks vulgarity with such pecuniary remarks, how much more does a mere reader with his brash commentary. James clearly invites us to marvel at the high bravery that can handle such a dangerous topic and turn it into delicacy and candour. James, too, like the Prince, is taking his risk in sounding topics so full of explosive irony. One could say it was rather like Shakespeare in *Pericles*, opening a play which is going to be about the beauty of a father's relation with his daughter with an act about incest between another father and daughter. One notes moreover – and this has its incalculable resonance throughout the book – ambiguities amounting almost to puns on words like 'price', 'risk', 'value', 'pay'. Commercial 'values' are pervasively transvalued, so that commerce can seem both contrasted with 'real' worth, and in some sense analogous and consubstantial with it. The same transvaluation is inherent in all the uses of gold throughout the novel, and of course in the title itself. That this is deeply ambiguous and also in some sense deliberate, there can be no doubt. It is the same ambiguity as to whether the novel is in some sense a romance or about, and even a critique of, the romanticism of the Ververs. Such questions are hardly troublesome while the illusion of their being integrated and worked through by the action persists. Yet they do seem to me to remain in fact unassimilated – the hidden flaw in what, as one reads, seems pure gold and crystal.

James comes nearest to some collision in his museum theme when he has Adam Verver representing his own daughter as a 'fine subject'.[21] The passage is curious and deserves study:

> ... she stood there before him with that particular suggestion in her aspect to which even the long habit of their life together hadn't closed his sense, kept sharp, year after year, by the collation of types and signs, the comparison of fine object with fine object, of one degree of finish, of one form of the exquisite with another – the appearance of some slight slim draped 'antique' of Vatican or Capitoline halls, late and refined, rare as a note and immortal as a link, set in motion by the miraculous infusion of a modern impulse and yet, for all the sudden freedom of folds and footsteps forsaken after centuries by their pedestal, keeping still the quality, the perfect felicity, of the statue; the blurred absent eyes, the smoothed elegant nameless head, the impersonal flit of a creature lost in an alien age and passing as an image in worn relief

round and round a precious vase. She had always had odd moments of striking him, daughter of his very own though she was, as a figure thus simplified, 'generalized' in its grace, a figure with which his human connexion was fairly interrupted by some vague analogy of turn and attitude, something shyly mythological and nymph-like. The trick, he wasn't uncomplacently aware, was mainly of his own mind; it came from him caring for precious vases only less than for precious daughters. (Pt. 3, Ch. 4)

Part of any difficulty here has to do with the final status of James's dramatized consciousness and our sense of the limits beyond which they are not open to interpretation. This passage could read as a damaging comment on Verver's collecting mania and its inherent tendency to reduce other people to desirable objects. Moreover, it might suggest a refusal to acknowledge Maggie as a grown woman, by substituting an asexual image. Is Verver – as our view of both his marriages rather suggests – unable to cope with his own sexuality except in suitable aestheticized terms? Or is James presenting one representative view of Maggie, in line with the 'clear brightness' which the Prince responds to in her and the nun-like, over-innocent, even prim 'little person' that the Assinghams thoughtfully masticate in their intent colloquies? His 'caring for precious vases only less than for precious daughters' may be no more than the play of Adam's usual, self-deprecating, drooling irony. Yet it remains a strange passage, with its sense of personal relations receding into a generalized aesthetic and mythic dimness. One suspects, from the *bravura* music of the prose, that we are in the presence of another epiphany – and it is notably Adam who has them (indeed, the similarity of Adam to Lambert Strether is marked, perhaps because both are slightly elderly American gentlemen with aesthetic proclivities) – this time, of the good life. Adam's vast accumulation purchases, as its ultimate refinement, a re-creation, in the very person of his own flesh and blood, of a 'generalized' sympathy with the human spirit in its widest and deepest mythological reach. In effect, his feeling for his daughter and for his fine things is identical, the one guaranteeing the value of the other.

A passage such as this should warn us that Adam cannot be simply dismissed as a robber-baron and that James did not intend him to be

viewed as one. His droll, American vernacular obviously links him
with the elder Mr Touchett in *The Portrait of a Lady*.[22] We are no
more meant to disapprove of Adam Verver's tycoonery than we are
of old Touchett's banking. Yet the imagery sometimes associated
with Adam Verver is fairly sinister. At the opening of the book, we
learn that 'Mr Verver had pitched a tent suggesting that of Alexander
furnished with the spoils of Darius' (Pt. 1, Ch. 1) in Portland Place.
The word 'spoils' was obviously a vibrating one for James; and if
Adam is Alexander, one wonders, who is Darius? Later in the
résumé of Verver's career, we are told that 'to rifle the Golden Isles
had become on the spot the business of his future' (Pt. 2, Ch. 1).
Inevitably, both the words 'rifle' and 'business' acquire questionable
overtones particularly in a passage which notes (in contrast to his
present role of collector which, he feels, makes him 'equal somehow
with the great seers, the invokers and encouragers of beauty – and he
didn't after all perhaps dangle so far below the great producers and
creators') what, as a businessman, he had 'too decidedly, too dread-
fully not' been.

What is at issue is the bearing that Adam's career of 'large
accumulation' is meant to have on his moral function within the book.
You could argue that here, as elsewhere, James simply preserves the
sense of paradox, of moral openness which characterizes any experience of human reality. This would be acceptable if, as we have
noted before, scrupulous attention were not paid to moral discrimin-
ations at so many other levels. *The Golden Bowl* is after all no loose
genial baggy monster rejoicing, in its excess of life, in a multiplicity
of sometimes contradictory ethical perspectives. On the contrary, its
formal tightness insists upon some equivalent intensity of moral
vision. The counter argument to this is that the very concentration of
its formal design suggests and even generates a complexity beyond
itself which will, however, be an organized and not random complexity. The novelist, in this view, does not order and prescribe each
movement of consciousness in his characters. On the contrary, he
provides a nutritious medium in which, in their interaction, they
can flower beyond his ordination and that of his readers. The
novelist holds the ring – the ring being the formal occasion in which
a free life can manifest itself. This is the Jamesian theory in its essence

as lucidly stated in a famous sentence in the Preface to *Roderick Hudson*:

> Really, universally, relations stop nowhere, and the exquisite problem of the artist is eternally to draw, by a geometry of his own, the circle within which they shall happily *appear* to do so.[23]

For 'relations' we can read 'ethical perspectives' and we arrive at the same point – that intricacy of design may come to signify the variousness of moral reality. But does it work like this in the case of Verver? While doing the theory justice, it is impossible to escape the impression that James really half believed in the redemptive power of some alliance between taste and money-power. Moreover, Adam Verver is a special kind of capitalist, whose fortune has been generated in the same mysterious and occult way that James sometimes represents his own fiction as having been. By some strange logic, James's ignorance comes also to symbolize Verver's mystery – the purely verbal means with which James has to conjure his career becoming the equivalent of the cerebral means with which Verver has conjured his fortune:

> The essential pulse of the flame, the very action of the cerebral temperature, brought to the highest point, yet extraordinarily contained – these facts themselves *were* the immensity of the result; they were one with the perfection of machinery, they had constituted the kind of acquisitive power engendered and applied, the necessary triumph of all operations. A dim explanation of phenomena once vivid must at all events for the moment suffice us. . . .   (Pt. 2, Ch. 1)

Several passages in the Prefaces advert to James's confessed incapacity to render 'downtown', the world of business; this, from the Preface to *The Reverberator*, is as frank as any:

> . . . before the American businessman, as I have been prompt to declare, I was absolutely and irredeemably helpless, with no fibre of my intelligence responding to his mystery. No approach I could make to him on his 'business side' really got near it. That is where I was fatally incompetent, and this in turn – the case goes into a nutshell – is so obviously why, for any decent documentation, I was simply shut up to what was left to me.[24]

Which is why, James explains, he had to deal with passionate young American females in his early stories – the fathers were impenetrably blank businessmen and the mothers nothing at all.

Mr Verver's blankness, whiteness, unassumingness stand for this business mystery to which James had no access. And he makes a kind of dramatic virtue out of the mystery by rendering it inaccessible to any of his characters either, perhaps not even to Adam himself. James knows well enough that, as he notes himself, Adam's fortune was not produced by 'amiability'. Hints and sly suggestions abound that Adam Verver conceals an iron will beneath an appearance of benign and helpless boyishness. It seems, despite the argument canvassed above, that Adam represents a yawning and intractable gap in James's experience within which various notions of power and authority waver and blur. Some instinct warned James that – as in the case of the abysmal poor – any attempt to render money-power in direct terms would necessitate the adoption of a naturalist externality of treatment which so easily becomes in turn an abdication to 'the perfection of machinery'. Both Conrad and Lawrence use highly oblique methods to deal with money-power. In Lawrence's case, it is already part of a highly organized counter-ideology. It is interesting to note that Gerald Crich, in *Women in Love*, accentuates and deepens Verver's dim whiteness into demonic brilliant whiteness of snow and ice. By 1900, a career of acquisition has long ceased for novelists to represent, with whatever moral ambiguity, the way to any possible notion of heroic self-fulfilment. Business energies become imaginatively negotiable by James only when applied, as in the collector's passion, to aesthetic ends. Otherwise an impenetrable monotony prevails, whose extent marks the degree of the unavailability of wide areas of social experience to James. All that he can do with the mass of Verver's business life is to explain that 'Mr Verver then, for a fresh full period, a period betraying, extraordinarily, no wasted year, had been inscrutably monotonous behind an iridescent cloud' (Pt. 2, Ch. 1). To counter this 'inscrutable monotony' he makes it an imaginative fact for his other characters and plays up the possible iridescence, making Verver the last of what James himself admitted to be 'sneaking attempts to substitute the American romantic for the American real'.[25] The complication in *The Golden Bowl* is that no-one knows which quantity they are dealing with, and the subversive possibility is that they are identical. This in turn opens up interesting possibilities for James's own fiction: *The Golden Bowl* itself being, in its inner significance, a western and capitalist version of Mann's 'power-protected inwardness' which the late fiction simultaneously exhibits and diagnoses. In any case, the equation of romantic and real works either way: the romantic dream may mask a brutality of applied will. This too is one of the latent, brooding ambiguities of the novel, one which again threatens the entire structure with incoherence and collapse.

James's romantic American innocents have come to look, by the time we arrive at *The Golden Bowl* a fairly predatory, even lethal lot. It is the calculators and designers who are themselves trapped and destroyed. The dead Millie works her corrosion on Kate Croy and Merton Densher. Fanny, an earlier emigrant, is as well equipped as any to locate the ferocity and brutality in Maggie's outraged innocence. Maggie betrays sinister manipulativeness in her dealings with the guilty pair:

> '. . . They move at any rate among the dangers I speak of – between that of their doing too much and that of their not having any longer the confidence or the nerve, or whatever you may call it, to do enough.' Her tone might by this time have shown a strangeness to match her smile; which was still more marked as she wound up: 'And that's how I make them do what I like!'
> It had an effect on Mrs Assingham, who rose with the deliberation that from point to point marked the widening of her grasp.
> 'My dear child, you're amazing.'
> 'Amazing –?'
> 'You're terrible.' (Pt. 4, Ch. 6)

Maggie counters this assertion by claiming to be 'surprisingly mild' which shows how far she is from assessing her own cold, mental violence, which is indeed 'strange' to her. It is in this context that Maggie's famous declaration that she bears it all 'for Love' is made: but one would have thought that Fanny's appalled reaction to the childish power-boast of 'I make them do what I like', would prevent our taking this at its face value. Much more dramatically, we are in the presence of Maggie tasting, for the first time, the strangeness of her own power. Mrs Assingham takes up, on our behalf as surprised readers, the word 'mildness':

> Is that what you call it when you make them, for terror as you say, do as you like? (Pt. 4, Ch. 6)

And, in a spasm of triumphant righteousness, Maggie whips back with unexpected sharpness: 'Ah, there wouldn't be any terror for them if they had nothing to hide.' Mrs Assingham confronts this Rhadamanthine rigour with 'Are you really conscious, love, of what you are saying?' It is difficult to believe that all that Fanny is asking is whether she really accuses the Prince and Charlotte of a liaison. Is she not rather registering Maggie's bitter and exhilarating taste of reality, power and blood, of 'Evil – with a capital E'.

Of course Maggie always experiences violence subjectively as a form of victimization. Charlotte becomes a ferocious, uncaged beast and she an insect, a sacrificial lamb, a consecrated victim. Certainly, the lurid light that plays over the dramatic encounters at Fawns depends a good deal on the deployment of such imagery:

> Of the 'advantage', it was perfectly enough, in truth, with Mrs Verver; for what was Maggie's own sense but that of having been thrown over on her back with her neck from the first half-broken and her helpless face staring up? That position only could account for the positive grimace of weakness and pain produced there by Charlotte's dignity. (Pt. 5, Ch. 2)

We are left to infer for ourselves what stress the preservation of her dignity must be occasioning Charlotte. And the violence of this image may really only be measuring the depth of Maggie's initial timidity rather than the menace of Charlotte's dignity. The conversation that ensues hardly consorts with Maggie's inward trauma:

> 'I've come to join you – I thought you would be here.'
> 'Oh yes, I'm here,' Maggie heard herself return a little flatly.
> 'It's too close indoors.'
> 'Very – but close even here.'

James was fascinated throughout all his later fiction with the currents of violence that swirl beneath and ripple polite surfaces. The pleasure he takes in polished and elaborate conversations coincides with his artist's obsession with operations of grand good form, which contains and yet betrays every latent turbulence. A word like 'close' begins to crackle with electrical energy: the excitement that attends the outcome of this confrontation is, as Maggie's image also hints, erotically charged. We hang on the volcanic tip of a blazing row, waiting for eruption. Indeed, closeness here describes not only the foetid jungle stench of danger, but a proximity to collision, which will blast away the veiled interiority of consciousness. We expect bodies to collide in a blow or an embrace. What happens in fact is a rather muffled and strained exchange followed by the Judas kiss between Maggie and Charlotte, which half resolves the violence, while keeping each consciousness sealed and intact. It is a triumph for both the women of the diplomatic ego, conceding the illusion of fleshly contact in order to conserve the real play of mental conflict. The 'close' heat turns into the 'coldness of their conscious perjury'. Maggie, beneath her passive submission, seems thrillingly to participate in Charlotte's desperate extremity of conduct.

At such a moment we are very close to the spiritual atmospherics of *The Turn of the Screw*. One recalls how, at the climax of that story, the Governess 'flashed into ice' at 'Miles's supreme surrender to the name [Peter Quint's] and his surrender to [her] devotion'.[26] Maggie's struggle with Charlotte and the Prince is frequently reminiscent of the Governess with Miss Jessel and Quint, though, in terms of that scheme, the Prince is both Quint and Miles. I have always – amid the press of competing interpretations – read *The Turn of the Screw* as essentially a fable about the suppression of sexual identity in the Governess and its impact upon her charges, though obviously the story is poised in a deliberate ambiguity which is the most haunting thing about it. The Governess is obsessed with the idea of innocence, and can no more accept that her innocents have sexual identities than she can accept sexuality in herself. What the Governess in her interrogations of Miles is asking him to confess to is nothing less than his own life's energies, most patently declared in his gender. These energies, when alienated, become demons. The struggle of the demons to possess the children is really her own struggle to possess them under the guise of preserving their innocence and her own too. For – and this is where James's fable beautifully relates sexuality to class – she too is possessed by her employer, robbed of her sexual identity and yet used, both economically and sexually, by being asked to devote her life to the convenience of others. Deep down she is as much a servant as Quint, and as essentially clad in her master's cast-offs. Indeed, Quint as a demon is her master, metamorphosed by the complex class illusions which mask the Governess's abasement and yet are the condition of its successful operation. The whole story itself works in terms of contradictory, irresolvable appearances which involve the reader directly in the experience of illusion, and so close the circle between the author, his audience and the Governess herself.

Charlotte and the Prince represent, within the formal society of the novel and the artifice of its own fiction, a similar set of energies, smouldering towards explosion and experienced by Maggie as demonic and alien. Indeed, the question of their duplicity slides over into a mental atmosphere in which they show as doubles: as both loving husband and responsible wife and as alien forces who simulate these roles. At the same time, they are also embodiments of Maggie's alienated experience of her own sexuality, and of the power of possession inescapably involved in her purchase of the Prince and, as a result of her prompting, her father's of Charlotte. The Prince and Charlotte behave, indeed, like prodigiously superior servants who do the Ververs' living for them and feel relatively little dishonour in enjoying each other as a perk that goes with the job.

It is Maggie's growing awareness of an intrusive alien intelligence within the apparently secure structure of her life that is enacted by the elaborate pagoda image with which the second book commences. This arrangement represents the childlike immunity purchased by great wealth – a fairy-tale life within what is itself a fairy tale. The pagoda is thus also James's own house of fiction, within which lurk the unutterable figures and realities with which he cannot directly communicate but which, as fundamental life forces, constitute the vitality of his art. It is also the system of lies and illusions which is civilization itself. The paradox is that Maggie cannot herself occupy this structure of civilized arrangement because it is constructed from her own alienated life. She can only enter it by entering herself and coming to some sort of terms with her power and her appetites. As it is, the alien presences are, in the last resort, embodiments of the productive and exploitive energies which, in sexual terms, have generated her life and in economic terms made it possible for her to be the fairy-tale Princess. The image itself smacks of childhood fantasy and seems blended out of *The Arabian Nights* and *Alice in Wonderland*. Maggie's anxious perception 'that no door appeared to give access from her garden level' reminds one of Alice's recurrent crises of exclusion. The size-shift is also very Alice-like:

> She had walked round and round it – that was what she felt; she had carried on her existence in the space left her for circulation, a space that sometimes seemed ample and sometimes narrow: looking up all the while at the fair structure that spread itself so amply and rose so high, but never quite making out as yet where she might have entered had she wished. (Pt. 4, Ch. 1)

The pagoda image serves to introduce the second book and at the same time becomes a pictorial analogy of its action, which can be seen as Maggie's entry into the pagoda and confrontation with the alien and deeply familiar forces that harbour there. It is a romantic image whose not so very distant ancestor is Xanadu, that dome of pleasure in which all the antinomies of heat and cold are held in musical balance but which immanent conflict threatens. Perhaps the pagoda suggests everything, which is clearly too much. As a metaphor it finally exhibits itself in its demonic, unattached concreteness – the *symboliste* construction squatting at the heart of the novel, waiting to be redeemed by bodily and mental suffering. Yet it arises as the autonomous and quasi-divine play of imagination itself. The Prince has already been likened to a Palladian church, and at still another level one could read the whole of the second half of *The Golden Bowl*, Maggie's half, as a kind of penetration by feminine consciousness of the male *superbia* – suggested by the pagoda being also likened to a Mahometan mosque, and admirably exhibited, as a form of materialized consciousness, in the first book. Only then can it become a fit temple for the marriage of action and contemplation, knowledge and reality. But finally the pagoda is the as yet virgin structure of Maggie's own self: constructed for her – until the moment when she realizes precisely that – by others, and now due to be infiltrated and finally occupied by herself. In almost every passage I have quoted the word 'strange' has appeared; and the strangeness which is the self seen newly for the first time as other than itself is the central characteristic of the pagoda. It 'had reared itself there like some tall *strange* tower of ivory' (my italics): one notes the colour, Adam Verver's colour. The reflexive tense enacts its apparently uncaused, autonomous existence. The metaphor become more intricate as Maggie contemplates its 'apertures and outlooks', for the pagoda also seems to be the body of others, perhaps most of all the body of the Prince and Charlotte – and even beyond that, your most deep-reaching Freudian would doubtless wish to speculate, the body of Adam, the primal parent himself. (We remember Maggie's subsequent imagining of 'the polished old ivory of her father's inattackable surface': Pt. 5, Ch. 5.)

That such metaphors of the body are well within his compass is suggested by such a passage as this one from *The Sacred Fount*, that voyeur's revelation of cannibal feasts in the dorms of high society:

> I saw as I have never seen before what consuming passion can make of the marked mortal on whom, with fixed beak and claws, it has settled as on a prey. She reminded me of a sponge wrung dry and with fine pores agape. Voided and scraped of everything, her shell was merely crushable.[27]

Maggie of course views Charlotte as 'fixed beak and claws', and both she and Charlotte herself – when in the grip of her erotic nemesis – are 'prey'. It is striking how absolutely Racinian James's conception of damaging passion is: *C'est Venus, toute entière, a sa proie attaché*. Within the tight, hysterically over-organized systems of Racine's drama, the passions short-circuit each other fatally, as they almost do in James. In James, Venus is largely, and for similar reasons, a beast. There is obviously a close connexion between high formality and explosive passion. James has returned, in certain respects, to the abstract movement of such very early, formal novels as *La Princesse de Clève*, associated, as formal art so often is, with themes of renunciation. Here another – and real – Princess feels herself '*surmonté par passion*', and the military and animal acts, looming in the linguistic underworld of the relatively abstract sign language of *surmonté* – stormed as in a seige or mounted as by a bull (as Phèdre's mother, Pasiphae has been) – are like a generic version of the whole process of metaphoric mirroring which James elaborates in his late fiction. Indeed, at the second and final confrontation of Maggie with Charlotte, James becomes as mythologically allusive as Racine himself:

> The Princess kept her for a few minutes in sight, watched her long enough to feel her, by the mere betrayal of her pace and direction, driven in a kind of flight, and then understood for herself why the act of sitting still had become impossible to either of them. There came to her, confusedly, some echo of an ancient fable – some vision of Io goaded by the gad-fly or Ariadne roaming the lone sea-strand. It brought with it all the sense of her own intention and desire; she too might have been for the hour some far-off harrassed heroine – only with a part to play for which she knew exactly no inspiring precedent. (Pt. 5, Ch. 5)

It is hard to say which is the more important – that Maggie imagines herself as a gad-fly (the insect turns at last) or Charlotte as a cow. Perhaps the really important item in these reflections is the intensity, at this stage, of Maggie's identification with Charlotte. She lives out the lot, is persecutor or persecuted, abandoned and abandoner. Her totality of imaginative involvement is the new heroism – 'for which she knew, exactly, no inspiring precedent'. What she is about to do is to manipulate Charlotte, as Charlotte initially has manipulated and managed the Prince. Yet Maggie's heroism involves an extra dimension. Her part, in a sense, is really not to have one. The demonic lovers have had the shared excitements of their complicity. And now they have the bodily reality of their separation. But Maggie's deed is the negative adventure of not having had one. She feels this as deprivation indeed; it is almost the core of her suffering. And, typically, she describes the adventure she has not had in images as exotic as the pagoda:

> She might fairly, as she watched them, have missed it as a lost thing; have yearned for it, for the straight vindictive view, the rights of resentment, the rages of jealousy, the protests of passion, as for something she had been cheated of not least: a range of feelings which for many women would have meant so much, but which for *her* husband's wife, for her father's daughter, figured nothing nearer to experience than a wild eastern caravan, looming into view with crude colours in the sun, fierce pipes in the air, high spears against the sky, all a thrill, a natural

joy to mingle with, but turning off short before it reached her and plunging into other defiles. (Pt. 5, Ch. 2)

Of course, in image, Maggie has the high exotic pleasures of passion which she denies herself in fact. It passes before her eyes like an opium vision. And there seems to be a connexion implied between the civilization represented by these wealthy cosmopolites and their parasites, playing bridge in a rented country house which they do not occupy as true aristocrats, and this vision of barbaric splendour. Again, one recoils to Adam as Alexander with the spoils of Darius (remembering not only now the spoils of Poynton but the way in which Quint *spoiled* little Miles in *The Turn of the Screw*), and likewise to the novel's opening chapter, where the newly-purchased Prince contemplated in the Bond Street shops 'objects massive and lumpish . . . tumbled together as if, in the insolence of Empire, they had been the loot of far-off victories' (Pt. 1, Ch. 1). The caravan loses itself, not only in a defile, but in imagery straight out of *The Turn of the Screw*:

> She saw at all events why horror itself had almost failed her; the horror that, foreshadowed in advance, would by her thought have made everything that was unaccustomed in her cry out with pain; the horror of finding evil seated all at its ease where she had only dreamed of good; the horror of the thing hideously *behind*, behind so much trusted, so much pretended, nobleness, cleverness, tenderness. It was the first sharp falsity she had known in her life, to touch at all, or be touched by; it had met her like some bad-faced stranger surprised in one of the thick-carpeted corridors of a house of quiet on a Sunday afternoon; and yet, yes, amazingly, she had been able to look at terror and disgust only to know that she must put away from her the bitter-sweet of their freshness. (Pt. 5, Ch. 2)

Again, one notes that it is precisely 'the bitter-sweet of their freshness' that is rendered so sharply as that which Maggie must renounce. In fact, or rather in metaphor, horror does not 'fail' her. Indeed her pursuit of it is rather active. The 'bad-faced stranger' (again the familiar strangeness!) is himself surprised. Part of the creepiness of the image arises from the thick carpeting that muffles the footfall of she who surprises him. The hesitation as to whether the 'bad-faced stranger' haunts or is haunted, if not actually hunted, is precisely caught in the wavering syntax of 'to touch . . . or be touched by'; while the horror's ease suggests that It, the fact of deceit and adultery, has more right to 'that house of quiet' than its appalled possessor. Surely in that haunted house Maggie is face to face with her own dispossessed energies, experiencing a phantom contact, through her experience of their duplicity, with the real carnal life of Charlotte and the Prince. But again, it is a contact inside the head, lived out as a vertiginous temptation to enjoy in actuality what she can contemplate only as the deed not done, foregone and abdicated.

Yet this comes over as an exercise in power, the more pleasurable because she chooses not to exert it. She revels in feeling, of the card players, that she is 'consciously, as might be said, holding them in her hand' (where 'consciously' and 'holding them in her hand' clang against each other with the force of oxymoron). Indeed, her most extreme form of pleasure is the overwhelming temptation that almost conquers her – to play the card that will crack the whole system apart as Fanny had cracked the golden bowl itself. She might so easily become a palpable focus of terror and anguish for all the others and assume an appalling substance in their gaze. It represents a supreme sacrifice that she does refrain from playing this last card. How fierce the temptation is, though, can be gauged by an earlier incident, the dinner given for the Matcham party:

> It wasn't that she wished she had been of the remembered party and possessed herself of its secrets; for she didn't care about its secrets – she could concern herself at present absolutely with no secret but her own. What occurred was simply that she became aware, at a stroke, of the quantity of further nourishment required by her own, and of the amount of it she might somehow extract from these people; whereby she rose of a sudden to the desire to possess and use them, even to the extent of braving, of fairly defying, of directly exploiting, of possibly quite enjoying, under cover of an evil duplicity, the felt element of curiosity with which they regarded her.   (Pt. 4, Ch. 3)

This is perhaps as clear an enactment of the evil in Maggie as any we are offered. Indeed, we experience its onset with Maggie in the mounting sequence of excited phrases. Maggie takes immense inward

pleasure in the idea of being watched, or suddenly becoming herself a
source of terror, consternation or plain fascination. She too can contemplate what it might be to possess; and in a sense she does possess,
in the most satisfactory way of all – in her own performing imagination, the sense of whose liveliness eventually leaks out to the Prince –
all that she denies in herself.

Yet once more one has to complain that this insight into Maggie's
participation in 'possession' and 'exploitation' is hardly the consciously focused concern of the novel. To say the least, James lays
plenty of false trails: enough, it appears, for critics to take seriously
the 'for love' speech and some of the grosser manifestations of Mrs
Assingham's sentimentality, which sit oddly – though perhaps not
surprisingly – with her sharp cynicism on other occasions. Maggie is
endowed by her with 'no small amount of character' and one begins
to wonder what character means, if not Maggie's half-roused violence.
Fanny explains to Maggie that it is:

> '. . . Somewhere *under*, I should simply have said – like that little silver
> cross you once showed me, blest by the Holy Father, that you always
> wear, out of sight, next your skin. That relic I've had a glimpse of' –
> with which she continued to invoke the privilege of humour. 'But the
> precious little innermost, say this time little golden personal nature of
> you – blest by a greater power I think, even than the Pope – *that* you've
> never consentingly shown me.'   (Pt. 4, Ch. 6)

Here Fanny seems to be part of the conspiracy to keep Maggie in
moral pinafores. The second book is the story of Maggie's emergence
from childhood, not only in respect to Adam, who is as much a play-
mate as a parent, but to all the other adults who keep her at the
nursery level. All these other adults lie to her, arrange her, handle her
as if she were their object. Charlotte and the Prince sometimes appear
like gay, young parents, made into demons in childish imagination by
their dimly divined sexual complicity. This turns them into appari-
tions as much as appearances, and gives a ghostly character to their
star turn on the balcony in Portland Place when Maggie and her
father return from their inconclusive colloquy in the Park. Maggie
has to crane upwards, as if she were indeed a child; and the impression
is strengthened by Maggie's recollection of the Prince, the previous

Christmas, having come out to stare at 'the dingy waifs' singing below for pennies, whose place she now occupies. In their triumph, Charlotte and the Prince act the part of genial and overseeing parents whose brightness conceals a horrid secret. Again, the atmospherics are essentially those of *The Turn of the Screw*.

Fanny, to return to the 'silver cross', is the grandest liar of the lot, with her sentimental religiosity, her determination to save appearances and her own skin, her possibly *louche* motivation in her crush for the Prince, which, like all the jokes, trembles on the rim of abysses. As Maggie's confidante, she virtually teaches her the power of the bare-faced lie. She emerges as rather like the madame of a bordello with a half sentimental, half prurient, but always shrewdly realistic interest in the behaviour of her girls and their clients. She is indeed a pander. Her exotic Jewish appearance connects her with the eastern caravan image that stands for the passion Maggie does not include herself in: '[Fanny's] eyes of the American city looked out, somehow . . . from under the lids of Jerusalem' (Pt. 1, Ch. 2). Her dealings with the Ververs, and most of all with Maggie, invest the main protagonists in a discreet ambience of buying and selling, which James seems to identify as Jewish. There is some similarity between James's portrait of the Gutermann-Suesses, and Pound's fascinated report on the familial intensities of Mitteleurope in *Canto XXXV*:

> . . . and Tsievitz
> has explained to me the warmth of affections,
> the intramural, the almost intravaginal warmth of
> hebrew affections in the family. . . .

Adam's regard for Charlotte comes as near to a responsive sensuality as it ever does, in the bosom of this Jewish family:

> . . . with their return to the room in which they had been received and the renewed encompassment of the tribe, he felt quite merged in the elated circle formed by the girl's free response to the collective caress of all the shining eyes, and by her genial acceptance of the heavy cake and port wine that, as she was afterwards to note, added to their transaction, for a finish, the touch of some mystic rite of old Jewry.   (Pt. 2, Ch. 6)

The suggestion of 'tribe' and 'rite' is suitably exotic and a shade sinister. The Jews are seen, in a conventional way, as a secret, underground race, exclusive and clannish, mingling commerce, ritual religion and familial piety, and hence the focus of excited curiosity, half fascinated, half paranoid. 'The collective caress of all the shining eyes' acknowledges Charlotte as a kind of honorary Jewess, in her subversive, concentrated rapaciousness and sensual generosity. It is these qualities that give her sympathy with 'low types' – she being virtually one herself – like the Jewish seller of the golden bowl on whom she and the Prince make such a fatal impression. It seems that Jewry, for James, concentrated all the exotic occult, darkly oriental and deeply commercial elements – which yet, with their tribes and rites suggest mysteries and secrecies not unlike the artist's own – at work within and beneath the structure of gentile society. 'The Jew' – as Eliot more tersely put it – 'is underneath the lot'.

The Jewish theme is one minor instance of the omnipresent awareness in all late James, and particularly in *The Golden Bowl*, of the surfaces of civilization as complex illusions, out of direct contact with their own illicit depths, yet in secret and fascinated commerce with them. The construction and themes of the novel itself simulate and explore this ambiguous realm of the knowledge of what is not known. The whole novel, then, is impossibly both an act and refusal of descent into its own depths, a submission to the necessity of preserving appearances in the knowledge of their unreality. Maggie embodies this paradoxical condition – one which can only be conceived if caught in the act of exploding itself. Maggie's story can be seen as a very slow explosion, which only appears to be a development or a growth, just as an actual explosion filmed in slow motion might resemble the silent unfolding of a flower. The novel's slowness of pace becomes a way of redeeming the violence of the explosion, a form of control over it, which permits an abstract beauty of form to survive the actual ugliness of disintegration.

For surely, with the couple's final separation, the utopian harmony for which the Ververs' arrangement in some sense stands is seen to have come to immedicable grief, just as the golden bowl itself is fractured beyond repair. And the further implication is that it could not be otherwise, because the utopian arrangement was deeply flawed and fraudulent. Maggie thought she could change power and possession into harmony and mutual freedom, whereas what she has to do, in the outcome, is to assume power herself, directly, and become herself the possessor if she is not to be possessed. This represents the re-emergence in the heart of this beautifully fashioned and elaborately conscientious work of the Balzacian dilemma that, in bourgeois society, a man must either be a fool or a rogue. Maggie buries her head in the Prince's breast at the end of the novel in knowledge that she has had to become a predator and he her prey. And the pity and terror she reads in his eyes are appropriate emotional responses to the condition of the victim and the worse condition of the victor. When at last the Prince fully acknowledges her supremacy, she encounters herself as the stranger that she has felt her beloved enemies until then to have been.

Yet James believes above all that though the bowl and everything it represents is broken, someone has to sacrifice himself to covering up – and in the process mitigating – the disaster. By so doing, Maggie enters the very heart of deceit, the knowledge of human darkness and duplicity. The problem seems to be how to live in the light with that haunting knowledge of the darkness locked within. She is constantly swept and assaulted by the temptation to let the darkness out, to confess the lie in the Conradian mode. One such occasion is the night of the card party at Fawns:

> Nothing in fact was *stranger* than the way in which, when she had remained there a little, her companions, watched by her through one of the windows, actually struck her as almost consciously and gratefully safer. . . . They might have been figures rehearsing some play of which she herself was the author; they might even, for the happy appearance they continued to present, have been such figures as would by the strong note of character in each fill any author with the certitude of success, especially of their own histrionic. They might in short have represented any mystery they would; the point being predominantly that the key to the mystery, the key that could wind and unwind it without a snap of the spring, was there in her pocket – or rather, no doubt, clasped at this crisis in her hand and pressed, as she walked back and forth, to her breast. She walked to the end and far out of the light; she returned and saw the others still where she had left them; she passed round the house and looked into the drawing-room, lighted also, but empty now, and seeing to speak the more in its own voice of all the possibilities she controlled. Spacious and splendid, like a stage again awaiting a drama, it was a scene she might people, by the

press of her spring, either with serenities and dignities and decencies, or with terrors and shames and ruins, things as ugly as those formless fragments of her golden bowl she was trying so hard to pick up. (Pt. 5, Ch. 2)

The oddest feature of this passage is that which makes Maggie into a creative dramatist by virtue of all that she does not let happen. James seems to be recalling here his own dramatic ambitions and disappointments. To have succeeded as a dramatist would have been to establish a public art, which would have a real worldly presence, something for which James obviously yearned. The impossibility of this amounted to a doom of privacy, isolation and loss of contact. This could only be sanctified by regarding that doom itself as a vocation, a sacrifice, one in which the burden of 'terrors, shames and ruins' was conscientiously assumed as that which the 'serenities and dignities' of the late style redeemed. James comes close here to recognizing how easily the artist, like Aschenbach or even more Leverkühn, can become demonic and Mephistophelian, a conjuror of alien (or *strange* – the word does not fail us here!) mysteries. The process of permitting the appearances of good form to prevail when, like Lazarus come back from the dead, she could if she wished tell all, allows Maggie to see the society of others as neither a source of solid reassurance nor of demonic haunting, but as a drama of which she, like all the others, is the author. This confers a terrible sense of freedom whose whole point is that it can never be exercised.

A passage such as this marks the extreme limit to which James allows his knowledge to go. Like Maggie, he walks 'far out of the light'; but like Maggie again, he returns. Yet darkness is a tempting element. As Maggie earlier watches the card players, she is forced to leave the room 'to get away in the outer darkness, from that provocation of opportunity which had assaulted her, within, on her sofa, as a beast might have leapt on her throat'. What is beautiful in that sentence is the way the prepositions *within* and *on* subtly disturb each other by insisting on their competing functions within metaphor and description – the static *on* being rudely jostled by the metaphorical and mental, and essentially more actual, *within*. Darkness becomes a shelter from dark impulses which are of course her own. Here the complex trafficking between surface and depth, darkness and light, becomes almost explicit. But it does not – quite. The suspense of the whole dangerous episode is located as much in what James's narrative may reveal in the sudden rupturing of its own formal design as in Maggie's bated, expectant consciousness. Fawns itself exists as much as a structure of metaphor as an actual location, though as a metaphor it is more actual than what it stands for. Thus the empty room, awaiting its drama, seems to represent the enigma of an unwritten future which is, there and then, about to declare itself. In a vastly mediated way, James presents Maggie's moment of moral crisis with all the force of an historical, an epochal crisis. Admittedly, such a reading cannot be demonstrated. It depends upon one's whole sense of where the book historically is, and equally on the assumptions that one brings to bear on it. It is also a question of how one takes the language – whether the generalizing vocabulary of 'serenities, decencies and dignities' seems merely abstract and musical, or designed to vibrate to any extent that you care to take it.

Indeed, in the other crucial temptation scene, it is hard not to feel that the issue has become one of civilization as against barbarism, rather than the ostensible issue of whether Maggie or Adam is going to mention Charlotte. At this stage, the question of Charlotte seems to have become itself a metaphor for more fundamental problems. To let the cat out of the bag and confess, or even hint at the hidden disaster, is to acknowledge the fact that the system is blown sky-high. To keep it tacit is to render it salvageable. At plot level, Adam's marriage will not have to show the otherwise inevitable face of crude failure. Maggie is sorely tempted to blow the gaff; again, one has the impression of the gaff blown, but as it were invisible and noiselessly – another negative act:

> At this it hung before her that she should have had as never yet her opportunity to say, and it held her for a minute as in a vise,[28] her impression of his now, with his strained smile, which touched her to deepest depths, sounding her in his secret unrest. This was the moment in the whole process of their mutual vigilance in which it decidedly *most* hung by a hair that their thin wall might be pierced by the lightest wrong touch. It shook between them, this transparency, with their very breath; it was an exquisite tissue, but stretched on a frame, and would give way the next instant if either so much as breathed too hard. She

held her breath, for she knew by his eyes, the light at the heart of which he couldn't blind, that he was, by his intention, making sure – sure whether or no her certainty was like his. The intensity of his dependence on it at that moment – this itself was what absolutely convinced her so that, as if perched up before him on her vertiginous point and in the very glare of his observation, she balanced for thirty seconds, she almost rocked: she might have been for the time, in all her conscious person, the very form of the equilibrium they were, in their different ways, equally trying to save. And they were saving it – yes, they were, or at least she was: that was still the workable issue, she could say, as she felt her dizziness drop.   (Pt. 5, Ch. 3)

The 'exquisite tissue, but stretched on a frame' might strike many readers of *The Golden Bowl* as an apt description of the novel itself, with its extreme tenuousness of dramatic motive billowing upon a rigid structure of relationships. Yet against this tenuousness juts the queer physicality of Jamesian metaphor. Innocently abstract terms like *impression*, *strained*, *intensity*, *dependence*, *issue* get returned to their remote origin in physical sensation. Our sense of the artist as constructor, maker of his world, is never allowed to lapse. We cross those Jamesian sentences, track down the huge slopes of his paragraphs, hang suspended in the cradle of his parentheses, turn and pause with his digressions, sustain the enormous weight of delayed periods. Sensations are handed over bodily through a series of linguistic acts. Why James has a cult – and one agrees with Geismar that he has – is not only for the questionable reasons that he enumerates, but because late James engages his reader so completely at the sympathetic bodily level, by endowing the bodiless abstractions and negations which can be felt as though they were bodied. Glancing through the pages, particularly of the second book, one is struck by the frequent articulation of unuttered thoughts. Whole paragraphs stand in a strange phantom visibility, against the shadow of negation and hypothesis. It is as though the ghostly world of the novel were the projected shadow of some much more vivid and active drama, which in turn haunts the novel and its characters as a latent adventure which all previous and subsequent novels depict in crude actuality. If one reads along the line of imagery right through the book one can extract an exotic Conrad novel, where the metaphors all become acts.

Examples abound. There is a whole, fairly consistent stream of boat and ocean imagery. In one instance, Maggie discovers that the Prince and Charlotte have been managing or, as she calls it, *treating* her. James's progression into his own metaphor appears to proceed at the same pace as Maggie's penetration of her insight, and both are landed in the same strange waters:

> Some such happily-provoked remarks as these from Charlotte at the other house had been in the air, but we have seen how there was also in the air, for our young woman, as an emanation from the same, a distilled difference of which the very principle was to keep down objections and retorts. That impression came back – it had its hours of doing so; and it may interest us on the ground of its have prompted in Maggie a final reflexion, a reflexion out of the heart of which a light flashed for her like a great flower grown in a night. As soon as this light had spread a little it produced in some quarters a surprising distinctness, made her of a sudden ask herself why there should have been even for three days the least obscurity. The perfection of her success, decidedly, was like some strange shore to which she had been noiselessly ferried and where, with a start, she found herself quaking at the thought that the boat might have put off again and left her.   (Pt. 4, Ch. 2)

That image conjures a Conradian seascape: one thinks, for example, of Martin Decoud left on his island in the Placid Gulf. Once again, of course, it is a *strange* shore to which, in metaphor and consciousness, Maggie finds herself ferried. Perhaps even more violently adventurous is the image that plays before Maggie at the dinner table in Fawns, while Father Mitchell, the Catholic priest to whom, typically, Maggie promises herself she will one day confess that she did not confess (and how James rejoices in that intricate casuistry), twiddles his thumbs and scoffs the wine:

> These shadows rose and fell for her while Father Mitchell prattled; with other shadows as well, those that hung over Charlotte herself, those that marked her as a prey to equal suspicions – to the idea in particular of a change, such a change as she didn't dare to face, in the relations of the two men. Or there were yet other possibilities as it seemed to Maggie; there were always too many, and all of them things of evil when one's nerves had at last done for one all that nerves could do; had left one in a darkness of prowling dangers that was like the

predicament of the night-watcher in a beast-haunted land who has no more means for a fire.   (Pt. 5, Ch. 5)

The non-fire fuses with the shadows that rise and fall like flames of darkness; while Charlotte, as '*prey* to equal suspicions', seems to generate the 'beast-haunted land'. One notices how one feature common to all these metaphors is the idea of being abandoned, as though a childhood anxiety of being left alone without light underlay Maggie's penetration of moral darkness. 'Night-watcher' should remind us, however, that Maggie's terror of the night cannot be separated from her complicity with it.

This double identity achieves a kind of resolution in the frequent metaphors of acting, associated particularly with Maggie throughout the second book. The idea of acting takes in all manner of performance – juggling, recitation, orthodox theatre, circus, pantomime and ballet. The metaphor does occur a couple of times in the first part, but not in connexion with Maggie. Charlotte with 'her strange gift of tongues' is likened to a 'conjuror at a show [who] juggled with balls or hoops or lighted brands' (Pt. 1, Ch. 3); while the Colonel watches his wife operate 'in her favourite element [of speculation] very much as he sometimes watched at the Aquarium the celebrated lady who, in a slight, though tight, bathing-suit, turned somersaults and did tricks in the tank of water which looked so cold and uncomfortable to the non-amphibious' (Pt. 1, Ch. 4). This nicely and comically accommodates the acting to the water and boat metaphors that normally buoy up Fanny's titanic speculations. Maggie's new-found consciousness involves her in a form of theatre, in acting in the performative sense, in terms of the gap between reality and illusion. Interestingly, she seems to come to consciousness when she realizes that she is being used as a puppet by others:

> . . . she was passed about . . . like a dressed doll held, in the right manner, by its firmly stuffed middle, for the account she could give. She might have been made to give it by pressure of her stomach. . . . (Pt. 4, Ch. 3)

It is a nursery image and delicately seizes Maggie's new-found awareness of herself being seen by others as a child, and not even a real child, but a child's toy child. She does however grow beyond this, to become an 'overworked little trapezist girl – the acrobatic support presumably of embarrassed and exacting parents' (Pt. 5, Ch. 5: shades of Verena Tarrant in *The Bostonians*); and later still she is found as 'a tired actress who has the good fortune to be "off", while her mates are on, almost long enough for a nap on the property sofa in the wing' (Pt. 5, Ch. 2). In her relationship to the Prince, at one stage of their silent stand-off, she feels herself like 'some panting dancer of a difficult step who had capered, before the footlights of an empty theatre, to a spectator lounging in a box' (Pt. 5, Ch. 1). When she finds herself committed to a course of consistent duplicity, she figures her situation is 'not unlike some young woman of the theatre who, engaged for a minor part in the play and having mastered her cues with anxious effort, should find herself suddenly promoted to leading lady and expected to appear in every act of the five' (Pt. 5, Ch. 1). Fanny becomes her ringmaster:

> Fanny Assingham might really have been there at all events, like one of the assistants in the ring at the circus, to keep up the pace of the sleek revolving animal on whose back the lady in short spangled skirts should brilliantly caper and posture. . . the collective hand had been held out to her with such alacrity, so that she might skip up into the light even, as seemed to her modest mind, with such a show of pink stocking and such an abbreviation of white petticoat. . . . (Pt. 4, Ch. 4)

Both these last images are like anxiety dreams: in the first Maggie is called upon to perform acts beyond her powers, and in the second there is a suggestion of being improperly or inappropriately dressed. Such dreams would be especially appropriate for Maggie in her condition of a child growing into awareness of an adult world, with consequent fear of exposure but also desire to shock.

In one powerful image the circus is joined to the haunted house. Here one feels that, at a deeply subjective level, *The Golden Bowl* has achieved a coherence beyond the level of its plot in its underworld of images. This time it is distinctly James the narrator reaching for an analogue of the strange interregnum between Charlotte's confrontation with Maggie and Maggie's successful pursuit and conquest of Charlotte:

They learned fairly to live in the perfunctory; they remained in it as many hours of the day as might be; it took on finally the likeness of some spacious central chamber in a haunted house, a great overarched and overglazed rotunda where gaiety might reign, but the doors of which opened into sinister circular passages. Here they turned up for each other, as they said, with the blank faces that denied any uneasiness felt in the approach; here they closed numerous doors carefully behind them – all save the door that connected the place, as by a straight tented corridor, with the outer world, and, encouraging thus the irruption of society, imitated the aperture through which the bedizened performers of the circus are poured into the ring.   (Pt. 5, Ch. 4)

The architecture – surely another version of the pagoda – of the arrangement has now been imaginatively occupied by Maggie – and it is a profoundly connective faculty that relates the 'rotunda', the *circular* passages and the *circus*. That it is also an image of James's own art and practice seems inescapable. The implication is that only the innocent imagination – which for these purposes is also an American imagination – only the frightened insight of childhood can expose the corruption of adult relationships in a steady, uncompromised light. Arguably, the fundamental dialectic of the novel itself as a form has been that of the romantic child and the worldly adult, the child as a full human potentiality which is doomed to wither into adult actuality, and by so doing bring it to knowledge and judgement. The virtue of riches, at least in Maggie's case, is that they enable her to recapitulate the whole human condition within her inner world. Not only is she all these performers, but also the lowest, most abject of the ghosts that haunt the 'overglazed rotunda'. She changes shape with the outcast denizens of a world which her father's wealth has created – but of course in image and imagination only. Perhaps this deeply metaphorical self-extension is one way in which the static, fixed, ahistorical point of view which John Goode sees as a limitation of the later fiction, is overcome.[29] It remains true of course that if the deprived and enslaved were really to erupt into her world, its surfaces would be shattered and, as happens in Conrad, the cyclone of the twentieth century would howl through the struts and wires of the now glassless rotunda. Still, within her nursery world Maggie goes a long way to living out the deep misery of the human condition:

She looked out as from under an improvised hood – the sole headgear of some poor woman at somebody's proud door; she waited even like the poor woman.... (Pt. 5, Ch. 2)

Even more drastically, Maggie can time travel: in the shadowy embodiments of metaphor, to be sure – outside historical time altogether and, remarkably, given her marked American fairness, outside white Western society:

> It was *strange* [my italics], if one had gone into it, but such a place as Amerigo's was like something made for him beforehand by innumerable facts, facts largely of the sort known as historical, made by ancestors, examples, traditions, habits; while Maggie's own had come to show simply as that improvised 'post' – a post of the kind spoken of as advanced – with which she was to have found herself connected in the fashion of a settler or a trader in a new country; in the likeness even of some Indian squaw with a papoose on her back and barbarous beadwork to sell. Maggie's own, in short, would have been sought in vain in the most rudimentary map of the social relations as such. The only geography marking it would be doubtless that of the fundamental passions. (Pt. 6, Ch. 1)

Yet not to be too elated by these last, we should also remember the servant whose presence is dismissed in an irritated parenthesis earlier in the novel, when Maggie is preparing to sound out her father ('the prime source of her haunted state'):

> She had made anxiety her stupid little idol; and absolutely now, while she stuck a long pin a trifle fallaciously into her hat – she had, with an approach to irritation, told her maid, a new woman whom she had lately found herself thinking of as abysmal, that she didn't want her – she tried to focus the possibility of some understanding between them in consequence of which he should cut loose. (Pt. 4, Ch. 4)

Of that passage about 'the fundamental passions', let he who can sort out the dense tangle of conditional tenses and speculative clauses. The image stands out clear and precise within the syntactical jungle. Amerigo represents a supreme instance of social fact, the given, the achieved, the subjugated and the established. As against this, Maggie's romantic consciousness attempts reconstitution and penetration. The process is, as a trajectory, revolutionary, though its end becomes an even more rigid petrification of the social fact. But in the process Maggie dreams through again, as does James, the whole fabric of civilization, the energies that have built it and that lie in wait to destroy it. As a last example of ideal constructive power, James presents the fabric of his own novels, tensed to the last tenuous elaboration and already deeply conversant of the destructive element in which they are about to dissolve. James's own novel, in this last instance, does not founder and it invents, as its last expedient, a female hero who assumes the burden of the structure, lying gloriously to preserve the lie and lying in the consciousness that nothing, finally, can be saved. *The Golden Bowl* is high literature's last refuge against the deluge: it contains high drama, deeply intestine struggles, 'high fights' of truly Balzacian proportions. Indeed, imaginatively it figures, in its imagery, the whole past and future of the novel form. Every subsequent novel can be viewed as in some way post-novelistic – parasitic, parodic, nostalgic, ironic – or in some more or less post-humous relationship to the great classical nineteenth century novel, whose last paradoxical example is *The Golden Bowl*.

Notes

1. *The Novels and Tales of Henry James*, New York, 1909, vols. 23 and 24. These volumes coincide with James's division of the novel into Book First, 'The Prince', and Book Second, 'The Princess'. In some modern editions, such as the Penguin, the chapters are numbered consecutively: thus in the first book the chapters of Part 2 are numbered 7–13 and Part 3, 14–24; in the second book those of Part 4 are numbered 25–34, Part 5, 35–9 and Part 6, 40–2.
2. *The Art of the Novel*, edited by R. P. Blackmur, New York, 1962, p. 76.
3. Ibid., pp. 77–8.
4. Literally, of course, it is Mrs Gereth, not Fleda, who reassembles 'the wretched thing', but it is Fleda who makes conscious and imaginative meaning of them as yielding 'the impression somehow of something dreamed and missed, something reduced, relinquished, resigned: the poetry, as it were, of something sensibly *gone*'. Such impressions – 'ghosts' as Fleda calls them – are only the final mastery of time; and in what could be the definitive vindication of Proust's enterprise, Fleda asserts that '. . . ghosts count double – for what they were and for what they are' (*The Spoils of Poynton*, London, 1947 ed., p. 171).

5. *The House of Fiction*, edited by Leon Edel, London, 1957, p. 84.

6. Ibid., p. 85.

7. *The Characters of Love*, London, 1968.

8. *Eight Modern Writers*, Oxford History of English Literature, vol. 12, Oxford, 1963, p. 71.

9. *The Art of the Novel*, pp. 60–1.

10. 'Emile Zola' in *The House of Fiction*, p. 223.

11. '. . . the fortune and felicity of the book [Madame Bovary] were assured by the stroke that made the central figure an embodiment of helpless romanticism. . . . Flaubert himself but narrowly escaped being such an embodiment after all, and he is thus able to express the romantic mind with extraordinary truth' ('Gustave Flaubert' in *The House of Fiction*, p. 195).

12. Though this does not, of course, make *The Bostonians* a naturalist novel, as Goode is at pains to point out. For a sharply focused and informed discussion of James's relationship to the naturalists, see John Goode, 'The Art of Fiction: Walter Besant and Henry James' in D. Howard, J. Lucas and J. Goode (eds.), *Tradition and Tolerance in Nineteenth-Century Fiction*, London, 1967, esp. pp. 266–7.

13. 'Nana' in *The House of Fiction*, p. 277.

14. Ibid.

15. Ibid.

16. 'Gustave Flaubert' in *The House of Fiction*, p. 199.

17. *The Art of the Novel*, p. 130.

18. *The Novels and Tales of Henry James*, vol. 10, p. 130.

19. 'Portents and betrayals' in the English editions.

20. Leavis puts the matter with his usual finality and authority, and one is only nagging away in his wake: '[In *The Golden Bowl*] James clearly counts on our taking towards his main persons attitudes that we cannot take without forgetting our finer moral sense – our finer discriminative feelings for life and personality' (F. R. Leavis, *The Great Tradition*, London, 1960, p. 159).

21. Leavis sees the main source of moral contradiction in Adam and Maggie collecting their respective spouses as they do their 'pieces'. But it is in Adam's 'aesthetic' view of his daughter that the contradiction comes to its acutest issue.

22. Touchett is older and earlier, but 'his American physiognomy' makes him one with Verver's type: 'He had a narrow, clean shaven face, with features evenly distributed and an expression of placid acuteness' (*The Portrait of a Lady*, Oxford, 1956 ed., p. 3).

23. *The Art of the Novel*, p. 5.

24. Ibid., p. 193.

25. Ibid., p. 194.

26. *The Two Magics*, London, 1898, p. 168.

27. *The Sacred Fount*, London, 1953 ed., pp. 135–6.
28. 'Vice' in the English editions.
29. Goode, op. cit. The problem of point of view is discussed in detail in the last section of Goode's essay, and with particular relevance for my purposes in the long central paragraph on p. 276.

INDEX

WITHDRAWN